M000289046

EVERY CITIZEN A STATESMAN

# *every*
# *citizen a*
# STATESMAN

### THE DREAM *of a*
### DEMOCRATIC FOREIGN POLICY
### *in the* AMERICAN CENTURY

DAVID ALLEN

Harvard University Press

Cambridge, Massachusetts & London, England    2023

First printing

Publication of this book has been supported through the generous
provisions of the Maurice and Lula Bradley Smith Memorial Fund

*Library of Congress Cataloging-in-Publication Data*

Names: Allen, David, 1989– author.
Title: Every citizen a statesman : the dream of a democratic foreign policy
in the American century / David Allen.
Description: Cambridge, Massachusetts : Harvard University Press, 2023. |
Includes bibliographical references and index.
Identifiers: LCCN 2022005446 | ISBN 9780674248984 (cloth)
Subjects: LCSH: Foreign Policy Association—History. | Political
Participation—United States—History—20th century. | Non-state actors
(International relations)—United States—History—20th century. |
International relations—Citizen participation—History—20th century. |
United States—Foreign relations—20th century.
Classification: LCC JZ27.F67 A55 2022 | DDC 327.73009/04—dc23/eng/20220628
LC record available at https://lccn.loc.gov/2022005446

*for Tian*

# CONTENTS

EVERY CITIZEN A STATESMAN

# Introduction: Destiny and Democracy

*L* *ife* magazine had always presented its millions of readers with a glossy, optimistic vision for the United States, but the edition of June 5, 1939, went further than normal. Published to mark the opening of the New York World's Fair, the issue showed the Statue of Liberty soaring from its cover, her beacon lighting the way towards "America's Future." The pages were filled with the photographs that made the magazine so popular, but there were also an unusual number of maps. One set of images, for instance, outlined the economic capacity of the United States, plotting its ability to produce iron, cotton, wheat, and electricity against the potential of the other great powers. The United States, the text declared, was now not only "'richer' and 'greater'" than its rivals, but "so basically different from the rest of the world's nations that it can hardly be compared with them." This was cartography with a purpose, the aim being to make American superiority in the world seem as much a part of everyday life as the cars and the cooking utensils, the drugs and the cigarettes that advertisers promoted on page after page of the magazine. "By examination of our heroic past and hopeful present," an editorial elaborated, the issue hoped to bring about "the richer and happier America which will be ours when we have nerved ourselves to accept our bounty and our destiny." Soon enough, *Life*'s publisher, Henry R. Luce, would announce the dawn of "The American Century."[1]

Luce's declaration was a year and a half away yet, though, and a long year and a half at that. In the summer of 1939, the ideal of an America regnant seemed distant. Explaining why it felt that way was a task that *Life*'s editors left for Walter Lippmann, who elaborated in an article entitled "The American Destiny." For Lippmann, the preeminent foreign policy commentator of the age, an understanding of why the United States was not yet acting like

1

the great power it so obviously appeared to be to him and other observers was in order. Americans must be "embarrassed" of their preeminence, he surmised; their reticent, ambiguous foreign policy was "an attempt to neutralize the fact that America has preponderant power and decisive influence in the affairs of the world." But Lippmann was certain that this situation was temporary, "the curious mood of a peculiar epoch." Surely Americans would one day accept the blessings of providence, and soon, for they lived amid "one of the greatest events in the history of mankind." "What Rome was to the ancient world, what Great Britain has been to the modern world, America is to be to the world of tomorrow," Lippmann declared. That fate was inescapable. "When the destiny of a nation is revealed to it," he wrote, "there is no choice but to accept that destiny and to make ready in order to be equal to it."

But there was a choice, and Lippmann knew it. For the United States was not Rome, nor even Great Britain. The United States was destined to become the leading power in the world not as a republic, not as a parliamentary monarchy, but as a mass democracy. That mattered. The fate of the world seemed, to Lippmann as to others, ultimately to rest not with America's diplomats or with its politicians, but with its citizenry. That fact made it easy enough to assign blame for the country's inertia at the time. "The indecision which pervades the American spirit," Lippmann argued, "has its root in the refusal by the American people to see themselves as they are, as a very great nation, and to act accordingly." But it also offered an opportunity. Americans could be taught to lead the world—indeed, they needed to be, for their own safety. And if that proved possible, Lippmann concluded, "the things that seem difficult will seem easy, and the willingness to be equal to their mission will restore their confidence and make whole their will."[2]

THIS IS A BOOK ABOUT how Americans like Walter Lippmann sought to reconcile their nation's power in the world with the problem of their democracy at home. The question of how to conduct foreign policy in a democracy is not new now, and it was not new in 1939. Debates about which Americans should be entrusted with diplomacy, and to whom they should be accountable and how, had run through the earliest years of the republic, as the United States tried to find its place in a world of warring empires. The Constitution handed the conduct of foreign affairs to the executive branch to ensure that "the power of making treaties should be committed to able and honest men," as John Jay wrote in 1788, men who could be kept insulated from the worst impulses of electoral politics. The fear of permitting popular views to interfere with diplomacy was a lasting one. Alexis de Tocqueville thought that foreign affairs would be the downfall of the nation he so admired; diplomacy, the French correspondent wrote in the 1830s, "requires virtually none of the distinctive virtues of democracy but does demand the development of nearly all that it lacks." While some American statesman agreed, others found ways to use democratic politics for their nation's cause. Secretary of State William Seward, for instance, began a tradition of transparency by starting the *Foreign Relations of the United States* series in 1861, releasing diplomatic documents to bolster confidence in Abraham Lincoln's prosecution of the Civil War in the belief that if "the Government continually depends upon the support of Congress and the People," as Seward said, such support could be "expected only in the condition of keeping them thoroughly and truthfully informed." If issues like these were as old as the United States itself, however, the dilemma took on a deeper, darker intensity as the world grew more connected, as the nation flourished economically, and as Americans felt both more influential and more insecure in international affairs. From the 1910s to the 1970s, the problem of a democratic foreign policy became an existential one, the solution to which felt as if it might assure world peace or cause a war. In that period, this book argues, to think about foreign policy in the United States was always to think about democracy, for behind debates over what the national interest might be lay assumptions about who should get to decide.[3]

Since the 1970s, it has been conventional wisdom that US foreign policy-making is, and long has been, the province of an "elite" or "establishment"—the "Blob," as Obama administration official Ben Rhodes scorned in 2016. These terms, though different in their critical force, invoke a network of professionals who move between the federal government, think tanks, and academia and are united in their belief in the righteousness of US world leadership. While arguments have periodically flared up about how powerful this elite really is, how far its mistakes should discredit it, and how closed it is to outsiders and outside ideas, there is little doubt about whether it exists. Where disagreement does persist and, if anything, has heightened, is on the question of how responsive that elite is—or should be—to the popular will. Does the foreign policy to which this elite subscribes, whatever its internal differences, match what Americans really want? Does the elite follow or ignore mass preferences? Does it suffer from a lack of accountability, or even a crisis of legitimacy? Does it care?[4]

The histories of the terms we currently use to describe those who run US foreign policy give the answers away. The idea of a secretive, even manipulative foreign policy "elite" or "establishment" pulling the strings was something of a joke until the worst years of the Vietnam War. When the *New Yorker* writer Richard H. Rovere brought the notion of "an Establishment in America"—with the Council on Foreign Relations as "a sort of Presidium"— into the mainstream in 1961, he was spoofing the conspiratorial thinking of the extreme right and the academic left. But by the end of the decade the idea had become common sense, as campus protestors, leftist writers, and even some past policymakers argued that the Vietnam disaster was not just an error, but symptomatic of a deeper refusal to submit foreign policy to democratic control. The phrase "foreign policy establishment" first entered the *New York Times* in 1970, when one of the war's architects, former national security advisor McGeorge Bundy, described the claims that he had been part of such an establishment as "nonsense." "Foreign policy elite" followed in 1971, in an exposé of the Council's fraught private debates about its place in public life. By then, academics and journalists had already started to write the same concepts back onto the past, causing what William Appleman Williams in 1972 called the "extensive elitism" of US policymaking to seem traditional, entrenched, even inevitable. Seemingly without irony, the terms have since been adopted wholesale—suggesting that the radical critique of the Watergate era is now simply taken for granted.[5]

Were things supposed to turn out this way? Was foreign policy always intended to be so cut off from the people that it is arguably even less susceptible today to democratic control than any other area of government policy? Many Americans have historically thought not. What this book defines as the foreign policy "community"—a less loaded term than "elite" or "establishment" for the amorphous, shifting networks of people and organizations who hold professional or significant voluntary interests in foreign affairs—has been more honestly dedicated to reconciling diplomacy with mass democracy than has often been allowed, but it has failed in its efforts to do so, with damaging, still dangerous consequences. Even at the core of the foreign policy community it was taken for granted well into the 1950s that the United States needed—for its own security and for the peace of the world—to create a uniquely democratic form of diplomacy in which an interested, informed public would participate actively, effectively, and meaningfully to influence basic policy. Democracy being an unstable concept, there were of course debates about who that public ought to include, what duties policymakers would owe to it, and how public opinion might be translated into policies. But until the frostiest years of the Cold War, the general premise remained that the United States must not conduct its policy in the secretive, insular manner of a traditional, European foreign office.

At the end of World War I, a rash of institutions emerged in response to that conviction, of which two were most important and enduring. One was the Council on Foreign Relations, which sought to restrict what it saw as legitimate discussion of world affairs to a select, male few—white, wealthy, and educated. The Council would eventually triumph as the private group most influential on policy and on notions of how it ought to be made, and it remains at the heart of the foreign policy community today. But until the middle of the century, its ascendancy was far from certain; the Council's partner and frequent rival, the much more open and participatory Foreign Policy Association, seemed to many to offer a wiser solution. The nonpartisan, nonprofit Association was, in fact, the primary institution through which many of the Americans most interested in world affairs explored what it meant to conduct foreign policy in a democracy. This book is the first to tell its story at any length, for its defeat was so thorough that its importance has been forgotten even among scholars. What makes it worth telling, among other reasons, is that the men and women of the Association did not offer one, singular answer to the problem they confronted. Some of its leaders believed that foreign policy was barely susceptible to mass participation in the slightest, or at least that to submit it to democratic control would require the safeguard of strong expert guidance. Some of its leaders sought, in the words of the most visionary of its presidents, to make "every citizen a statesman." Recovering the history of the Foreign Policy Association and setting it in the context of the wider debate in which it operated therefore restores much of the complexity, contingency, and contention of a complex narrative that is often reduced to a flat, default elitism.[6]

Still active today, though in diminished form, the Association was founded in 1918 by a group of progressives who supported Woodrow Wilson's efforts to create and join the League of Nations. Working closely with the State Department, benefitting from big philanthropy, and presiding over a branch network that took world affairs debates into cities nationwide, the Association was the single most important private group dedicated purely to foreign policy issues from the 1920s to the 1940s, and it remained influential into the 1960s. Existing as both an expression of a broader, societal commitment to a democratic foreign policy and the chief means of realizing it, the mature

Association aimed to educate an "ever-widening public" on issues in world affairs, a task it undertook largely through the production, dissemination, and discussion of "essential information of a non-partisan and objective character," as it wrote in 1943. But considered over time, the changing work of the Association and its allies reflected the shifting ways in which the foreign policy community as a whole thought about the public. Concentrating on the Association therefore allows the telling of a broader story—one that takes us from Oval Office meetings to debates on porches in rural Oregon, from studious assessments of opinion polls in the seminar rooms of the Ivy League to protests at school board meetings in Pasadena, California.[7]

For the Association was not a trivial or uninfluential group, despite its underappreciated past. Presidents of the United States were involved, offering public support from the White House and sometimes giving private, tactical advice. All but one or two of the men who served as secretary of state from Frank B. Kellogg in the 1920s to Cyrus Vance in the 1970s had their hands in it at one point or another, to a greater or lesser extent. Few of the leading personalities in US foreign relations in this period escaped it, whether coughing up their membership dues, serving on its board, or speaking from its stages. The richest foundations in the world provided up to half of its budget, the trustees of the Rockefeller, Carnegie, and Ford inheritances in turn giving millions of dollars over four decades to shape a project that was among the more durable in the history of US philanthropy. Scholars paid attention, shaping their theories of public opinion in light of its successes and failures, and sometimes reshaping its course in turn. Countless volunteers were true believers in its cause, praying that their work might make for a safer world or a fairer democracy. Countless of their neighbors went along with them, perhaps to join the effort themselves, perhaps to make like-minded friends, or perhaps just to take up the offer of a decent lunch.

But the story of the Foreign Policy Association is a story of failure all the same, and not just in retrospect. However unfair it might be to blame a single institution for the ills of an entire nation, over the decades the Association's failure to create the public it hoped for strengthened increasingly widespread perceptions that the citizenry could not be educated, reasoned with, or trusted at all. Such convictions lurked behind many turning points in the history of US foreign policy, from Franklin Roosevelt's inflation of real threats to aid Great Britain in fighting its Nazi foe, to Harry Truman's effort to garner support for his standoff with the Soviet Union by escalating it into a militarized, apocalyptic Cold War. Come the 1960s, there seemed to be so little

evidence that the public of the foreign policy community's intent was a reality that scholars felt free to argue that the ideal itself might be false, even
reckless—that democracy did not and should not depend on the participation of its people, but on its institutions, its values, its elites, bulwarks saving
the republic from the apathetic masses who might drag it into totalitarianism.
Even the Association's more ardent supporters agreed that their dream had
become a nightmare. The rise of the "establishment" critique was evidence
enough that their slogan—"world affairs are your affairs!"—had resonated
with too few Americans for a culture of democratic control to take hold.[8]

Why did this dream die? Any number of reasons emerge from this story.
There was the dismaying paternalism of experts who swore that the unfiltered views of the people could not be trusted. There was the racism that
simply refused to treat Black and other Americans of color as able to engage
with foreign policy as experts defined it, the class politics that declined to see
why it might matter to union leaders to advance a "labor" point of view.
There were the ever-more implausible standards of knowledge and action
that foreign policy elites set, and the ever-more impenetrable language with
which they talked. The whole notion of creating a participatory, democratic
foreign policy through processes of top-down education was flawed, even ar-
rogant, and it ignored the anti-intellectualism that has scarred American history. None of those explanations would be wrong, even without considering
an activist incompetence that was at times almost derisory. But what must be
resisted is the suggestion that the ideal was deficient *per se*—the conviction
that foreign policy is simply, inevitably not susceptible to democratic control.
Some Americans believed that, to be sure, and some still do. Some thought
the United States had a "democratic foreign policy" just because it had a
foreign policy and it was a democracy, or because it had elections, even as
they admitted that few citizens voted with foreign policy foremost in mind.
But a powerful group of Americans thought otherwise. Their vision shaped
how the most powerful nation in history approached the world. We live with
the consequences still.[9]

ALTHOUGH THERE WAS ONCE wide agreement that the United States required an exceptional sort of foreign policy, there was always considerably
less agreement on what that meant. That lack of consensus was especially
true when it came to "public opinion," the concept through which much of
the debate played out. We think of public opinion today as a statistical entity,

one created through opinion polling that gives us insight into aggregated popular preferences, but the meanings of "public opinion" have historically been disparate and contentious. Political scientist Harwood Childs was expert enough on the subject to found a journal called the *Public Opinion Quarterly*, but even he had to concede in 1939 that the phrase "by itself has very little meaning" suggesting anything from "a collection of individual opinions" to "some mystical entity floating about in the atmosphere over our heads." When it has come to foreign policy specifically, there has rarely been clarity on a definition at all. Some analysts, like the League of Women Voters writer Anne Hartwell Johnstone, saw public opinion simply as "what people collectively think about foreign policies." Others, such as the Carnegie Endowment for International Peace president Nicholas Murray Butler, defined it as almost the opposite of mass preferences, a trait bred into men of character and wisdom who could withstand popular whims. Some have thought of public opinion as a weapon to be wielded in power politics; others have believed it to be a radical force, capable of ending power politics forever. Scholars have often suggested that the term be abandoned. Pierre Bourdieu once declared that "public opinion" of the sort imagined in polls "simply does not exist."[10]

Something called "public opinion" clearly did and does exist, though. Presidents, after all, have put it at the heart of their plans for peace, as Woodrow Wilson did; have felt unable to follow their view of the national interest because of it, as Franklin Roosevelt did; have sent men to their deaths for fear of it, as Lyndon Johnson did. This tension between the ephemeral and the real senses of public opinion has exasperated scholars. Bernard C. Cohen, a political scientist whose thinking had significant impact on the Foreign Policy Association, spent two decades working on the subject before publishing *The Public's Impact on Foreign Policy* in 1972. He admitted he could do no better than "the unsatisfactory conclusion that public opinion is important in the policymaking process, though we cannot say with confidence how, why, or when." Melvin Small, a historian, wrote in 1991 that proving the "impact" of public opinion on diplomacy was "arduous"; he turned to studying partisan politics instead. Ernest R. May, a historian of unusual insight and an architect of Harvard's public policy program to boot, wrote several books on public opinion and foreign policy, but he once conceded that he remained perplexed by the matter. May doubted that "public opinion is an entity which can be described, dissected, and analyzed at all" in 1964, calling it an "invention," a "construction." "Perhaps at least some studies of it," he concluded, "ought to begin not with what is observed but with the observers."[11]

With those injunctions in mind, this book does not claim to demonstrate that "public opinion" did or did not impact foreign policy at any given point, nor does it make the dubious claim that the public is a fount of wise judgment that can be entrusted with the path to peace. Instead, it takes May's advice and treats "public opinion" as a construction, and a crucial one at that. Scarce has been the policymaker who did not appreciate the importance of public support for their policies, after all, and many Americans have believed they have some role to play in the making of foreign policy. In the past few decades, in fact, historians have detailed how specific publics involved themselves in foreign relations, especially historians who have approached the past through the categories of race, class, gender, and religion. Historians have also studied in some depth how cultural artifacts like films, books, and television shows taught their audiences certain lessons about the world and America's dominant place within it. This book does not challenge the importance of that scholarship; it depends on it. What is striking about that work, however, is the problem it leaves us: if historians today imagine Americans as having been "in the world" in every conceivable way, why did those closest to the making of US foreign policy always believe that those same Americans were out of it?[12]

Resolving this dilemma historically rather than simply assuming the answer lies in an inbuilt privilege or supercilious elitism means charting how the foreign policy community constructed its understanding of public opinion over time—how it defined, produced, used, and ultimately ignored the publics that mattered to it. Seeing public opinion and concepts associated with it not as things with a stable definition or an innate reality, but as constructions subject to contestation in theory and practice, helps us see how those close to policymaking classified facts, views, actions, and even people as relevant to their work, and others as beneath them. Treating public opinion as a construction does not, however, mean treating it as if it exists solely in the realm of ideas. What matters in this history is how theories met operational practicalities to make some kinds of activism seem plausible and others not. For that reason, it would be insufficient to conceive of public opinion scholars, however influential, as the only people thinking about these issues. The theories of social scientists like Harold Lasswell about how foreign policy ideas move through the polity were important, of course. But so too, and often more so, were the ideas of the women who met in the 1920s to discuss which members of their high-society set needed to attend a luncheon to make foreign policy more fashionable, or of the housewife in San Mateo, California, who took politicians at their word that everyone had a role to play in foreign policy and mounted a discussion program that swept across the San Francisco Bay in the late 1950s, to the anger of officials at the local World Affairs Council who raged that such zeal was irresponsible. If democracy is a practice and not merely an idea, then studying its practices, even its failed ones, is important to its story.[13]

As those examples might suggest, expanding our vision from a foreign policy "elite" to a broader, if more amorphous foreign policy community exposes the gender politics of foreign policymaking, another central theme of this book. Traditionally, histories of the foreign policy elite have assumed that it was the province entirely of men, which is true enough if one correlates that elite with policymakers, academics, and the members of the Council of Foreign Relations and imagines it to have been static over time. But the gender politics of the foreign policy community in fact changed markedly, and that change bore critical implications for the problem of a democratic foreign policy. The rise from mere power to clear dominance of an insular, secretive male elite around the Second World War was, this book argues, in part a response to the unmistakable visibility and even influence of white women within the foreign policy community as a whole, white women who championed a far more ambitious approach to public engagement than many of the men of the Council were prepared to countenance. It was the Council's rival, the Association, that embodied the worldview and prominence of those women, who in the first instance were suffragists and pacifists of the most significant stature. White women powered the Association, made up most of its members, and were its first researchers. Without the networks, labor, and expertise of these women, the creation of the foreign policy community was unimaginable, as was its educational style and orientation towards the public. But this was never an equal world, nor one diverse in race or class. If the making of the foreign policy community was initially a story about white male internationalists plugging into white women's networks to create a public sphere, it was a sphere that male internationalists then professionalized, masculinized, and eventually abandoned. In their cultivation of a male policymaking class in the face of a public in which women were so prominent, lies not just the lamentable difficulty with diversity from which the foreign policy community has suffered since, but its outlook on public engagement as well.[14]

If ideas about public opinion were never stable, nor were the institutions that took up the ideal of a democratic foreign policy monoliths. Far from offering a single, coherent vision for their work, the Association and its allies were often paralyzed with debate about what to do and how to do it. Was it proper to target civic leaders, academic experts, and elites of other kinds on the belief that opinions trickled down from such people to the rest of society? Was it better to work from the bottom up? Did one method make more sense when war loomed or when peace seemed at hand? Was it wiser to take a carefully balanced approach to an issue, so that readers of a pamphlet might feel they were making up their own minds on German rearmament or Soviet adventurism? Was it more sensible to take a more adamant line and provide a more explicit framework through which readers might interpret facts? Did the answer change based on the perceived readership of a report or on the subject at hand? When did "education" turn into "manipulation"? What were the limits of information? What were the mechanisms through which public opinion might influence policy and policy influence public opinion? These questions and more were constants in the Association's history, but the Association could not answer them on its own. Even if its leaders could agree among themselves on their approach, they still needed to convince a range of partners, from voluntary leaders to scholars and other experts, and they depended on the well-meaning but often confused aid of the philanthropists who funded them. Telling the story of the Foreign Policy Association, then, requires combining intellectual history with political and foreign relations history and also demands that attention be closely paid to the specific contexts of a wide array of actors—global, national, and local.

For all these reasons, this book avoids imposing set definitions on the past, trying instead to reveal history through how definitions have changed over time. There is one crucial exception. When this book talks about a "democratic foreign policy," it means a form of foreign policy that emerges from the active, informed, meaningful participation of some part of the citizenry. There are practical reasons for that definition, to be sure, for this is a book about institutions that conceived of a democratic foreign policy in that way. But there are properly historical reasons for it too. Even the toughest critics of the ideals embodied by the Association explicitly granted that those ideals were "democratic" and that their own, competing proposals for how to conduct foreign policy were likely to be construed as undemocratic, even if those critics disagreed with that premise. Gabriel Almond, the preeminent academic theorist of foreign policy and democracy during the early Cold War, might have written in 1950 that the notion "that the people are inherently wise and just, and that they are the real rulers of the republic" was a "myth," but he conceded that it remained "the democratic myth" all the same.[15]

One important distinction, additionally, is the separation of an active "public" from a passive "audience." Jürgen Habermas's classic evocation of the "public"— a closer translation of the German *Öffentlichkeit* than the typical "public sphere"—defines it as including "organized discussion among private people that tended to be ongoing," which "presupposed the problematization of areas that until then had not been questioned" and that "became 'general' not merely in their significance, but also in their accessibility." As that scheme implies, publics do not naturally exist around any issue, nor do they emerge simply because they are addressed or because information is released into the world. The publics that have long been at the heart of democratic theory have had to be built; they have been projects, often flawed ones, founded in exclusions as much as inclusions. Writing in the early 1960s, Habermas reflected that such publics were implausible in modern, mass societies in which rational, critical debate was impeded by the media, the public relations industry, and consumerism; in this view, the commanding power of publics at the end of the eighteenth century had already faded in the nineteenth. If that fact seemed obvious half a century ago, half a century before that such pessimism seemed unwarranted. One of Habermas's main influences, philosopher John Dewey, wrote then of his belief that citizens could, in fact, be educated and empowered towards a more perfect democracy. For a long time, the Foreign Policy Association that Dewey had a role in founding tried to do just that.[16]


HOW, THEN, DID THE Foreign Policy Association, its allies, and its rivals grapple with the problem of a democratic foreign policy? The first two chapters of this book argue that the Association's first instinct was to help build a foreign policy community among elites, one in which predominantly wealthy or highly educated citizens interested in foreign policy could discuss it formally, in the hope of shaping both state action and public impulses. As Chapter 1 shows after a brief account of the origins of the Association in 1918, white progressives—especially former suffragists—were the main force behind the creation of institutions dedicated to informing publics about foreign affairs, whether in New York, Boston, Chicago, or cities elsewhere. The men and women of the Association initially sought to make foreign policy fashionable, bringing full-throated, often raucous debates about world issues to high society in luxurious hotels on the widely held assumption that ideas would trickle down from a social, financial, and political elite. Far from representing a heroic defense against a dominant "isolationism," this Wilsonian internationalism was ascendent immediately after the Great War. It had "public opinion" at its heart, a force thought capable, if suitably led, of transcending power politics and ushering in peace; along with other institutions, the Association attempted to create it.

Chapter 2 explores how this form of internationalism matured into something more self-consciously scientific—a process shaped, accelerated, and funded in partnership with the Rockefeller Foundation. This period was the nascent age of the foreign policy "expert," a nonpartisan figure who might discover the causes of war through research and work toward peace through public opinion. In 1925, the Association formed a research department to supply basic, "objective" information to educated readers, particularly those close to policymaking or to means of mass communications. This research department was arguably the first foreign policy think tank on the modern model, albeit with a permanent staff of scholars that appealed as much to the public as to policymakers. Those researchers at first were almost all women plucked straight from graduate schools, but as the think tank infrastructure became less precarious, the staff began to adhere more to prevailing social structures. Their readership was small, however authoritative their work became as they gained the respect of the State Department. The question remained open, though, as to whether such experts were ultimately responsible to policymakers on the one hand or to publics on the other, and how much to each. As the Great Depression struck and fascism challenged those who kept faith in participatory democracy, that question became still more difficult to answer. Working amid a vast movement for adult education, the Association turned to a much broader public, pioneering on the radio and writing "popular" pamphlets for a general, reading public. But as the world order centered on the League of Nations broke down in the 1930s, faith in the public opinion that been at the heart of that order grew harder to come by, not least for the Association's president, Raymond Leslie Buell. That disillusionment would only heighten among scholars over the next three decades, a crucial trend beginning in the 1920s that, when joined with traditional diplomatic elitism and an ever-more warlike foreign policy, brought the ideals of progressive internationalism into question.

When war came, the Association was forced to make a choice. It had pledged to remain neutral in debates about US foreign policy, even if it believed that the righteousness of progressive internationalism would become apparent to any American who studied the facts. Adolf Hitler made that stance all but impossible. Following the line of an avowed supporter, President Franklin D. Roosevelt, the Association pushed those who held to non-interventionist approaches to security—"isolationists," as they were now called—out of the realm of legitimate debate that its stages and publications had come to represent. But as the United States marshaled its power to defeat the Axis, as Chapter 3 shows, the rise of the national security state all but destroyed the Association. The Council on Foreign Relations vaulted above it in policymaking influence after 1939, while the State Department, under significant public pressure, set up structures that embodied its own idea of what a democratic foreign policy might look like in practice. State no longer needed the Association in the way it had a few years earlier, and it quickly reconciled itself to methods of rousing the public that were far more propagandistic than the educational approach the Association favored, methods it had defined itself against. At the crucial moment when the United States was sketching a template to guide its global primacy, the Association was diminished.

Nonetheless, although the United States was now fully engaged with the world, few experts thought that its people were ready to govern their own foreign policy. The conviction that educational methods had gone not nearly far enough was not novel, but the Association now needed a fresh approach. Chapter 4 offers a history of the Cleveland Council on World Affairs, which since the mid-1930s had joined progressive internationalists with hard-power realists around the belief that more could be done. This chapter shows how national visions met local realities, and how a very particular sort of success became a model for the rest of the country despite the struggle that the Council's guiding spirit, Brooks Emeny, faced in gaining serious support for his ideas. Emeny became the president of the Foreign Policy Association in 1947, but his dream of founding a nationwide network of community World Affairs Councils faltered, as Chapter 5 shows. While the Ford Foundation threw its wealth at the problem, McCarthyism swept through the internationalist infrastructure, tarnishing reputations, ruining livelihoods, and even making public debate about foreign policy physically dangerous in some parts of the country. The World Affairs Council model turned out to fit only a few cities, cities that were themselves changing rapidly as the white, wealthy, and educated citizens who were the Association's traditional target dispersed to the suburbs. The Association had to abandon the Cleveland example, and it lost more than just time in the process.

The damage had been done. Chapter 6 shows that the intellectual doubts that had been muttered quietly in the 1920s and 1930s spoke loudly from academic scholarship in the late 1940s and early 1950s. Opinion polls and other statistical surveys seemed to suggest to many observers that not only were the American people deeply ignorant about foreign policy, but that many were incurably apathetic about the issue too. Political scientists advised that the educational ideal was wrong headed; it had failed to such a degree that experts who appeared to share a set of core values with the rest of the country would have to be delegated to work in the public's place. If institutions like the Association were to survive, such scholars argued, they should focus their energies only on an elite, promoting the interests of policymakers rather than creating a public that could act to define the national interest of its own accord. Even at this point, though, what sociologist C. Wright Mills in 1956 called the "fairy tale" of American democracy continued to exert its sway, and the older ideal of a democratic foreign policy remained powerful enough for the Association to mount a counterattack. Great Decisions was its weapon, an attempt to take foreign policy to the people through home discussion groups, mass media programming, and assurances that public opinion really did matter to policymakers. But Great Decisions was too weak to bear such a burden, even if it reached tens of thousands of Americans each year after 1955. It ended up proving the new social science not wrong, but right, as an attempt to rubbish an "elitist theory of democracy" fell prey to a different kind of elitism: the Association's, with its high-society origins and its deference to expertise. Theoretical concerns about the mission were therefore joined in the early 1960s by the sense that it was also a practical impossibility. Chapter 7 details how the dream of a democratic foreign policy died, with the nation in uproar over Vietnam, US foreign policy in tatters, and the Association tarred as just another part of an "establishment" that it had labored for decades to prevent.[17]

SINCE THE 1970s, the question of how to conduct a foreign policy in a democracy has not been as fraught as in the half century before. Although the fundamental nature of American leadership is up for debate in a way that it arguably has not been since the Vietnam War, that debate is usually posed in terms of what specific policies the public might support, how diplomats might better serve the middle class, or how hard it will be for the United States to secure its interests or promote order abroad if it is divided at home. The idea that every citizen might be made a statesman, however blinkered that idea's content was when Brooks Emeny advanced it in 1946, seems as far-fetched now as his motto that "it is the essence of a democracy that the people decide on foreign policy" and "the peril of a democracy that they decide in ignorance." Is it? Has it been? Could it be? The questions have almost been forgotten, and while this book offers no clear answers, it suggests that in telling how Americans approached them in the century gone by, they now might be raised again. For that reason, even if this story is one of failure, it nonetheless remains instructive at a time when America's foreign policy confronts yet another a crisis of legitimacy, and when its own democracy is under siege.[18]

# 1

# "Foreign Relations Was Something for Women"

Herbert Croly and Alvin Johnson were there from the *New Republic*. Editors from the *Public*, the *Dial*, and the *Independent* were there too, men of impeccable progressive credentials all. Charles Beard, the historian who had quit Columbia University in disgust at its restriction of academic freedom when the United States had gone to war, came, as did Henry R. Mussey of the *Nation*, who had resigned from Columbia in disgust at its treatment of Beard. British allies arrived, prime among them Norman Angell, who had helped to found the Union of Democratic Control, which had rocked Whitehall with its calls for diplomacy to be subjected to popular consent. Although entirely male, it was a politically broad group of reformers that met at the Columbia University Club on April 23, 1918, and surprisingly so. All these men claimed the mantle of progressivism, and some might have constituted its leadership not so long before, but their recent divisions over whether the United States should enter the Great War and what that fight meant for democracy had been so rancorous that few causes and fewer men could now bring them together. Paul U. Kellogg was one. He chaired the meeting that evening on West Forty-Third Street.[1]

Kellogg held an exalted position among progressives male and female alike. Famed for a muckraking exposé of the Pittsburgh steel industry that had helped end the seven-day work week, he had campaigned against intervention in the Great War as editor of the *Survey*, then reconciled himself to it once America joined the fray. After starting to collaborate with men he considered reactionaries to plan for the peace that would follow the war, Kellogg set sail for France in September 1917 as a volunteer for the Red Cross. On his way back, he stopped in Britain. What struck him everywhere he traveled, he told his friends once back in New York, was the inspirational impact

of Woodrow Wilson. People abroad, Kellogg said, spoke of the president's Fourteen Points "as if the whole new world were ablaze with them." Far from it, he
complained. Wilson was already a hero overseas, but at home he faced dissension. While the League to Enforce Peace was promoting a conservative view of
international law as the salve for a warring world, progressives—"democrats,"
in Kellogg's words—quarreled in "ignorance of foreign affairs." What was
needed, Kellogg thought, was an organization that would offer the backing of
"thinking democratic citizens" to a White House proposing a "democratic
order of world relations." Open to all, this group would try to influence policy
through public education, ensuring that foreign policy was rooted in the
popular participation that progressives thought essential to democratic culture. Such an institution might, in time, claim Wilsonianism as its own.[2]

Over the next few months, more journalists and more academics joined
this Committee on American Policy, meeting privately to learn the catechism
of internationalism. Beard wrote a reading list, teaching the group about a
world connected through trade and ruled through racial hierarchies. Kellogg
invited speakers to give lectures, prime among them Tomas Masaryk, who
was just months from becoming president of the new state of Czechoslovakia.
Stephen Duggan, a historian and veteran of the peace movement, drafted
plans for an institution that "liberally minded men" could use to educate the
"provincial and ignorant" towards "the international mind," a phrase borrowed
from Nicholas Murray Butler, Columbia's president and a director of the
Carnegie Endowment for International Peace. Seeing themselves as part of a
movement sweeping across borders, the members of this Committee took
cues from their British colleagues. They formed a League of Nations Society
in October, then replaced that name with another in use across the Atlantic.
With the ink just about dry on the Armistice and the former *Harper's* editor
Norman Hapgood elected as their leader, the League of Free Nations Association went public on November 27, 1918.[3]

The Association announced itself with a statement of principles vague
enough that men and women from all parts of the progressive movement
could sign it, from philosopher John Dewey to J.P. Morgan partner Thomas
W. Lamont, suffragist Jane Addams to future Supreme Court justice Felix
Frankfurter. The signatories accepted the use of force in international affairs,
but sought to transcend it through "security" and "justice." Security, they agreed,
would come when states abandoned power politics and combined their
strength to uphold "fair treatment for all." Justice, they argued, would come
when competition was replaced with cooperation, as "interdependence" and

"equality of economic opportunity" were vouchsafed in an unequal world. Just as these progressives had sought to use the federal government to create a more perfect union among the several states, so a similar institution was needed to create a more perfect world beyond. The Association hoped that Wilson's League of Nations would end the secrecy and duplicity surrounding diplomacy that seemed to make wars more likely, becoming a "democratic union of peoples" through publicity and "effective popular representation" rather than "an immense bureaucratic union of governments." These progressives sought, they said, thereby to reform the world through an extension of "the principles that have been woven into the fabric of our national life"— America, leading the world through its ideals, if not yet its might.[4]

The Association was comprised of people prominent enough to draw immediate fire, with a *New York Times* editorial joking that its plea for free trade meant it might better be called the "League for the Resuscitation of German Commerce at the Expense of the Allies." But as a compromise among squabbling progressive factions, the Association was far too weak to withstand the collision of principles with realities. Powerless to influence the peace negotiations in Paris, where Angell, its representative, found himself unable to get a hearing, it condemned the draft League of Nations Covenant as a product "of governments not of peoples," a fatal concession to an old, undemocratic world. Even as the Association applauded the more liberal aspects of Wilson's peace, the president saw the threat. Assistant Secretary of the Navy Franklin D. Roosevelt was sent to address the Association at the Commodore, a glitzy new hotel near Grand Central Terminal, before Wilson himself cajoled Hapgood and Duggan at the White House on March 1, bribing Hapgood a couple of days in advance with a nomination as US minister to Denmark, one the Senate would never take up because of his supposed sympathy for the Bolsheviks. Practicing the participation they preached, the few hundred members of the Association voted later that month to support Wilson, with some caveats. The president's opponents, including the *New Republic* and *Nation* editors who had attended the Columbia Club meeting a year earlier, promptly quit.[5]

Progressive splits widened when Wilson unveiled the full, punitive Treaty of Versailles in May. The Treaty, outraged Association leaders cabled the White House, was "unfavorable to future peace and incompatible with principles mutually accepted as a basis for the armistice." The Association nevertheless voted for the Treaty's ratification in July, albeit on the condition that the Senate declare it would interpret the Treaty in a liberal light, an unlikely prospect given that the Republican majority leader, Senator Henry Cabot Lodge, was threatening reservations to protect US sovereignty, not share it still further than Wilson proposed. Even that compromise at the Association could not last, though, as Attorney General A. Mitchell Palmer authorized raids on radical organizations, horrifying progressives, and as an anticommunist scare chilled speech. Wilson's authority among liberals collapsed; so did the Association, or near enough. Soon it found itself in the hands of historian James Grover McDonald, a nobody in progressive circles born in 1886 in Coldwater, Ohio—population, about one thousand—who had, before joining the staff of the Civil Service Reform League in 1918, been a lecturer at Indiana University, his Harvard doctoral thesis on an obscure order of Spanish monks left incomplete. When the Senate voted the Treaty down in November, McDonald urged Wilson to pay Lodge's price. Wilson refused. McDonald warned that "the entire League of Nations Covenant may be lost." When the Senate voted again in March 1920, it was. "To speak frankly," the Association's executive committee wrote to the ailing president, "we have all of us failed."[6]

## "Foreign Politics Shall Be Subject to Democratic Control"

Though it seemed unlikely at the time, the failure of 1920 led to the continuation of an internationalist moment in the United States. Describing the decade that followed that way might seem odd given that Americans claiming the heritage of internationalism have since dubbed it an "isolationist" era. But if we read the past forward rather than back, the framing is correct. Wilson's League was extraordinarily popular among Americans. The Treaty of Versailles had a strong majority in the Senate, just not the two-thirds majority necessary to ratify it. The League had the support of most newspaper editors, most major voluntary associations, and most state legislatures. While there was opposition to the League from nationalists who sought a freer hand for the United States to wield its power, more damage was done by internationalists who felt secure enough to quarrel among themselves. As Stephen Wertheim has shown, "internationalism" at this point did not mean the use of overwhelming US power to solve problems, as it would come to mean from the 1940s on, but rather the transcendence of power politics through peaceful intercourse and especially through the cultivation and application of public opinion. This sort of internationalism was a consensus position in US politics at the time; where Wilson failed was in satisfying sufficient senators that the

League represented the right *kind* of internationalism. Gilbert Hitchcock, Wilson's floor leader throughout the fight, was right to tell the Senate in February 1919 that "internationalism has come, and we must choose what form the internationalism shall take." The trouble was that the choice remained an intractable one; no solution would come until the 1940s, when Roosevelt would use the legacy of internationalism to give the primacy of American arms a moral mask.[7]

The United States never joined the League, and some of its advocates eventually came to accept that Wilson's ambition to substitute "discussion for fight" had been naïve, but the political culture of what John A. Thompson has called this "restrained superpower" was not generally hostile to internationalism in the 1920s. US foreign policy remained engaged. Diplomats, united in a reformed United States Foreign Service in 1924, came to a working relationship with the League, particularly its judicial, economic, and "technical" arms. Americans flocked to Geneva, giddily partaking in its intoxicating atmosphere as tourists, working on the League's staff, or ensuring it was properly funded. The United States took the lead in disarmament negotiations, above all at the Washington Naval Conference of 1921–1922, and championed the outlawry of war, the Kellogg-Briand Pact of 1928 winning near-unanimous Senate assent. US influence was simply a fact to the New York financiers whose credit made global finance work, to the titans of industry whose outputs and methods came to dominate the world economy, and to onlookers across the waters, who perceived a hegemon on the rise and began to act accordingly. Americans meanwhile created myriad groups that expressed their persistent interest in the world, continuing the peace movement at home, joining professional organizations that crossed borders, and studying "scientific" solutions to the scourge of war. At the center of these developing networks emerged a handful of institutions that embodied progressive principles but outlasted progressives themselves, surviving for decades as the heart of the foreign policy community. Although few Americans were eager to get involved in a second major war, and though traditional ideas about non-entanglement continued to shape policy debates, there was little "isolationism" of this organized, institutionalized, resourced sort.[8]

Much of this activity had explicit roots in progressive politics. Histories of the progressive era tend to end with the sweeping Republican victories in the elections of 1920, but even if prewar progressivism did not recover as a recognizable electoral force, it still set the terms for the political and intellectual debates of the 1920s. Progressives lived on, after all. Long attentive to the overseas contexts of their work, they now applied what they were still learning in municipal reform, settlement houses, and industrial relations to a larger geographical space. They brought with them their obsessions with expertise and efficiency in governance, as well as a fear of the masses that complicated their ultimate faith in public opinion, suitably managed. Conscious that the increasing power of the United States required a more sustained, coherent approach to world affairs than the nineteenth century had demanded, they started to bind some of the ways in which they engaged beyond their borders—law, trade, empire, religion, feminism, and much more—into a novel field of policy whose boundaries and outlooks they defined and contested. Distinguishing this field from "peace" and day-to-day "diplomacy," they called it "foreign affairs," "foreign relations," or "foreign policy."[9]

Who should control that foreign policy? If one of the animating questions of progressive reformism had been who ought to govern various aspects of American life and how, it was only natural that progressives would ask this question about their diplomacy too. Wilsonians believed that a degree of democratic deliberation among nations would bring peace where secrecy and force had once brought war, but their commitment to reforming international politics came with the conviction that it was also essential to reform how foreign policies were made at home. Even if Wilson held a cavalier disregard for popular opinion himself, he told Congress in January 1918 that a US war aim was that diplomacy "shall proceed always frankly and in the public view." It showed the strength of allegiance to that ideal that his fellow progressives became so irate when the president later betrayed his commitment to "open covenants, openly arrived at" in Paris. Part of that reaction might be attributed to the old-world shadows in the Covenant itself, but part spoke, too, to the success of a transnational movement for the "democratic control" of foreign relations during the war. The demands had been loudest in Britain, where the *hauteur* of the Foreign Office had led a million people to join the Union of Democratic Control by 1918. Similar calls had been made in the United States as well, even if Congress historically enjoyed far greater power over foreign relations than Parliament. Union ideas also circulated among *New Republic* and *Nation* progressives; after lobbying from activists such as educator Fannie Fern Andrews, Wilson embraced parts of the Union's platform. Conservative internationalists had long spoken a similar language, too, if for less radical purposes. "Why labor the point!" scholar Quincy Wright exclaimed in 1922. "Democracy is convinced of the merits of democratic diplomacy."[10]

What might that mean? Men and women with strikingly different politics claimed the same words for strikingly different purposes. Their answers were as much implicit as explicit, offered through institutional action more than worked-out theories of public opinion, which were bafflingly scarce and maddeningly vague given that they described an entity that internationalists thought could save the world. The institutions that worked on the problem of public opinion were not unfettered expressions of the ideas behind them, moreover, but compromises with the banal contingencies of budgets and staffing, the limits of technology and geography. Even so, there were some areas of consensus among progressives. The most basic was that while the unfiltered will of the people could not be trusted, susceptible as it was to nationalism and militarism, the collective intelligence of some of them could, if properly instructed. Those closest to foreign policymaking agreed that their first task was to educate themselves and those like them. Partly attributable to the natural inclination of elites, this view also followed academic theories of public opinion that saw opinions trickle down from leaders to the people, a model that had been widely adopted after being advanced by James Bryce, who had presided over the American Political Science Association in 1907–1908 while serving as British ambassador to the United States. Bryce, a supporter of the Union of Democratic Control, argued in London after the war that more information needed to be made available about foreign affairs, and more opportunities offered for sustained discussion of it. Wilsonian internationalists assumed that both tasks would entail forming voluntary associations, the form of political and civic organization that had done so much to teach Americans how to subject issues of common importance to common concern.[11]

One path forward was suggested by the most prominent statesman writing on the subject, Elihu Root. Secretary of war from 1899 to 1904, secretary of state from 1905 to 1909, and Nobel laureate in 1912 for his promotion of judicial arbitration to resolve disputes, Root had been urging broader understanding of world affairs since the turn of the century, offering plenty of clever lines that liberals could borrow as an endorsement. "A democracy which undertakes to control its own foreign relations ought to know something about the subject," he said in 1916. What this Republican founder of the League to Enforce Peace meant, however, was that a group of men ought to be trained to resist the "popular diplomacy" that was, he said in 1922, an irreversible consequence of "the exercise of universal suffrage, the spread of elementary education, and the revelation of the power of organization." If the ignorant masses were inevitably to have their say, Root thought, disaster could be averted only if the many felt the sure hand of an enlightened few, of public-spirited men who possessed such Victorian virtues as "politeness," "restraint," and "responsibility" and engaged in the "laborious and difficult undertaking" of "long and attentive study." Root's vision of a democratic diplomacy hardly meant empowering the citizenry, but rather the opposite. "What is everybody's business is nobody's business," he fumed in 1925 as the situation further escaped his control. "To get things done some human agency must be designated to give effect to the general desire that they be done."[12]

This vision of a democratic foreign policy found its home at the Council on Foreign Relations, which Root said in 1931 showed "the right method by which the path is to be found and to be followed." Founded in 1921, the Council was reserved for a few hundred, carefully selected men of stature who met for genteel dinners at the Harvard Club, the Council's home until it acquired premises on East Sixty-Fifth Street in 1930. Its events served as a meeting point through which diplomatic practitioners and outside experts could share knowledge, foster networks, and generate consensus; its membership constituted a pool of suitably vetted talent that could serve in senior policy positions whenever called upon. In time, the Council would be identified as the core of the foreign policy establishment, but in the aftermath of the Great War, it was a far less significant enterprise, however distinguished was the readership of its journal, *Foreign Affairs*. Before 1939, indeed, the Council is best thought of as a social haunt for predominantly wealthy men with professional interests in foreign affairs, one they modeled on the clubs that they and their fathers had started during the Gilded Age to insulate themselves from a public sphere in which women were becoming ever more prominent. Not all Council men shared Root's politics, to be sure, but it was hardly a coincidence that he had been such a vocal opponent of the Nineteenth Amendment that one critic called him an "ancient cave man" who would "not only oppose the extension of the suffrage to women," but "its extension to anybody." Hostility to "popular diplomacy," in other words, was intrinsically related to a specific hostility toward women in public life.[13]

The Council's origin story is just as revealing of its reactionary basis as the aristocratic theory of public opinion that supported it. Its founding was not an inevitable replication of patriarchal structures, as is often imagined, but an explicit response to the rising visibility of women in foreign relations and the expansive culture of participation they embodied and worked to further. Its genesis lay in two separate enterprises. One initiative was Root's, a group of bankers, lawyers, and others paying one hundred dollars in dues to attend the dinner meetings of a "Council on Foreign Relations" in 1918. That Council met at the ritziest of all Manhattan clubs, the Metropolitan, but became moribund after the summer of 1919. The other initiative lasted little longer after its founding event, a meeting of the more scholarly British and American delegates to the Paris Peace Conference on May 30, 1919, which planned out a transatlantic Institute of International Affairs. The British cadres went on to set up the Royal Institute of International Affairs, better known as Chatham House, but their American peers — mostly men who had worked in New York for The Inquiry, Wilson's postwar planning staff, before going to Paris without their thirty or so female colleagues — prevaricated. Only when lawyer Frances Kellor, exasperated with their inaction, tried to found an American Institute of International Affairs of her own in 1921 were a few quiet words had with her sponsors to head off the threat so that the two groups could merge to form the Council proper, with Root as honorary president. From then until 1969, when an eventual decision to admit women left some old-timers in tears, policing the gender line was the focal point of the Council's defense against the involvement in foreign relations of a broader public that it saw, as Robert Schulzinger has written, as "always stupid and usually wrong." Putting the Council at the heart of the story of democratic control would merely replicate its exclusionary vision.[14]

There is another story to be told, though, one that pays due attention to the women whose activism prompted such a response. After all, it has long been clear that women were making their voices heard on foreign affairs around the time of the Great War. Suffrage had been an international effort, for one thing, and it was embroiled in debates about imperialism. Women had always been important in the peace movement and continued to be after the Armistice, whether in domestic groups like Carrie Chapman Catt's Committee on the Cause and Cure of War or transnational organizations like the Women's International League for Peace and Freedom, for whose work Jane Addams won a Nobel prize in 1931. Even the crustiest of diplomats admired the ability of the League of Women Voters — the successor to the National American Woman Suffrage Association — to generate interest in foreign policy issues. Women in the 1920s were meanwhile entering universities in numbers that would not again be approached for decades; alumni networks were crucibles of internationalism. As Martha Jones has written, Black women were "marginalized, rebuffed, and overlooked" among white suffragists, and they would continue to be, but their own internationalism persisted all the same. So, if we are to ask "where are the women," as international relations theorist Cynthia Enloe has encouraged us to do, the answer is that, in this period, they were almost everywhere.[15]

In fact, the networks, labors, and methods of white women spilled from suffragism and pacifism into the effort to subject foreign policy to democratic control, and hence into the early foreign policy community. Certainly, there were parts of this community in which women struggled to break through, as well as areas towards which they dared not look even as opportunities opened with a new dawn of peace. But if this world was not at all an equal one, when it came to the democratization at the heart of postwar internationalism, suffragists came to the fore. "Since war is commonly brought about not by the mass of the people, who do not desire it," the International Congress of Women had declared at The Hague in 1915, with Addams presiding, "Foreign Politics shall be subject to Democratic Control." Marshalling these energies, former suffragists would join with sympathetic male allies to build an institution so towering that the less chauvinist of the Council's members felt they had to join it as well. Radical enough to combine men and women in common cause but not to overthrow the social structures of the time, that institution took its style from the women's movement and set to work "for popular education in foreign affairs," as it declared in June 1921. To that end, it took steps to obscure its origins, relieving itself of a name that to some onlookers suggested an alliance with "the Sinn Feiners, the Bolsheviks," and others striving for independence. Come March 1921, the League of Free Nations Association became the Foreign Policy Association.[16]

## Trickle-Down Diplomacy

Seven years later, in 1928, the Foreign Policy Association celebrated its tenth anniversary with a meal for a thousand guests in the grand ballroom of the Hotel Astor. It was the 109th luncheon it had held in Manhattan, where the events had become such a sensation in the social scene that they had spread to fourteen other cities, as far west as Minneapolis and as far south as Richmond. Sitting on the Association's national council were lawyers, educators, and bankers, as well as a who's who of the women's movement. The Association was not a mass organization, whatever the reach of its pioneering radio broadcasts; despite a budget of $160,000 its rosters listed only nine thousand members or so, which meant that the weekly *Bulletin* they received enjoyed a comparable circulation to the *New Republic*. The Association had its

**1.1** James G. McDonald aboard the *SS Paris*, 1933. Travel was an important symbol of authority for foreign policy experts after the Great War, marking firsthand expertise of issues that remained distant to most Americans. McDonald spent many summers touring the diplomatic hotspots of Europe, reporting back in speeches in the fall.
United States Holocaust Memorial Museum.

competitors too. The Council on Foreign Relations attracted wealthier men. The Institute of Pacific Relations, founded in 1925 under Stanford University president Ray Lyman Wilbur, had opened a San Francisco branch in 1927 and would soon expand. The Chicago Council on Foreign Relations and the Social Science Foundation in Denver worked from the luncheon model. But the Association alone aimed for national reach, drawing notices across the press and receiving telegrams from all over the world on special occasions, praising its work for peace and understanding. At its head remained James McDonald, a wry, debonair speaker who had, somewhat unexpectedly, become one of the most famous experts on international affairs in the country.[17]

This success was more of an organizational triumph than the miracle of policy influence the Association's founders had hoped for. Dedicated to "a liberal and constructive American foreign policy," as its letterhead and constitution put it, the Association had most notably promoted the League of Nations, sending out reports from the annual meeting of the Assembly in Geneva, keeping in close contact with its officials and advocates, and honoring League personalities at public events in New York and elsewhere. It had courted controversy over more pressing issues in US foreign policy, demanding disarmament, urging formal recognition of the Soviet Union, and decrying Washington's more brutal efforts at imperialism. It had even made temporary cause with politicians opposed to the League when their interests overlapped, not least Senator William Borah, leader of the irreconcilables. If the Association had not taken a stance on an issue, then it had been sufficiently confident to let its staff do so on their own time, while also using its offices as a neutral party to coordinate causes like the crusade to join the World Court. In these years, the Association still defined "education" as meaning instructing activists towards a certain objective rather than the broader, subtler sense it would soon adopt. Even amid the internationalist moment of the 1920s, however, it had achieved little it could claim as its own.[18]

Where the Association did find its niche was in creating cohesion among disparate sets of internationalists, forging unlikely alliances around its attempt to define and discuss "all sides of every important international question affecting the United States," as its formal constitution promised in 1922. It cobbled together funding from where it could. In time, the Association would come to depend on the philanthropies named for those who had prospered most from the nation's economic expansion—the Rockefellers, Carnegies, and Fords—and whose foundations leveraged unfathomable resources to promote particular visions of peace. But before then, the Association relied on donors who connected high-society reformism to the interests of finance. Women's wealth was invaluable. The Association's earliest significant bene-factor was Dorothy Payne Whitney, an heiress who supported causes from the settlement house movement to educational reform. Whitney was the principal backer of the *New Republic*, the journal of choice among Associa-tion supporters; the magazine's managing editor, Bruce Bliven, was an Asso-ciation trustee from 1922 to 1943. Whitney was joined among the leading contributors by Agnes Goddard Leach, a pacifist who, as well as working on New York State commissions on health, education, and welfare, at one point combined serving on the Association's board with her chairmanship of the New York State League of Women Voters.[19]

Wall Street quickly exerted its influence despite the awkward position bankers occupied in the progressive imagination. Felix Warburg and Otto Kahn of Kuhn, Loeb & Co. both contributed with their wives, Frieda and Addie, as they did to most major New York charities, but their role was overshadowed by that of Thomas W. and Florence Lamont. Florence was a committed in-ternationalist in her own right, serving as one of the more active members of the Association's board from 1926 to 1951 and contributing more in total to its finances than her husband. Even so, it was Thomas's role that gave rise to rumors. "Some people told me the F.P.A. was a Morgan organization," an As-sociation official reported after taking soundings in Washington in 1927, "while other people said that it was extremely radical, which is, I suppose, what we want them to say." Private bankers played a key role in US foreign policy in the 1920s, their lending used as the crucial lubricant in dollar diplomacy, war debts, and reparations; no bank was more important than J. P. Morgan & Co., and no banker more important than its senior partner, Lamont. Morgan financiers were involved across the foreign policy infrastructure—Russell C. Leffingwell would chair the Council on Foreign Relations from 1946 to 1953— but Lamont was always closest to the Association. There was a political affinity to the relationship, but the reality was bluntly transactional. McDonald re-ceived cash, *entrée* into the social circle around Florence, and access to one of the most powerful men in the world. Lamont could launder the reputation of the House of Morgan, promote banking as nonpartisan expertise, and sate his prodigious ego. It was a privilege that could backfire. At a Hotel Astor luncheon in 1926, Lamont stood next to the president of the Fascist League of North America, declared his admiration for Benito Mussolini, and asked whether the Association's membership was "liberal enough to let Italy have the kind of government she seems to want." General outrage ensued.[20]

1.2 Florence Lamont, 1928. The wife of J. P. Morgan banker Thomas W. Lamont, Florence was a devoted internationalist in her own right: one of the principal financial backers of the Foreign Policy Association, she served with several other women of distinction on its board of directors from 1926 to 1950. Smith College Special Collections.

What was a fascist doing speaking to these apostles of liberalism, over three courses and in white tie? Part of the answer lies in the progressive desire to restore free speech after Wilson's wartime censorship, the excesses of George Creel's Committee on Public Information, and the distaste for the Red Scare that had swept through the left in 1919 and 1920, leading to the founding of the American Civil Liberties Union. When the Association declared that it was "working for real freedom of thought and discussion" and putting in place rules that guaranteed radical positions a hearing, it was therefore drawing on harsh experience; one of its first events saw *New Republic* editor Walter Lippmann and Harvard free-speech advocate Zachariah Chafee Jr. denounce anti-sedition legislation in 1920. But another aspect of the reasoning behind the luncheons testifies to the lasting power of philosophical pragmatism. As Throntveit has argued, the pragmatist legacy had been central both to Wilson's plans for the League and to liberals' rejection of them; pragmatism was claimed by reformers promoting deliberative forms of politics long after it had become unfashionable among other intellectuals. Among those activists were those at the Association, who based the luncheons that made its reputation on the belief that citizens could be led towards a truer understanding of their common interests through the open discussion of ideas, and the feistier the better. A luncheon at which two, three, four, or even five speakers offered competing views on a subject in foreign relations, with an often raucous question period to follow, was therefore much more than just a luncheon.[21]

The Association started its luncheon series with a meeting of ninety guests on January 11, 1919, at the Café Boulevard, an exclusive Hungarian restaurant. Already wedded to the multi-speaker format that would define its first two decades, three men addressed different sides of "The Problem of the Adriatic"; the next week, three more discussed "Poland and Danzig"; the week after that, five discussed the Russian Revolution, three anti-Bolshevik, and two pro. One internal history recounted that "the various topics under debate were presented to them by experts representing every national interest, every racial cause, every territorial, political and economical problem," and that "scrupulous care was taken to hear all sides." This was not always strictly true, and the Association would sometimes claim a little too conveniently that it could not find speakers eager to challenge liberal orthodoxies before tables of notable reformers baying for embarrassment. Still, the luncheons were an immediate hit, drawing unusually large crowds. By April 1919, Lippmann, Hamilton Holt, and David Lawrence were debating the relationship between Wilson's Fourteen Points and the proposed League in front of 1,400 people at the Hotel Commodore, to wide press coverage. Three years later, the luncheons moved permanently to the Hotel Astor, the new playground for plutocrats that anchored the entertainment district of Times Square.[22]

Though the Association's constitution committed it to reaching "as large a number of the American people as possible," high society was its first target, the product of the privilege that progressive reforms had only heightened in New York. Even this form of internationalism, like its Council on Foreign Relations rival, coalesced in the clubs and ballrooms that had prospered in the Gilded Age and remained intended to close off an elite from the mass. Once McDonald had made his reputation, the day was rare when he did not take both meals at a club, or as an invited guest at a salon with his wife. But the club networks from which the Association emerged were tellingly different to those behind the Council. The Association's board met not at the Metropolitan or Harvard, Council haunts where women were banned, but at the Cosmopolitan Club or the Women's City Club. The former, founded in 1909, was central to New York's networks of educated, professional women; the latter, founded in 1915, was a crucible of activist reform that shared leaders like Frances Hand, Lillian Wald, and Mary Simkhovitch with the Association. Although broader public engagement was a core part of these women's politics, the ballrooms in which they heard McDonald speak tended to limit that engagement to a predictable crowd. Even if the luncheons were open to the public, participating in them—and therefore participating in foreign policy debate in the ways these progressives endorsed—was demanding. It required significant free time, awareness of social codes, and some wealth. Membership in the Association cost a minimum of five dollars, and discounts were available to teachers and students, but a ticket to one of the twelve or so luncheons held each season cost a further two to three dollars for members. Those lunching elsewhere could pay a dollar or so to watch the spectacle from the galleries, roughly the same price as a grandstand seat at Yankee Stadium.[23]

And a spectacle the luncheons certainly were. McDonald was a witty, urbane chairman, and under his gavel foreign policy became a potent brew of high-society glamor and highbrow academic combat, a "clash of wit and feeling" as Kellogg described it in 1926. The luncheons physically staged the deliberation that Wilsonian progressives hoped would transform domestic and international politics alike. Education was the name of the game—maps, reading lists, and even treaty texts were set out on the tables for reference—but drama was the weapon of choice. "I understand that the exigencies of the budget require that these discussions become intellectual battles," Edwin Borchard of Yale told one luncheon in 1928, "and that people do not feel they have been a success unless there has been a very sharp and acrimonious, if not bloody, contest." Borchard was not joking; plain-clothed police officers sometimes patrolled the walls of the Astor, and meetings grew heated as a matter of course. One luncheon devolved into "little short of a riot" in 1925, McDonald noted in his diary, as "unprecedented hissing" erupted amid an argument between the US correspondent of the Soviet newspaper *Izvestia* and an Irish journalist who had once been captured by the Red Army. "Boos mingled with derisive laughter" at another when a former Mexican official accused the United States of promoting banditry to support oil interests. Proceedings seethed with particular fury when attendees were brave enough to breach the lines of race and class that typically protected speakers. The chairman of the British League of Nations Union, Gilbert Murray, once endured such hostility from "representatives of subject portions of the Empire," McDonald noted, that he became "a little explosive, particularly as he answered the Negro."[24]

Such interventions were rare, however, and the luncheons were hardly intended to reach beyond a monied class. Kellogg accepted that the attendees were "not the man in the street," but rather a community "with a common thread of interest," men and women possessed of "as much intelligence but not so much information to the subject in hand as the small group of experts." Steep barriers to entry remained, even if the Association told donors in 1925 that it hoped "the thinking of millions of our fellow citizens on international affairs" could be supplied with sufficient facts to make public opinion "a sure and constant source of strength." The connection was taken on faith, however. Little serious thought was put into the mechanisms through which facts might trickle down from the lunching few, or indeed trickle up towards policymakers. It was "our work" to reveal facts "free from the import tariff of prejudice, self-interest and narrow nationalism," the Association secretary Christina Merriman told members in 1927, but it was "your work to help us get them out to a wider and wider public." How that might happen was left unsaid, the responsibility outsourced, but if the members were "laboring under the illusion that your business with foreign policy ends when you have listened to a lively debate," Kellogg said in 1928, they were wrong. "You can't lunch your way into either the Kingdom of Heaven or a world safe for democracy."[25]

Even the radio, widely seen as having the potential to transform democracy at home and reknit the fabric of peace abroad, offered for the moment a similar kind of public to the one that gathered at the Astor. The Association first appeared on the airwaves on April 2, 1923, when New York's WEAF network broadcast a dinner in honor of Lord Robert Cecil, an author of the League Covenant whose tour of the United States that month the Association sponsored with a blank check from Thomas Lamont. McDonald, who traveled as Cecil's chaperone, told the Astor to a standing ovation that evening that eight hundred thousand people were listening in, among them Woodrow Wilson himself. If that number stretched credulity at a time when only a few million radio sets had been sold, the luncheons became a staple of early radio programming. They were popular enough to withstand the buffeting of commercialism and were protected by McDonald's golf-buddy relationship with James Harbord, president of the Radio Corporation of America, and his friendship with Owen D. Young, the General Electric chairman who was an Association council member as well as a key figure in the plan to renegotiate German reparations that bore his name.[26]

Still, if the radio allowed McDonald to imagine a community of internationalists beyond the walls of the Astor's ballroom and gave evidence of interest from what he thought of as unexpected places, at this point it offered
returns barely less rarefied than those from the luncheons. Basic sets cost
about twenty dollars to purchase in 1925, a price steep enough that the Association could not hope to use the technology to do much more than extend
the reach of its usual techniques, not least because the geographical range of
the major networks was still limited. It suggested instead that the radio might
be made a social concern rather than a radical one. A Mrs. Walter Read of Indian Hill, New Jersey, drew praise in the *Bulletin* for hosting a luncheon as the
international relations committee of her local women's club listened to the
discussion from the Astor, then talked over what they had heard. While fears
lingered that the broadcasts might cut attendances in Manhattan, and would
do so when the radio became a mass medium in the 1930s and 1940s, Mc-
Donald remained satisfied in 1928 that "there is an audience for serious discussion of international affairs, an audience which will listen to such discussion
even in competition with the latest African syncopation." As that comment
implies, the Association was anxious to ensure that racial lines were protected
even as it promoted the occasional Black speaker. One debate on Haiti in
1929 turned into a farce when the white speaker defending the US occupation of the island, W. W. Cumberland, was hooked up to seven more stations
than W. E. B. DuBois had been for his remarks. "No discrimination was intended," a National Broadcasting Corporation spokesman assured the press.[27]

Even so, the listening groups the Association praised suggest that it approached the radio in the same spirit of pragmatism as its in-person discussions, hoping to create an active, if still white and educated public fully
engaged with what it was hearing. As McDonald's fame grew, he started a
weekly, fifteen-minute show on NBC's Red Network, a slot Young arranged
for him in 1928 and defended until 1933. One of the first regular commentators on foreign affairs, McDonald experimented with radio as if the airwaves
were simply an extension of his ballroom. "Ladies and gentlemen," he began
his first show, "this is not a lecture," but "the first of a series of informal discussion conferences" aiming for "a mutual exchange of impressions and experiences" that might produce "for me as much as for you a fuller understanding
of our rapidly changing world." Just as McDonald incorporated questions
that radio listeners telegrammed to the Astor into luncheon discussion periods, he quoted and answered listeners who wrote with comments after his
shows. He had maps and transcripts ready for those who wanted them, as

well as bibliographies to send to the teachers who used his broadcasts as a basis for the more internationalist pedagogy many sought. But while Mc-Donald admitted that he sought "quality listeners" rather than those whom he presumed preferred baser offerings, he still used his mailbag to draw maps drawn that visualized the popular engagement he created beyond the Northeast. The success of his "experiment," McDonald wrote in another set of maps that NBC made available to listeners, depended "upon the degree of your cooperation." He learned to be pleased that just dozens of letters arrived each week.[28]

## Women and the Creation of the Foreign Policy Community

The Association's radio broadcasts were most useful, it turned out, in spreading the luncheon model beyond Manhattan, as listeners decided to replicate what they heard in their own cities. Postwar reformism remained intensely, proudly local even as internationalist networks took on global reach, and for that reason the Association struggled outside New York at first. Manhattan's internationalists bickered initially with their friends in Boston, whose own, semi-independent League of Free Nations Association ran into so much trouble after the defeat of the Treaty of Versailles that they were forced to affiliate with the main Association in December 1922. The Chicago Council on Foreign Relations looked to New York for guidance throughout its founding year of 1922, but eventually declined to join formally with it. As turbulence among internationalists settled down, though, a more cohesive network became possible. First the citizens of Cincinnati asked to set up an Association branch, then Philadelphia, then Hartford; Providence and Springfield followed, then Columbus. By 1928, New York was supporting fourteen branches, which held sixty-seven luncheons between them that season, their rolls counting anywhere from 644 members in Philadelphia to ninety-three in Rochester, upstate. Radio played a role in this growth, but far more important was the role of women activists. In fact, the extent to which the Association was able to wire itself into pre-existing women's networks—those left from the suffrage campaign and those that worked for peace—decided its fate, locally and nationally. Suffrage, in this way, shaped the form of the early foreign policy community.[29]

Although the Association could not boast the support of men of the stature of those who led the Council on Foreign Relations, it had the assistance of some of the most prominent, influential women in US politics, benefitting from the advice, skills, and labor of tested activists as well as the ideas of pioneering international thinkers. Carrie Chapman Catt and Jane Addams did little more than offer their endorsements, but under the sponsorship of such towering figures the Association could count on the cooperation of the more mainstream factions of the women's movement, Catt's League of Women Voters above all. Women with deep experience in campaigns for suffrage and peace quickly took charge of the Association's day-to-day administration. Its first secretary was Christina Merriman, an activist and photographer whose elevated position among pacifists dated to her stint as acting chairman of the National Council for Limitation of Armament during the Washington Naval Conference of 1921–1922. When Merriman resigned in 1928 due to the ill health that would take her life two years later, her place was taken by Esther G. Ogden, who as membership secretary after 1921 played a leading role in internal debates about who the "public" in "public opinion" ought to be. Ogden was prominent enough in the peace movement to sit on the executive committee of Catt's Committee on the Cause and Cure of War and the board of the Woodrow Wilson Foundation, and her *bona fides* from the suffrage campaign were unquestionable. Elected to the board of the National American Woman Suffrage Association on two separate occasions, Ogden had served as president of its publishing arm throughout the climactic years of the struggle, overseeing the production of millions of pieces of campaign literature. At the time, there were few operatives savvier than Ogden in the practical creation and direction of public opinion.[30]

While colleagues from the women's movement oversaw the Association's work—none more revealingly than Ruth Morgan, who was concurrently vice chairman of the Association's board and chief of the League of Women Voters' admired department of international cooperation—Merriman and then Ogden staffed their office with women serving in positions from assistant treasurer to promotion bureau chief. Arguably the most important department was the speaker's bureau, led initially on a voluntary basis by Mrs. Henry James, then run for more than three decades by Frances J. Pratt, a Barnard College graduate who joined the staff in 1926. Even in the 1926–1927 season, before Pratt fully took over, the task required hundreds of letters, telegrams, and phone calls to potential speakers and their secretaries, knowing that two-thirds of inquiries would be declined. By 1929, the bureau had become a professional outfit, contracting with forty-five experts, diplomats, and personalities to plot appearances around the country, managing their diaries and tracking their fees. One year later, the bureau was not only sending speakers to ninety-two branch meetings with a total attendance of more than

**1.3** Members of the board of the Foreign Policy Association with the Italian fascist and Minister of Foreign Affairs Dino Grandi at a tea following Grandi's broadcast address to the Association at the Waldorf-Astoria, November 26, 1931. McDonald welcomed Grandi as a "vigorous advocate of disarmament and international cooperation." *From left:* Ruth Morgan, vice chairman of the board; Esther G. Ogden, secretary; Eustace Seligman; Mrs. Grandi; Grandi; James G. McDonald, chairman of the board; Agnes Goddard Leach; Charles W. Kellogg. United States Holocaust Memorial Museum.

thirty-seven thousand, but to three hundred or so engagements for outside groups too. Here was the start of the foreign policy lecture circuit, with a new breed of experts circulating around the country as never before; no single person was more responsible for its creation than Pratt, who thought up potential topics for debate, identified the key players in those debates, cajoled them to address those subjects, and wrote up long lists of speakers from which branch and other officials could select their programs. The speakers Ogden promoted were not the only experts involved in taking foreign policy to the public, to put it another way.[31]

If women were at the heart of the Association's office in New York, women's networks were central to its efforts outside Manhattan. Their importance makes sense: even if the League of Women Voters was small compared to its predecessor—for the women's movement fractured after the passage of the Nineteenth Amendment—the suffrage campaign left cadres of talented activists across the country, most of them committed to the voluntary, educational, nonpartisan approach to politics that women helped the Association embrace. Everywhere Association officials went, they found women eager to take the initiative or already doing so. In Philadelphia, the city's League chapter had begun its own luncheon series by 1922; its women at first invited the Association to cooperate on their terms, electing to form a branch in 1924. When McDonald took trains to Providence and Springfield in the hope of founding outposts in February 1925, he was primarily hosted by groups of women who sought to have the Association join their work, not the other way around. When the Association's board hired a field agent, a former director of relief efforts for the World Christian Student Federation named Raymond T. Rich, he filled his reports with praise for the women he encountered. And if the Association found a target city intractable, the cause either seemed to be that its women were already so active in peace activism that they did not need or want its help, or because women's networks for some reason faltered. Cleveland was the prime case, a city in which women dominated a vibrant pacifist scene and McDonald struggled to connect with "any of the women with whom we would naturally be associated." From this point onward, the changing fortunes of the League of Women Voters and its allies in the women's and peace movements would be an important component in the Association's success or lack thereof.[32]

The Association offered these women access to an otherwise inaccessible world of male diplomats, scholars, and writers, as well as an outlet through which they could fashion opportunities even within ongoing constraints. While the Manhattan office drew plaudits, the Boston branch provided the most striking example of what was possible after it appointed Marguerite Hopkins as its chair in November 1923. A former leader of the Women's City Club who possessed what McDonald admired as a "rigorously effective manner," Hopkins turned the branch's luncheons at the Copley Plaza hotel into events "so fashionable that they were oversubscribed before the announcement was given," as one attendee put it. Although Hopkins was acknowledged as a formidable administrator, however, she could accomplish little without the branch's program committee, which decided what issues in world affairs were current, who should speak on them, and what line the chosen speakers would take in debate. The committee changed from year to year and it often included women such as Fannie Fern Andrews, the education reformer who had lobbied Wilson on democratic control during the war, and Bernice Brown, dean of Radcliffe College. But at the committee's core tended to be four men: Harvard historian William Yandell Elliot; *Christian Science Monitor* editor Willis J. Abbot; another editor, Christian A. Herter, who had been a delegate at the Paris Peace Conference and later an advisor to Commerce Secretary Herbert Hoover; and, most importantly and durably, its chair, Manley O. Hudson, Bemis Professor of International Law at Harvard and the leading international lawyer in the United States, possibly beyond.[33]

Hopkins and Hudson formed an unusual but productive partnership, each depending on the expertise of the other to fuse and extend Boston's disparate internationalist communities. Hudson was no revolutionary and Hopkins was surprised at his faith in her, as if acknowledging the radical act of collaboration their alliance indeed was. "I have a good deal of faith in the gods myself," she told him in February 1924, praying that a schedule they had agreed on would work out; "you seem to have faith both in gods and in women as well." But the pair came to a fruitful working relationship, no doubt helped by the coy wit Hopkins deployed when needing to "assail the monk in his cell." Their correspondence suggests that Hopkins's knowledge of how to organize publics was just as intrinsic a part of Wilsonian internationalism as Hudson's erudite disquisitions on the law. "I do not know how much experience you have had in organizing or re-organizing an organization which needed cultivation of the most harrowing kind from the very depth of the soil to its surface," she wrote in 1924, before instructing him on how newspaper publicity actually worked. Hudson, for his part, offered his vast address book, habitually claiming to potential speakers that the Association offered "the best audience in New England." Hopkins was just as aware that Hudson could connect Bostonians to worlds she could not as she was that she possessed talents he lacked. "For the Annual Meeting, would you be willing to make the contact with Sweetzer," she asked in April 1929, shortly before her exhausted retirement, meaning the American League of Nations official Arthur Sweetser. "He might be willing to do it for you, knowing you, rather than for me, who proves to him merely a myth."[34]

Similar collaborations within unsettled but unequal gender dynamics played out in the Boston branch more generally, as in the Association as a whole. The branch was unusual in having a large governing council rather

39

than a small board of directors, in part because so many local constituencies had to be built into its work. Many of the luminaries invited to join the council were male lawyers, bankers, businessmen, clergy, and academics, but ordinarily about one-third—twenty-nine out of eighty in the 1928–1929 season—were women. They included several teachers, academic administrators, and socialites of the caliber of Harriet Hemenway, whose portrait was painted by John Singer Sargent, but also scholars of the prominence of Alice Hamilton, the former associate of Jane Addams who served on the League of Nations' Health Committee and was the first woman to join Harvard's faculty, and members of groups like the Women's International League for Peace and Freedom, not least the architect Rose Standish Nichols. The role of such women would continue into the 1930s, when the branch was chaired by former Assistant Secretary of State Harvey H. Bundy. And if the governance of the branch reflected the significance of Boston women's engagement with foreign affairs, so too did its rank and file illustrate its size. About two-thirds of the 1,564 branch members were women at the end of April 1928, roughly the same proportion as in the Association as a whole. Without the interest of these women, their labor in attendance and their generosity in dues, the branch—and the Association—would not have been viable.[35]

Even if Hudson and Herter saw the importance of their female colleagues, though, the Boston branch was hardly a place where women could advance themselves. Hudson would be recognized as an expert or an intellectual worthy of contemporary and later historical interest, not Hopkins; her skills, after all, did not come with the authority of a doctorate. Speaking at a luncheon offered male scholars opportunities to cultivate an aura of expertise, build networks, and add their twenty minutes to the world of ideas. Chairing an Association branch or leading its program committee offered men a way into society and often a platform for higher office. Both men who succeeded Hopkins saw it that way, Herter using the branch as a base for his election to the Massachusetts House in 1930 and Bundy using it to stay active in the foreign policy community before heading back to Washington in 1941. Several women chaired Association branches, but their service was the high point of their voluntary careers, not a stepping-stone to other things. For many women after suffrage, with their focus on civic life—including the peace movement—as an extension of the home, that was sufficient. But the prominence of women in early foreign policy institutions was no help to the few women who did seek careers in the field. Not a single woman gave a speech in Boston's 1927–1928, 1928–1929, or 1929–1930 seasons; just one, the British member of parliament

Margaret Bonfield, spoke in 1926–1927, while four would speak in 1930–1931, including the jurist Cornelia Sorabji and the disarmament expert Laura Puffer Morgan. Even if the creation and the dissemination of expertise were two sides of the same coin for progressives, education being the guarantor of democracy and even peace, the inequities were obvious and, to some, increasingly frustrating.[36]

## The Backlash Begins

It was not those continuing inequities that struck most observers of the Foreign Policy Association, however, but rather its radical quality that made it seem so out of place, perhaps untenably so if the dream of a democratic foreign policy were to become a reality. Late in 1928, an article appeared in the *Outlook and Independent*, the Boston magazine that Herter edited before running for the Massachusetts state legislature, the first step in a career that would span the US Congress, Massachusetts State House, and Department of State, where he would serve as secretary of state from 1959 to 1961. "Foreign Policy on the Half-Shell" was written by John Franklin Carter, a *New York Times* journalist who had form when it came to internationalism. Carter's *Man is War* had savaged the Association in 1926 for presenting the "thinking man" with "realists," "scare-mongers," and "horror-boys" under the guise of impartiality, attempting to drag America into foreign problems without good reason. But Carter's real issue became clear in his polemic in Herter's periodical, which took aim at a "Foreign Relations Group, Inc., with its thirty branches, its twenty thousand members, its advisory committee of three bankers, two former Democratic Ambassadors, five wealthy and unemployed ladies, four absentee editors, and one very able publicity man." This "hypothetical" fooled nobody.[37]

For Carter, the freedom the United States enjoyed from immediate danger had left a "comfortable intellectual vacuum" in its foreign policy, one now capitalized on by "that section of the American people which really believes that after dinner speeches create public opinion and that it is possible to run a government by public oratory." Many of their initiatives were "interesting and amusing," he granted, "but none approaches the high comedy of the food-plus-oratory formula for hampering the administration of our foreign policy." The Foreign Relations Group, he quipped, drawing on the Association's connections to the peace movement, wanted to "knock the arrows from the claw of the eagle on our coins and to substitute an oyster-fork, prefatory to changing our national emblem from the Bird of Freedom to a Soft-Shelled

Crab." This was no place, he wrote, for the "impartial and disinterested inquiries into the actual character of American foreign policy" that McDonald
promised. And Carter thought he could explain why. "At bottom," he continued, "the trouble seems to be due to the women who form 90 per cent of
the Group's membership"—an exaggeration, but a telling one. Look at a luncheon, he suggested. "You will see more beauty than brains, more furs and
platinum than pencils and note-books, more white kid gloves than square
chins." Such "plump rich women" wanted "a sort of moral bull-fight in
which Error shall be slain by the Toreador of Truth"; they sought new foreign
policies for the same reason they sought "new hats," not to "protect her head
but because she is bored with the old ones." Serious advocates of government
policy could hardly defend themselves in this atmosphere, so "the wretched
opponents of the cause of sweetness and light are lucky if they escape without
being hissed." Thankfully, Carter thought, while such women flattered themselves "that by a slight palpitation of their emotions they are really contributing to public opinion," policymakers were oblivious to their cause. "The
Department of State," he wrote, "has never been worried by the oyster-fork
type of diplomacy." And Carter would know. After he filed his article, he left
the *Times* for the department.[38]

Marguerite Hopkins struggled to understand this "innuendo attack" on the
Association, coming as it did from a journal under the control of one of its
most active supporters. Either way, it hardly bothered her; as she told Hudson,
"we grow beyond being disturbed by pricks of this kind." But what Carter's
extraordinary broadside—and Herter's tolerance or promotion of it—did reveal
was lingering, significant unease about what the Association was doing, an anx-
iety that came as much from within the movement as from critics outside.
The first decade of the Association's work left numerous questions open, all
of which would have to be confronted in the decades to come. There was the
question of whether its origins and sympathies meant that it was as objective
or nonpartisan as it claimed, whether it was delivering on its promise to take
foreign policy out of the partisan politics that were thought to have doomed
the Treaty of Versailles. There was the question of whether a democratic foreign policy could be built by fostering community among those who knew
their oyster forks from their soup spoons, of whether it was enough simply to
involve and educate an elite in the hope of influencing the broader citizenry.
There was also the question, if rarely asked, of how to get the State Department to take any of this seriously, of how a foreign policy public, if it could
be created, might demonstrably influence diplomacy itself. Most pressingly,

there was the question of gender, on which all these issues for the moment converged.

Concerns about gender did not just come from the chauvinist right and the diplomatic old guard; even the women of the New York staff wondered whether the extent of their dependence on suffrage and pacifist networks would do more harm than good in the end. At one executive committee meeting as early as 1924, for instance, Ogden brought up the "preponderance of two-thirds women in the membership," asking whether she should concentrate for a while "on circularizing lists of men." But the committee members who met at the Women's City Club that night—McDonald, Bliven, four other men, and the settlement house pioneer Lillian Wald—vetoed the idea, knowing where their strength already lay. The same concerns intensified over time. The gender divide was so stark between male speakers and female audiences in Chicago that its Council eventually found it could generate press coverage only in the society pages of the local newspapers, much of that coverage focusing more on fashion than on fascism. Discussions there came to a head in October 1936, when the Council's president, future Illinois governor and perennial White House candidate Adlai Stevenson, demanded that its board campaign to "get more men to Council meetings." His fellow trustees agreed with the aim but feared it was too late. Economist Harry Gideonse went so far as to say, to no opposition, that there now existed a "general feeling among men that foreign relations was something for women."[39]

It was in the shadow of this sense that participation was becoming too gendered that the foreign policy community began to change course. New and potentially more insular forms of expertise seemed to be in order—necessarily coded male if they were to be rooted in academic credentials—as the world grew more connected and as US interests seemed to touch on ever more of it. New and potentially more restrictive models for public opinion might be required for discussions of foreign policy to appeal more precisely to the imagined social mores of male elites. Potentially, that is. For the moment, while the United States lacked much of a foreign policy for which it would need to generate support, investment in such questions remained limited, and it was unclear what form these or other developments might take when America faced a more ominous world. When that day came, it was a mark of just how powerful Wilsonian language had become and how successful the Association had been that progressive, participatory ideals would set the terms of the debate, however more circumscribed their reality had been than their rhetoric might suggest.

# 2

# The Fact Cult

They set off at the end of July 1929, John and James. Named after his father and his father's father before that, John was heir to the richest man in history. Just graduated from Princeton and up for a good time, he wanted to see the world with his friends, but there was no chance that his parents would bow to his wishes. Abby, his mother, wanted a chaperone, someone who could be trusted, someone who might teach her son a thing or two, perhaps someone whose own fame might even draw the spotlight a little from him. James would be that man: sensible, an intellect, a darling of Manhattan high society. They barely knew one another, let alone the French tutor they took with them, but they shared an interest in foreign affairs; they had met once before to prepare for their addresses to a Model League of Nations Assembly, John as a participant, James as the keynote speaker. John had spent the summer of 1928 in Geneva, working at the League of Nations not long after his father had handed it $2 million to build a library. James had seen plenty of the League himself, having spent most of his recent summers touring the capitals of Europe. So it was that John D. Rockefeller III would journey around the world with James G. McDonald, the scion supposedly serving as a secretary.

Four months they were gone, a whistle-stop diary of dances and dignitaries, much of it giddily reported in the newspapers back home at the conniving of the Rockefellers' publicity man, Ivy Lee, still burnishing the family's image years after their violent breakup of miners' strikes in the 1910s. They landed at Gibraltar on August 3, swept on to Tangiers, then headed back to Santander for lunch with the king and queen of Spain. Paris was next, then The Hague, then London before a visit to Lossiemouth, Scotland, the birthplace and summer retreat of the British prime minister, Labour leader Ramsay MacDonald.

James ordered a new suit to meet MacDonald, a hero to him as to many on the American left; John did not. Next came Geneva to see the League in session, before a long journey east at the start of September. They stopped in Moscow, where they met with the Soviet foreign minister, Maxim Litvinov, and went to the Bolshoi theater. James, a dedicated operagoer, was shocked to see "workers and functionaries" in the stalls and shadowy figures sitting in the czar's old box. "Perhaps bakers," he noted in his diary. "Perhaps dictators."

It took a week and a half for Rockefeller and McDonald to reach Vladivostok in the Soviet far east; from there they headed for Osaka, Busan, and Mukden, where they met Chang Hsueh-Liang, the young marshal of Manchuria, son of a man the Japanese had assassinated a year before. Next came Beijing, Nanking, Shanghai, and finally Kyoto, their ostensible destination, for the third international conference of the Institute of Pacific Relations, to which McDonald was a delegate. Business taken care of, they sailed from Yokohama back to San Francisco, a voyage on which John had a brief romance that lasted until James intervened with the young lady in question, having what he called a "long confidential talk re Rockefellers." Safely ashore, John reported to his father's office in New York on December 2 "for work," as the newspapers put it. McDonald took a detour to make some speeches on the transcontinental train back, met his wife at Penn Station on December 3, and took a room at the Commodore, "for the day and the night."[1]

What a display this was of just how connected the world had become since the end of the Great War, and of just how enmeshed Americans had become within it. Almost everywhere McDonald and Rockefeller had gone they had dined and met with their countrymen, some from the foreign service, to be sure, but some either part of the high-society internationalist set McDonald was so familiar with, or part of the world of expertise represented at the luncheons he commanded. Even Moscow offered a reminder of home when the two men bumped into journalist Anna Louise Strong at a salon, chatting with a regular if controversial speaker. The official, semi-official, and corporate United States intersected, overlapped: if it was not a *chargé d'affaires* who met the pair at a train station or on a gangplank, then it was a Standard Oil employee, hotel reservation in hand. More than once, John graciously accepted thanks for the generosity of his parents offered by some local enterprise that had profited from their philanthropy. More than once, James took congratulations from a diplomat or even a foreign leader for some pamphlet his Association had published, or some other contribution it was perceived to have made. At this apogee of scientific internationalism, the apparent interests of these men and the United States that they were seen to represent seemed hard to separate.

The ties that bound the Foreign Policy Association to the Rockefeller family symbolized one of the defining, most enduring projects of major philanthropy in the United States, one in which vast reserves of private capital shaped the public goal of a democratic foreign policy. That effort involved many more institutions than just the Association. It had arguably started with the establishment of the Carnegie Endowment for International Peace in 1910, if not earlier, and it continues today. But at its peak between 1924, when the Rockefellers' Bureau of Social Hygiene first cut a check to the Association, and 1967, when the Ford Foundation cut its last and ended the project in this form, philanthropy was the glue that held the movement together. The Rockefeller, Carnegie, and Ford foundations among others saw in the Association and its allies a way to demonstrate their commitments to the promotion of peace and the protection of democracy. The Rockefeller name dominated at first, as the personal initiatives of the Rockefeller family and then the more deliberate work of the Rockefeller Foundation supported, formed, and shaped institutions, ideas, and networks to such an extent that it is difficult to trace their full influence even now. One of the clearest and most consequential successes of that influence, however, was to push an ideal that foundations had already woven into social policy at home into the realm of foreign affairs: the contrived authority of "the neutral, highly trained 'expert,'" as historian Judith Sealander has put it. Creating that expert—the physical, professional embodiment of the scientific approach to world affairs that internationalists thought might bring peace through the League of Nations—required building think tanks, tending to knowledge networks, developing and acting on theories, and supporting scholars in all manner of pursuits.[2]

This effort also required making a choice about public opinion. Who would these experts be? Who would they serve? Trained to possess an international mind and to be immune to partisan passions, it might seem inevitable that such experts would hold themselves high above the people; that they would act on behalf of the citizenry rather than on instructions from them. That indictment did indeed become truer over time, but in the early foreign policy community it was rarely thought to be the aim. Not only was the foreign policy community conceived in reform but during a great experiment in adult education, one that swept through academia, mass media, civic culture, and even the New Deal state. This was a time when it was widely and genuinely thought that knowledge could and should be taken to the people so that citizens might gain the facts, skills, and outlooks to master their fast-changing, interdependent world through participation in the political process. The place of expertise in this effort to form a democracy worthy of the name was of crucial importance, not only for the role experts would have to play in the creation and dissemination of knowledge, but because their eventual position would speak to the success or the failure of the project—to whether knowledge could serve democracy, even in foreign policy. Could experts be trained to value publics? Could their research be distributed at scale? Could it be made usable? Could it have an impact? What if publics did not listen? What would it mean if the people rejected the advice of those who insisted that they knew best? With fascism and communism offering a frightful contest for the future, contemporaries put vast effort into solving these problems and creating a "scientific democracy," as historian Andrew Jewett has called it. And with public opinion remaining at the heart of thinking about US diplomacy, the stakes for a democratic foreign policy were high, and heightening.[3]

## *"What Is Research?"*

In May 1932, James McDonald wrote in triumph to John D. Rockefeller Jr., John's father. Five years earlier, the leader of the Foreign Policy Association told his most generous benefactor, the State Department had thought the Association to be "of little consequence." Now, twenty or so of the department's staff were members, and senior officials kept its publications on hand. While the Hoover administration was struggling in the face of economic collapse, McDonald wrote, it had made clear that the Association should work on its behalf to undermine the "narrow, isolationist attitude" that was usurping the internationalism of the 1920s. All this and more, McDonald said, had come from the $151,500 that Junior, as he was nicknamed to distinguish him from the Rockefeller patriarch, had donated since 1925. Close to officialdom and peerless among the public, the Association was so important to the political culture of US foreign policy that even Nazis cared what it published. Later that summer, McDonald would find himself upbraided in Berlin, where the future economics minister to Adolf Hitler, Hjalmar Schacht, would take an article from the Association's *Bulletin* from his pocket and rage that its writer "does not understand the Hitler movement, and belittles it."[4]

That the Association built this reputation so quickly was surprising. McDonald might have become as much of a matinee idol as a scholar could be, but he was also a campaigner associated with the effort to join the World

Court among other causes. Observers would have needed short memories indeed to forget that the Association had been born in radicalism. Avowedly liberal ends had indeed informed its first efforts at research, as it muckraked world affairs just as progressive journalists had used reporting to prompt action on the railway monopolies, the breakup of the steel corporations, or the need for public health initiatives. But the Association's early appeals had gone unheard in the cacophony of internationalist demands, and the research on which they were based was shoddy. Its committee on Russia had fallen into disrepute when Acting Secretary of State Norman Davis accused McDonald of falsely describing government policy in questions sent to candidates for the White House in 1920. McDonald fared worse still when charging oil firms of engagement in a "shameless effort" to gin up a "war of loot" against Mexico in 1919, claims for which he was ridiculed while testifying before the Senate Foreign Relations Committee. Secretary of State Charles Evans Hughes had joined the fun in 1922, describing an Association memo on the illegality of the US occupation of Haiti as "most inadequate and one-sided." Embarrassed, the Association had contented itself that these setbacks were nonetheless outstanding examples of democratic control. However "controversial" the debate over Russia had been, it replied to Davis, "open and frank discussion of exactly this sort is the soundest American method of arriving at an enlightened foreign policy."[5]

If pamphleteering brought nothing but trouble, the Association had made quiet progress in one obscure field. Internationalists made an example of drug control, seeing it as an area in which the United States and the League of Nations might work together with little political risk. Private actors were important in that collaboration. The Association had set up an opium committee in 1922, and the committee's main figures—Helen Howell Moorhead, a Bryn Mawr graduate and aid worker, and Herbert May, a druggist and lawyer—used it as a platform to claim expertise, observe at conferences, and even, in May's case, gain appointment as a member of the Permanent Central Opium Board, making him one of the few Americans to serve in an official League role. May and Moorhead's success was peripheral to the Association's main concerns in all but one way: in 1924, the Rockefellers' Bureau of Social Hygiene gave them $10,000 to mail information about opium issues to newspapers. Word came back from editors that what was needed much more urgently were explanatory introductions to basic issues in world affairs, the kind of thing that would help them understand the reports that came in from wire services. Given that newspapers were central to political discourse and civic life, this was an opportunity the Association could not miss. With the aid of Abby Rockefeller and Raymond Blaine Fosdick, the former League adminis-trator and Association supporter who advised Abby's husband on interna-tional relations, McDonald convinced Junior to support the founding of a research department in April 1925. He gave $10,000.[6]

Publishing its first issue on October 5, 1925, the Association's *Editorial In-formation Service*—quickly renamed the *Information Service* and later the *Foreign Policy Reports*, in 1931—promised to offer "essential facts on interna-tional questions, gathered from reliable sources and assembled without bias," and to do so, crucially, in a timely way. Making good on that idea required a staff of writers able to meet constant deadlines, a very different proposition to the irregular cast of otherwise-employed authors who wrote in *Foreign Af-fairs*. For his research director, McDonald first tried to hire Raymond Leslie Buell, a prolific and idealistic Harvard lecturer. Not yet thirty years old, Buell had already published two monographs and was about to bring out *Interna-tional Relations*, a textbook that would dominate its new field for a decade. But Buell was setting sail to do fieldwork in Africa when McDonald met him in March 1925, so the Association made do with Edward Mead Earle, a Co-lumbia historian continuing the present-minded scholarship of his mentor, Association founder Charles A. Beard. Earle would eventually become a pio-neering theorist of "national security," words that meant little in the 1920s; for now, he brought the research staff to life. It was not an easy task. Despite the Rockefellers' cash, the idea of such a staff was experimental, though it had its inspiration in progressive traditions that cherished independent expertise. There was no competition for the *Service* as a product, and for good reason; though McDonald and Earle took care to develop its format in consultation with journalists including Walter Lippmann, there was no guarantee of a market for it at all.[7]

The precarity of the Association's research department, as well as the orga-nization's basic sympathies, opened doors for scholars who found others closed. Earle's first hires were all white women, plucked straight from the graduate schools where female enrollment in subjects like history was booming, or from the institutions where women were already taking advantage of the new, if limited opportunities available in postwar world affairs. Earle's first offer was to Elizabeth MacCallum, a Canadian expert on the Near East who was training at Barnard College under Carlton Hayes, an Association director and Columbia historian who would later serve as US ambassador to Spain. Earle's second was Ruth Bache-Wiig, a Norwegian who had worked for

2.1 Vera Micheles Dean in an undated portrait by Barbara Sutro. Initially a Russianist, Dean joined the research department of the Foreign Policy Association in 1928. She was hugely popular with the women who made up much of the Association's membership and became one of the most prominent speakers on foreign policy in the United States up to the early 1950s. She remained at the Association until 1961. Schlesinger Library, Harvard Radcliffe Institute.

Wilson's Inquiry and the League of Nations Secretariat before moving to Cambridge to assist Manley Hudson at Harvard Law School. Earle's third was Mildred Wertheimer, another Inquiry veteran who had written a thesis on German nationalism under Hayes. Later came Vera Micheles, a gifted Russianist fresh from a doctorate at Radcliffe College. Male colleagues came and went, their work not normally up to the standard these women set, and as late as 1929 just one permanent member of the nine-strong research staff was a man, its director aside. The position of these women was the product of discrimination, that of the universities unwilling to hire them to posts befitting their talents and of the men unwilling to work for the wages they had to suffer. Though the Association was already known for the visibility of women among its staff and members, observers were still surprised that such prominence extended to its research department.[8]

The work was hard, and it exposed these women to withering criticism. The staff selected subjects to write on as a collective, taking turns to publish a *Report* that might sometimes scarcely have seemed relevant to immediate

US policy but nonetheless revealed the breadth of interest that the foreign policy community was starting to sustain in matters overseas, even as the Association defined for its members what the field of "foreign policy" should include. The first editions were titled "The Locarno Security Conference," "The Turco-Iraq Boundary Dispute," and "The French Mandate in Syria"; the second volume had a little more focus, with "The International Credit Position of the United States" and "Open Diplomacy and American Foreign Relations" joining issues such as "Colonial vs. Mandate Administration," "The International Problem of Tangier," and "Recent Legislation in Italy." Each *Report* emerged from a process more rigorous than most scholarship at the time. "Our instructions were these," MacCallum recalled. "Your next monograph, perhaps 25,000 words, is on such-and-such a subject. You are to go for the facts. You must not slant them. You must read all round the subject so as to avoid giving the reader an unbalanced impression." Then came peer review. "If you have been dealing with an issue where there are perhaps four or five different views, strongly held," MacCallum remembered, "you must find a leading proponent of each of these views, send him or her copies of your draft, and wait for the criticism." With the views of the most senior lawyers, bankers, and eventually State Department diplomats thus considered, one *Report* would be printed each fortnight.[9]

The stringency of the *Reports* had a purpose, rooted in the philosophy behind them and the imagined mores of those reading them. Most basically, the *Reports* spoke to the widespread belief that even active, committed internationalists—let alone broader publics—had much to learn about the world, that there was a gulf between the power of the United States and the knowledge required to use it in the name of peace. "Facts are our scarcest raw material," Owen D. Young warned at Johns Hopkins in 1925, proposing a school of international relations to create a science that would outlaw war just as "the plague and yellow fever, typhoid and diphtheria, the hookworm and malaria are outlawed in the world today." Even the noninterventionist *Chicago Tribune* felt it necessary to subscribe to the *Reports*; newspapers of all viewpoints wrote stories about their contents and sometimes reprinted entire sections of them. Every newspaper with a circulation of ten thousand or more was receiving the *Reports* for free by 1927, and the State Department was handing out copies to Washington correspondents. Association officials were astonished to find editors keeping the indexes to the *Reports* close at hand for reference. If the *Reports* had a distribution of no more than a few thousand people, then, they intended to influence far more. As McDonald told his

Rockefeller patron in 1926, their readers were supposed to be the "men and women who, through their pens and voices, are reaching the minds of millions of Americans every day," desperate for information to do so.[10]

What separated the *Reports* from other publications through which Americans might have looked upon the world was their success in seeming "objective." While the social sciences generally shifted towards positivism in the 1920s, the *Reports* were also able to tap into the general revulsion towards propaganda that had built up since the war. With the zealotry of the Committee on Public Information still burned into liberal minds, "propaganda" had become a dirty word in political culture as well as in academic theory despite the arguments of boosters like Edward Bernays and Harold Lasswell. "My chief impression from the trip is that this country is utterly weary of propaganda," wrote field agent Raymond T. Rich after covering thirteen thousand miles for the Association in 1926. Charles Howland, a former State Department official who led the League of Nations' Greek Refugee Settlement Commission, advised his fellow Association board members that while "crusading" for peace would backfire, "fact-finding and fact-presenting" would now be "accepted at its face." The Association willed that acceptance into being, joining its assurances that the *Reports* contained nothing but facts to an attempt to strip all authorial personality from them, forcing the driest of writing styles on the staff and refusing even to publish their names until 1929. Success then bred success. Surveying the subscription lists, one foundation official surmised in 1927 that "these different groups could only have been secured on the basis of an objective and well-grounded program." After reading a *Report*, former Secretary of War Newton D. Baker wrote in 1929, "I have the sensation of having read widely on the subject and made up my own mind on it." Soon enough, complaints started to arrive if a researcher was felt to have deviated from their promised course.[11]

This turn to "objectivity" was a maturation of internationalist strategy, though, not an abandonment of its ends. "The growth of a wider and more intelligent public interest in foreign affairs waits not upon propaganda but upon facts," the Association's board declared in 1925, before it deleted the word "liberal" from the constitution three years later. The tradeoffs involved were clear to the old guard. No less an authority than Carrie Chapman Catt warned McDonald, over dinner, of the "danger of organizations going in for search after truth as an easier way out than to fight for any given cause." Unless the public had a "sound philosophy of international relations," Norman Angell asked him, might endowing it with firmer facts not serve to make it "remain as much an isolationist opinion as at present, only more able to defend that attitude?" McDonald saw the risk, but took it. Even if an "objective" stance meant that the Association would now forego explicit policy positions, its sympathies would still be clear. Promotional materials from 1926, for instance, said that the provision of basic information would, in itself, "make more Americans see our stake in international affairs." It would in any case be wrong, McDonald told a member in 1928, to think of "objectivity" as a "neutral" space rather than as a methodology that guided readers towards proper views. "Our suggestion," he said at the annual meeting that year, "is that the facts in a controversy are important, and usually right has less to fear from them than wrong."[12]

When McDonald was finally able to hire Buell as his research director in March 1927, this precarious balance was certain to collapse. Buell was as much the prototypical foreign policy expert as anybody, exemplifying the complexities that ran through scientific internationalism. Distrustful of mass politics yet earnest in his appeals for public engagement, the workaholic Buell yearned to make a difference in the world but was never happier than in the quiet company of his books. *The Native Problem in Africa*, his study of the effects of empire on colonized peoples, made him an infamous critic of imperialism upon its publication in 1928, even if its 2,146 pages seemed to Quincy Wright to be a "model of objectivity." Beyond an unmatched erudition, Buell's distinctive talent was to perform nonpartisanship while leaving little doubt where he stood. He was proud of a 1929 *Report* on "The American Occupation of Haiti," for instance, precisely because its one hundred thousand words appeared to be reasonable both to Charles Evans Hughes, the former secretary of state who defended the occupation, and to the Haitians who opposed it. But Buell chafed at his restraints. "Perhaps F.P.A. propaganda methods have been responsible for the fiction that facts exist without interpretation," he complained in 1930, but "there can be no sound understanding of facts without interpretation."[13]

Buell went further at the Association's annual meeting in April 1931, with a speech entitled "What is Research?" In it he praised the acolytes of the "new faith," the idea that the "social good which research in the physical sciences has produced" could be extended to human life, as if to "diagnose its ills and prescribe remedies." But research had a purpose, this most devoted of Wilsonians insisted, and there was no point hiding it. Buell so resented being subjected to the "fact cult" that meant his writers often found themselves attacked as "'partisan,' 'propagandist' or lacking in 'objectivity'" that he declared himself a "heretic." Writers inevitably made judgments in selecting facts, he said, and to make such judgments required "a sense of values." Buell confessed that his researchers "put our own interpretations in the mouths of others," using weasel words like "it is contended by certain observers." This was not just excusable; it was essential. After all, it was through research that the world might "gradually discard the harrowed, cynically hopeless exterior in which it now lives and bit by bit take on the garments of Utopia." For the moment, Buell's plea fell flat; the board member Eustace Seligman stood up after his speech to admonish him for being "a little selfish," for wanting to dictate to people rather than trust them. Buell himself would never solve that conundrum, his faith in the citizenry cutting against the frustration he felt at his inability to convince them of his views. Many of his successors would prove less squeamish.[14]

## Professionalism for Professionals

The summer of 1932 felt uneasy. McDonald went to Geneva, as ever. He was able to talk with Secretary-General Joseph Avenol and keep his usual appointments with other officials at the League, but something was off in the mountains. The diplomats seemed troubled, the social scene stilted, as if Geneva were not the center of attention it had once been. McDonald knew why; his real destination that year was not Switzerland, but Germany. He had never seen Adolf Hitler speak, but he felt he had to see the man who had led the Nazi Party to first place in Reichstag elections in July in action. None of McDonald's conversations in Berlin went well. He lunched with Ernst Hanfstaengl, Hitler's foreign press agent. "It was clear that he and, I presume, many of the other leaders of the Nazis really believe all of these charges against the Jews," McDonald noted in his diary, astounded. On September 1, he walked to the Sportpalast, a vast auditorium often used for rallies during the Weimar Republic, or what was left of it. "Perhaps 25,000 people were in the audience," McDonald wrote, perturbed that brown-shirted "shock troops" lined the aisles. When Hitler arrived in the hall, "his reception was the most extraordinary I have ever seen given a public man." McDonald knew charisma, but Hitler stunned him. "The experience of the evening," he wrote, "had given me a new picture of him and his movement." Just as chilling as the speech were the banners around the hall. "Gebt Hitler die Macht," one demanded, "Give Hitler Power." "Deutschland Erwacht," read another—"Germany Awakes."[15]

German fascism would tear through the world and worldview that men and women like McDonald had built since the war. That "public opinion"

wilted in the face of a Blitzkrieg would explode the philosophical underpin-
nings of internationalist foreign policy; that people might willingly hand
power to a man like this, and then seem so manipulable to him, would tear at
its faith in popular consent. All that was yet to come. For now, McDonald
tried to avert the worst. Dining with Hanfstaengl when he rushed back to
Berlin in March 1933, Hitler having since become chancellor, McDonald
heard the Führer's confidante remark roughly that "each Jew has his S.A.,"
that "in a single night it could be finished." McDonald met Hitler on April 8.
He told his diary that night that he felt he had peered into "the eyes of a fa-
natic," albeit one with "much more reserve and control and intelligence than
most fanatics." That frightened him. He had failed to convince Franklin Roosevelt to appoint him to the senior State Department post he thought his stature
deserved, but now he used his relationship with the president's wife, Eleanor,
to try to win the embassy to Berlin, lobbying personally at the White House
and even sleeping in the Lincoln Bedroom as a friend of the family. Despite
Eleanor's three years of service on the Association's board, McDonald had no
luck. Raising the specter on his radio programs of a "threat to civilization," he
tried the League instead. After touring the Dachau concentration camp, in
October he became the League's High Commissioner for Refugees (Jewish
and Other) Coming from Germany. His failure was inevitable, if honorable;
he resigned in a fury in December 1935, denouncing the apathy of the great
powers to the fate of the Jews and warning of "impending tragedies" to come.
After the Holocaust, he would be appointed the first US ambassador to Israel
in 1949.[16]

While McDonald was off "looking for new worlds to conquer," as Buell
ruefully put it, the Association grappled with the Great Depression, which
offered an intellectual challenge as well as a financial one. As the League
buckled and New Dealers started to build a federal state of unprecedented
power, progressives questioned their trust in public opinion. Could the politics of deliberation really keep the peace? Could talk really hold back the
armies of authoritarianism? Growing numbers assumed not, as fascist powers
withdrew from the League and ever more internationalists turned to what
they called "collective security." Would democracies have to find some other
means than participation to prove themselves in the battle of ideas against
fascism and communism? Some feared so; others protested not. What, then,
did a call for an informed public opinion now entail? Did it mean, as more
conservative progressives implied, the creation of a class of leaders and intellectuals who could stand athwart popular desires, resisting the baser instincts

**2.2** *From left:* James G. McDonald, Alfred Zimmern, and Raymond Leslie Buell in front of an exhibit of Foreign Policy Association materials on the occasion of its twentieth-anniversary luncheon at the Hotel Astor, December 10, 1938. Copies of the Headline Books are at the *bottom left;* copies of the *Foreign Policy Reports* are behind Buell. Wisconsin Historical Society.

of human nature or at least guiding them with a firmer hand? Did it mean, as liberals hoped, that more and better democracy was the answer? The fluid network of people and institutions that made up the foreign policy community offered no one answer. Nor did the Association, which struggled to reconcile both impulses, as torn as its senior officials.[17]

Buell took up the presidency when McDonald quit, and the scholar was the Association's most likely candidate to join those who "lost their international mind," as Stephen Wertheim has described those whose faith in postwar internationalism died. Confrontational, stubborn, and impractical, Buell had little of McDonald's political ability and none of his social cachet; he lived, as one of his closest friends wrote, "in a world of documents," and was never long without his portable typewriter. Conceiving of politics as merely intelligence properly applied and believing that "the people form their opinions from their leaders," no Wilsonian was surer than Buell that smarts could make a difference. He wrote in 1935 that "intellectual" forms of politics were the best means of dealing with "unreasoning and unintelligent nationalism," with the "demagoguery represented by Father Coughlin, Huey Long and others." All the major initiatives Buell oversaw at the Association—that is, those that he took a significant personal interest in—were intended to bolster the claims, methods, and power of enlightened expertise so that leaders could apply its teachings to politics.[18]

Professionalizing the research department had been Buell's mission since 1927, and it intensified through the 1930s. Working more than full time despite also holding lectureships at Harvard, Princeton, and elsewhere, Buell sought to put his staff on a more systematic basis to produce timelier analytical work. He hired a librarian in 1928, a *New York Times* indexer named Ona Ringwood, whose ability to catalogue the ever-vaster troves of information becoming available as transnational knowledge networks developed was crucial for the speed and completeness with which the staff could write. Ringwood subscribed to dozens of periodicals, and as newspapers from all over the world came in, the researchers read, clipped, and classified them, creating a reference library that served callers of all kinds. Every major book on world affairs arrived at headquarters, the staff reviewing some in the *Bulletin*, others in the *New York Times* and the *New Republic*. The researchers went searching for information too, meeting statesmen, senior officials, and other figures abroad at a time when extensive foreign travel, still rare, was a strong component of authority. The staff were welcome the world over—at the Quai d'Orsay in Paris and the Foreign Office in London, of course, but in the hills above Yan'an too, at the mountain redoubt of Mao Zedong—and the insights they gained were crucial to their influence. "As a result" of their interviews, the Association wrote in 1932, "the *Reports* reflect an understanding of the questions dealt with which could not be obtained by mere documentary work within a library."[19]

Professionalism required professionals, however, and as the Association rose in reputation Buell sought to fit his department more snugly within prevailing social structures, despite his admiration for thinkers neither white nor male. While Buell did what he could for Black scholars such as Alain Locke, Ralph Bunche, and W. E. B. DuBois, and while he ranked his female colleagues as highly as any of their male competitors, he was guarded in his hiring. Buell appointed no women to permanent posts on the research staff after Micheles, eager as he was "to attract the best graduates of our leading universities," as he put it in 1934. It was a criterion that inevitably cut against women. McDonald had written in 1929 that the department would need "first-rate" researchers, men who would not be forced to leave to start a family, who would want the wages and the tenure they would gain at universities. Though Buell never sealed the deal with targets like historian Herbert Feis and economist Jacob Viner, men of lesser initial fame such as T. A. Bisson and Charles A. Thomson rose through his ranks, while Micheles, who became Vera Micheles Dean upon her marriage in 1929, used her position to fashion herself into a significant public intellectual, as did Wertheimer before her tragically early death in 1937, at just forty-one.[20]

Meanwhile, Buell moved the Association closer to power, taking it into the elite ranks of transnational research institutions by joining the International Studies Conference, trying to use his staff to enliven the League's think tank, the Geneva Research Center, and making the Association inescapable in diplomatic circles. "If I had my way about it, we would move the Research Department of the F.P.A. to Washington," Buell wrote in 1927; he settled for a liaison office there under William T. Stone, a former journalist. At first, Stone's task in Washington was to promote the *Reports*, but that was supplanted when it became clear how limited official Washington's knowledge was of what the Association considered to be foreign affairs. The State Department had a mere 1,347 personnel in 1930, 714 of them in Washington; lacking the facilities, funding, and time to conduct or process research, they left such work to others. Secretary of State Frank B. Kellogg told McDonald in 1927 that he would happily receive materials "for the purpose of corroborating or supplementing information derived from official sources here and abroad," and ties between State and the Association strengthened when board member Joseph P. Cotton became undersecretary to another admirer, Henry Stimson, in 1929. State's senior officials were soon acting as confidential sources, forcing their juniors to serve as off-the-record peer reviewers, and lavishing praise on the Association for its work raising public awareness of diplomacy. Stone struck up close relationships on Capitol Hill, too, reporting that twenty senators had personally expressed their approval of the *Reports* as early as May 1927. Soon enough, Stone became a one-man reference service for senators, who until the Legislative Reorganization Act of 1946 lacked significant personal or committee staffs.[21]

If the Association had therefore become "the most important educational force in this country in the field of international affairs," as Rockefeller's advisors told him in 1932, its education was pointed inward as much as outward. The five thousand or so *Reports* printed each fortnight were intended to meet "the most exacting requirements of the scholar, the international lawyer, the educator, the administrative official, and the statesman," the Association wrote. Most of the rank and file found the *Reports* far too abstruse for their tastes: barely one-tenth of the 12,500 men and women who had joined by 1931 mailed in the extra three dollars members could pay to receive the *Reports* as well as the briefer, more opinionated *Bulletin*. Instead, the staff had created a new market, dispensing facts to the growing number of Americans who had a professional stake in foreign affairs. Universities were a crucial outlet as international relations courses became more common; Harvard and Columbia had joined fifty-three other colleges in adding the *Reports* to their syllabi by 1932, and special subscriptions were available for students enrolled in specific courses. "Recent Defaults of Government Loans" (1932) was covered in fifty newspapers; even a topic as impenetrable as "Silver: Its International Aspects" (1931) received notices in the *New York Times*, *Wall Street Journal*, and *Chicago News*, as well as dailies from Beijing to Buenos Aires. Buell added a final target: "key men," those with influence in Washington and New York, or who chaired voluntary associations, led political parties, and so on—men from whom opinions were thought to spread. In that way, Buell wrote in 1932, the staff could be imagined as "an unofficial civil service" for "the organs and leaders of public opinion."[22]

Attractive to social, financial, and political elites alike, the Association easily withstood the aftershocks of the stock market crash of 1929, dispelling the dark prediction of its finance chair, Goldman Sachs banker Arthur Sachs, that it was a "luxury charity" and could not expect to survive. Although its membership, attendances, and contributions dropped after 1932 and would not recover until 1936, its problems were relatively minor: when even John D. Rockefeller Jr. had to reduce his subsidies, the Rockefeller Foundation simply stepped in to fill the gap, guaranteeing the research staff $25,000 per year and offering fellowships for its writers to travel. "Substantial support from the Foundation, now and for some years to come, seems essential," its officials wrote of the Association in 1935, praising "the relevance of its research program to intelligent and realistic thinking upon international affairs." So central had the Association become that the Carnegie Endowment for International Peace argued that it should take the lead in restructuring the entire internationalist infrastructure in 1933, when the financial threat to lesser institutions had become mortal. It was a sign of how far the Association had come, in both size and orientation, that it found collaboration difficult with even the more think-tank-like World Peace Foundation and Institute of Pacific Relations, let alone the more activist Woodrow Wilson Foundation and the League of Nations Association.[23]

Even so, Buell's discussions with senior officials suggested that the Association could now contribute more to policy, shielded by its reputation for rigor. Fearful for the fate of democracies amid a global economic catastrophe, in his personal capacity Buell started to launch bitter attacks on US neutrality policy, and as his own stature grew, he insisted the Association also do more. "Although during the last ten years research in facts has been of primary importance," he wrote in March 1933, "the future will depend upon how facts are interpreted and policies defined." Buell had ideas, too, about who should do that defining, even as he failed to gain a policymaking post for himself. With the World Peace Foundation, he sponsored committees of mostly male experts that made suggestions on topics such as Filipino independence. Rockefeller grants allowed him to accept an invitation from the US-backed president of Cuba to lead a delegation in surveying the island's conditions in 1934; his report, filling five hundred pages or so, was politely written up in the press but made little impact. Dangers lurked in drawing closer to policy, however, as Buell found when the Dominican ambassador to the United States lodged a complaint over a publication in which a researcher labeled President Trujillo a dictator in 1936. It was a spat that spoke to the close relationship that had grown between progressives and power, for the Dominicans treated the Association as if it were an organ of officialdom; the fallout forced Ernest Gruening, then director of the Interior Department's Division of Territories and Island Possessions, to resign from the Association's board.[24]

But the bigger risk, as Buell's colleagues saw it, was the elitist streak that started to infect the models of public opinion he advocated. The path he mapped for the branches was instructive. Working with former World Student Christian Federation chairman Francis Pickens Miller, who served as the Association's field director in 1934–1935, Buell sought to use the branches to create hundreds of small "policy groups," which he imagined gathering prominent citizens to forge consensus and then submit ideas to the government and the public. Conscious of the links between foreign and domestic policies, Buell proposed to convert the Foreign Policy Association into a Public Policy Association, a suggestion his board humored until 1935, when it demurred. What was striking about plans like these, however much they appealed to those who sought to tighten the publics around expertise, was how unrealistic Buell's ideas often appeared to be. At a conference in 1934, one branch chairman complained that he had "great difficulty in imagining just what sort of people will be included"; Miller replied that perhaps "a dozen or two" of a branch's members would "like to go into some subject a little more thoroughly and fully with men and women of other points of view." It was telling that this extremely limited conception of participatory democracy, along with Miller himself, found a more germane home at the Council on Foreign Relations after 1937, if necessarily stripped of its pretense of gender equality. But if the roots of the more frankly elitist policymaking vision that would emerge in decades to come can be found in these years, Buell's doubts remained. For while he was pulling the Association in one direction, he also let the Association pull him in another, one more consistent with the dominant intellectual convictions of the time.[25]

## Deweyans for Democracy

Progressives had long placed their faith in an educated public, sufficiently managed, to create the society of their dreams, and that faith flourished in the 1920s. Often intellectual historians frame this period as a time when "realist" thinkers came to the fore, profoundly pessimistic of democracy, or as the era of a great debate between John Dewey and Walter Lippmann, their disagreement thought to center on whether a democratic public could be created or whether the barriers to its creation were implausibly high. But the "realists" were in fact few, and there was little debate. Men like Lippmann, the most famous purported skeptic, found apostasy hard to muster, and their influence came only as a foil for true believers. Lippmann's first two books after his tortured service in the Wilson administration, *Liberty and the News* (1920) and *Public Opinion* (1922), dwelled on how hard it was for citizens living far from events to escape the "stereotypes" that made up their worldview. But Lippmann still agreed in 1920 that "to claim that the mass of men is impervious to education" was "to deny the postulate of democracy, and to seek salvation in a dictatorship," and described "the administration of public information toward greater accuracy and more successful analysis" as "the highway of liberty." Only with *The Phantom Public* (1925) did he become more forcefully cynical, arguing that "the usual appeal to education as the remedy for the incompetence of democracy" had become "barren," that the people were just too ignorant, too uninterested, too busy to care. Even then, few saw such critiques as fatal. Dewey simply built Lippmann's thinking into his own; it would take three decades more for Lippmann's work to be invoked as part of a wholesale turn against traditional democratic theory.[26]

All the momentum in the postwar years was with those who believed that the public of progressive dreams could still be created, that modern technologies meant that knowledge could be democratized and advanced at the same time. Adult education was the movement through which such hopes coalesced, a vast attempt to lead the populace to the standards that democratic theory demanded. Dewey provided the ideas. He agreed that rapid developments in communications, travel, and trade meant that the things shaping modern lives happened far beyond the places in which people lived them, involving forces so far removed from the circumstances of everyday life that they were difficult to comprehend, let alone manage. Corporate advertising and state propaganda, Dewey thought, had profited from this gap, filling it with a "hokum" being "swallowed more eagerly and more indiscriminately than ever before" as people struggled to explain their world. Was it a shock that people were indifferent to, or prejudiced about, matters of public affairs, when those matters could not be understood through the childhood education most had received? It was not. But unlike later theorists, Dewey saw no reason to mistake democracy as it existed for democracy as it could be. Education would simply have to step up, so that it could "cultivate the habit of suspended judgment, of skepticism, of desire for evidence, of appeal to observation rather than sentiment, discussion rather than bias, inquiry rather than conventional idealizations." Face to face, town to town, a great society could be built in which the intelligence of the collective would overcome the weaknesses of its individuals.[27]

Dewey knew that "the democratic public is still largely inchoate," but he offered few practical suggestions to organize it. Others he admired had been experimenting with educational techniques for decades, including pioneers in the settlement house movement, like Jane Addams, and those associated with him in New York, particularly at Teachers College. Most influential among the latter was Frederick Keppel, a former dean of Columbia College who had created the educational aspects of the Commission on Training Camp Activities as an assistant to Newton Baker; one beneficiary of that work had been Buell, who while serving in Europe after the Armistice had studied at the University of Grenoble, where he wrote a book on French politics. Keppel became president of the Carnegie Corporation in 1923 and made adult education a primary focus for the foundation, using the scientific knowledge his grants to scholars were creating to solve public problems through public opinion. The newspapers, radio, and much else educated adults in all kinds of ways, Keppel argued in his "Education for Adults" (1926), but not systematically or sufficiently—new methods would have to be found. Carnegie therefore created the American Association for Adult Education (AAAE), which distributed $4.85 million from 1926 to 1941.[28]

Under Carnegie's leadership, adult education became a sprawling affair ranging from philosophy and music appreciation to needlework and child-drearing, its inspiration tracing back to the colonial-era direct democracy of the New England "town meeting." Civic or political education was just a small part of this overall effort, but one fraught with hopes of creating a more perfect democracy, if only among the white middle and upper-middle classes that Carnegie targeted. "Such special problems as the education of the Negro, of the Indian, of the mountain white were set aside," AAAE director Morse Cartwright recalled. Deweyan educators agreed with Lippmann that it was time to abandon "the theory of the omnicompetent citizen" who could gain sufficient expertise across sufficient policy areas to participate fully in democratic politics. Lyman Bryson, a Teachers College professor who became influential on radio programming, admitted in 1936 that "the complication and formidable quantity of public business have made it very difficult for the average man, even with the best of intentions, to keep up with public affairs." But Bryson and other Deweyans were convinced that Americans could still participate in a more meaningful manner than simply assenting to expertise or, worse, submitting to demagoguery. "Those who believe in democracy are determined that it shall have its opportunity to prove its capacity," said the head of the Social Science Foundation, Ben Cherrington, who earned a Teachers College doctorate testing cutting-edge methods in world affairs programs in Denver. "If we will summon the collective will and the collective intelligence," Cherrington concluded, Americans might "set men—not some men, but all men—free to live like gods."[29]

Adult educators made a start in the 1920s, setting up institutions, building networks, and trying out techniques, but their work became more ambitious and more urgent in the 1930s. Like other social scientists, they believed that fascism preyed on the popular apathy and ignorance that had long been thought to undermine democracy; in their thinking, education became as much a shield for the republic as a force for positive change. Adult education was "fundamental to the defense of our cherished ideals of democracy," wrote John W. Studebaker, whose success running public discussion forums in Iowa led to him creating a chain of government-sponsored forums as the New Deal's federal Commissioner of Education. "The enemy of democracy is civic ignorance," he wrote in 1935, which could be overcome only through "full, free, carefully organized, and professionally and impartially managed public discussion of national affairs." Others similarly saw democracy at risk. "If we continue to attempt to manage an adult, ever-changing civilization with the static education of adolescence, America will probably soon follow Europe into the tyranny of either Fascism or Communism," wrote one Cleveland adult educator, A. Caswell Ellis. "It seems to be truly a race between adult education and disaster," he wrote in 1935, "and disaster seems just now to have the lead."[30]

Adult education offered more than a way to inoculate the public against propaganda, then, but a means to arm it in a battle of ideologies, work that inevitably came close to being propagandistic itself. What separated education from propaganda, in the view of educators, was its careful emphasis on the procedures of discussion through which facts alchemize into opinions. These processes would be slow, imperfect, and diffuse, but their celebration of tolerance and of the minority view was cherished. "Authoritarian adult education," Cherrington wrote in 1939, after joining the State Department as the chief of its Division of Cultural Relations, "seeks to inculcate unquestioning obedience to the policy and authority of the government." Democratic adult education, on the other hand, sought "a qualified acceptance of the policy and authority of government on the ground that it is temporary and always subject to revision." Much as McDonald had responded to critics of the Association's turn to objectivity, Studebaker wrote in 1936 that adult educators believed that "truth is the answer to error, that right triumphs eventually in a free market of thoroughgoing discussion and study." How far educators would have to rig that market as the prospects for democracy darkened was, for the moment, an unspoken dilemma.[31]

Seeing the survival and expansion of democracy as a matter of technique, adult educators worked to perfect their processes of persuasion. They experimented to see how well different subjects were served by different learning techniques, whether lectures, institutes, conferences, or forums, and they invented new methods like the panel discussion, which debuted in 1932. Pride of place in their work, however, went to the discussion group, a meeting of a few citizens in which all could speak and all would be heard, in which a consensus might be reached, or differences at least aired. Imagined as both miniscule representations of, and the basic building blocks for, the democratic polity, discussion groups were freighted with political symbolism, and educators theorized their workings to the last detail, from how comfortable the chairs in a meeting ought to be to how warm the room should be kept.

Discussions were assumed to have a designated leader, who had the tricky role of remaining neutral while ensuring that facts were kept to, challenging prejudices but not taking sides, and insisting that no participant dominate while not talking too much themselves. Their role was to help citizens make sense of issues in the context of their own lives; their duty, wrote Eduard Lindeman, a favored educator among *New Republic* liberals, was "not to profess but to evoke."[32]

As it was hoped that authorities of some kind would chair discussions, Deweyan discussion theory promised to resolve a core progressive dilemma, namely the role of expertise in democracy. "Persons with special experience close to the matters in question" were the ideal discussion leaders, the Teachers College professor Alfred Sheffield wrote, but it was essential that those authorities encourage "everyday folk to respect their own experience" while also genuinely valuing that experience as a contribution to their expertise. The experiment, he went on, therefore sought "to use 'authorities' without succumbing to their prestige." Lindeman put it another way, suggesting that while it was "all very wholesome to join with world societies dedicated to bring peace to mankind," that would come "only when individual human beings learn to act, to behave in the direction of peace." Democracy in this view would survive if knowledge were democratized rather than merely popularized, if citizens gained the skills and confidence to do more than shop among products of expertise. Adult educators sought to bring the citizenry up to scratch, but also, crucially, to demand that experts understand that their responsibilities ultimately lay with the people. Without publics, experts would be powerless; without experts, publics would be lost. Fusing publics and experts meant, as historian David Goodman has written, that "for the Deweyans, there was no clear line between educational and democratic work"; for Cherrington, democracy was no more than "government by discussion." More discussion, better discussion, meant more democracy, better democracy—to subject a field of policy like foreign affairs to more and better discussion was to subject it to more and better democratic control.[33]

## A Popular Foreign Policy

Whatever Buell's instincts, and whatever the slim likelihood that those like him would agree that publics should educate them as much as the other way around, adult education was inescapable, whether in its formal techniques or simply as the fashionable expression of a deep commitment democracy.

Adult educators tapped into themes and rhetoric of primeval attraction to progressives, and with no satisfying answers available to the crisis of democracy that Buell perceived all around him, he tolerated broader approaches than those he personally preferred. Even he had to admit the Association's focus on elites had its limits, after all. With the United States unwilling to mount the collective, international response he thought the Great Depression demanded, he was disheartened to see that a decade of work on the "people at the top" had made policy "more irrational," Buell told his board in 1932. "Where we have failed is at the bottom," he said. Six years later, with the world situation still worse, Buell thought it yet more crucial to help "the man or woman in the street" to "form intelligent opinions concerning America's interest in the outside world," certain as he was that the United States would soon "be called upon to make grave decisions affecting its national life."[34]

What Buell meant by "the bottom" or "the street" became clear in 1935, when he asked his Rockefeller patrons to bankroll an experiment. For the most part, the Foundation had left adult education to the Carnegie Corporation, focusing its work on social scientific researchers, think tanks, and international organizations, but it made an exception for the Association it trusted so much, granting the same $25,000 it gave each year to the research department for the formation of an equivalent education department. Placed under Stone, the education department worked to convert expert knowledge to "popular form," Buell wrote, teaching a reading public "the significance and complexity of world interrelationships." Stone hired the adult educator Ryllis Alexander Goslin as his editor, and in September she oversaw the release of the first of the Headline Books series, the initial issues of which she wrote or co-wrote. Carefully edited to ensure that the prose was readable, and filled with maps, charts, and images, the Headlines were intended to appeal to those who wanted to learn more about events in the news. Sometimes written by the research staff but more often produced by specialist writers like Varian Fry and Delia Goetz, these short books were priced at twenty-five to thirty-five cents, the five or six of them that came out annually costing far less than the Association's five-dollar dues. Although a large proportion of the Headlines were sent to the membership, which seemed to appreciate easier texts to read than the *Bulletin* and the *Reports*, the Association would distribute 2.5 million Headline Books over the next decade.[35]

As the Association discovered in its radio work and in later efforts to reach large numbers of citizens, it found that creating a paperback public for foreign affairs was not simple: setting aside the question of whether such citizens were interested, there were formidable technological and infrastructural obstacles to success. Although newspaper readership remained high, the United States was not a nation of bookworms, for one thing. Few Americans had high school diplomas at this point, and literacy levels were far lower than they would be in the 1950s, when mass-market paperbacks became ubiquitous. For another thing, no supply chain existed through which the Headlines could be sold. The Association correctly estimated that there were just six hundred bookstores in the nation in 1935, of which about two hundred were major outlets. Much of their stock was priced as a luxury good and cost two dollars or more, and if mysteries, comedies, and smuttier tales than the shifting distribution of naval forces in the Far East were available for less, the few titles that did sell well usually reached readers through book clubs or mailing lists. There were thousands of libraries across the country, and their circulation was on the up, but a market through which the Association could break close to even on the Headlines did not exist until the late 1940s. The Association also had no experience with the volume it aimed to deal with here, regardless of pamphleteering skills left over from the suffrage campaign. As an *Atlantic Monthly* review of the earliest Headlines noted, sales were slow "because the publishers have undertaken a type of book unusual for them, one which their ordinary system of promotion and distribution is not geared to handle." There were 115,000 Headlines printed in the first year; 5,500 were sold in stores. The Association had some success mounting books on newsstands, albeit at such a severe loss that John D. Rockefeller III had to step in to cover the balance personally, but retailers saw little benefit, yet, in promoting titles with such small profit margins.[36]

Where the Headline Books did their best work was as literature for voluntary associations, as tools for citizens who were already engaged in civic and political life as the Association defined it. Few foreign affairs organizations could provide their members with texts of consistent quality, and groups like the National Peace Conference and the National Council for Prevention of War therefore placed large orders; there was also considerable demand from partners not exclusively interested in diplomacy such as the League of Women Voters, the YM and YWCAs, and the International Ladies Garment Workers Union, a key player in the labor struggles of the 1930s. Such groups used the Headlines in their regular meetings, a process the New York office helped by providing study kits, reading lists, and even scripts for public hearings and mock trials. The education department sponsored its own programs in New York, trying to inculcate discussion techniques among teachers, clubwomen, and students, and it also tried out prizes for club initiatives, sent exhibits to conferences and conventions, and sought to work with schools. Although this work thrilled some of the junior staff, none of it provided Rockefeller with sufficient proof that the experiment was worthwhile. If a market existed for this kind of material, as one Foundation official put it, it would be filled through "normal academic and publishers' activities." Rockefeller staffers anyway still believed that public opinion was created from the top down, and it felt that the Headlines were unlikely to be "the type of material really needed by the opinion forming groups in this country." The greater their distribution, in this view, the less useful they would really be.[37]

The most striking of the Association's efforts at renewed popular engagement came through its return to the radio, which had come of age since McDonald's day. Fifty-one million receivers were in use in 1940, nine in ten households possessing a set and most counting it among their most cherished possessions, whereas just three million sets had been sold when the Association broadcast its first event in 1923. Lacking McDonald's relationship with the higher-ups at NBC, and with a principled disdain of the corporate sponsorship that made other educational programming possible, Buell could not convince the networks to give him a show after McDonald left for Europe. But Buell thought it was essential that the Association offer its services, for while he believed, like Dewey, that the medium had significant promise in a world that radio technology was itself shrinking, he feared that its tendencies to commercialism and sensationalism might work to the detriment of an informed public opinion. Buell presumed that radio was making public affairs more pervasive in daily life, even if the effect was attenuated by class, education, and geography. "Today a great change has come over the United States," he told the Women's National Radio Committee in 1939, for radio meant that "what happens in the little kingdom of Albania interests housewives in Montana." Or it could, at least; Americans, he assumed with little evidence, now followed events abroad "with deep interest and even passion." But the risks of incomplete, superficial, or propagandistic information were clear, especially among what he thought of as less "discriminating" audiences. Educators like Bryson had taken to the airwaves to solve precisely that issue, replicating physical discussion formats in programs such as the *Town Meeting of the Air* and the *Chicago Round Table* to see whether the radio could in fact become a "two-way instrument of democracy," as McDonald once put it, or whether it would deaden listeners into an audience ripe for manipulation.[38]

When the Association finally won a contract on NBC's Blue Network in the fall of 1939, with the help of the State Department, its programs were a quiet test of the potential for world affairs education. Rotating through their fields of expertise, members of the research staff read out an analysis of a current event for fifteen minutes each Sunday on a program called *America Looks Abroad*. Each broadcast featured the slogan "foreign affairs are your affairs" and implored listeners to write to the research staff to offer their views, just as McDonald had in his earlier broadcasts, with the idea of stimulating a dialogue between publics and experts in Deweyan fashion. Some listeners did. Seventy-two stations in the Blue Network carried *America Looks Abroad* by October 1941, and up to 350 listeners per week were by then responding with letters. One February 1940 report noted that the mailbag bulged with postcards from "working people" as well as clubwomen, teachers, and "professional people generally," a public the Association's radio secretary was convinced it had "never contacted before and probably never would reach except through the radio."[39]

Whether the Association was genuinely reaching a different kind of American or just expanding its reach to the same sorts of people in new areas of the country was nonetheless unclear. Some letters suggested as much. "We live out on the Arizona desert, the radio playing a major part in our daily life," one listener wrote in April 1941. "I listen to all your broadcasts and like them very much." Another correspondent, from California, reported that "these programs are of great public interest and serve as the 'meat' of the news for those who can't read the news." But even if the Association took pleasure in reaching people previously beyond the sway of foreign policy institutions, it took much more notice of correspondents who fit into its trickle-down model for how public opinion really worked. One letter picked out for attention came from Salem, Kentucky, in which a "pastor of two rural churches" wrote that he had a "keen interest" in the shows because he always tried "to guide the thinking of my people on such matters into current channels." The radio secretary noted in October 1941 that "while we receive only about 200 requests weekly for the broadcast copies, the quality of the comments, and the fact that many of the requests come from teachers in schools and colleges, would indicate the usefulness of the program."[40]

Even as the Association assumed it was reaching millions of people through the radio, though, it became hard to deny that the number of listeners who sought to do more than tune in was limited. With audience research techniques still in their infancy, despite scholars such as Paul Lazarsfeld warning that programs mainly reached people with preexisting interests in their subject matter, the Association could look only to its own metrics to see what it had achieved. The mailbag was offered anecdotes, but not much data: in February 1941, after sixty-four broadcasts, 11,401 letters had come into headquarters, an average of 178 per show. (The State Department's later NBC show, *Our Foreign Policy*, garnered more than four hundred letters per broadcast in 1945.) More ominous than these inconclusive numbers was that listeners saw little reason to translate their interest in the programs into a deeper relationship with the Association. Just eighty-three members had been added as a direct result of the radio broadcasts by that February, earning a paltry $492. Evidence also suggested that branch members were citing the broadcasts as a reason not to attend meetings. One did not have to be a media critic of the caliber of Theodor Adorno to fear that radio, despite the efforts of educators, was transforming public culture for the worse, making audiences where once there had been publics.[41]

## The Breaking of Raymond Leslie Buell

What did all this add up to? Nobody really knew, a frustration that led to significant dissension, even if all agreed that the Association's role had been supreme in whatever internationalists had or had not accomplished. As Americans watched storm clouds grow in Europe, there were observers, including at the Rockefeller Foundation, who wondered whether the Association had been so successful in getting information into newspapers and other outlets that it might have worked itself out of a job. There were others who knew that it had made little impression outside its core clientele of the wealthy and highly educated. There were those who thought that that target population was sufficient, proper, wise; there were those who thought such a limited objective irresponsible. And then there were those who connected all these questions to questions broader still, who could draw a line from the content of a single *Report* to pressing issues of war and peace, who connected their work building an informed public opinion to the transcendence of power politics abroad, and who consequently could see little but failure now that men who thought that might made right were trying to dominate the world again. Buell was one of the few men capable of seeing the question whole; his fate as president of the group most attuned to both foreign policy and public opinion was illustrative.

Buell never quite lost his faith in the common sense of the people, not as much as more conservative men; he could in fact be touchingly naïve about the democratic process. His move towards the Republican party and his decision to become an advisor to Wendell Willkie in the 1940 election campaign emerged from his distaste for what he perceived as the authoritarianism of the New Deal, as well as from his embarrassment at the Roosevelt administration's rejection of his efforts to ingratiate himself, which had included an elegant if implausible plan for an "international new deal" that entailed the United States joining the League followed by Germany and Japan. But what else except Buell's idealistic streak could explain the primary challenge he launched in 1942, from the left, against Republican Allen T. Treadway, a fifteen-term noninterventionist congressman and dean of the Massachusetts delegation to the US House? Buell could not bring himself to appeal to the pocketbooks of his constituents and had no understanding of how political power worked; he stumped with abstract arguments about the future of managerial capitalism, the duties of the representative, and the importance of a legislative check against "the rise of dictatorship and the one party system in this country." "A Man of Vision, Knowledge and Action," Buell's campaign leaflets announced—his Berkshire County neighbors disagreed, and he was crushed.[42]

While similarly prominent internationalists turned to geopolitics and various other forms of repudiation of Wilsonianism during the war, Buell held the line, steadfast in his commitment to a certain understanding of public opinion and its power. "If democracy in this country is going to function," he wrote in *Isolated America* (1940), a surgical dissection of what he had long called isolationism, "it must do so not only in the domestic but in the foreign field." Perhaps, he asked, US strategy should not be made behind closed doors, but hashed out in a joint committee of Congress, with the executive branch and the "general public" present? Even in the League of Nations, whose faults drove some of his peers to outright cynicism, Buell saw a failure of democratization, not of democracy. "Its defects," he wrote, were "due not to its construction but to the treason of its members." Buell proposed to bolster the League's administrative powers and give it an armed force to prosecute its sanctions, but he also sought broader public participation in its delegations, for example through the inclusion of opposition parties or voluntary association officials, a proposal that recalled those of his Association predecessors who thought Wilson's League too undemocratic back in 1919. Whether the United States joined the League or not, for Buell the fate of democracy at home and the fate of a democratic world order were still tied. "When international relations are dominated by power politics, democracies cannot compete with the dictatorships without adopting dictatorial methods," he argued. "While every effort must be made to democratize the conduct of foreign relations," he concluded nonetheless, "every American friend of democracy should realize that this is extremely difficult so long as we live in a jungle world."[43]

Buell was troubled that the methods he and the Association used appeared not to have worked: creating and disseminating facts about international relations had not brought about the policy responses he thought followed from them. "As a result of the work of such bodies as the Foreign Policy Association," he wrote in *Isolated America*, Americans now had "a knowledge of international affairs far greater than at any other time in their history, and as far as information was concerned, more extensive than what was available to the public in any other country." But what had been the result? Politicians had capitulated to "pseudo-pacifism," to a "new isolationism" that had been "strong enough to prevent the United States from accepting an international program which might have averted the outbreak of war," even if it had not been able "to sterilize the 'moral' concern of the country with the fate of the outside world." Unwilling or unable to accept that facts might not be sufficient to change minds, Buell questioned his techniques, not his theories. Perhaps, he suggested, citing Dewey's *Freedom and Culture* (1939), too much information was now available, for the "average individual is confronted with an immense number of unrelated facts on the one hand and untested generalities on the other," all spewing forth from "giant radio, movie, and newspaper chains constituting semi-monopolies." The answer, Buell thought, was to seek both "greater popular participation in public life" and "stronger intellectual leadership." For this Deweyan, Deweyan problems still required Deweyan solutions.[44]

Buell knew and read men who thought otherwise, men who would abandon adult education and throw participatory theories of democracies out with it, leaving expert leadership in their place. Buell paid particular attention to Joseph Schumpeter, an Austrian economist who had spoken from Association stages and whose wife was active in the foreign affairs activities of the League of Women Voters. Schumpeter wrote in 1942 that no amount of "meritorious" discussion groups would improve an "infantile" mass, arguing that democracy amounted to no more than a routine competition for votes. Buell would not go so far, but he did change tack. He took a leave of absence from the Association in September 1938, quitting the following summer to join *Fortune*, a magazine in Henry R. Luce's empire aimed at corporate elites. Buell edited its roundtable, a feature that gathered leaders from business, labor, agriculture, and other fields to find areas of compromise, much as his "policy groups" had planned. If *Fortune*'s experiment reduced the "public" of public opinion to few enough men that they could sit around a single table, Buell later turned to write explicitly for an audience of one, albeit one who spoke to millions: he spent World War II for the most part in Luce's postwar department, a brain trust that advised the Republican powerbroker on the line *Time, Life,* and *Fortune* should take on global affairs. A Wilsonian in a less and less Wilsonian world, Buell's stature wanted. He refused to join his colleagues in supporting armed US primacy as the guarantor of peace; he insisted that primacy—imperialism, in his view—was "morally wrong" and "a threat to our own interests" however cleverly the Roosevelt administration couched it in the language of internationalism that Buell had done so much to promote.[45]

So angry was Buell at the wartime drift of US policy that he refused to join the postwar planning staff the State Department put together in 1943, pleading the need to recover from initial treatment for the brain cancer that would take his life in 1946, at just forty-nine. By then, Buell had become an even more bitter critic of Roosevelt, who he saw as an inadequate internationalist in prewar terms—his failure to buttress the League now deepened with the concessions to power in the veto clauses of the United Nations Security Council—and also in postwar terms, Roosevelt's cowardly failure to stand up to the Soviet Union evidently having led to the "surrender" of Eastern Europe. With that critique of policy necessarily came the critique of the form of democratic foreign policy the president had adopted, linked as the two always were in Buell's mind. Roosevelt had appeared to Buell to turn to dictatorial methods to sell his peace, masking "misleading propaganda" as a purely educational campaign, as Buell put it in 1945 to the chief architect of that effort, Assistant Secretary of State for Public Affairs Archibald MacLeish. But if Buell confronted a markedly different world at his death, the dilemmas he had spent his life thinking about had not at all gone away. If anything, the problems involved in reconciling US democracy, still at risk, to US power, now overwhelming, had intensified. What would be the duties of expertise now? Of citizenship? Of statesmanship? If Buell was troubled by the answers Roosevelt had come to, the solutions the president's successors came to would have horrified him.[46]

# 3

# The War for Democracy

May 1941. The United States was not yet a full combatant in what was becoming known as the Second World War, but in the Foreign Policy Association's offices above East Thirty-Eighth Street, its research director Vera Micheles Dean was already planning for the peace to follow. With the war raging so destructively, its end seemed such a distant prospect that Dean doubted her deepest convictions. Might the twentieth century not be destined for the peace and prosperity of which she and her fellow internationalists had dreamed? Might peace be impossible if the war became "a contest of mutual annihilation"? Might her times even reprise the sixteenth century, its wars lasting decades, its truces uneasy and brief?

Faith, after all, was hard to keep. German forces occupied Poland, Denmark, Norway, Belgium, the Netherlands, Luxembourg, France, Yugoslavia, and Greece. Northern Africa was tottering; Russia would be next. The Atlantic frothed with foes, the Mediterranean no less. The pilots of the Royal Air Force may have beaten back their enemy, but not even that finest hour could hide the mortal threat to the British Empire as a whole. If the Empire fell, the United States would be defenseless. Sensing the danger, America had come to Britain's aid in March when, after rancorous debate, President Roosevelt had signed "An Act to Promote the Defense of the United States," which lent materiel in return for the lease of strategic bases. It was enough that Dean could just about see reason for hope. "The United States has already abandoned all pretense of isolation within its own continental borders," she typed. Whether it fought in the war or not, after all, when the peace came America would have the power to "determine the new world order." And this time, it looked like it might.

What kind of world would the United States then make? Returning to the *status quo ante* would be impossible. "Too many things have happened,"

Dean argued, "too many systems have been crushed, too many leaders and ideas have been discredited." She knew what kind of peace she sought, one that would confront the inequities of the industrial age and promise freedom for all. Security would be collective. Empires would fall. Welfare would offer stability. People would never again fall to the "despair and defeatism" on which fascism and communism had feasted, would see no need to hand their destinies to those ruling for a "master race" or a "master class." Dean's vision was far from mainstream, she knew, sitting somewhere on the Democratic left if even there, but the basic problem she foresaw was on the minds of her colleagues, too. If the United States was to lead, she wrote, it would have to summon the "will to act"—and summon it, ultimately, from the depths of public opinion.

Could Americans be made aware of what Dean saw as their duties in the world, and agree to them? Could they be taught to lead? Could they learn that compromise in foreign affairs was inevitable, that no peace could be "eternal or unassailably just"? Could the government be made responsible to the people, if the people could be so taught? Could America break with the customs of diplomatic history and forge a new kind of foreign policy, one worthy of a democracy, at the critical moment at which it grasped its power? The stakes seemed higher than ever; the shape of what Henry R. Luce had just christened the "American Century," Dean felt, hung on the answer.[1]

## *"Objectivity" and Power*

"No people are now as a whole better informed on world affairs than is the case with citizens of the United States," the *Washington Post* wrote in December 1938, marking the Foreign Policy Association's twentieth anniversary. The claim was rash, speaking to the widespread availability of information rather than the indeterminate extent to which citizens availed themselves of it, but the *Post* was not alone in making it, nor in handing out the credit. "Today all foreigners who travel through the United States are surprised to see how wide the interest is in international questions," Sonia Tomara reported in the *New York Herald Tribune*, declaring that "newspapers, the radio and the Foreign Policy Association are responsible for having made Americans 'foreign minded.'" Even those who feared what such an achievement might mean had to applaud. Charles A. Beard, the historian who had joined the earliest meetings of the League of Free Nations Association and whose scholarly methods inspired many of the Association's researchers, would soon savagely indict the "heavy industry" that had cropped up to create "frenetic preoccupation with foreign quarrels." But even Beard was among the seventeen thousand or so members of the group at that industry's core, a long-standing admirer of the "exacting care" of its publications and the "catholicity of opinion" on show at its meetings.[2]

The Association was lauded from all sides of the foreign policy community it had done so much to create. Birthday greetings came from Henry Stimson, Cordell Hull, and John Foster Dulles, secretaries of state past, present, and future. Walter Lippmann sent a telegram in congratulations; John Dewey wrote in a tribute that he knew of "no organization which has combined more effectively than the F.P.A. research work and dissemination of the results of its studies." The Association's staff found their *Reports* read as carefully at the State Department as in the international relations classes that had spread across campuses nationwide, and they found themselves as welcome for private discussions at the great European foreign offices as for public addresses in the school halls and women's club rooms where they so often spoke. Seventeen branches now held luncheons in some of the finest hotels in the land, their cachet undimmed, their leaders men like Harvey H. Bundy of Boston, the erstwhile assistant secretary of state who would soon become special assistant to Stimson at the War Department, and Francis Biddle, a Philadelphia lawyer who would enter the coming war as Roosevelt's attorney general and end it exacting justice from the bench at the Nuremberg trials.[3]

Decades later, this period would be remembered as the Association's golden age, its work "valiant" at a time when "Mussolini's armies were chasing Haile Selassie's warriors in Ethiopia or Hitler was reoccupying the Rhineland," as a foundation official recalled in 1964. Such notions came from another era, a time in which it would be deliberately misremembered that the 1930s as a whole had pitted an embattled "internationalism" against "isolationism," with agencies like the Association holding the line against disaster. But it was clearer in 1939 that the Association had built such a commanding reputation precisely because it had not explicit chosen sides in a struggle that did not yet exist. It had left room for debate; both the interventionist Lippmann and the continentalist Beard could admire it, after all. Its board and staff had hoped that the United States might play a more constructive role in the world, but as late as 1940 there was no clear, corporate sense as to what that might mean. Did the internationalism that the Association had championed really now entail fighting another European war? Discussion, it thought, would bring clarity; its meetings for the moment remained tolerant of competing views. That was true when its events focused on core issues in US foreign policy, as in a March 1939 luncheon that saw Lewis Mumford, Samuel Flagg Bemis, and John Foster Dulles offer divergent futures for the nation: intervening with imperial ambition, guarding "the United States first," or transcending power with the "triumph of democratic ideals." The Association's prewar commitment to freedom of speech even extended to inviting a Nazi to promote Hitler's cause: the fascist writer Colin Ross declared his "love" for the dictator at the Astor that January, to loud jeers.[4]

Not even after Germany invaded Poland in September 1939 did the Association's highest officials agree on the correct response to Nazi aggression, a sign of just how unclear the fate of the nation remained. Raymond Leslie Buell, its president until that summer, had championed intervention for years, with force if necessary. Dean had likewise never believed in the "fallacy" of neutrality. But others took the opposite view. William T. Stone had to remain friendly with policymakers of all views to direct the Washington bureau successfully, but Buell's deputy had become personally influential only among noninterventionists. When Senator Gerald Nye started, in 1934, to investigate the role of armaments manufacturers in Wilson's intervention of 1917, Stone not only provided research assistance, but detailed Nye's findings so favorably in a *Report* that DuPont, the munitions giant, threatened to sue the Association. When Congress drafted the Neutrality Act in the spring of 1935, Stone helped write it. When Senate investigators turned to the role of financiers in Wilson's declaration of war later that year, Stone authored a pamphlet that so angered the House of Morgan that the Association's most generous individual benefactors, Thomas and Florence Lamont, almost ended their support. So central had Stone become in noninterventionist circles by 1938 that the *Nation* went so far as to name him the "quarterback" of "the isolationist team" that March. And plenty of men and women tied to the Association were on the field beside him. Many of the staff and board members volunteered for the National Peace Conference. Some of the junior researchers also held—and were permitted publicly to argue for—far more constrained understandings of US interests than Buell and Dean. None of the core institutions of the foreign policy community represented a globalism-in-waiting in 1939, the Association perhaps least of all.[5]

Hitler changed that. Although the Association promised it would continue to act with "objectivity" after the fall of Poland, the range of opinions it endorsed in its publications and on its stages quickly narrowed. How could the Association not show its hand if Dean was warning that the Wehrmacht would shake "the foundation on which millions of Americans had built their

EVERY    CITIZEN    A    STATESMAN

way of life?" By April 1940, Lamont was praising the researchers for their efforts to teach Americans that "we may have a peaceful world only if we are
willing to pay a part of the price for it," a message that implied the backing of
the White House for which he was an intermediary. Stone supported the
Lend-Lease Act with the zeal of a convert, despite having insisted a year and
a half before its passage that he would never countenance loans to the British
Empire. By September 1941, Stone was assaulting the "isolationist" position
in its entirety, arguing that "the United States must prepare to assume a new
and responsible role in a world that will not be the familiar, secure world we
have known for the past hundred years." After the Association hosted Henry
Wallace for a speech in April 1941, in which the vice president called on all
Americans to take their "second chance to make the world safe for democracy," Dean began sketching out her blueprint for a new world order, insisting that "a great power cannot indefinitely avoid responsibility" though
stopping short of explicitly advocating a declaration of war.[6]

What kind of "objectivity" was this? Not the old commitment to balancing
competing, presumptively equally legitimate views, however much men like
James McDonald had assured critics that balance had always been a sly means
to internationalist ends. There were trustees who wondered whether the Association was wise to take such an open stance, but its researchers now worked
from assumptions far removed from the "fact cult" of the 1920s, fearing that the
crisis was sufficiently grave that the public required firmer guidance. Dean
thought it patently obvious that "every writer of integrity has a point of view toward his material," for "otherwise he would be merely a well-articulated robot."
Rockefeller's Tracy Kittredge similarly found nothing objectionable in the
idea that the researchers would make "certain assumptions as to the foreign
policy and interest of the United States" in their choice of topics, collection of
materials, or final analyses. Either way, the Association came under little pressure in 1939, 1940, or 1941 to curb its instincts. Most of its supporters, schooled
through years of luncheons in the necessity of US responsibility, turned to the
Committee to Defend America by Aiding the Allies and even more belligerent groups. By late 1940, the Committee had more members in New York
state alone than the Association had nationwide. And as the Association's attendance and sales figures plummeted in the rush to intervention, it became
painfully clear that nonpartisanship would not be profitable in political, intellectual, or financial terms amid a fractious debate on US policy.[7]

The Association was left with a more subtle task. While its researchers inveighed in print and on the airwaves against the intellectual assumptions of

noninterventionism, its administrative staff cast noninterventionists themselves from the semi-official debate that the Association's pages and stages had come to represent, aiming to make their views seem illegitimate. Buell might have had qualms about this, given his philosophical commitments, but his successor had few. Appointed president of the Association in July 1939, Frank R. McCoy was not a scholar as Buell had been, nor a charismatic speaker like McDonald, but a stiff-backed major-general. He had spent his life on the frontiers of the US empire; he needed no instruction in the righteousness of American power. Protégé to Henry Stimson, who likely made sure of White House support before placing McCoy at the Association, McCoy had trained as a colonial administrator in the Philippines, served as a White House military aide to Theodore Roosevelt, and commanded men on the Western front. After another spell in Manila, he had become a uniformed diplomat of sorts, leading a detachment of Marines to supervise elections as "the Mussolini of Nicaragua," as one outlet dubbed him, and ensuring that the League of Nations' inquiry into Japan's invasion of Manchuria in 1931 reflected US interests. McCoy was trusted enough in Washington to sit on the commission designated to investigate the attack on Pearl Harbor and, not coincidentally, he was a friend of Franklin and Eleanor Roosevelt. What he was not was a thinker. As his biographer Andrew Bacevich has put it, McCoy was a soldier "lacking intellectual originality" to whom "eloquence never came easily." He was a follower, and follow he would.[8]

The Association therefore echoed the Roosevelt administration's message. Where once the branches had showcased fiery arguments about the future of US foreign policy, in September 1939 they were instructed to avoid the "violent conflicts" that had made their luncheons so popular. Their two-speaker rule, which had guaranteed debate at every event, was weakened; a single speaker might be followed with a panel of local experts, or face no rebuttal at all if they were a member of the research staff. With the Association's finances suffering as competition rose for internationalist cash, a particularly intractable problem at the local level, luncheons featuring more than one speaker became rare outside Manhattan; it was the noninterventionist view that was typically left unspoken. McCoy then tightened the screws as Roosevelt sought to intervene further in the European conflict. The America First Committee, founded in September 1940 to advocate traditional noninterventionism, was simply ignored. When one of its chapters asked the following summer whether a researcher might give a speech on a "purely objective" factual question like the statistical balance of raw materials among the nations, McCoy refused.[9]

Once Lend-Lease tied US policy to the defense of Britain, and especially after Roosevelt declared a national emergency in May 1941, the Association's board felt liberated to restrict the bounds of discussion permanently. Confirming a procedure McCoy had informally followed for months, the board agreed that September that "within our framework of objectivity we can be forward-looking along the line of settled American policy and not add confusion to confusion by useless discussion and re-hash of old policies." One month later, the Association permitted Roosevelt to use one of its regular forums to say that those who sought "to lull us into a false sense of security, to tell us that we are not threatened"—like Beard—were "Hitler's agents and Quislings." Pearl Harbor confirmed a new reality in which the United States was assumed to be abidingly insecure, its safety therefore requiring that its power be used to underwrite the peace. After Congress declared war on the Axis, the Association announced that its stance would be "informative" rather than "argumentative," quoting Roosevelt to declare that education "must be begun 'by abandoning once and for all the illusion that we can ever again isolate ourselves from the rest of humanity.'" There would be no going back. Not for decades would opponents of US primacy again have access to the platforms of the Association or any similar group.[10]

That the Association felt it necessary to rig the debate in this way spoke to the radicalism of the interventionist cause and the weakness of prewar internationalist education. How, after all, did Roosevelt convince much of the public that US interests required Nazism's defeat and the establishment of a US-led order? He claimed in March 1941 that these decisions were settled "by the American people themselves" after debates "in every newspaper, on every wavelength, over every cracker barrel in all the land." True enough, to some extent, but Roosevelt and his acolytes had skewed that discussion, employing methods more forceful than the educational techniques the president knew plenty about from watching the Association at work. Believing fully in the need for popular support and the malleability of the public mind, Roosevelt inflated real fears of the German threat, exaggerating the nation's vulnerability and promoting boundless conceptions of "national security," a neologism resonant with Depression-era anxieties that added the global defense of democratic values to traditional definitions of security that emphasized the defense of physical territory. Deploying new ideas, Roosevelt also armed himself with new technologies, tailoring his messaging in his radio broadcasts after a careful reading of opinion polls, some of them secret. His allies outside government wielded the latest methods in corporate advertising, methods explicitly intended to manipulate publics rather than reason with them. If progressive interventionists had not supported the ends to which these tactics were put, they might well have wondered whether the propaganda they had once feared as a ruinous threat to democratic politics had not returned. Their former colleagues who favored noninterventionism certainly did.[11]

Were pure facts then not enough to separate right from wrong? Few educators dared ask the question, but Dean did grapple with it. More than aware of the limited reach of her work, the failure of information to generate what she saw as the proper policy response troubled her, as it troubled Buell. When the war ended, she would reflect that the United States had shown "little more than academic interest" in the collapse of the League of Nations system after 1933, its "aloofness" inexplicable given that "at no other time in history" had its citizenry been so well supplied with "first-rate, penetrating newspaper and radio analyses." But the availability of information had not led to its processing and to consequent action, at least not quickly or adequately enough. Some, though not Dean, would blame the American people for this, their scapegoating the result of a worldview that saw public opinion as the guardian of security and yet also belittled the masses as ignorant and apathetic, if not incurably so. The State Department frequently engaged in this tactic to deflect from its own failures, shaming citizens with the argument that their complacency had prevented the United States from facing down its foes. But blame was not enough. Policymakers needed to be sure that public opinion would never again constrain them, whether through facts or some other means.[12]

Public opinion might not have transcended power as Wilsonians had hoped, then, but it remained at the core of their latest solution to the problem of peace: the use of US power. Not for nothing did Archibald MacLeish, the poet and Librarian of Congress who Roosevelt asked to help lead his wartime propaganda agencies, say in April 1942 that "the real battleground of this war is the field of American opinion."[13]

## What the National Security State Wrought

When German troops had blitzed their way through Poland, it had been unclear what role the Association might play in a world at war. At the highest levels, it represented an incomplete ideal for what might be possible in terms of a democratic foreign policy. Secretary of State Cordell Hull had told Buell in 1934 to consider himself a member "of the State Department staff," and that bond had tightened as war had loomed. Senior policymakers spent more of their time talking with Stone, on and off the record; assistant secretaries of state and their subordinates took more care over the Association's publications, offering advice on drafts and reading articles in print; the embassies abroad were told to do more to support the research staff on its travels, for it was making a "real" and "responsible" contribution to "the development of an enlightened public opinion," as a cable from Undersecretary of State Sumner Welles confirmed. Generous public praise followed, too. Welles, who took day-to-day control of diplomacy in 1937, had told a luncheon a year earlier that the modern State Department believed, unlike its predecessors, that the "more our citizenry knows, debates, and thinks about the foreign policy of their Government, the greater the security of this democracy will be." It therefore "strongly" valued the Association's work.[14]

But the Association knew its position was precarious. Even supportive State Department officials preferred to speak in the safety of the Council on Foreign Relations when they traveled to New York, rather than at the Association's rowdy public meetings. "The same old story, the Council gets the big shots though we could give them a better audience," Buell scrawled on one of several letters of apology from Hull. And would the Association be able to operate at all if free speech was curtailed, if debating policy was again deemed unwise, even seditious, in a nation at war? Progressive fears of propaganda remained visceral, and they grew stronger in light of the example of Joseph Goebbels. The Association told the Rockefeller Foundation in 1941 that "the task of educating American public opinion cannot be left to the government alone without inviting regimentation and dangerous restrictions on traditional democratic freedoms," but it made the argument more in hope than certainty. Anxieties also rose that the government would have to hire staff to administer Lend-Lease and similar programs, even if America did not join the war. The Association's staff would be an easy target. The Council on Foreign Relations and the Institute of Pacific Relations relied on outside experts and temporary fellows to produce much of the knowledge they distributed; they functioned as private forums for a policymaking class that was spread across multiple professions, adding to the dismal capabilities of the official bureaucracy. But the Association's structure made it far more vulnerable. Its researchers were permanent, well-traveled, and held to the astronomically high standards demanded by Buell and Dean. The research staff was a "college faculty," as one report to Rockefeller put it, and one with a unique sense of public responsibility. When the State Department was small and civil service were salaries low, government work was unattractive for the men of the Association. When the crisis began, and the state desperately needed expertise, that changed.[15]

The turning point came in the first two weeks of European fighting. When Great Britain and France declared war, officials at the major foreign policy institutions recognized that the State Department would want to begin planning for the peace. But State could not do the job itself: it had no research facilities of its own and it could not risk annoying Congress by prejudicing debate on America's future strategic posture. Buell smelled an opening. He knew that the United States would end the war dominant, for it had "become the world's greatest power without knowing it," as he said in a speech that fall. But if it ended the war without a "program for future world organization," he wrote to McCoy on September 3, it might again succumb to withdrawal. Here was a chance to learn from the past. Wilson's Inquiry had been too little, too late; worse, and offensive to those who championed public participation and voluntary initiatives, it had been "a government commission financed by government funds," giving the citizenry little input. McCoy might therefore offer to coordinate private work to "formulate suggestions" on all aspects of US policy. "Time is of the essence," Buell warned. "Other organizations or universities may get the same idea."[16]

McCoy dithered, characteristically; others moved. *Foreign Affairs* editor and longtime Association critic Hamilton Fish Armstrong telephoned Assistant Secretary of State George Messersmith on September 10, making much the same argument to his fellow Council on Foreign Relations member as Buell had made to McCoy. The difference was that Armstrong and Messersmith believed that the Council alone could be trusted to take on the task in the right way, quietly and in confidence. On September 12, Armstrong and a colleague took a train to Washington and secured approval from Welles and Messersmith for what became the Council's War and Peace Studies program, in which the United States' plans for the postwar world were drawn up. On September 14, Stone told McCoy that the State Department officials to whom he had spoken claimed not to have given the matter much thought, even if they felt that "competent research bodies like the FPA" might well do the job; he would see "Messersmith and several others tomorrow." It was already too late. Over the next six years, the Council would churn out some 682 memoranda for the government, at a cost to the Rockefeller Foundation of $300,000.[17]

This was an epochal decision, not that it seemed like it then. Postwar planning became something of a craze after the war began, engaging everything from the Federal Council of Churches to the editorial committee of Time Inc.; such groups evidently did not believe that the United States should plot its path in private, without public input. But the State Department's decision to conduct the planning that really mattered in secret set a precedent. Desperate to avoid Wilson's fate, policymakers improvised a process through which they foreclosed meaningful debate about the peace, avoiding the messiness of the Great War and enabling them to present Congress and the public with a take-it-or-leave-it choice at the end of the fight. Even so, it was not initially obvious that the Council should take responsibility for such an initiative, still less sole charge, on which the Foundation insisted when McCoy suggested a collaborative approach. Clearly the commitment to public participation Welles and Messersmith had professed had its limits, especially if women might get involved. The Department could have faith that "groups of men with the proper background and understanding" were doing this work, Messersmith told Hull; other proposals were not of "quite the same caliber" and might "cause the Department considerable concern." The stench of sexism lingered; elitism too. McCoy, McDonald, and some of the Association's male staff took part in the Council's deliberations on a personal basis, but the Foundation heard rumors that others at the Association "resent being completely ignored in the work which they know to be under way under the auspices of the CFR." Dean was furious.[18]

While the Council's war work pulled it to the heart of the foreign policy community and laid the groundwork for the rise of an "establishment," the consequences for the Association were stark. Lacking any specially protected role in policymaking, the growing national security state could ransack its offices for talent. Charles A. Thomson was the first researcher to leave, and the Latin American specialist's appointment as deputy director of State's Division of Cultural Relations in October 1938 struck Buell as an honor at the time. But Buell's pride soon turned into McCoy's worry. Thomson's replacement, Howard Trueblood, left for State in 1940, as did Frederick Merrill, a narcotics specialist. James Frederick Green, an expert on Britain, left soon after. "We must work out some way of not being crippled by losing our staff to the government," McCoy warned in May 1941; Stone reported that "every government agency is looking for research people and can offer from $500 to $1,500 more." T. A. Bisson, a leading authority on Asia who had been hired in 1929, quit for Henry Wallace's Board of Economic Warfare soon after Pearl Harbor, as did John C. de Wilde, who studied Europe. Louis Frechtling, a Rhodes scholar, joined Green at a forerunner of the Office of Strategic Services (OSS), the precursor to the Central Intelligence Agency. "It seems impossible to get any young men at the moment," Dean wrote in May 1942, complaining that "government agencies have already made such forays into university and journalistic circles that only second and third-rate people are available." David Popper, a Harvard valedictorian, reported to Fort Dix; Howard Whidden, fresh from his own studies on the Charles, lasted barely a few months on the staff; William Maddox, McCoy's erstwhile assistant, went to the OSS. The most devastating loss was Stone, who had gone to work for Wallace just before Bisson, leaving the Washington office empty and in disrepair—a fitting illustration of the Association's diminished role.[19]

Whether the federal government had torn the research department apart for good was not yet known; other men at the Association took the chance to serve as well, none more heroically than education department editor Varian Fry, who risked his life to rescue Jewish refugees from Marseille, France. "We have been able to carry on at least within the framework of the women in our organization," McCoy told the board in May 1943. Dorothy Leet, the new secretary, and Florence Pratt of the speakers bureau became ever more crucial. Dean found a couple of women to hire as researchers, but she was put in an impossible position. She was among the nation's most insightful writers on foreign affairs and she was prominent enough in the women's movement to be offered the presidency of her alma mater, Radcliffe College, early in 1943. She declined that post, arguably the most prestigious in women's education, citing her "dominant passion" of writing and her "equally overwhelming desire to participate, in some small way, in the tasks of post-war reconstruction." But that desire went unfulfilled. Often named among the women best qualified to serve on US delegations to peace conferences, her input was limited to a brief role consulting for the United Nations Relief and Rehabilitation Administration. Either way, Dean could not risk losing her place on the lecture circuit, on which she was so popular that her fees sometimes doubled her salary, irreplaceable earnings for a widowed mother of two. Even if she had felt able to leave the Association, her gender meant that her other options were few.[20]

Although Dean and her colleagues continued to write their *Reports* and their *Bulletin*, their broader educational work became more pressing as they pushed to make the Association's rhetoric more of a reality. Far too often, Dean had said in 1939, scholars had been content to reach "a pitifully small group of educated men and women, on the theory that leaders would leaven the masses." Seeing the collapse of the Weimar Republic as a failure of democratic technique, she insisted that experts needed to "abandon their scholarly formulas" and "speak the vernacular" to storekeepers, farmers, and housewives. She tried to do just that, despite her struggle to find the right tone. She sought to push further, telling Rockefeller in 1942 that foreign policy institutions had reached "saturation point" with "'elite' groups," and that they should address themselves to "the 96 per cent or so who do not receive college education." McCoy agreed, though the Association did not much change its approach. Losing its radio broadcasts in July 1942, it invested in its more popular publications, distributing 1.6 million Headline Books from 1941 to 1945, a quarter million of which were sent to the War Department as literature for troops. Dean wrote ever more, her most successful piece being a United Nations discussion guide for the Office of War Information that *Reader's Digest, Time,* and *Newsweek* sent to their readers for free. But the public the Association sought was primarily, still, a reading public.[21]

Soon it became hard to distinguish even Dean's work from the deluge of information that rained down on citizens about the state of the war and the prospects for peace. "There are a hundred sources which are engaged today in adult education in international relations in this country for every one there was when FPA started in 1918," wrote Joseph Willits, director of the Rockefeller Foundation's Division of Social Sciences, in 1943. Was there not an argument that the Association had done its job, and perhaps too well for its own good? After all, Buell himself had taken his post at Time Inc. at the same time as journalists had started to report from bureaus around the globe as they never had before. And *Time* and *Life* were just one part of a broader information infrastructure. "The Government, the political parties, the press, the radio, the magazines, the colleges and universities, and the numerous books from scholars and men of affairs such as Willkie and Lippmann—all testify that the effort in which the FPA pioneered has now permeated the educational media of the country," Willits went on. What more could the Association do?[22]

Quite a lot, it was thought, a conviction held not just in the office of Willits's superior, Foundation president Raymond Blaine Fosdick, but in the most important offices in the land. What precisely President Roosevelt and Secretary Hull instructed their man on Thirty-Eighth Street to do during the war is unclear, but the message from those two Association supporters was nonetheless forceful. At the request of the White House, McCoy spent the summer of 1942 presiding over the military tribunal of eight Nazi saboteurs, sentencing six to death. While he was in Washington, he later told his board, he spoke with "high government officials" who asked him to "reach the great mass of American people rather than only the groups which were already aware of international problems." What Roosevelt and Hull meant, it turned out in further talks, was that the Association should set up more branches. "The more you spread, the better it will be for our general work in foreign

**3.1** Franklin D. Roosevelt, seated, speaks to the Foreign Policy Association at the Waldorf-Astoria, October 21, 1944. *From left:* Mayor Fiorello LaGuardia of New York; William W. Lancaster, chairman of the Association's board; Roosevelt; Frank R. McCoy, president of the Association; Secretary of War Henry L. Stimson; Secretary of the Navy James Forrestal (behind Stimson); Herbert H. Lehman, director of the United Nations Relief and Rehabilitation Administration; Senator Robert F. Wagner of New York; Agnes Goddard Leach.
Anthony Camerano, Associated Press, Shutterstock.

affairs," Roosevelt told McCoy over dinner at the Waldorf Astoria Hotel in October 1944, before he gave a speech so partisan that McCoy had to fend off complaints that the Association had taken sides in an election campaign. When asked, the Rockefeller Foundation insisted that McCoy should follow the orders of his commander-in-chief.[23]

It spoke to the Association's lasting prestige that the White House and State Department thought an expansion of its branch network would be worthwhile, but even McCoy could see it was waste of time and resources. Unlike Roosevelt and Hull, he knew the realities behind the Association's reputation. It might have had seventeen branches at the start of the war, but most

were flimsy at best. Several lost large numbers of members in the intervention debate and all reported that their meetings were attended poorly well
into 1943, as reputable speakers became hard to find. Members had their gas
and tires rationed, making driving to luncheons difficult; activists turned
to more immediate, tangible causes such as civil defense or relief; branch
chairmen were plucked for government posts. When New York headquarters
called a branch conference in May 1942, the reports it heard were dire. "We
are broke all the time," attendees from Providence complained, their outfit
having become a "moribund mutual admiration society of old fogies." The
few branches with more ambition found expansion impossible. Delegates
from Baltimore sighed in another conference in October 1943 that they could
find no way to reach beyond "the 'stuffed shirt' crowd who simply want to
come to dinner."[24]

Whatever McCoy's doubts about the branches and the "very fine results"
he thought other policies had earned, he pressed on—or, rather, the women
who worked for him did. With no money available to hire a field secretary,
the duties fell on Leet, who had succeeded Esther Ogden as secretary in
1937. Close to Virginia Gildersleeve, the Barnard College dean who would
be the sole woman to sit on the US delegation to the San Francisco Conference in 1945, Leet had graduated from Barnard in 1917 and then made her
name directing the American University Women's Club in Paris, better
known as Reid Hall. The position had put Leet at the heart of international
women's networks, hosting tourists, students, and academics on their jour-
neys across Europe; after the war, her towering reputation would be reflected
in a spell as president of the International Federation of University Women.
In between, she traveled the United States for the Association. Often following in Dean's wake, she scouted out endless towns and cities, interviewing
civic leaders, attending teas, doing the hard work of building a public for
foreign affairs one city at a time.[25]

Take New Orleans, a rare target in the South on account of the port that
connected its business community to growing international trade. Dean visited in May 1942 for a speech on postwar plans that drew national attention.
Leet followed in April, carrying recommendation letters from McCoy and
his allies, including Dave Hennen Morris, then the US ambassador to Belgium. Scholarly interest was vital to the success of any branch, so Leet first
saw the president of Tulane University to set up a luncheon with faculty; the
academics told her to see a rabbi. One friend from Paris, a sculptor, held a
tea for twenty women, including the director of the public library system.

One contact had to be dropped "because of the pressure which she is using on the colored question," in line with the Association's quiescent approach to race. Corporate leaders were hesitant, as the Chamber of Commerce already had a foreign trade committee. Edward Rightor, counsel to the mayor, pointed out the need to involve the Catholic hierarchy. Hennen Morris unlocked access to the editors of the *Times-Picayune*, who promised cooperation. The State Department had to be brought in at a tricky moment, with a letter from Secretary Hull assuring a fretful candidate for the chairmanship of his "appreciation of the past achievements of the Association in creating a wide public understanding of international problems." It took until April 1944 for the branch to hold its first luncheon, at which Leet introduced William K. Jackson, vice president of the US Chamber of Commerce. At the war's end, the branch had four hundred or so members, most of them women, with a history professor as its program chair and a banker as its finance chief. This work Leet repeated, over and over again.[26]

The Association ended 1945 with thirty-two branches. There had been progress in the South, the Midwest, and even in the far West; where there had been success, the cooperation of the League of Women Voters or similar groups had been crucial. Some branches, as in Houston, Omaha, and St. Louis, depended on banking interests; others, as in Indianapolis, depended on favorable press coverage. Academics were important for their connections and their intellectual leadership; historians such as Julian Park in Buffalo, Arthur Lovejoy in Baltimore, and Dexter Perkins in Rochester took posts. There were places that resisted Leet's overtures, most disappointingly Kansas City, Nashville, and Dallas. Some target cities recoiled in the face of hostile, often conservative activism; others lacked a voluntary infrastructure for the Association to collaborate with; more were already over-organized or had another agency doing similar work, whether a dedicated group like the Chicago Council on Foreign Relations or a local offshoot of the (New York) Council on Foreign Relations, a Committee on Foreign Relations that was sufficient to satisfy its male members without getting the rabble—or women—involved. Even so, the Association had built a presence in eighteen states, growing its branch membership to almost fifteen thousand, half of a total membership of around thirty-one thousand.[27]

Had Roosevelt been right, then, and McCoy wrong? The statistics might have suggested so, but the branches still seemed terribly weak to those who knew them well. Dean complained that the branches left out too many citizens for comfort, with "labor and the Negroes"—and even women—"remembered at the last minute," if at all. Segregation limited the default audience to whites across the South, though if the Association had any desire to challenge Jim Crow, it was hardly advancing the idea that Black perspectives on the world counted as "foreign policy" in cities in the North. And the effort was fatally impoverished. Branch chairmen could not afford to expense their travel to New York, a minor issue compared to the small fortune that was required to lure prestigious speakers out of Washington or Manhattan. "Now that I am out where the Indians are," one member who had moved from Boston to St. Paul complained, "I can realize how difficult it is in the East to picture the conditions in the Far West." Speakers had to be found locally, but only a handful of cities yet had serious scholars of world affairs on hand, despite the philanthropic investment in such expertise since the Great War. All that left the question of what a branch ought to do with its events, as even the most devoted internationalists from the past two decades found themselves challenged with new subjects, new ideas, and new responsibilities as US forces fanned out across the globe. "There are so many present problems where opinion needs to be guided," historian Kenneth Holmes lamented at one branch conference, "especially when focused on the United States as a world power."[28]

While the White House and the State Department pushed the Association toward one kind of work, aimed somewhat into the future, the government was meanwhile working with a largely separate network of activists to promote more immediate causes. Leet found herself battling for the time and interest of the few citizens who were eager to lead world affairs efforts in their communities, a fight she usually lost. "We are finding a new difficulty in forming branches," she told the board in February 1945, "due to the fact that the groups working for the United Nations plans are anxious not to have other organizations interested in international affairs established at this time." Nonpartisan even if it was internationalist, the Association could not for philosophical or legal reasons make a formal alliance with the American Association for the United Nations, whose chapters were springing up nationwide in 1944 and 1945. "We are trying to develop the idea that the F.P.A. is a long-range organization with an education program not only for the immediate future," Leet sighed, "but for the long continued interest of Americans in the foreign policy of their country." It was no use. The years 1944 and 1945 repeated the experience of 1940 and 1941: at a crucial moment, an approach to public opinion that valued deliberation, however imperfect, was being pushed aside by the need to sell a specific policy, fast. Would this be the way future foreign policy would work? The question was ultimately one for the federal government.[29]

## "The Cooperative Method of Making Foreign Policy"

As it became clear that the United States would decide to lead the world, the feeling grew that inherited constitutional arrangements for the making of foreign policy were unfit for the task. Strangely enough, this was quite a novel concern: even among those who thought most about the relationship between democracy and diplomacy, explicit calls for structural reform were as rare as fleshed-out theories of the problem. But if the nation was indeed to take up the burdens of global responsibility, if diplomats, troops, and dollars were needed without end, and if diplomacy was to impinge on domestic life in wholly new ways, was it right to grant the executive such power as the founding fathers allowed? Should not the citizenry, or at least its elected representatives, have more input? "It is high time for the State Department to enter into diplomatic relations with the American people," the chair of the Time Inc. postwar department admonished in *Life* in September 1943, for while there remained "doubt in some quarters as to whether a democratic foreign policy is possible, since diplomacy is a secret and devious profession," any "true" policy would need to "be understood and approved by the majority of the American people." Wilson had failed at this, or so the story was now told; Roosevelt must not.[30]

Long before US troops set foot in Europe, proposals floated around Washington to root foreign policy more firmly in public opinion. These initially addressed the relationship between the legislative and executive branches of government and came from Republican critics of the administration. Senator Alexander Wiley of Wisconsin was the most vocal, proposing to avoid the "disaster" of the Treaty of Versailles through the creation of a Foreign Relations Advisory Committee comprised of the secretary of state, his major deputies, and the chairmen and ranking members of the Senate Committee on Foreign Relations and the House Committee on Foreign Affairs. Secretary Hull refused, even as he came to an informal arrangement along similar lines, but the sense remained that there was a problem to be solved that went beyond partisan politics and separation-of-powers concerns. By the time retired diplomat Hugh Gibson proposed a Council of National Defense in 1944— bringing the major cabinet secretaries together with congressional representation and a dedicated staff—he had to argue against a host of competing ideas, whether those as minor as forcing the secretary of state to testify regularly to Congress, as sensible as creating an undersecretary position for legislative liaison, or as radical as amending the constitutional requirement that

91

two-thirds of senators approve treaties down to a majority. The breadth of the debate spoke to the significance of the concern.[31]

With these proposals going nowhere, attention turned to the State Department itself. As State's planners settled on their blueprint for the postwar world, calls for its reform became so widespread that the quip about it needing to enter diplomatic relations with the American people became a cliché. Compared to the rest of the New Deal state, which had put significant effort into smoothing its extension of government into everyday life, State's public engagement apparatus was antiquated, involving nothing more than private press conferences, cryptic news releases, and the odd official speech. Revealingly, the strongest critiques came from within, most loudly from Joseph M. Jones, an economist who had introduced State's special research division to public opinion scholarship in 1942, only to quit in protest at its lack of use. "It is fashionable in some quarters to label the Department or individuals therein purely and simply as fascist in sympathy," Jones fumed in *Fortune* in 1943, but he suggested that State was in fact simply a nineteenth-century institution out of place in a twentieth-century world. "They have no faith in the people," Jones wrote of the diplomats he had seen "give the wordiest of lip service to democracy and proceed to deny it in their day-to-day actions." Attitudes as well as institutions needed reform, Jones warned; without it, "we are certain either to lose our democracy, or to fail in the task of world leadership, or, more probably, both."[32]

Facing the interrelated tasks of selling the peace, improving its reputation, and addressing these damning critiques, State embarked on a series of reorganizations. It created an Office of the Special Consultant in June 1943, then a larger Office of Public Information in January 1944, and finally a full Office of Public Affairs under MacLeish, who that December became assistant secretary of state for public and cultural relations, a title that soon shrank to assistant secretary of state for public affairs. Along with these innovations, which were shadowed by a Council on Foreign Relations group that studied public opinion under the leadership of pollster George Gallup, came a dramatic shift in rhetoric. While men like Walter Lippmann were still defining policymaking as a top-down process that needed to be undertaken long in advance of popular input, Secretary Hull could be heard on the radio in April 1944 defining "foreign policy" as the "task of focusing and giving effect in the world outside our borders to the will of 135 million people through the constitutional processes which govern our democracy." Assistant Secretary of State Dean Acheson went even further, announcing that "foreign policy in a democracy is merely the expression of the people's purpose." These declarations bore little resemblance to State's day-to-day operations, but it was telling that the need was felt to genuflect before the ideals of a democratic foreign policy, even if Hull left himself cavernous room to "focus" and "give effect" to the popular desires policymakers chose to perceive. Vera Micheles Dean applauded the sentiment.[33]

The State Department left open the means it would use to create the democratic foreign policy it now claimed to seek. Deweyans interested in foreign policy had drafted few blueprints; in general, such progressives thought "surprisingly little about the formal mechanisms of governance," Andrew Jewett has argued. The question was a familiar one, though: should State then take up the educational approach of the Association, which was the most participatory means advocated within the core foreign policy community, or should it favor something closer to corporate marketing, even outright propaganda? Personnel changes implied the second course. Much of the impetus for State's reforms came from Edward Stettinius, who replaced Welles as undersecretary in October 1943 and Hull as secretary in December 1944. Once in charge of public relations at General Motors and later chairman of US Steel, Stettinius was quite familiar with modern marketing techniques, and he insisted that State should stand up to the scrutiny of the private sector. MacLeish's successor as assistant secretary, indeed, would be William Benton, an ad man whose company, Benton & Bowles Inc., was a Madison Avenue pioneer. But before Benton's arrival in August 1945, MacLeish had already unleashed a crusade to promote the United Nations so successful that a debate in time emerged about whether the organization had been "oversold" as a panacea for peace. When the dust settled, polls indicated that nineteen in twenty Americans had heard of the San Francisco Conference at which the United Nations Charter would be agreed to, and fully 80 to 90 percent supported the Charter's ratification — numbers that indicated practical unanimity.[34]

Channeling the globalist commentary that marked academic debate, "middlebrow" texts, and much more in popular culture from 1941 onwards, MacLeish drew on his experience as former director of the Office of Facts and Figures and assistant director of the Office of War Information to saturate public consciousness with a more specific vision for US internationalism. State started its own NBC radio show, *Our Foreign Policy*, sponsored an Alfred Hitchcock film, *Watchtower Over Tomorrow*, and printed 1.75 million copies of the Dumbarton Oaks agreement. Adding a patina of spontaneity, State's campaign took strength from voluntary associations that distributed literature,

from mayors who sponsored town meetings to discuss the proposals and wondered whether their cities might host the United Nations itself, and from
partnerships with the mass media, not least with the film studio Fox, which
made a hagiography of the man now beatified as a fallen hero, *Wilson*. Even
the *New York Herald Tribune*, a newspaper of impeccable internationalist
credentials, thought it was all a bit much, deriding "peace by propaganda," a
"first-class publicity campaign" that took obvious inspiration from the selling
of "breakfast foods, B-29 bombers, laxatives, war for democracy, automobiles,
nail polish, blood banks, dress fabrics and gyro-controlled tank turrets." Dean
snarked that to say one believed in internationalism amid all this was "like
saying one believes in the Rockettes"—but that was in essence MacLeish's
intention, to make the United Nations seem as natural and uncontroversial a
part of daily life as a toothbrush.[35]

State was sensitive to the criticism that it had gone too far, though, even as
it made the United Nations campaign the reference point for its later efforts to
sell the Marshall Plan and the North Atlantic Treaty. Acheson, for one, told a
Carnegie Endowment conference in November 1945 that State was "damned
if it does and it's damned if it doesn't," finding itself accused of "propagan-
dizing" in the manner of the Nazis if it took an active stance towards public
opinion but attacked as "cynically denying your right as citizens to know what
is going on behind these musty old walls" if it did not. Behind closed doors,
too, were those within the department who felt a deeper, more genuine at-
tachment to the "cooperative method of making foreign policy" that Acheson
claimed was his goal, to the "two-way communication with the American
people" that was, he said, "the essence of the democratic process." Had Deweyan ideals made more of an impact at State than Jones had allowed?[36]

Given that adult education had been the dominant means through which
the foreign policy community had approached the public, adult educators
inevitably found work at State, their priorities and practices present even as
MacLeish took a harder line. Former Association officials including Charles
Thomson and William Stone were invited to assist in setting up the department's new institutional infrastructure, although they exerted stronger influence over the foreign information apparatus that MacLeish also helmed,
their experience appealing to citizens at home now put to work appealing to
those overseas. The two men who first led State's Office of Public Affairs had
almost certainly been Association members, and were in any case familiar
with the participatory, educational outlook. John Sloan Dickey, who had
done public affairs work for State's free trade legislation since 1934 and joined

the department formally in 1943, was a Boston lawyer and protégé of Francis Sayre, a former assistant secretary of state and son-in-law to Woodrow Wilson who sat on the council of the Association's Boston branch. After Dickey left State in 1945, his post was taken by his friend Francis H. Russell, a lawyer who had led the Boston chapters of the League of Nations Association and the American Union for Concerted Peace Efforts, which called for a unilateral declaration of war after the fall of France. The *Boston Globe* reported in 1946 that Russell was also "a member of other groups interested in foreign policy." Dickey and Russell had the assistance of other Association graduates as well.[37]

These men came of political age as progressive liberals and they struggled with familiar anxieties about propaganda, none more so than Russell, who was always fearful of the "high-pressuring, button-holing, trick persuasiveness and mere slogan-thinking" that he would try and fail to avoid using in the early Cold War. Russell's more educational instincts had an outlet in his office's Division of Public Liaison, the centerpiece of State's claims to be engaging in democratic policymaking on the Association's model. The Division comprised four branches: one compiled the *Foreign Relations of the United States* series of historical documents; another answered hundreds of thousands of pieces of mail per year; a third worked on radio and television shows. Balancing the mass media approach was the Group Relations Branch, which traced its roots to the New Deal's Federal Forum Project, the zenith of prewar adult education efforts. Chester S. Williams, the Branch's director, had in fact been John Studebaker's assistant in the heady days a decade earlier when education had seemed to stand between democracy and disaster. Williams tried to continue the use of similar educational methods at the Office of War Information and the United Nations Relief and Rehabilitation Administration. He also worked to apply participatory processes to the drafting of the United Nations Charter, looking after the 187 representatives of forty-two voluntary associations who served as consultants to the delegation in San Francisco, and making some impact on the Charter as a result. It was an experience that gave him hope.[38]

If most educators shied away from thinking about the machinery through which public opinion could be brought to bear on the government, whether because they saw the state as part of the public—as Dewey did—or for some other reason, Williams was one of the few who did not. Stating his branch's operating philosophy in July 1946, he accepted the importance of "one-way" media like the press and radio in shaping public views but insisted that "the strength of a self-governing society depends on more than reading, listening and looking." What was required was "two-way" democracy, the longstanding concern of Deweyans, comprised of "the weighing of conflicting opinions, the testing of facts, the questioning of conclusions and the rephrasing of the argument" that "elevates the individual from the position of mere spectator to participant." The State Department would find cooperation with associations, forums, and the endless tapestry of voluntary life essential, Williams said, and he insisted that such cooperation should happen on the terms of private groups, not those of the government. It was not for the Group Relations Branch "to secure public *support* for the Department's policies," he wrote, but to "help the public *understand* what the policies are and why the Department projects them, inviting critical examination of them." Part of that would mean promoting "the practical expression of representative opinion to the Department." Part would mean taking it seriously.[39]

What did "practical" expression entail? All kinds of ideas circulated through the State Department after 1944 as to how citizens might meaningfully contribute to policy; Williams discerned no fewer than eleven such means in a memo in November 1945. Some of those became central to State's eventual public affairs effort: regular analyses of the mail; advisory committees and roundtables that engaged outside experts in private conversations with officials; a variety of formal public events, of which the most important was the National Conference on US Foreign Policy, which drew 240 voluntary-association and other civil-society representatives to its first, three-day iteration in 1947. Soon enough, State would expand a speakers bureau that sent officials to address eighteen hundred organization meetings from 1945 to 1947, add a calendar of regional conferences outside Washington, and develop systematic contact with the two or three hundred voluntary associations it thought best to pay attention to. Most of this work was intended to give State a good sense of elite or educated opinion rather than to connect it to the masses; the regional conferences were collaborations with Association branches or similar organizations, and the voluntary association leaders that the department talked to tended not to be terribly representative of the views of their members. Wanting to go further, Williams urged the department to place its trust in opinion polling.[40]

Opinion polls and their academic offshoot, the more granular analyses called statistical surveys, were a new, controversial technology in the 1940s, intellectually as well as politically. They offered what appeared to be an easy way to keep the wartime state within the bounds of public consent, however, and

# YOUR PART IN U.S. FOREIGN POLICY

**3.2** "Your Part in U.S. Foreign Policy," a cartoon outlining ways in which citizens can contribute to their foreign policy, from a Headline Book published toward the end of World War II. Note that it was left unclear in which direction the lines between the government and the people ran. Vera Micheles Dean, *After Victory* . . . (New York: Foreign Policy Association, 1945), 70.
Foreign Policy Association.

they had become indispensable to the growing national security bureaucracy, which secured their future as an authoritative means of discerning public views. Consistent with its commitment to managing public opinion, the Rockefeller Foundation had forged the networks and supplied the cash that made this prominence possible at the same time as it funded the Association. Late in

1939, it funded the Princeton social psychologist Hadley Cantril, whose analyses of Gallup poll data at his Office of Public Opinion Research had become so influential that President Roosevelt was soon supplying him with questions he wanted tracked. Certain that scholars of public attitudes had to be seen as useful for their discipline to survive, Cantril had contracted with twenty-two government agencies by 1943, including the State Department, and he was far from the only such specialist working in Washington. While the war seemed to prove the benefits of social science for the state generally, survey data and modern governance seemed to fit together particularly well. In 1945, one analyst found that 63 percent of executive officials found polls and surveys "helpful," far more than legislative leaders; the "warmest" supporters were at State, where opinion reports were used to sell the peace.[41]

When the Rockefeller Foundation started to fund Cantril, it was not clear what the polls, surveys, and research they allowed into the effects of mass communications might mean, an unease that reflected broader confusion about the properly "democratic" solution to the problem of public opinion. Technologies never have inherent meanings, and pollsters held differing, often antithetical understandings of the contributions they could make. Gallup, the most famous of them, argued that polls offered a continual referendum through which the people could discover and express their aggregated, collective will. Polling would add to "the continuous educative process that is at the heart of effective popular government," Gallup wrote, warding off fascism and restoring faith in democracy through a constant demonstration of the interest, capacity, and intelligence of the people; he even borrowed the words of participatory democracy, suggesting that polls were a New England "town meeting" for the modern age, if without the face-to-face aspect of discussion so important to most Deweyans. The first polls might have perpetuated biases of race, gender, and class in their sampling methods, but Gallup's trust that polling might simulate—or even be—the participation of progressive dreams was one that educators shared. Russell, for instance, approved a Division of Public Liaison memo that said that polling could "bring the 'common man'—millions of common men—right into the Department," without even dirtying the carpets.[42]

Even so, policymakers initially valued polls not as a peacetime solution to a participation problem, but as a wartime solution to a communications problem. Rather than supporting the strand of progressivism that placed faith in popular abilities, surveys therefore buttressed the competing inheritance, one founded on a darker view of the populace and pushed the balance of power towards administrative efficiency, expert rule, and state power. Polls in this view offered unique, unprecedented insight into the public mind; to those intellectuals and practitioners who saw elite management as the only viable path through a crisis, they offered a tool through which that mind might be led. The means would be propaganda, thought of not as the antidemocratic technique of the consensus educational view, but as a morally neutral means through which elites could acquire—or manipulate, in the word of public relations theorist Edward Bernays—consent to achieve political ends without resorting to violence. This was a theory with clear utility for policymakers, above all those dealing with foreign threats about which the public was thought to have little interest and less knowledge; and if democracy was in any case a system run through its elites, the theory could be conceived of as democratic too.[43]

Shared at first among a small number of scholars and advocates who challenged the anti-propaganda consensus in the 1920s and 1930s, this view was best developed in academia by communications theorist Harold Lasswell, who found a berth at MacLeish's Library of Congress after the University of Chicago denied him tenure in 1938. Lasswell had no personal influence on policy, but his ideas became potent as his students and acolytes spread out across the federal government during the war. Representing Chicago political scientists who had spent the interwar years exploring the possibilities of social control, Lasswell thought Lippmann had not gone far enough in his evisceration of participatory ideals, writing in 1935 that the "'omnicompetent' theory of democracy"—which few Deweyans actually held—"seems more and more absurd." Skeptical of publics, Lasswell was far less so of social scientists, who he thought should take the techniques the Committee on Public Information had employed in the Great War, improve them, and put them to use. Propaganda was not taboo to Lasswell, but a reality of modern politics, one which would benefit from the charting of the public psyche surveys might provide. Warding off the "probable" future of the "garrison state" he wrote of in 1941—in which the masses would be controlled through a "monopoly of opinion" and decisions would be "more dictatorial than democratic"—might, it seemed, require borrowing its methods. So might defeating Nazism.[44]

For a while, the ideas that Lasswell, Bernays, and others propounded in books like their *Propaganda Technique in the World War* (1927) and *Propaganda* (1928) were so far from the mainstream that adult educators could treat them as a straw man, though their influence on corporate marketing grew. Even after the Rockefeller Foundation grew interested in Lasswell at the end of the 1930s, for the same reasons that it grew interested in Cantril, critiques of his theories were hardly in short supply. When the Foundation convened a study group to discuss innovations in communications research in 1940, the educators involved explicitly called one Lasswellian report fascist; even Willits, no friend of mass prerogatives, attacked it for being concerned not with "the critical examination and improvement of what is to be decided upon and put over by government, but with the 'putting over' of what has already been decided." But Willits knew that a war would make these methods more appealing, whatever legal or political constraints lingered on their use. As Lasswellians learned to write about their methods in the progressive language of "two-way" democracy and the benefits of "information," as Lasswell did in *Democracy Through Public Opinion* (1941), so the use of such methods became more routine, the thin wall that had separated educational and propagandistic approaches collapsing under the pressure of national security imperatives.[45]

In no single person was the tension between these approaches to public opinion more obvious than in H. Schuyler Foster, who led the State Department's Office of Public Opinion Studies from 1943 until his retirement more than two decades later. Foster might have been an Association branch chairman while he taught at Ohio State before the war, but he had done his graduate study under Lasswell at Chicago, specializing in assessing whether propaganda campaigns actually worked. That was also part of Foster's job at State, where he oversaw a large staff that wrote up daily, weekly, and monthly reports on trends in popular views. The office subscribed to every newspaper and magazine of significance, received transcriptions of mass media broadcasts, pored over the *Congressional Record*, and catalogued the foreign policy resolutions of myriad voluntary associations. But polls and surveys were the most useful tool Foster possessed, whether the Gallup and Roper polls reported in the newspapers, the samples Cantril and others passed privately along, or the surveys Foster commissioned—without informing Congress—from the National Opinion Research Center, the first of a breed of academic, non-profit survey institutes that depended on federal contracts for their work.[46]

What State might do with this data, which amounted to a database surveilling the public mood, was a difficult question; the answers depended on which theories about public opinion took hold, what kind of bureaucratic foothold the Office of Public Affairs could find, and which foreign policy the department chose. But was there something latent in polling itself? The basic function of pollsters at the time, after all, was to help officials "shape the contours of the public sphere," Susan Herbst has written; they owed their funding, careers, and even discipline to the federal government, and they were eager to serve it. Their talent was to reduce complexities to simple binaries. "Which of these two things do you think the United States should try to do when the war is over," went the query that became the standard assessment of the public's mood after 1940, "stay out of world affairs as much as we can, or take an active part in world affairs?" If polls really were intended to encourage and represent participation, these questions were hardly empowering. The wording of that question framed issues in the same way that Roosevelt and his successors would falsely frame the choice before Americans: in or out. Citizens did not write the questions, nor the answers; polls offered few means for them to give a sense of their worldview except by assigning themselves to categories set elsewhere, and pollsters excised "don't know" responses from their published results for clarity. On an issue like foreign policy where popular views were diffuse at best, polls and surveys merely offered insight into how well citizens had taken in the information rushing at them across all media—or, to put it another way, of how Americans were coming to grips with foreign policy as their leaders had defined it for them.[47]

At the moment when the State Department was at its most open, then, it was not true that it thought foreign policy should rise from the bottom up, whatever Assistant Secretary Acheson claimed. The most participatory means at State's disposal, polling, in practice reinforced its power. Nor was the Office of Public Affairs bureaucratically secure—it struggled to find desk space within the department's main building, let alone influence diplomacy. "Do you have any evidence," Benton asked Russell in 1947, "to indicate that the *policy* officers are really making any use of these 'Public Opinion Reports'?" The idea was preposterous. Foster, indeed, had told the American Political Science Association in March 1946 that the real utility of polling came not in feeding popular views into policy debates, but in fixing areas of "public confusion or ignorance" that might put policies at risk. Foster's studies offered evidence that confusion and ignorance were common, that "people are not only uninformed about some of our foreign policies," but "frankly say that they haven't attempted to follow them." Russell hinted at how the dilemma would be resolved in September 1946, telling an audience that "if the American people are to have a will which can be focused and given effect"—Hull's words from 1944, rephrased in the conditional tense—then State would have to define the problems relevant to the citizenry, and provide the necessary facts, so that there could be "continuous, purposeful, constructive thinking upon these questions by, as nearly as may be possible, all of the people of the land." If the public "will" needed to exist, and it was not clear that it did, then it would have to be created. The State Department would be its creator.[48]

Although the direction in which State was headed was not quite settled, it was evident enough by 1946 that Williams left Washington for the US mission to the United Nations. Around the United Nations and especially UNESCO, Williams and others would help a more genuinely participatory culture grow, something that spoke to the diminished status that the international organizations held for policymakers, if not for engaged activists. On core policies, public opinion would be a "powerful instrument of national policy," as a Council on Foreign Relations report put it in 1949; it would be treated as the problem of communications that Lasswell had imagined, not the participation question it posed for the Deweyans. "Our present task," Lasswell had said in 1941, was to use "the magnificent instruments of modern communication for the purpose of clarifying a common view of the society in which we live," a task he defined as "sharing the insight of the few with the many." But even that path forward, so appealing to policymakers, left questions. What would happen if the State Department stopped handing out information? What if its skepticism about the public hardened into cynicism? What if the faith that social scientists could manipulate consent was misplaced? Even Lasswell had to admit, after all, that his vision for democracy still depended on the popular discussion he otherwise mocked. "If the practice of discussion does not create a sense of achievement," he wrote in 1941, "there is contempt for talk." What would happen if Americans felt they were not being heard? Either way, a moment had passed; State's brief, limited commitment to "two-way" democracy had dissipated. "May I say that you stay out from underfoot absolutely wonderfully," Benton wrote to Russell on March 10, 1947, welcoming the domestic public affairs chief's invisibility in the department. Two days later, President Harry Truman would announce that a situation in Greece and Turkey threatened the peace of the world.[49]

## "Harvest Time"

World War II tied Americans to their state and its foreign policy in unprecedented ways. Millions of them donned uniforms and traveled across the seas to fight and die; many left their shores for the first time, seeing the world as never before. Those who stayed on the home front were told that their homes were at risk in a new age of warfare, that their livelihoods were in danger, that their labor in factories and in fields matched sacrifices made on fronts far away. They paid for the war, too. Much of the $350 billion needed for the fight — $4 trillion today — came from federal debt, but much came from the sale of war bonds, which most families bought under severe societal pressure. Those Americans subject to income taxes paid more; millions came into a direct fiscal relationship with their government for the first time, filing with the Internal Revenue Service despite its inability to enforce the law. The taxpaying citizenry acquired a significant stake in foreign policy.[50]

Even so, the United States had not fought the same war as its adversaries or its allies. It was the sole power able to wage a truly global war, but its war was never a total one. There were places the stars and stripes flew where there had been real destruction, but as Daniel Immerwahr has argued, that empire was hidden in the metropole, imagined as outside the bounds of the nation proper. The continental United States escaped such a fate. That the war had been a remote concern to so many not fighting it, so far from the stenches and sins of the struggle, meant that extraordinary efforts had been necessary to maintain public support for it. Whether wartime propaganda had worked would be debated for years, but observers feared that even the unanimity that had been forged around the United Nations—and, through it, America's new world role—was brittle at best. "Let no one assume," wrote Jerome Bruner, Cantril's deputy at the Office of Public Opinion Research, "that because opinion is favorable to internationalism today, there are no worries for the future." Even Council on Foreign Relations officials fretted at the "great gap between the ideal of a public sufficiently well informed to influence foreign policy effectively, as it should in a democracy, and the actuality of a public largely indifferent to critical institutions in our foreign policy."[51]

Similar unease was felt across the foreign policy community, but the solution was as unclear in the philanthropic offices of New York as within the hallways of the State Department. With State now taking responsibility for public opinion, the media now invested in world affairs, and voluntary associations now talking about diplomatic developments, what was left for the Foreign Policy Association to do? State had become distinctly wary of the prewar infrastructure, for its part. George F. Kennan, a quiet diplomat who had just sent a long telegram to Washington from his Moscow sickbed, spent a few weeks riding the lecture circuit in 1946 and complained that the "women's clubs and organizations devoted to the study of international problems have a large percentage of members for whom 'foreign affairs' are apparently a form of escape from the boredom, frustration and faintly guilty conscience which seem to afflict many well-to-do and insufficiently occupied people in the country." Margaret Carter, a public affairs official who was familiar with these groups from her work in philanthropy, agreed. There was "an inertia and an exhausted enthusiasm," she wrote, "among people who have worked in the international affairs field for the last twenty-five years." The time had come, she said, for the State Department "to plow new fields."[52]

Right on cue, the Rockefeller Foundation stepped back. It had come a long way in a little more than a decade. Once beholden to solutions to the problem of war that were based on the power of public opinion and reflected in support for the League of Nations, Rockefeller leaders now equated the search for peace with the primacy of US arms, something that was reflected in their support for the United Nations, which, with its veto rights for the permanent members of the Security Council, was a far more power-political institution than the League had ever been. What the United States now needed was not so much an informed public opinion, on which the Foundation thought it could make little impact given the dramatic transformation of the mass media, but expert knowledge to lead a world that even the most educated Americans knew little about. "RF's first responsibility," Willits had noted in 1943, referring to the Foundation, was not "merely to bring the mass up to a still low level," but "to discover higher levels." The Association would have "to be established on their own feet, so that RF can be free to strengthen the centers of advanced, and undergraduate, training." Fosdick, the Foundation's president, had managed to resist Willits's plans to move purely into academic research up to 1945. "What good is it going to do to add a little bit to knowledge here and there around the periphery of things," Fosdick had asked then, "if our whole world is going to be kicked into a cocked hat by a public opinion that doesn't understand what time it is in human history?" But this archetypal Wilsonian, who had been undersecretary of the League of Nations before quitting after the debacle in the US Senate, could not hold the line forever. The Association's membership and budget were at historic peaks, Willits told McCoy soon after Japan had surrendered; now it was "harvest time." Rockefeller grants would continue as they had until 1948, when Fosdick retired, before winding down to nothing in 1950.[53]

The end of Rockefeller largesse shocked the Association. The Association had done its fair share to sell the United Nations, assuming its interests to be the same as those of a State Department with which it was eager to work. Dickey had come to New York in December 1944 to ask for its help with a "cooperative foreign policy," and the Association had jumped at the chance. Dean had her own vision for what that might entail, but it was a surprisingly unambitious one, even if she was almost alone in calling for the foreign service "to include men and women from all walks of life and all economic levels of the nation." It was not to be. When McCoy and Dean had traveled to the San Francisco Conference, it was McCoy who had served as an official consultant to the US delegation, and Dean who had observed from the press pool. State's public affairs officials would still occasionally coordinate with the Association, but the old closeness would never return after 1945. McDonald sailed for the Middle East and the Anglo-American Committee of Inquiry on Palestine; Buell was dead; McCoy resigned from the Association for a post in the Far East. Dean was suddenly the Association's most powerful figure, and her ascent led to further departures from the staff. The membership rolls plateaued at roughly thirty-two thousand after the war, but as inflation drove costs higher and the unionized staff insisted that wages rise, publication sales fell. Several of the branches no longer met the number of members their charters required for their survival. The activists who had sustained the Association for so long had retired; many had died. At the end of 1946 the Association was using its reserves to cover a tenth of expenditures. Board members muttered about closing it for good.[54]

Once at the core of a consensus about the place of public opinion in foreign policy and the importance of education within it, the Association was lost at the heart of fresh confusion as Americans had won themselves an empire without yet finding their role. The Association existed in part to promote the idea of a more engaged United States and it had achieved that goal, too much so for some of its stalwarts. But US engagement with the world had never been the Association's sole aim. It also existed to create the informed public opinion it thought would be the basis of a democratic foreign policy. There, its achievements were mixed. What it needed now was a program, an idea. Research was out of the question. Education was left. Pursuing it would mean turning to a man with a vision that left the board "with much trepidation."[55]

# 4

# How to Teach a City to Lead the World

On the first Tuesday in February, 1943, the more senior members of the Cleveland Foreign Affairs Council gathered for a business meeting at the Mid-Day Club, the preferred social haunt of the local Chamber of Commerce. Half a world away, Soviet forces were accepting the surrender of the German Sixth Army outside Stalingrad, preparing their arduous drive west. These Clevelanders were not up to anything quite so momentous, but their meeting did point to something equally defining of the times to come. Their Council needed a title that reflected new realities. Perhaps there were some who thought that it made no difference "what title a local organization might assume, whether it was a Foreign Policy Association, a World Affairs Council, or a Foreign Affairs Institute," the Council's leader, Brooks Emeny, told the Rockefeller Foundation a few weeks later, relaying news of the meeting. But to Emeny, it did. Americans were fighting all over the globe, the entire planet now their domain. *One World*, a travelogue by Emeny's friend, former White House candidate Wendell Willkie, was about to sell faster than any nonfiction book had ever sold before, a craze one reviewer thought testified to "a world opening up." Foreign affairs were no longer "foreign," or ought not be. The Council needed a name "more in keeping with the change which has taken place in the foreign relations of the United States with respect to the world as a whole," the *Cleveland Plain Dealer* reported. Gone was the Foreign Affairs Council, with its motto, "Foreign Affairs Are Your Affairs!" In its place stood a Council on World Affairs, with a new slogan—"World Affairs Are Your Affairs!"[1]

The Cleveland Council was one of many community groups working to educate adults about foreign affairs at the time, but nowhere else was the effort so far advanced. Most similar institutions were based on the luncheon model of the Foreign Policy Association; they were struggling to keep their old members, let alone attract new ones. Groups more devoted to scholarship and study, like the Seattle and San Francisco branches of the Institute of Pacific Relations, were also stumbling. Denver's Social Science Foundation was offering a rare example of success under the leadership of Ben M. Cherrington and a fellow professor at the University of Denver, Elizabeth Fackt, with unusually popular discussion groups and a weekly radio show that statistics suggested reached a fifth of Denver families. The Foundation, though, enjoyed an endowment that largely freed it from financial constraints, a luxury that meant it had made "that Rocky Mountain capital world-minded to a degree which cannot be duplicated in scores of other cities," as the *Christian Century* put it in 1938. Educators would have to look elsewhere for a model that could be replicated at scale.[2]

Founded in 1933, the Cleveland Council had its roots in suffrage and pacifism, like so many similar institutions, but the ambitions of its maturity were those of two men. One was Newton D. Baker, a towering progressive often rumored as a possible Democratic candidate for the White House who had been Woodrow Wilson's secretary of war and remained a leading Wilsonian internationalist until his death in 1937. If Baker hoped to transcend power politics through public reason, the man who put his ideas into practice sought merely to apply public reason to power politics. Brooks Emeny was a Republican, a scholar of the new science of international relations who saw the world in bleak geopolitical terms, its peoples waging a ceaseless battle for resources. These men were so different personally, politically, and intellectually that they might be said to have come from entirely separate wings of the foreign policy community, but they shared a great deal. Both were members of the Council on Foreign Relations. Both declined ambassadorships from Cordell Hull's State Department. Both hated the New Deal, fearing its impact on cherished progressive traditions of democracy. Together, they believed that the world would be in danger until US foreign policy was subjected to the control of an active, informed public, like almost all experts on the subject at the time. Together, they offered a critique of foreign policy education as it stood, and thought that debate about world affairs needed to become an inescapable part of community life. They set about creating an alternative—not just for Clevelanders, but for the rest of the nation.

## Wilson's Fool in Christ

No man had a stronger claim on the Wilsonian spirit than Baker. Born in 1871, this prototypical progressive had moved step by step from urban to national to international politics, serving first as Cleveland's city solicitor from 1901 to 1909, then as its mayor from 1912 to 1915, and then as the US secretary of war from 1916 to 1921. Long slurred incorrectly as a pacifist, Baker oversaw the conscription, training, deployment, and demobilization of US troops during the Great War, a mammoth task that made him a wartime leader second in fame only to Wilson himself. When Wilson died, Baker was seen as his natural successor even as he returned to Cleveland to earn his keep at the law firm that bore his name, Baker Hostetler. What kept Baker from the White House, in the end, was his unwavering commitment to exactly the Wilsonianism that made him so prominent. At the Democratic convention at Madison Square Garden in 1924, Baker ended his chances of the nomination with a futile, hour-long call for the party to commit to joining the League, one he delivered with "the spirit of prophecy upon him" as the *New York Times* put it, and in which he imagined that the fallen president was "using me to say to you, 'Save mankind! Do America's duty!'" Come the 1932 convention in Chicago, by which point Baker had been a judge on the Permanent Court for International Justice for four years, he was again a possibility for the nomination. But while Franklin Roosevelt was willing to compromise his rather shallower ideals, renouncing the League to win the prize, Baker refused. "The time has come for somebody to be 'a fool in Christ' if necessary," he wrote in an essay on internationalism in *Foreign Affairs* a year later; he surely knew that "somebody" was him.[3]

Even so, no man was better connected within the foreign policy community than Baker, no insider more aware of its faults. An active member of both the Foreign Policy Association and the Council on Foreign Relations, Baker was also at various points the chairman of the American Institute of Pacific Relations, the president of the Woodrow Wilson Foundation, and a trustee of the World Peace Foundation, all while staying involved in the League of Nations Association. Baker inspired the loyalty of the two men who controlled the funding some of these groups relied on, both former advisors at the War Department: Raymond Blaine Fosdick, counsel to John D. Rockefeller Jr. and then president of the Rockefeller Foundation, and Frederick Keppel of the Carnegie Corporation, who appointed Baker as a Corporation trustee. Unusually able to see the effort to create a democratic foreign policy as a whole, Baker appreciated its basic difficulty. After a decade or so of efforts to inform public opinion, he wrote in 1934, it was clear that the problem Wilsonian internationalists faced was not "a lack of knowledge" about the world, but an inability to make that knowledge "a common and therefore an effective possession in America." Baker was no populist: he swore that mass stupidity had killed the League and he once described the Ludlow Amendment, which would have required a referendum before Congress declared war, as "incredibly wrongheaded." Like most progressives, however, Baker believed the public could be lifted from its manifest ignorance. What was required was a "consecutive, continuous, and disinterested" form of adult education that ensured that "every man, woman, and child" could learn the "economic, racial, social and political" outlines of the world, he wrote. If they did, then America would attain "that ideal of democracy, an informed public opinion."[4]

Uniquely among the diplomatic class, Baker felt strongly enough about the benefits of participation that he engaged as seriously with the institutions of the formal adult education movement as he did with the institutions of the foreign policy community. With the rise of modern communications, he told Carnegie's American Association for Adult Education as its president in 1931, the fate of peace was "governed by the spontaneous responses of the people of the world, simultaneously receiving and reacting to great and crucial ideas." That might have its benefits, but he feared that if the people were "prejudiced in their point of view or ill-advised in their action, a world conflagration may blaze up." Baker thought education was crucial to the efficiency of democracy at home, but he valued it above all for what it could bring in the name of peace. "We must hold a man who abstains from acquainting himself with public affairs," he therefore said, "not merely as useless but as dangerous." With the stakes were so fearsomely high, Baker was prone to lashing out at his opponents as irrational or malevolent, unsurprisingly for a man who had taken responsibility for the deaths of American soldiers at war. But he saw no reason to give in to idiocy, nor to give up on a public he never entirely trusted; the lesson he took from the League debacle, he told a conference in 1931, was that "the nature of democracy necessitates an educated electorate in order to provide for its own safety."[5]

Baker found that creating the public of his dreams was easier said than done, though, even in the city he dominated politically. By the end of the postwar decade, Cleveland was notable for its lack of foreign policy institutions on the nonpartisan model. The Association had started branches in Cincinnati and Columbus but made no headway in Cleveland, for the simple reason that the city's women pacifists needed no assistance from New York. Cleveland's suffragists had formed a Women's Council for the Prevention of War in 1923, soon renaming it the Women's Council for the Promotion of Peace. Controversial enough that the local Chamber of Commerce dubbed it "unpatriotic" for holding a mass parade in 1924—one Baker defended so staunchly he was invited to march in its front ranks—the Women's Council was supporting the world affairs activities of over a hundred groups by 1926. So successful was it, in fact, that it declared victory and wound itself up in 1929, in part because the Kellogg-Briand Pact of 1928 had "definitely outlawed war," its president, Mrs. Charles Prescott, told the press. With the Pact certain to be as important "as the Magna Charta and the Declaration of Independence," as the women's page of the *Cleveland Plain Dealer* put it, the Women's Council sought to move away from agitation and into education, a campaign it would wage with and for men. Prescott asked Baker to lead the charge.[6]

By then Baker had already made Cleveland a pioneer in community adult education. Civic grandees had joined him in founding Cleveland College in 1925 and within two years its downtown campus was enrolling thousands of adults in classes on everything from parenting to metaphysics. Baker was besotted with the College, personally teaching its night course on international relations, arranging for Carnegie patronage, and bequeathing it his library. Baker also presided over a local Adult Education Association, which cultivated interest in subjects neither widely perceived to be relevant to everyday life nor part of the routine of civic life. Foreign policy was prime among these, and it was into the Association's Foreign Affairs Committee that the Women's Council decided to fold in 1929. The Committee distributed literature, experimented with forums, and arranged for public lectures from residents who had traveled abroad, but its centerpiece was an annual institute. Combining set-piece speeches, panel discussions, and roundtables over two or three days, institutes were vital for "gaining new recruits to the army of those who 'want to know,'" the Committee's activists said, because they were so easily promoted and drew on widespread community cooperation. Cleveland's first Foreign Affairs Institute, held in 1927, starred the treasurer of the League of Nations and attracted fifteen hundred people, mostly the usual suspects from the peace movement. Baker took charge of the second institute himself a year later, stoking a vigorous debate on US imperialism.[7]

But just as the Foreign Affairs Committee was starting to strengthen, the Depression hit. Cleveland was struck hard, its heavy industries suffering and its wealthier citizens withdrawing from civic philanthropy. Cleveland

College survived, just, and Baker attached the Foreign Affairs Committee to it when the Adult Education Association collapsed in 1933. The renamed Foreign Affairs Council dedicated itself to creating "an intelligent and informed public opinion in international affairs by providing opportunities for study and discussion as an effective means of promoting peace through understanding," a purpose closer to pacifism than most groups with similar names that nonetheless embraced the nonpartisan methods of the foreign policy community. The Council was small, carrying on its luncheons and the institute. It started a men's discussion group to go with a women's group that had persevered since the suffrage years under the leadership of Mrs. L. J. Wolf, at which women submitted a paper based on extensive research to the criticism of their peers, often a hundred or more women at a time. Baker would never witness the Council mature, but even before his death he had seen enough to refuse to allow Raymond Leslie Buell to set up an Association branch in the city, insisting on protecting his Council. Part of Baker's reasoning, aside from local pride, was that he had met a young man who dreamed of inspiring the nation with his vision of a democratic foreign policy.[8]

## Geopolitics and Public Opinion

Brooks Emeny hailed from Salem, Ohio, a small town on the train tracks from Cleveland to Pittsburgh. Descended from Joshua Twing Brooks, general counsel of the Pennsylvania Railroad when it was the largest private corporation in the world, Brooks was born on July 29, 1901, the eldest son of Frederick and Elizabeth Emeny. His mother died in 1915, so Brooks was cared for as a teen by his extended family. He came under the influence of his cousin, Theodate Pope Riddle, an architect who survived the sinking of the *Lusitania* to marry a former US ambassador to Russia, John Wallace Riddle. Eagle Scout though Brooks became, he was a bored student and was sent to boarding school in Pennsylvania. There he fell for Woodrow Wilson and decided to study international affairs at the president's Princeton rather than his father's Cornell.[9]

At Princeton, Emeny started to make his way through the infrastructure that Baker and his colleagues built after the Great War to train scientific experts in the study of world affairs. Before the summer of 1923, Emeny was elected chair of the roundtable of the International Polity Club, one of many groups on college campuses nationwide that had the support of the Carnegie Endowment for International Peace and worked, as the *Daily Princetonian*

**4.1** Brooks Emeny in his office at the Cleveland Council on World Affairs, 1947. Constantin Joffé, Condé Nast, Shutterstock.

put it, to "disturb undergraduate lethargy toward the affairs of the world." Emeny then attended that mecca for the politically inclined, the Institute of Public Affairs at Williamstown, and won a scholarship from the Endowment that gave him three years to travel abroad, granting him entry into the rarefied world of elite internationalists. He studied at the Sorbonne, the London School of Economics, and the Konsular Akademie in Vienna, but his most intense experiences came on the pilgrimages he took each summer to watch the League of Nations at work.[10]

Emeny spent most of his time in Geneva studying in the Rockefeller-funded library or sneaking into the League's sessions, carrying a briefcase to disguise himself as a diplomat, but he also enrolled in the seminars and lecture series that senior internationalists ran to explain the League to those who passed through town, especially American tourists. In 1927, Emeny signed up for the Geneva School of International Studies, a graduate-level summer school, and became friends with its deputy director, Nicholas Spykman, a Dutch-born sociologist who taught at Yale. Spykman invited Emeny to become his assistant and student. Soon to become the godfather of modern geopolitical thinking, Spykman was still an apostle of Wilsonian internationalism at that point, though an unusual one. Whereas his friends in the League of Nations Association sought to end to power politics, Spykman was already starting to view power politics as the inevitable result of geography and international cooperation as the only way to avoid the use of force. During the Second World War, that insight would make Spykman an influential theorist of US leadership, inverting the views of New Haven colleagues such as A. Whitney Griswold, Edwin Borchard, and Samuel Flagg Bemis to insist that the location and resources of the United States made it not secure—as the traditional noninterventionist argument ran—but insecure, so much so that it needed to intervene permanently in Asia and Europe for its own safety. But Spykman did not come to this conclusion alone: he worked out his ideas with Emeny, who wrote upon his graduation in 1934—with the first doctorate in international relations that Yale ever granted—that he was Spykman's "ardent follower."[11]

Most students with Emeny's interests might have been expected to write a dissertation on some arcane aspect of the League's internal workings, but he saw his thesis as the prelude to an eventual study of nothing less than "The United States as a World Power." In that, he planned to make the Spykman-esque argument that although the United States possessed "predominance" as it was unconquerable and had sufficient resources to make it "the greatest existing single unit of concentrated power in the world," the sheer extent of its influence and the reach of its economy gave it interests that were "seriously endangered" by a policy of isolation that unrealistically denied its "fundamental qualities." Emeny's ambitions outran his abilities though, as those of graduate students often do, and his doctoral thesis in the end did the duller work of mining facts about the basics of US strength. Published as *The Strategy of Raw Materials* in 1934, it offered statistical comparisons of the availability to the great powers of innumerable physical resources, from manganese and tungsten to silk and sugar. Emeny found that the United States stood alone. The "formidable character of our inherent national strength," he wrote, in contrast to Spykman's later arguments, "must give pause for thought on the part of any nation contemplating the risk of hostilities with us." Emeny's was a pioneering study, reprinted repeatedly and translated widely, not least by the Japanese government. Fumimaro Konoe, twice prime minister of Japan between 1937 and 1941, questioned Emeny in detail in Tokyo in 1940, ruminating on the limited benefits that the occupation of Manchuria had brought and asking about the treasures that might be found if Japan elsewhere. Flying back from that visit, Emeny diverted his Pan Am captain over Clark Field, a US air base in the Philippines, and was baffled to see that planes gathered so closely on the ground. Japanese pilots would find them an easy target on the day their countrymen attacked Pearl Harbor.[12]

Emeny's early scholarship was intended to demonstrate that the United States had power its people knew not, and his second book, written with columnist Frank Simonds, took on that discrepancy more directly than his first. *The Great Powers in World Politics* (1935) described an international anarchy of states, "Haves" and "Have-nots" competing unendingly for strength. Geography determined all, for if a state could support itself it would have "security"; if not, it would seek it. The United States was a "Have" power, with such "absolute" security for itself and such dominance over its hemisphere that other powers were no more likely "to attempt imperialistic adventures in the Americas than in the moon." But there was a mismatch between America's capabilities and its policies, an inconsistency Emeny and Simonds thought was rooted not in partisan politics or in inescapable traditions but in mass beliefs. "Public opinion in the United States," they argued, "has not kept pace with the physical change in the circumstance of the nation." External observers expected America to follow its real interests and assure peace in Asia and Europe, but it was not doing so. "'Intervention in words, isolation in action,' sums up the proper policy for the country in the eyes of the American people," they wrote. Something had to be done.[13]

At the heart of Emeny's realist theory of power politics, then, was the people. If America was to fulfil its responsibilities, its citizens would have to reconcile themselves to its power. But how? Once, at the Sorbonne, Emeny had met Myron Herrick, then US ambassador to France and a former Republican governor of Ohio. Herrick, Emeny recalled, "told me that if he had it to do all over again he would go to some community, identify himself there, and become interested in the instruction of public affairs." Emeny was rich enough to fund that task himself, having married Winifred Rockefeller, daughter of Percy A. Rockefeller and grandniece of John D. Rockefeller, in 1928. What finally prompted Brooks to action, though, was personal tragedy. Percy died in September 1934; Winifred learned at the same time that her mother and her four-year-old child with Brooks, Elizabeth, were fatally ill. "I could be of no use in the household of the dying," Emeny later wrote, so he went off to tour Asia for the Institute of Pacific Relations. When he returned, the Emenys and their remaining daughter, Faith, fled their compound in Greenwich, Connecticut, to start again in Cleveland. It would not be the last time that Emeny's private suffering reshaped the public project of a democratic foreign policy.[14]

## *Cleveland's Experiment in Democracy*

Baker and Emeny had quite different understandings of how the world worked, but like much of the rest of the foreign policy community, they agreed on both the centrality of American public opinion to world order and the proper means of cultivating it. Neither was terribly bothered by their theoretical disagreements. Baker wrote to a friend that he was unmoved by Emeny's *Great Powers in World Politics*, for he had "enough idealism to withstand all the assaults of all the realists there are." Emeny had been an idealist himself, and if over time he became the "realist" Baker saw, he was nothing like the realists who claimed the term after the Second World War—men such as Hans Morgenthau and George F. Kennan who, like Emeny, saw untutored public opinion as irrational but demanded that policymakers insulate the "national interest" from mass influence altogether, rather than try to unite publics and policies as Emeny sought. Without an educated citizenry, Emeny worried, no policy could prevent war.[15]

Baker first met Emeny at the end of 1931. "We are in complete agreement," the younger man wrote afterwards, that communities must "be awakened to the *profound* change which has come about in the World Position of the United States bringing in its train a *new* set of interests as well as obligations." Their fears of propaganda's effects on society limited the tools at their disposal; they eschewed "emotional appeal, high-powered salesmanship or lobby methods" and sought instead the "presentation and free discussion of the basic factors of the problems involved." Emeny proposed a Cleveland Institute of International Relations, complete with auditorium, seminar rooms, library, and offices for local representatives of the Institute of Pacific Relations, the Foreign Policy Association, and the like. The Institute would offer lectures, forums, and study groups while sending speakers out to schools, clubs, and civic associations. Emeny asked Baker if an endowment might be raised, but knew that would only be possible once the basic, initial task was accomplished and Clevelanders came to understand that foreign policy was of significant consequence to their city and of personal importance to themselves.[16]

Cleveland seemed the perfect place to try this experiment in democracy, and not just because of the progressive traditions in its politics. The nation's fifth or sixth largest city by population, depending on the year, its prosperity was built on an influx of immigrants from Central and Eastern Europe around the Great War, who sweated their labor into the city's steel, iron, and coal works and eventually its automobile, electrical, and chemical industries.

Corporate growth and international trade had stimulated financial networks, including a Federal Reserve Bank, and the city had thriving sectors in accountancy, law, and education. Wealthy elites and a booming professional class had fostered to a burgeoning civic spirit, one not strong enough to alleviate the depths of the Depression through its Community Chest, maybe, but one immensely proud of its cultural life, with its Museum of Art, Cleveland Orchestra, and regular visits from the Metropolitan Opera of New York. Rail connections to Manhattan and Washington, crowned by the Union Terminal station completed in 1930, meant that Clevelanders could be assured of hearing the big-ticket speakers who introduce them to major policy and scholarly debates.[17]

Cleveland also offered an opportunity to challenge the myth that the great cities of the Midwest, let alone its agricultural plains, were in some way backward when it came to world affairs. This myth lasted deep into the Cold War, when one historian attributed the region's reticence to the "certain inner security" that came "from having thousands of miles of land, in addition to the oceans, act as a buffer to the outside world." This reputation was more fiction than fact. Scholars in the 1930s and 1940s found little evidence that the Midwest was more prone to "isolation" than other regions in terms of polling data, volume of foreign news in the papers, or even syllabi for university courses. Nor did internationalists struggle to create a foreign policy infrastructure in Midwestern cities before the Second World War, nonpartisan or otherwise. Still, the notion that the Midwest was "the backbone of American isolationism," as historian Thomas Bailey wrote in 1948, was as persistent as the "isolationist" slur generally, and its history was an old one, long predating the fight over the Treaty of Versailles. Emeny played on the stereotype, though never so much that it made his work seem destined to fail. All efforts to educate the public on foreign policy, he told the Carnegie Endowment in 1943, "should be concentrated upon the American industrial Ruhr, located in the area bounded by Buffalo, Pittsburgh, St. Louis and Chicago." Not only was this "the most important area in America from the point of view of public opinion," Emeny continued, "but the success of the project here would guarantee its success elsewhere." The reference to the Ruhr was suggestive: if the fate of the world had once turned on the coal buried under the Franco-German border, it was increasingly thought to turn on attitudes deep in the minds of the American Midwest.[18]

Emeny took charge of the Cleveland Council in October 1935, at first as its educational director. He found it more connected than influential. Its institute that March had opened with an ill-tempered argument about US policy between Baker, Quincy Wright, and Hamilton Fish Jr., the staunchly unilateralist Republican ranking member of the House Foreign Affairs Committee. Baker could draw impressive names, it seemed, but not raise money: the Council was so poor that it could barely cover the salary of its secretary, Polly Prescott. Emeny thought he could see the problem. Like his colleagues — including Buell, who tried to hire him as the Association's secretary in 1937, a post otherwise reserved for grandees of the women's movement — Emeny was disturbed that the Council was so gendered, or at least so gendered in what he saw as the wrong direction: women made up two-thirds of its membership and dominated its operations. Its consequent ties to the peace movement made Emeny equally uncomfortable. Baker had written upon Emeny's arrival that the Council's "constituency" was comprised of "people who want to do something constructive for the preservation of peace," that its aim was therefore not "an abstract educational program" but "a program of education directed toward the greater object of peace." But at the same time as Emeny moved the Council from the hallways of Cleveland College to offices on the ninth floor of a bank overlooking Public Square, he committed it constitutionally to "open discussion of international problems" based on a "serious and honest understanding of the world position of the U.S." Recasting the Council's aims in the language of the new social science, he recast its content too, turning it from discussions of peace and cooperation towards debates on geography and power.[19]

Freshly credentialled with his doctorate, Emeny launched himself into his task. He taught an introductory course on world affairs at Cleveland College, sending the enrollment fees of ten dollars into the Council's budget. He filled his schedule with addresses to groups like the Export-Import Club and the Chamber of Commerce, giving up to ten speeches a week. He armed himself with charts and statistics, making sure that the maps he had published in *The Great Powers* — with the United States centered in their projections — were reprinted in the newspapers. He told the *Cleveland Press* that raw materials mattered more to world affairs than race. He told the League of Women Voters that in any analysis of peace "only the industrial centers of the world must be considered." Emeny did not convince everybody, particularly those he made no effort to convince at all. David H. Pierce, a columnist and president of the local branch of the National Association for the Advancement of Colored People, mocked him as "Cleveland's synthetic authority on international problems," who "furnished information known to every intelligent fifteen year-old child." But Emeny found at least one adoring audience, albeit the one he was unhappy remained so crucial to the Council's fate. "One of the most handsome public speakers who ever raised the pulse-beats of Cleveland women's club members," the *Plain Dealer* reported in a profile, "speaks language that many women's clubs never heard, and he speaks it well."[20]

Rooting foreign policy in women's networks was not Emeny's aim, much as he enjoyed the attention. At the moment that peace had again become "the current concern of the women," as the *Plain Dealer* reported in 1936, Emeny worked to make foreign affairs more of a concern for men. He reinvigorated the men's discussion group, tried out dinner events more amenable to corporate schedules than luncheons, and had a telephone marketer cold call the city's rich and famous, only to find that three in four of the men who answered had never heard of the Council. By the end of Emeny's first year in charge, the gender disparity in the membership had widened, comprising 482 women and 148 men. What little success he had in the next two years came from providing opportunities for men to talk in private, away from the women who dominated public events. The difference between the discussion groups suggested what this meant more generally. The women's discussion group had always been an open forum, theoretically accessible even to Black women, and it drew a weekly attendance of 225 by 1938; the men's "rather resembled a seminar," as Emeny put it. Other initiatives intended to attract men followed the same pattern. Bankers, 169 of them by 1938, joined a private international finance committee; businessmen proved more reticent, perhaps because Emeny tried the most public means at his disposal to woo them, making rearmament the topic of the annual institute in 1939. Significantly, male members preferred to communicate what they learned at the Council to a broader public through methods less amenable to face-to-face participation than those of their female counterparts. The more engaged of the Council's women often spoke in settlement houses, subjecting themselves to physical debate; the men started a radio series, performing their authority in the comfortable solitude of the studio, insulating themselves from the people they sought to influence. Women always occupied key leadership positions in the Council, but the rank and file saw Emeny's intentions and began to leave. In April 1937, the rolls counted 991 women and 381 men; a year later, there were 773 women and 670 men.[21]

The problem was not just gender in itself, but access to money. Regardless of female philanthropy, Emeny thought that men of means were needed to make the Council sustainable. The Council's annual report for 1938 noted that "there seems to be a permanent discrepancy between the amount of money which can be raised through memberships and the actual amount necessary to run an educational organization," something that was clear elsewhere in the country too, including at the Foreign Policy Association itself. The search for private capital and the demands that such capital imposed— on the rare occasions it could be found—always shaped the campaign for a democratic foreign policy. Emeny had asked Baker about raising an endowment for precisely this reason. Without one, and with the major foundations unwilling to fund local groups at this point, the Emenys stepped in personally. Paying salaries and meeting deficits, they spent roughly $7,000 in their first year in Cleveland, $8,577 in their second, and $9,570 in their third, covering half the Council's expenditures. These were huge sums, and they were kept quiet, for the secret risked the viability of their project. Foundations would never spend that kind of money on this kind of thing, and in most places Rockefeller heiresses were not available to underwrite the dreams of their husbands. So often, as here, the question of a democratic foreign policy was a matter of the mundane realities of budgeting and staffing, of how finances matched with ideals. Seeing public opinion as trickling down from male civic leaders, and policy from the scholarly perspective cultivated in male intellectual networks, Emeny chose to seek salvation in a concept of a democratic foreign policy far more limited than his own.[22]

## Committees on Foreign Relations

As the world tottered towards war, not even the Council on Foreign Relations could escape the pressure to make foreign policy a more popular concern. Characteristically, however, it aimed to restrict the participation it endorsed as legitimate to a select male few. With Carnegie Endowment backing, the Council began to hold conferences for "university men" in 1935–1936; the small, private gatherings of mostly Ivy League students were "unique," it argued, "in a world that suffers from an exuberance of conferences." When the Carnegie Corporation asked in 1937 whether the Council might start operating outside New York, it responded similarly. Carnegie initially asked the Council to sponsor public meetings that would emphasize "the need for American collaboration in the solution of world problems." This horrified Council dons, not least because Carnegie insisted that cooperation with women's groups would be essential in making the arrangements. Walter Mallory, the Council's executive director, instead proposed "popular education" for "selected leading individuals" in various cities. This was not necessarily the oxymoron it seemed, for it followed from the theory that the more influential the people the Council chose to work with, the more likely they might in turn "affect the opinion and action of the masses." Or not, of course—others at the Council saw in the same proposals an opportunity to root foreign policy even more firmly in an elite. "I do not think much about the possibility of organizing any class as broad as adults to an understanding of foreign affairs," J. P. Morgan partner and Council bigwig Russell C. Leffingwell explained. Carnegie relented; the Council chose Francis Pickens Miller, Buell's close friend, to create a network of Committees on Foreign Relations under the supervision of future Central Intelligence Agency director Allen Dulles.[23]

Miller saw the Council's Committees as experiments in participatory democracy, in the same roundtable tradition that increasingly appealed to Buell. The Committees were technically autonomous, but the Council supplied a suggested agenda, a list of speakers, and subscriptions to *Foreign Affairs* and the *Foreign Policy Reports*. Miller took care selecting their membership, aiming for "a cross-section of responsible opinion" that would include businessmen, lawyers, bankers, faculty, clergy, and editors. He could not convince most Committees to include even a "responsible" labor unionist; admitting a woman was out of the question, as was admitting anyone of color. With threats to the intimacy that the Council thought supported frank exchanges of views duly fended off, the groups of twenty to thirty white men met for dinners at clubs or in hotels, followed by confidential chats with invited guests. For Miller, the Committees were "first class demonstrations of the democratic process of formulating public policy" as much because of their exclusionary nature as despite it. There were seven Committees at first, then thirteen by 1941 and twenty by 1944.[24]

Conceived following the example of Elihu Root to inoculate "popular diplomacy" with a drastic elitism, and employing the language of participatory democracy to do so, the Committees satisfied nobody. The State Department supported them as an "instrument" for promoting its policies and sometimes gained useful feedback from them. The Carnegie Corporation wondered by 1946 whether the scheme had created more than "superficial" interest, a question the more earnest members asked themselves too. Chairmen complained that attendance was sporadic, attention hard to maintain, and discussion less than vigorous, not least because the speakers the Council supplied tended to impose their views on the members rather than hear them out. The more alert Committee secretaries knew that the groups were little more than social clubs and that few of their colleagues cared whether their secret, off-the-record meetings actually promoted a specific foreign policy, let alone a more democratic one. The Council merely assumed that Committee members would spread the facts they learned and the views they formed "in daily contact with scores of their fellow townsmen," as director of studies Percy Bidwell put it, though some secretaries thought the Committees could do more to make that process explicit. Most of the time, though, they concluded that it would be rash to gamble what they had built. The men of Louisville, for instance, admitted in 1942 to "some twinges of conscience from time to time," but decided not to risk "the informality of discussion which has been one of the best features of our meetings."[25]

Emeny disagreed. The Cleveland Committee on Foreign Relations was among the first to be founded, in April 1938, and Miller left its running to his friend. Emeny bent the Council's black-tie brand to his own purposes, seeking to attract men of means "by sheer snob appeal, though more hopefully by intellectual stimulus," as he later wrote. Affiliating the Committee to his Council, he gathered a group even more unrepresentative than those that met in cities elsewhere. Filled with businessmen, it also included Eliot Ness, the city safety director; Harold Burton, the Republican mayor who sponsored crucial foreign policy bills after his election to the US Senate in 1940; and Chester Bolton, a five-term Republican congressman who died in 1939 and turned his seat over to his wife, Frances, a Council director whose fifteen-term political career ended as the ranking member of the House Foreign Affairs Committee. (Naturally, that did not qualify her to join the Cleveland Committee.) Emeny expanded the Committee far beyond the number of members the New York Council thought appropriate and charged dues of one hundred dollars—twenty times the Cleveland Council membership rate—so that he could turn the resulting spare cash into Council revenue. The New York Council raised its eyebrows but severed ties only in 1947.[26]

Emeny's creativity righted the finances of his Council and wove it more firmly into the city's governing class. While the small number of foreign policy activists in cities elsewhere were split among different voluntary associations, alliances like these meant that Emeny could centralize debate. During the war, the Cleveland Council acted as the agent of the Council on Foreign Relations, the Institute of Pacific Relations, the Foreign Policy Association, the Commission to Study the Organization of Peace, the Carnegie Endowment, and even the Office of the Coordinator of Inter-American Affairs, a federal information agency. All these groups worked from different theories of public opinion, but Emeny forged them into a single whole on the ground. That meant he was often able to convince speakers traveling under the auspices—and the expense account—of the Council on Foreign Relations or another group to spend an extra day in town, so that they might address a luncheon audience. He was also able to break down some of the injustices of the foreign policy community, inviting Vera Micheles Dean, for instance, to address his Committee in 1941. For the most part, however, Emeny's arrangement entrenched inequalities. If the women of the luncheons gained an opportunity to hear State Department speakers such as Stanley Hornbeck and Sumner Welles that they would otherwise have lacked, they did not receive the chance to talk privately with officials that was granted to the men of the Committee. Regular Council members had no more contact with policymakers than ordinary citizens; Committee men had their views reported to the State Department. So if Emeny achieved a parity of numbers among men and women by 1940, that parity concealed a widening disparity of power. Emeny's project to ensure that "world affairs were no longer largely a matter of concern for women" encouraged tendencies that would only accelerate in the years to come.[27]

## The Expert and His Problems

Emeny struggled to convince Clevelanders that foreign affairs were, in fact, their affairs, though his Council became more elaborate than any similar institution elsewhere in the effort. It took until the spring of 1941 for the Council's membership to near three thousand in a city of forty thousand college graduates. The 1940–1941 season offered thirteen luncheons as well as nine afternoon or evening speeches, which were intended to attract professionals more than the high society set. The women's and men's discussion groups met weekly, and there were Junior Foreign Affairs Councils in sixteen high schools. If there were signs of progress for this "scholarly crusader," as the *Cleveland Press* called him, there were too few to convince him that an adequate public for foreign policy had yet been built. It was a view that was shared widely among Emeny's peers, but one that did not quite matter enough to most educators for them to let it interfere with their views on foreign policy itself. Buell, for instance, championed intervention despite his fears that the public was not ready for the world leadership it would hasten. Emeny, however, converted his belief in the deficiency of public opinion into a policy position. He suffered for it.[28]

Emeny opposed the Roosevelt administration's drift towards war after 1939 for strategic rather than partisan reasons. His research had argued that the United States was fundamentally safe, and he was convinced that interventionists were exaggerating the danger that aggressors posed to the nation. Even if he understood that global power brought global responsibility, he saw no reason that such duties should include making war; as he did not agree with Spykman that there was "no safe defensive position" for the United States, he equally did not agree on the need to launch the "great offensive across the oceans" that his mentor championed. Better, Emeny thought, to avoid what he told Baker in 1936 would be "the disasters of involvement" and wait out any future war so that the United States could lead the peace to follow, as Woodrow Wilson had hoped before his intervention in 1917. "Economically, strategically and politically it is to our interest to remain aloof," Emeny told the Cleveland Council in October 1939. What distinguished Emeny from the many other noninterventionists who made similar arguments—and strengthened his noninterventionism as the debate continued—was the centrality of public opinion in his views.[29]

For Emeny, the bitterly emotional tenor of the intervention debate was proof that Americans were not ready for the burdens of world leadership. "I am not prepared to impose our armed will either upon Europe or Asia until it is evident that the American people have come to the conclusion that they are going to remain permanently," he told the National Peace Conference in October 1940. Memories of the Wilsonian debacle weighed so heavily upon him that he suggested in St. Louis the following May that "a greater tragedy to mankind than the victory of Hitler would be the withdrawal of America, after the peace." By then, Emeny had testified against the Lend-Lease Bill on the same January day as Charles Lindbergh spoke before Congress. "We waged the last war, and we lost the peace," Emeny told the House Foreign Affairs Committee, answering a question from fellow holdout Congresswoman Bolton. "What is so very overwhelming about it is that it has to be our peace that has to be waged, and imposed; and I am not so sure that we have made up our minds as to what our peace has to be."[30]

Emeny feared that Lend-Lease sealed America's fate: in setting off what he called "the greatest blood business in the world's history," arming the Allies was tantamount to a declaration of a "crusade." He still held to the theory that the United States was physically safe from danger, he told the Cleveland Council's annual meeting at the Hotel Statler shortly afterward, though "realism" demanded that he accept that "the majority of the American people have, wisely or otherwise, decided against its validity." But his argument about the inadequacy of public opinion continued. If Congress had truly understood the consequences of its actions, Emeny said, it would have demanded "any air or naval base in the British Empire we might desire," appropriated half a billion dollars for "propaganda, sabotage and espionage," and started to make plans for a new, "Anglo-American" world order. It had not. Polls meanwhile revealed that 89 percent of citizens opposed entering the war, at the same time as they found, perplexingly, that 68 percent favored doing exactly that if intervening in the conflict was the only way to defeat the Axis powers. "Colonel Lindbergh is thus far correct," Emeny concluded, invoking a name that was anathema to his members. "We are not as yet prepared as a nation for the policies already adopted, and the lack of our preparedness is due largely to our national habit of wishful thinking."[31]

Here was a test case for Deweyan arguments about the role of publics in the education of experts, for Emeny now learned that he had trained some of his members in the imperatives of US power all too well. The noninterventionist America First Committee was strong enough in Cleveland to rent out the twelve thousand-seat Public Hall for speeches by Congressman Fish, Senator Burton Wheeler, and even Lindbergh himself, but Emeny had nothing to do with that organization, nor was its leadership drawn from the Council's hierarchy. But it was revealing that the Cleveland chapter of the interventionist Committee to Defend America by Aiding the Allies was a Council offshoot in all but name. Back in June 1940, Cleveland College sociology professor Henry Miller Busch had quit as a Council board member to become the Committee's chairman; on the way out, he had denounced as "either ignorant or vicious or both" those people who deplored interventionism as "hysteria," the exact word Emeny had used in a speech one month earlier. Busch's deputy chairman was Lucia McCurdy McBride, a suffragist of significant reputation and a former president of the League of Women Voters of Cleveland who had been among the founders of the Women's Council for the Prevention of War in 1923. Fully half of the Committee's initial executive board were prominent in Emeny's Council; its launch event was attended by Mrs. L. J. Wolf, who had just retired from leading the women's discussion group.[32]

By May 1941, when Emeny gave his Hotel Statler speech in praise of Lindbergh, his interventionist friends had heard enough. "Lindbergh Right, Says Dr. Emeny" ran the headline of a *Plain Dealer* story by editor Spencer D. Irwin, a Council board member and the secretary of the Committee on Foreign Relations. Irwin was likely also behind an editorial insisting it would be "national suicide" not to see the "tragic warning" all Europe offered to "indifference and complacency," whether Americans understood what the consequences of any intervention might ultimately be. The most scorching attack came from McBride's successor at the Committee to Defend America, Josephine Irwin. Apparently no relation to the *Plain Dealer* editor, Irwin had been a regular at Mrs. Wolf's discussion group and was heavily involved in the world affairs work of the Cuyahoga Country League of Women Voters and the Cleveland Federation of Women's Clubs. She was incensed that Emeny had charged interventionists like her with "ignorance or dishonesty." "Having studiously followed his leadership, I cannot be ignorant," Irwin wrote of Emeny in a biting letter to the *Plain Dealer*, "therefore, I must be dishonest." What did her "dishonesty" entail? Following Baker's teaching that "the world must choose between world organization and world anarchy?" Following Emeny's lesson that "until the United States assumes a role in world politics which is commensurate with its vast power, there can be no peace?" Having learned from both, Irwin knew that until such "facts" were acted upon, "our dearest enemies cannot save America. Our dearest enemies: the America First Committee, the Communists, the Bundists, the Social Action Committee of the Northeast Ohio Synod of the Evangelical Reformed Church, a young man who has become a profound authority on international relations because he had the wind at his back when he flew the Atlantic in 1927, the United Mothers of America who are having such a gloriously exciting time aiding Hitler with their martyrdom, and Dr. Emeny."[33]

These words hurt—Irwin, like Busch, rarely appeared on Council programs again—but Emeny paid no price for sticking to his views. His power and wealth meant that his public could mount no real accountability against him nor demand much of an apology. So much for the democratic control of expertise; only events would force Emeny to change his mind, and even then, he was able to use his relationships to pretend he had been on the right side all along. Glossing over the incident, he wrote in his unpublished memoirs that the "vituperations of the past were forgotten" after Pearl Harbor. Emeny remained welcome at the State Department, and he was never shunned even by his most interventionist friends. Nor was Emeny easily slurred as an "isolationist," for he had always made clear that he understood the necessity of US power and worked to create a public that would support its exercise. Within two years, the *Plain Dealer* was gossiping that "rabid pre-Pearl Harbor internationalists" were considering running the supposedly like-minded Emeny in a primary against the unrepentant Senator Robert A.

Taft, with the backing of Wendell Willkie, for whom Emeny had worked as a speechwriter in the 1940 campaign. Emeny denied any interest in running for office, but Taft was worried enough to seek out a meeting with him in March 1944. It was one sign among many that Emeny's recalcitrance had been forgotten, as if someone in his position could not possibly have held such views.[34]

Emeny's dissent was revealing, though. For one thing, the incident uncovered how easily outflanked educators could be by activists wielding more direct means of appealing to the public, whether in terms of technologies like advertising and petition campaigns or in terms of the power of simple messages. For another, it demonstrated that not all internationalists abandoned their commitment to education and open debate in pursuit of interventionist goals, as the Foreign Policy Association had. Stubborn, haughty, and prone like so many of his fellow experts to dismiss his opponents as merely ignorant, Emeny learned no lessons about the dream of a democratic foreign policy itself, or how easily publics could be ignored if necessary. Whatever the success of "pressure groups" he saw inhibiting the "intelligent study of our problems," the great debate suggested to him only that there was much more to do.[35]

## Community Education in World Affairs

The war that followed changed Cleveland. Soon Emeny could look down from his office window to a War Services Center that dominated Public Square, offering citizens information about the conflict. Manufacturing jobs almost doubled even as thousands of Clevelanders left for the armed services, with existing factories retooled to produce war supplies and new works springing up to forge materiel, especially aircraft parts. Cuyahoga County residents bought $2.5 billion in war bonds, tying themselves to the state and its global ambitions. If Emeny took hope from such things, he was unable to see other ways in which the city was changing. Defense industries saved the local economy but at the same time encouraged cheaper, less union-dependent manufacturing in the South and West, setting up conditions that would soon haunt Cleveland, like so many industrial cities in the North. War production depended on Black migration from the South, which accelerated white flight to the suburbs once housing controls were lifted. The educated, white public Emeny had sought not only started to leave town, but took up new leisure pursuits as it went, partaking in a culture of consumerism; cities would no longer be the hotbeds of (white) reformism they had once been.[36]

The conflict changed Emeny's personal circumstances as well. His message that "no higher duty exists upon every citizen than to familiarize himself with these realities of America's world position," as he put it in 1942, took on fresh power in a nation at war. But Emeny was more a spectator than a participant in the fight. He could have accepted a formal government post and finished the war with a major policymaking position, but he chose not to. Before Pearl Harbor, he had declined an offer from his in-law Nelson A. Rockefeller to join the Office of the Coordinator of Inter-American Affairs, an agency that operated as a propaganda outfit abroad but paid more deference to liberal anxieties at home: the man who took it instead, Walter Laves, was deputy director-general of UNESCO by 1947. Emeny did seek voluntary service, badgering Welles until he was invited to sit on the legal and economic panels of the State Department's Advisory Committee on Postwar Foreign Policy in June 1942, but then played a minor role. That work nonetheless kept him in Washington most weeks until October 1943, a period when he was also teaching to cover for the ailing Spykman at Yale and writing a book on geopolitics for the Association that at last accepted his mentor's arguments; slyly mentioning no names, Emeny noted that geography had once given some Americans a "false sense of security." But Emeny for the most part was left to critique Roosevelt from the stalls, usually for what he saw as the dangerous unilateralism of postwar plans he had helped to design.[37]

On the rare occasions Emeny was in Cleveland during the war, he sought to expand the Council's work. "We have enjoyed seven happy, interesting years," he told its members before he left for Washington, hearing "some of the more distinguished authorities on world relations from this and other lands." He set up a Newton D. Baker Memorial Lecture Fund and convinced Walter Lippmann to launch it. He gave attention to the European and Pacific fronts alike in his luncheon schedule, making room for postwar planning, the future of colonialism, and even "The Negro in Two World Wars," a subject to which W. E. B. DuBois spoke. There were celebrities like Welles, military broadcaster George Fielding Eliot, and Republican grandee John Foster Dulles, but the bulk of the speakers were of a more studious type, academics like Spykman and Arnold Wolfers, or men closer to the grind of the war, such as Herbert Feis, William Yandell Elliott, and Ralph Bunche. The Council's finances became sounder and its speakers bureau busier, but overall it remained "more or less of a closed corporation," Emeny thought. He dreamed, he said in June 1942, of a Council that might "encourage members of this community" at all levels to "prepare for the role of America in the future."[38]

Like Baker, Emeny was no populist by inclination. He intended to create a situation in which "leading citizens recruited from all walks of life" could learn about and promote world affairs, he told the Carnegie Endowment in April 1943, "as a necessary part both of their own professions and their duties as citizens." The Council's structure encouraged stratification: its members entered worlds of people and information that were walled off to those uninterested, unwilling, or unable to pay, let alone unfamiliar with the subjects at hand. The kinds of people interested in taking out membership proved hard to come by, as if there were some invisible limit on the number of Clevelanders who sought to participate in foreign policy as Emeny defined it. 3,588 adults were members by the summer of 1943, but only a few more had joined by the end of the war. Emeny had neither the temperament nor the expertise in educational methods to push further: his innovations either borrowed from the work of friends elsewhere or extended what Baker had set up years earlier, and he spoke about public opinion in an aristocratic, willfully unspecific way. He took the Council's presidency in October 1943, hiring as his operational successor the following June a Yale-trained political scientist better known as an educator than as a researcher, a former director of the Omaha Public Affairs Forum and the Public Affairs Institute of Kansas City.[39]

Shepherd Witman was a true believer like Baker had been before him, and like Baker he spoke Deweyanism as a second tongue. Discussion was "the essence of democracy in the intricate, modern world," he wrote shortly after arriving in Cleveland, a means of overcoming "citizen lethargy." Witman also believed in letting people take command of their own education, far more so than Emeny. "Too often programs suffer from subject selection by 'superior,' 'objective' executives who determine plans on 'what the people need,'" Witman wrote. "Nothing could be more false and dangerous." Hired by Emeny to start a forum series, Witman instead tried to devolve power away from the Council while insisting on the use of methods that would "extract the maximum value from public discussion" and avoid "the charge that we just 'sit around and talk.'" He still held firm to the old urge "to make available without prejudice all facts and evidence needed for the study and evaluation of world affairs," he told his board in a proposal he also sent to the Carnegie Endowment in May 1945, but thought that it was not enough to make facts available to the few. The Council should help civic leaders "carry on under their own momentum," he said. While Emeny trusted that opinions forged at Council meetings would circulate beyond them, Witman was not prepared to leave that dynamic to faith.[40]

The result was the Council's Community Education Program. The first step was for the Council to sponsor neighborhood discussions, forums, and panels, under its own auspices or as part of the regular programming of libraries, churches, parent-teacher associations, and the like. Eighty-six such events took place in 1945, each of them led by volunteers who had been trained in facts and methods at special sessions in the Council's library. The speakers bureau, run by one of the Council's eight paid staff members—all women—placed lecturers for 106 events that year, mostly at churches, clubs, and professional groups. A Rotarian himself, Witman set up Program Planning Clinics, helping forty-nine groups from the Knights of Columbus to the Junior Chamber of Commerce find ways to start programs that would encourage their members to talk about the world. Emeny was particularly proud of a partnership Witman struck up with Crile General Hospital, training convalescent military officers to lead discussions among their fellow injured veterans. By 1951, the Council was sponsoring more than twelve hundred community programs a year, a wealth of courses, discussion groups, radio shows, film screenings, lectures, high-school programs, after-school clubs, clinics, weekend institutes, workshops, model United Nations Assemblies, and more.[41]

Promoting discussion on such a scale necessarily took that discussion further away from the experts Deweyan educators had always sought to constrain. The Council offered differentiated layers of access to power, whether the direct *entrée* to policymakers and leading thinkers enjoyed by the men on its Committee, or the question period open to those paying four-dollar dues to hear a roster of lecturers of steadily diminishing fame speak at luncheons. The discussion leaders sent out from the speakers bureau and promoted through the Community Education Program had a less-credentialled kind of expertise. One speakers bureau flyer from 1949 offered the services of local academics, journalists, and lawyers, as well as citizens who had traveled widely or spent the war in junior positions at the Strategic Bombing Survey or the Office of Military Government in Germany. Such people tended to relay facts rather than create them: social scientists at the time called them "opinion leaders," citizens who took in information from authoritative sources and passed it on, but the opinion leaders of academic theory operated at more levels of society than the Council's speakers, and less formally. Either way, making the Council into an institution with deeper roots in its community involved separating participation from the physical presence of experts and policymakers—at exactly the moment when those experts and policymakers began to hold more power over American life than ever before.[42]

Although Witman made sure that the Council joined forces with municipal institutions, he mostly conceived of community life working through voluntary associations. Contemporaries imagined voluntary associations as embracing "all ages, classes, creeds, and ethnic groups" in the people's "greatest school of self-government," as historian Arthur M. Schlesinger put it in 1944; the limits to educating the public in this way would be revealed with statistical precision only later. With some exceptions, Rotary included, Witman tended to cooperate with groups that had the same clientele as the Council, one which, as an observer noted at the time, might well have included "representatives of most economic classes, creeds, colors, and nationalities in the community" but "hardly approximates a true cross section of the population." Pushing further involved compromises too difficult for those beholden to a particular, scientific way of seeing the world to bear. It was easy enough to reach the college-educated staffs of labor groups, for example, but elected labor leaders, let alone workers, were impossible. "It is so difficult," Emeny told Congresswoman Bolton in 1947, asking if she could "vet" labor representatives Witman wanted to work with, "for them to get out of their minds the fact that foreign policy is the concern of citizens and does not need to be interpreted purely in terms of labor politics."[43]

Witman's efforts to make the Council less racist also faltered. The mature Council did have some Black members, but the limited extent of that involvement before Witman's arrival can be inferred from the scant notice the Council received in the Black press. In 1936, the *Call and Post* had urged Black women to attend the discussion group, and some did, but the Council was otherwise of little relevance to the Black community, receiving no publicity even when it invited DuBois and Bunche to speak. When Witman arrived in town, he met "racial leaders to discuss plans for postwar work in international affairs with racial groups," he told the Carnegie Endowment, but, in a *de facto* segregated city, the Council still left its outreach to libraries and schools. The *Call and Post* praised students who joined the Junior Council on World Affairs, which by 1948 had chapters in almost every high school in the city, and its editors sent reporters to hear Black speakers at the Council more often after the war. The newspaper was pleased that the National Association for the Advancement of Colored People was finally invited to send delegates to the annual institute in 1950, on the subject of foreign aid, and that "approximately 75 American Negroes" attended the institute in 1953, on Africa. Even so, it attacked the latter event for emphasizing "how much the British and the Belgians have done for the natives" in Kenya and

130

Congo, as well as for a panel discussion that saw the sole "African spokesman," a graduate student, face up to a career diplomat, a senior State Department official, and a future Moroccan ambassador to the United States. Clearly there was more to do—if more, in fact, was desired.[44]

## Brooks Emeny and the Foreign Policy Community

"This is the day that Newton D. Baker should have lived to see," the *Plain Dealer* said on its front page on January 9, 1947. Emeny stepped onto the platform of the Public Music Hall that evening, the flags of the United Nations behind him, three thousand men and women before him. His suit was dark, his face pale, his manner serious. The audience had just watched a film, *Where in the World is America?* Now, the *Plain Dealer* wrote, it became so quiet that "the proverbial pin falling would have sounded like an atom bomb." Winifred had hosted a *soirée* earlier; reporters were present, radio commentators, newsreel men; spotlights beat down upon the stage. "I need hardly say to you here that this opening meeting of our Twenty-First Institute is indeed a very happy occasion," Emeny said. "I think it may be said to our satisfaction that we in Cleveland have carried community education in world affairs as far—and I believe further—than any other American community."[45]

Emeny introduced Henry R. Luce to open the "Report from the World," three days of festivities sponsored by Time Inc. "Fundamentally this is the kind of meeting that no American needs to have explained," Luce said, but in his view that made it no less "extraordinary." That night Wellington Koo, Chinese ambassador to the United States, led off speeches from Filipino diplomat Carlos Romulo, Episcopalian preacher Henry Van Dusen, and Secretary of the Navy James Forrestal. The next day the premier of Italy, Alcide de Gasperi, left the foreign ministers of Uruguay and Czechoslovakia in the shade, as well as Omar Bradley, one of the great generals of the US Army. On Saturday night, in the hall America Firsters had once crammed to hear Charles Lindbergh, the Republican chairman of the Senate Foreign Relations Committee, Senator Arthur Vandenberg, spoke alongside Secretary of State James F. Byrnes, marking the first time those architects of their "bipartisan foreign policy" shared a stage. Ten thousand people looked on while an estimated fifteen million more listened in at home. Only in Cleveland could this have been possible, Luce had declared, as "eminent personalities and other leadership" spoke to the people on whose capacity to be "responsible" democracy would stand or fall. The Cleveland Council, after

**4.2** Republican Senator Arthur H. Vandenberg of Michigan, Chairman of the Senate Foreign Relations Committee, speaks to the "Report from the World," Cleveland Public Hall, January 1947. Brooks Emeny is at bottom right. Herbert Gehr, The Life Picture Collection, Shutterstock.

all, had not been "an eclectic society," Luce said, but had "spread its branches of enlightenment over your whole metropolis."[46]

The "Report from the World" was the summit of Emeny's achievements, and it testified to his place within the foreign policy community. Luce, who Emeny guessed had spent "well in excess of $125,000" on the event, knew him from the Institute of Pacific Relations. Secretary Byrnes had just announced his forthcoming retirement, but his speech made the front page of the *New York Times*, and his endorsement still mattered. "The community of Cleveland has come to regard world problems not as the affairs of far-distant countries, but as the affairs of the world of which the community of Cleveland is a part," Byrnes said, suggesting every city in the nation should do the same. State Department propaganda relayed the proceedings overseas, promoting not just the democratic foreign policy the United States claimed to wield, but Emeny's specific vision for it. Others were unconvinced. Edward

132

C. Carter of the Institute of Pacific Relations snarked that this was "mass education by celebrity," even if Emeny was "planning innumerable side shows where free discussion will be organized." The *Chicago Tribune*, which had lauded Emeny for his noninterventionism just six years earlier, blasted the "lickspittle members of the Cleveland Council" for "war mongering and America Last." Communists set up a picket, passing out flyers decrying Byrnes's betrayal of wartime internationalism and attacking the "Hitlerite dream of world conquest" Luce was apparently in town to promote. Emeny cared not.[47]

The foreign policy community had been looking to the Council as an example for some time, not least because of Emeny's relentless promotion of his work. "Other people, as well as Emeny himself, feel that the Cleveland Council has developed in a remarkable way," former Council on Foreign Relations staffer Whitney Shepardson told colleagues at the Carnegie Corporation in 1946. Praise came from internationalists, of course, but also from men still queasy about US primacy who naively saw the Council as a way to ensure that "worthwhile people who bear the reputation of being outspoken and radical" could be heard, as Oswald Garrison Villard told Emeny. Meanwhile, the Council model started to spread. Emeny's personal assistant, Phyllis Parker, married another scholar of raw materials, Eugene Staley, and moved to San Francisco to help him found the World Affairs Council of Northern California. Requests for advice arrived from Indianapolis, Seattle, and Cincinnati. The Carnegie Corporation cut a check in 1947 for a program that gave young activists work experience in Cleveland, while Witman conceived an MA in "Citizenship and World Affairs" at Western Reserve University, teaching the dual expertise in international relations and adult education its graduates would need to succeed. Students from these programs fanned out; one, Howard A. Cook, went from Cleveland to San Francisco and on to Washington, where he would take charge of the State Department's Public Services Division, its key link between policymakers and the public, in 1952.[48]

Even Emeny's strongest admirers still had concerns, however. "What this country needs is more Emenys," Raymond Blaine Fosdick told John D. Rockefeller Jr., as if the Council's success had come from the force of its president's personality alone. Vice Admiral John Greenslade, a self-described "fellow traveler" of Emeny's who had commanded the defense of the West Coast while helping to run the San Francisco branch of the Institute of Pacific Relations, warned that the "Cleveland method might not work nationwide," as it required "the leadership of an outstanding individual" and "means other than those normally obtainable." Greenslade knew the Cleveland secret. Winifred and Brooks had contributed more than $56,000 to the Council's operating costs over twelve years, and they had started an endowment after the war. Their total outlay came close to six figures, not including the salary Brooks had foregone, and they likely covered almost a third of the Council's expenditures between 1935 and 1944. Emeny was prepared to invest still more to purchase a permanent home for the Council: with no sense of irony or tribute, he made million-dollar plans to tear down the Women's City Club and build a center with two auditoriums, conference rooms, and a travel agency. Although that plan fell through, the Emenys' investment clouded the Cleveland model's prospects. Rockefeller and Carnegie were not fully informed of the extent of the couple's support; the foundations expected other cities to replicate the Council's success without anything like the same resources. Emeny disingenuously argued that every Council should be able to break even after a brief period of limited aid, but no memorandum set out how long or how much it had taken for the Cleveland Council to sustain itself. His dissimulation would have severe consequences in the years to come, fatally weakening the movement as a whole.[49]

Philanthropic funding was hard to come by in any case, which Emeny knew because he had spent years appealing to the major foundations, the leading foreign policy institutions, and even the federal government without much success. Revealingly, he met with less resistance in principle than in practice. He kept things in the family at first. Having consulted for Nelson A. Rockefeller's White House outfit in 1941, he told his in-law that to root foreign policy securely in public opinion, the government must "establish an elaborate system of Federally financed bureaus of education throughout the country as a means of distributing desired information," or else work through "efficiently organized private groups in communities throughout the nation, groups which unfortunately, with few exceptions, do not exist at present." The first option entailed government "control" of public opinion, a "negation of democracy"; the second, which diluted state power, was "the democratic way." Every community should have a Council, he wrote, served by a central headquarters that would train "competent young men" to direct them. Emeny thought that $700,000 would be needed over three years, including $170,000 for seed grants to help create forty to fifty Councils, which would receive a measly $3,000 to $4,000 each.[50]

Like most of Emeny's missives, this proposal went nowhere. Nelson took the plan to the family philanthropy, which oddly denounced it as overly propagandistic. Emeny retorted that he was merely trying to promote the research in which the Foundation was investing beyond its typical scholarly audience. "I cannot accept the proposition that there is only one Brooks Emeny to be found in these United States," he told Nelson, tabling his approach. He received still less of a hearing at the Carnegie Corporation before getting into a spat with the Carnegie Endowment, which he accused of wasting twenty years to "little avail." Emeny's proposal for a "complete and drastic" overhaul of the Foreign Policy Association caused a stink too. Only a handful of the branches, Emeny complained to General McCoy, had "passed beyond the primitive stage" of leadership by "an over-worked, badly-paid lady secretary" who caused "the male population to fight shy of meetings unless dragooned to attend from the social rather than the educational angle." The women of the Association were outraged. One snapped that "lady-secretaries" ran the best branches, that the "lady-secretary" in charge of the branch program was a renowned educator, and that if world affairs education was in fact "a man's task," as Emeny had claimed, then somebody had better tell Virginia Gildersleeve, Mary Woolley, and women internationalists "ad infinitum." McCoy, for his part, muttered that the plan was "very elaborate." Emeny's other correspondents had a similar reaction. *Des Moines Register and Tribune* editor W. W. Waymack, for one, assured Emeny that he sympathized but told Carnegie that the ideas were "grandiose."[51]

Emeny tried the Council on Foreign Relations next. In March 1942, he wrote to the entire Council membership, along with the membership of every Committee on Foreign Relations, to ask for support to expand the Committee program to a hundred cities and to mandate that they initiate "a wider program of public education." Nothing could have irritated Council officials more than such an impertinent misuse of its mailing list, and they sent out a circular making clear their disapproval of Emeny's missive. It went without saying that Council grandees hated the idea. "Foreign relations is a subject about which, particularly in war time and indeed at any time, the greatest circumspection needs to be observed," Leffingwell sputtered, for "miscellaneous chatter about foreign affairs is likely to do more harm than good." Still, Council staffers found latent approval for some aspects of Emeny's proposals when they made inquiries with a handful of Committee members, and they recognized that if there was "no perceptible support" for the Committees to do more, that did not mean the members were indifferent to the underlying goal.[52]

Emeny put his efforts on hold while he was working in Washington, but his frustrations boiled over with victory in sight in 1944. The spark was a letter from the Council on Foreign Relations that June, which said that since the Council had been gifted a new home at 58 East Sixty-Eighth Street, it needed to raise $77,500 in addition to the $222,500 it had already obtained for renovations to prepare the property for the "tremendous responsibilities which the Council should soon shoulder." The greed infuriated Emeny. "There is a very decided danger," he wrote back, copying everyone he could think of, "that the members, while enjoying their new and luxurious surroundings, may become unmindful of their deep moral obligation to aid in every way possible the extension of general public knowledge and understanding of world affairs." The Committees were proof of this delinquency, he said. "During the next three years the whole pattern of postwar adult education in American foreign relations is going to be set," he wrote, cautioning that time was running out. Emeny proposed that the Council's members should "collectively guarantee" $50,000 per year—matched by Rockefeller and Carnegie—to fund fifty Committees responsible for broader efforts in their communities. "This is a problem which we failed to solve between World War I and World War II," he reminded his colleagues sharply. "If we cannot solve it now, America will again lose the peace and the fault will rest heavily upon those who are in a position today to realize these facts."[53]

Council House reacted in its usual manner. John W. Davis, the Council's first president and a former Democratic candidate for the White House, admonished Emeny that "we must do one thing at the time." Officials plotted ways to ostracize him and claimed to Rockefeller associates that any such plan would be "extremely wasteful," but this time Emeny found more support from the Council's rank and file. More of the foreign policy community agreed on the need to do something about public opinion as the war neared its end, as the State Department's internal reorganization also implied. Will Clayton, an Office of War Mobilization administrator who was shortly to become assistant secretary of state, promised Emeny he would participate "in a substantial way," hoping for "not fifty or a hundred but at least five hundred" Committees as well as "some few score" Councils. Leland Goodrich, director of the World Peace Foundation in Boston, expressed his "unqualified approval." Owen Lattimore, the leading American scholar of Asian affairs, agreed that "however expert an expert may be, he cannot function efficiently unless he represents a society, or community which as a whole is well-informed." Philip Jessup, an international lawyer, nonetheless advised that there was not "the slightest possibility of the Council on Foreign Relations taking that kind of position." He and others had "given up hope."[54]

136

Emeny's campaign touched a nerve, but he came off as a crank. John D. Rockefeller Jr., whose initial $150,000 donation to the Council had caused Emeny such grief, responded only after Winifred had borne another child months later. "Your letter will afford the Council food for thought" was all he could muster. Emeny circulated another letter in March 1945, this time offering to host a conference to discuss how foreign policy institutions could cooperate. "I am getting quite a dossier of valuable suggestions from you," McCoy snipped. Emeny now soured at the baleful influence of a Northeastern elite. "What is it that makes New York associations suffer under the illusion that they are the tail that wags the American dog," he asked Buell. Meanwhile, pressure groups took control of the debate. Emeny had told Welles back in 1943 that a "people's peace" would be lost if the "general public" lacked a "sense of participating in the determination of these policies," and he was disquieted by the propagandistic means that State eventually used to sell the United Nations. He refused to attend the San Francisco Conference. "I am perfectly appalled when I remember the number of people representing this and that who intend to crowd the corridors of the Conference anterooms to try to wield their influence," he wrote to a friend at the Carnegie Endowment. He went fishing in the Canadian wilderness instead.[55]

By the time Emeny had come down from the high of the "Report from the World," then, his place within the foreign policy community was awkward. He was taken somewhat seriously, some of the time. The Cleveland story, cleverly told, offered an example of what the foreign policy community could achieve at the community level. In fact, the Council offered the only such example. If the Association continued with the educational approach that most within the foreign policy community still preferred to the problem of public opinion—a problem that grew with each new commitment the United States made abroad—then the Cleveland Council was the sole successful alternative to the luncheon society. But Emeny was not seen as someone to be trusted. He was a man with a plan, but not one that seemed to many of his peers to be practical; it had been rejected, repeatedly and in various forms, over the course of several years. For those reasons and more, he was a surprising selection to lead the Foreign Policy Association.

Come the spring of 1947, however, the Association felt it had no choice, not least because of Emeny's willingness to use his personal wealth in the cause. The Association still garnered support from the Rockefeller Foundation, and the Carnegie Corporation had become interested in increasing its support, with the encouragement of the State Department. It still had a significant membership and a large budget. When it launched a membership campaign that year, it convinced James Byrnes, John Foster Dulles, and Warren Austin, the serving US ambassador to the United Nations, to lend their names. But the board was old and tired, still stacked with progressives from a bygone era; its chairman, banker William W. Lancaster, was well into his seventies and the more active directors were relics of an earlier war and an earlier peace. The finances were in dire shape. The research staff was of no comparison with its former self. The branches were inept. If there was a man with the stature necessary to rescue it, he was likely to be able to take a significant government post, or else have his pick of similar roles that paid more and troubled less.[56]

Few within the foreign policy community doubted that the work of the Association was necessary, given the gap most still saw between public opinion and the new position of the United States. Nobody, however, was much interested in doing that work. Henry Stimson, the secretary of war who had proffered McCoy in 1939, suggested the board approach State Department hands such as Joseph Grew and Herbert Feis, to no avail. For two or three months, the board tried out James Grafton Rogers, former assistant secretary of state and deputy director of the Office of Strategic Services, but he was a miserable failure in the post. Allen Dulles was asked, and he declined. Adlai Stevenson was asked twice, and twice he declined. Alger Hiss was a viable candidate, but the secretary-general of the San Francisco Conference took the presidency of the Carnegie Endowment, though not before offering a list of names for Undersecretary of State Dean Acheson to look over. The Hiss list comprised sixteen men from the broadcasters Edward Murrow and Raymond Swing to veteran diplomats like Francis B. Sayre. Hiss knew, however, that "the Board is considering names without any evident plan as to the future work of the Association." Only one of the men had such a plan, yet even he, Emeny, was fearful of taking on the task. He told Dean he wished somebody else would do it, and he told the board, when he met it in the days after the festivities in Cleveland, that its offer would have to be all or nothing if he were to be convinced. The board gave in. Carnegie sent $20,000 as a vote of confidence; a week later, at the end of March 1947, Emeny became the Association's fourth president.[57]

# 5

# World Affairs Are Your Affairs

George Marshall stepped toward the podium. The speech the secretary of state was about to give to the Harvard Alumni Association, its members suitably fed and watered after commencement exercises that morning, was intended to be historic. It would declare that the United States was willing to fund a plan to rebuild Europe. The plan was humanitarian, aimed "against hunger, poverty, desperation and chaos," Marshall would say, but it was also directed at states, systems, even whole ways of life. "Governments, political parties or groups which seek to perpetuate human misery in order to profit therefrom politically or otherwise," he would warn, "will encounter the opposition of the United States." The Soviet Union would get the message.

But the students, faculty, and alumni who gathered in Harvard Yard that afternoon in June 1947 could be forgiven for thinking that Marshall was going to speak about something else. He started, after all, not by talking about the threat of communism abroad, but the plight of democracy at home: in fact, he offered his audience a theory of public opinion and foreign policy. "I need not tell you gentlemen that the world situation is very serious," Marshall began, for "that must be apparent to all intelligent people." The retired general feared that it had become "exceedingly difficult for the man in the street to reach a clear appraisement of the situation." The problem of a democratic foreign policy was not a lack of information, Marshall said, but the opposite, that the "very mass of facts presented to the public by press and radio" now made it hard for people to know what was important. More difficult still was that most Americans were affluent and insulated from a world that had been destroyed, so it was hard for them to "comprehend the plight and consequent reactions of the long-suffering peoples" and to understand what their suffering meant for "our efforts to promote peace in the world."

139

For Marshall, making foreign policy and making public opinion were therefore the same thing. "An essential part of any successful action on the part of the United States," he said, "is an understanding on the part of the people of America of the character of the problem and the remedies to be applied"— an understanding that they must "face up to the vast responsibility which history has clearly placed on our country."[1]

That was not all. With his prepared remarks about the State Department's proposed aid package complete, Marshall returned to the issue of public opinion, improvising on his original theme. He was sorry for giving such a political speech, he said, but he thought it of such "vast importance that our people reach some general understanding of what the complications really are, rather than react from a passion or a prejudice or an emotion of the moment." He reiterated the problem of distance, which he worried could not be overcome by "reading, or listening, or even seeing photographs or motion pictures." "The whole world of the future hangs on a proper judgment" by the American people, he concluded. Fitting words from a man who had considered, and declined, the presidency of the Foreign Policy Association a few months earlier.[2]

Part of what made the conflict with the Soviet Union into the militaristic, Manichean Cold War to come was the effort that Marshall and other officials put into ensuring that Americans came to the "proper judgment" they sought. Policymakers took extraordinary steps to mobilize the public against communism, steps based on a distinct theory of public opinion: either because Americans were ignorant about world affairs despite waging a war and making a peace, or because they were now bombarded with so much information that clarity escaped them, the citizenry would have to be rallied to the cause of US primacy as if they were entering another war. Policymakers spoke privately of the need to "shock," to "electrify," to "scare the hell out of" the American people. Dean Acheson, Marshall's deputy and later secretary of state himself, admitted in his later memoirs that "we made our points clearer than truth," that nuance had given way "to bluntness, almost brutality, in carrying home a point." That insight was based on explicit ideas about public opinion, too. How long, Acheson asked foundation officials who met at the State Department in 1951, did the "average citizen" spend thinking about foreign affairs? He had to wake up, shave, shower, dress, breakfast, commute, work. Perhaps he had five minutes a day, at a best guess, "and that is dealing with problems which have to do with the survival of our country," the secretary of state complained.[3]

Cold Warriors often operated from a skeptical understanding of public opinion, but many did not entirely give up on improving it. World War II had strengthened the idea that diplomacy ought to be democratic, that the people ought to be informed and that they could and even should participate in the making of foreign policy. Harry Truman had no connection at all to the major foreign policy institutions, but their language was sufficiently common that the president knew how to speak to them. Truman told the Association late in 1945 that "there is, in my opinion, no more urgent task before us at this time than the building of an informed public opinion on the problems of foreign policy," a line he would echo throughout his presidency. Of course, the world had changed. The United States possessed vast power, including a destructive capability unmatched in history to this point, yet the risks it faced in the world were felt to be increasing drastically, and would become intolerable should a competitor learn the secrets it had tried to keep about the atomic bomb. Perhaps there were policies that had to be made now that might be too dangerous, too dirty ever to reveal, let alone to subject to popular debate in advance of their execution. But the imperative to create an informed, active public remained, even if technologies like polling and the mass media seemed to make that public potentially more manipulable than ever—the Association had made sure that the conduct of foreign policy in a democracy was inconceivable without it.[4]

Maintaining the support of Americans for US primacy in general and the Cold War in particular became big business as the ideological conflict was pushed into all aspects of everyday life. There were propaganda programs to sell policies like Atoms for Peace, to bring home the dangers of a nuclear world, and to engage citizens in public diplomacy, whether by hosting foreign visitors or writing letters to pen-friends abroad. Books, magazines, films, plays, cartoons, and more embodied and imbued the tropes of global, even imperial hegemony. Defense spending created jobs, reshaping the geographies, economies, and politics of whole communities, while more citizens than ever were required to contribute taxes to a federal budget that provided for a preponderance of military power. World affairs came for God in the sky above, who found Himself invoked against totalitarians stamping out faith in anything but man, and it came for the bedrooms on the ground below, where investigators snooped in search of a perversion that might suggest sedition. Some of this activity might be considered participation of a sort, the constant coproduction and reproduction of a political culture that backed US power, but it was not the active, deliberative participation in core decisions that parts of the foreign policy community had long sought. For some, like Marshall at Harvard, the rise of the Cold War made that kind of meaningful participation far less likely, as the world overwhelmed the citizenry and created not engagement, but apathy—not discussion, but dissuasion.[5]

At this crucial moment when the policies, patterns, and procedures of US leadership were being set, the Foreign Policy Association and its allies had their chance to make good on their promise. Brooks Emeny had the right words, at least. Months before Marshall stepped onto the Harvard stage, Emeny had warned the Cleveland Council on World Affairs of "the educational unpreparedness of America for world leadership." He had harped on the same theme for years, of course, but atomic weapons made the perils of failure radioactive. "Either means must be devised whereby an organization of world peace shall be assured," he wrote in *Vogue* magazine in April 1947, "or we have only to contemplate the inevitable destruction of civilization through World War III." He now had the pulpit from which to preach his gospel. "Community education in world relations is the most challenging and important task of the political life of this nation today," he wrote. "Every American must learn to analyze international events as a special obligation and privilege of citizenship."[6]

Emeny would fail, by his own admission. Although the Cleveland model or something like it inspired activists across the country, appealing as a map that might guide them deep into their communities, Emeny scrambled at this key juncture to find the backing he needed to make his ideas a practical reality. Even as the language of progressive reform continued to exert some sway well into the postwar period, Emeny struggled to defend his vision from alternatives that, to most, were less palatable, whether academic elitism or rigid anticommunism. However attractive his vision might have been, he could not rescue the institutions through it was to be enacted; in time, he became the Foreign Policy Association's most intractable problem. By the time he left New York, five years after he arrived, he was a dispirited, exhausted, lonely figure, his dreams discredited, his personal life a tragedy. His successors would fare no better, coming to understand that Emeny's plans for a national movement of World Affairs Councils had been flawed all along. The Association missed its moment. The consequences were stark.

## *"Operation Rat Hole"*

When Brooks Emeny took over the Foreign Policy Association, it was still a central institution in the foreign policy community. It was a trusted partner of the State Department. It drew support from the Rockefeller Foundation and the Carnegie Corporation, the two most active foundations in the world affairs field. It received thirtieth anniversary greetings from President Truman, Secretary Marshall, and United Nations Secretary-General Trygve Lie, as well as personalities from Eleanor Roosevelt to Walter Lippmann. What the Association now lacked, however, was dominance. Central to Emeny's vision was the monopoly over semi-official discussion that the Cleveland Council had maintained as the licensed local agent of national organizations. What that monopoly avoided was clear from a Council on Foreign Relations survey taken in 1945, which reported on the resources available in the cities served by its Committees. The (white) citizens of Detroit, to take one city at random, could avail themselves of a Committee on Foreign Relations, an Association branch, an Institute of Pacific Relations outpost, an International Relations Club, an Inter-American Center, an East and West Association, and a World Study Council, as well as a chapter of Americans United for World Organization, a Foreign Trade Club, and various committees attached to the Board of Commerce and similar groups. This sprawl could have been celebrated as testament to the democratic nature of US foreign policy, and it did represent significant popular curiosity about foreign affairs, but it seemed to Emeny wasteful, suggestive of vested interests. "Manhattan can afford the luxury of multiplicity," he told Alger Hiss of the Carnegie Endowment, "but no other American communities, with the possible exception of Chicago, can do so."[7]

Emeny imagined founding a single national institution to deal with this problem, an idea with which foundation officials had historically sympathized. Early in his tenure, he therefore found himself in the strange position of arguing for the closure of the Association he ran. He resurrected his plans from the first half of the decade, proposing a Foreign Policy Foundation to bring together the libraries and staffs of the major world affairs groups on premises near the new, Rockefeller-donated United Nations complex in Manhattan. Thirty million dollars ought to do it, he told the Carnegie Corporation, a sum which one member of the Association's board dryly called "ambitious." Emeny pinned his hopes on Hiss, who was advocating the amalgamation of the national groups while offering direct funding to new World Affairs Councils. Emeny and Hiss did come close to integrating the Association and the Institute of Pacific Relations, which already shared researchers, board members, and office space. Internal fracturing at the Institute made that path plausible, as its regional affiliates expressed resentment at the control wielded over their work from headquarters in New York. Members in Seattle and San Francisco argued, not unreasonably, that those who actually lived on the shores of the Pacific should set the agenda of an Institute of Pacific Relations. San Francisco officials therefore suggested merging the Association and the Institute to create a single national organization that would delegate greater autonomy to local branches, on Emeny's Council model. But at a conference at the Coronado resort in San Diego Bay in April 1947, a majority of Institute delegates voted down a resolution for "organic union," prompting the San Francisco cadre to break off and form the World Affairs Council of Northern California, with the assistance of some of Emeny's former staff. Emeny and Hiss tried to force the issue, convening a meeting at Winifred's luxurious mansion at Overhills, North Carolina, without success.[8]

Lurking behind all this insider maneuvering were brutal financial realities. Neither the Rockefeller Foundation nor the Carnegie Corporation were yet certain how they would proceed in the postwar era, with the US participation in world affairs they had long sought now assured, if tenuously so. For Emeny, Carnegie looked the brighter prospect, with Hiss already plunging the Endowment into education and Devereux Josephs, the Office of Strategic Services veteran who now led the Corporation, declaring that "adult appreciation of international responsibilities" was the "double-starred" item on his agenda. But the Endowment's budget for external grants was minuscule and the Corporation was moving towards academic inquiry, targeting its grants in a way that the federal government, which now dwarfed foundational spending on international relations research, could not. Between 1946 and 1953 the Corporation funded area studies programs at twenty-five universities, seeking a detailed understanding of regions overseas and making no effort to democratize the specialist knowledge thereby created, while it was also encouraging the development of international relations departments and advanced research institutes. With the G. I. Bill drawing veterans into universities, the prospect of a generation of college graduates competent in world affairs issues was alluring and widely thought likely to create an informed public opinion of some kind. But this solution to the problem of a democratic foreign policy was not what Emeny had in mind: in what ways, after all, would such students stay involved after their graduation without a World Affairs Council to keep them engaged?[9]

Over at Rockefeller Plaza the writing had been on the wall for some time, the continuing personal interest of the Rockefeller family notwithstanding. Joseph Willits of the Rockefeller Foundation had promised the Association five more years of funding at the end of the war, but he remained convinced of the need to change tack after that. "I know that one may argue, as Brooks

Emeny does," he wrote in 1945, that world developments called "for a gigantic program of adult education," but even Rockefeller grants could make little real contribution to that process amid a deluge of "newspaper services, radio, public discussion, books, magazines and the educational effect of a Second World War." Where philanthropy could make more of a difference was in the higher realms of knowledge, Willits thought. The published results of specialized research would of course remain "available to all," Rockefeller official Bryce Wood wrote in 1947, but the Foundation would no longer fund "specialized methods of presenting it to the public." Wood belittled Emeny's plans to the contrary, dubbing educational efforts "operation rat hole." Adults could never be made to go to public meetings or read pamphlets, Wood argued, and they would have to be reached through the press and the radio instead; schoolchildren, who were forced to go to class "unless they can outrun the probation officers," might be taught the consequences of global responsibility more properly, but that was a project for the longer term, and for someone else to fund.[10]

As the Rockefeller Foundation sank its grants into academic research, including "realist" theories that denigrated the potential of public opinion and saw successful foreign policies as those capable of withstanding popular influence, Emeny watched on, furious. "Academicians do not rule the world," he had once huffed to Nelson Rockefeller, and he protested this generational shift in the structures and sensibilities of scholarly inquiry with appreciable foresight. "Hundreds of thousands of dollars are to be put annually in the universities and colleges of the country for the financing of international studies in general and regional research in particular," he warned his board in April 1948, but the private foundations were abandoning their duties to the common good. "The pouring of money solely into institutions of advanced research and for the training of specialized scholars will prove of little avail in the development of sound democratic thinking about foreign policy," he told the Corporation that December, "unless the products of such research as well as the trained scholars who are engaged in research activities can be brought into closer touch with the public as a whole." If expertise was not democratized, in Deweyan vein, then the risks to the United States would be grave.[11]

But Emeny was grappling with forces that he could only dimly perceive. Wood, who was invited to the Overhills summit and heard nothing from Emeny to change his mind, was one of the few to understand the basic causes of this shift. When the United States had played an officially diffident role in the major questions of war and peace, Wood wrote in February 1948, the Rockefeller

Foundation had been forced to adopt a "broadly international program" to promote peace, one that had sought to reduce frictions through the League of Nations, the creation of transnational networks of enlightened expertise, and appeals to public opinion. Now that the United States had taken responsibility for world order, the Foundation could promote peace by reinforcing US foreign policy itself: the Foundation had already turned the League essentially into a think tank as fascism dimmed its faith in public opinion and deliberation, and it would reorient the US foreign policy community in the same way. The consequent rise of the "military-intellectual complex," as historian Ron Robin has called it, came laced with bitter consequences. Even setting secret, government-funded research aside, the think tanks and other institutions created around the end of World War II that aspired to create useful knowledge—above all the RAND Corporation, founded in 1948—emerged from a profound distrust of democratic politics, Daniel Bessner has argued, indeed on the premise that experts could and should stand in where incompetent, apathetic publics could not. Research once valued for its contributions to public debate was of little worth when *Time* magazine, with its millions of readers, had dozens of its own foreign correspondents. The Association was cut off not just from the classified information on which ever more policy was formulated, but from policymakers too. Raymond Leslie Buell and William Stone had roamed the State Department at will; Brooks Emeny and Vera Micheles Dean had no hope of a brief appointment with an assistant secretary of state, let alone an intimate discussion with a senior official. There was a world to run, after all.[12]

If there was no money available for Emeny's wildest plans, then, there was no money for the public facing research that had made the Association's reputation either. Rockefeller pulled the plug on the education and research departments alike when it bade the Association farewell with a terminal grant of $20,000 in 1950, the last tranche in a total of at least $870,000 since 1933, not including travel fellowships and other minor grants, nor the donations of Rockefellers great and small, most notably the $201,500 that John D. Rockefeller Jr. had given after 1925. The withdrawal of a quarter of the Association's annual budget required harsh cuts. Emeny targeted the research department, proposing to disband the staff. Dean had approved the hiring of her friend a year earlier, but "wrecking" the Association as she knew it was too much for her to bear. Half the staff stayed, the other half left, mostly for the State Department. While the national security bureaucracy and the university sector grew, offering opportunities for male scholars that had been unheard of a decade earlier, there was little hope of resurrecting the towering position that the Association's research department had once held. What hope was left, another conflict waged in the name of democracy would soon kill off.[13]

## McCarthyism and the Cold War

Vera Micheles Dean was the voice of the Association, and she spoke with a Russian accent. Born in 1903 to Alexander Micheles, a Jewish businessman who had lived in New York City for a while before returning to St. Petersburg to represent American companies in Russia, and Nadine, who translated *Peter Pan* and other children's literature from English, Vera had a comfortable childhood. Schooled at home, her teacher "embodied the most ardent and inspiring qualities of the Russia spirit," she later wrote. He joined the Bolsheviks in 1917. Perfectly aware of the injustices of czarism, the Micheles were nonetheless no friends of the Party, and the five of them fled before the October revolution, heading for their summer house in Terijoki, Finland. The revolution came all the same. They hid as the Red Army scavenged for food and hunted for opponents; looters ravaged their home in Petrograd. Even so, Vera later looked fondly on these difficult years. "The Bolshevik revolution left no residue of bitterness or resentment in my life," she wrote in 1947, for in the end she "benefited" from it: she was sent to the United States.[14]

Micheles arrived in New York aged sixteen and alone. She was profoundly gifted, speaking eight languages, and worked as a stenographer before heading to Cambridge to study at Radcliffe College. She continued into graduate work, first at Yale on a Carnegie Endowment fellowship, then back at Radcliffe, where she wrote a doctorate on the international law of governments *de facto*, focusing on potential international recognition of the Soviet Union. Buell hired her as a Russianist before she had finished her thesis in 1928, but she eventually started speaking and writing on much broader themes, in part out of necessity. The New York attorney she had married, William Johnson Dean, died unexpectedly in 1936, forcing her to earn enough to support their two young children, one with whom she was still pregnant when William passed away. Unable to take up a role at the League of Women Voters or a similar group, where white women extended their authority in world affairs on a voluntary rather than a professional basis, Dean wrote voluminously, penning contemporary histories, freelancing for the *Nation* and the *New Republic*, and embarking on a lucrative speaking career. Long before Pearl Harbor she had become one of the most recognizable foreign policy experts in the land, a genuinely public intellectual whose expertise stemmed from popular acclaim. Dean was hugely admired among the educated white women who dominated world affairs audiences and drew bigger crowds than almost all her male peers—whether columnists, foreign leaders, or even, as the Cleveland Council found in its 1940–1941 season, Undersecretary of State Sumner Welles.[15]

If Dean became celebrated as a general internationalist, it was as a Russianist that her fame made her notorious after World War II. She had often downplayed Stalinist repression to praise the economic growth that accompanied it, as many Russianists did before the end of the war, but as views of the Soviet Union soured with the rise of Cold War antagonisms, she became distinctive in her willingness to see the best in Russian motives, refusing to stick to clear moral divisions and instead drawing parallels between her ancestral and adoptive homelands. "The Russians resemble the Americans more than any other people," she wrote in one of several wartime pamphlets that she hoped would solidify the bond. She tracked the Red Army's march to Berlin without concern, believing that the alliance foreshadowed great-power cooperation after the war, a view that earned her a private "spanking" from Buell, as he put it, for abandoning her "former belief in collective security in favor of Soviet unilateralism." She lost Buell's friendship before he died, but not her confidence in her analysis. "In spite of setbacks and mistakes," she wrote in 1947 in *Russia: Menace or Promise*, her most controversial book, "Russia is traveling in a direction that will eventually bring it out on the high road of spiritual and political, as well as material, progress."[16]

Holding firm to prewar attitudes towards objectivity and free speech that became less tenable as anticommunism swept through intellectual circles, Dean tried to right the balance by launching an attack not on Soviet endeavors, but on US foreign policy, the flaws of which she thought demonstrated the citizenry's unpreparedness for world leadership. She did not advocate a pro-Soviet view by habit, but she did see that communism might offer something capitalism—short of the social democracy she championed—as of yet did not. "The kind of society the Russians are striving to create in the USSR," she wrote in critique of Winston Churchill's "iron curtain" speech in March 1946, "is a society to which masses of people in other, even more backward, areas of the world have been aspiring." She maintained that the United States was not only failing to compete ideologically with the Soviet Union in what she perceived would quickly turn into a global conflict, but was making the situation worse by casting dark aspersions about the center-left in Europe, allying with colonial powers against independence movements, and buttressing white supremacy at home. Even the Marshall Plan disappointed her in its unilateral sidestepping of the United Nations, though she sufficiently admired its generosity to lead the research staff in writing a supportive explanatory pull-out for the *Washington Post*, which the Committee for the Marshall Plan reprinted one hundred thousand times.[17]

What really bothered Dean about early Cold War foreign policy was its abandonment of genuine internationalism for ill-concealed power politics. She saw internationalism not as the synonym for US primacy that it had recently become for others within the foreign policy community, but as a more modest spirit that could guide diplomacy, one that would keep the United States from "isolationism" on the one hand and "imperialism" on the other. Dean was anything but a utopian, and she drew on a pragmatism that she wrote came from the gendered realities of rearing a family. "It might not be amiss," she ventured to suggest in 1942, to "learn a few lessons from a section of the world's population which, in the past, has found it practically impossible to affect the course of world affairs, although forced to endure the ill-effects of their mismanagement." The "average" woman did not "assume that her loved ones are perfect," she said: mothers hoped for the "ultimate improvement and success for the least promising ugly duckling" and knew, or learned, that compromises were needed, that solving one problem often brought on another, and that resorting to force was ultimately unavoidable. But a mother also knew, Dean said, that idealism was essential to sustain people through the "trivial, often sordid, details of day-to-day living." And nobody could survive alone.[18]

Combine Dean's views of the Soviet Union with her commitment to internationalism in the prewar style, and a critique of postwar US foreign policy was unavoidable. The Truman Doctrine, as she saw it, might well have meant that "American intervention in world affairs is inevitable," but it also meant that such intervention would "assume the character of what we once denounced as imperialism." Dean reserved particular ire for containment policy, seeing that communists were unlikely converts to capitalist democracy and arguing that the strategy made no tactical or historical sense. As the czars had "sought again and again to break through the containment levees thrown up during the eighteenth and nineteenth centuries," she wrote, Stalin would surely follow suit. Containment above all revealed the hypocrisy of US policy. Russia, as she always called it, had undermined the Yalta accords, she admitted, but "it would be well to bear in mind that Russia—if perhaps less concerned with the niceties of diplomatic usages—is not essentially different in its great-power manifestations from Britain and the United States."

149

Russia often used political violence at home and abroad, she conceded, but "we forget that both we and the British passed through revolutions and civil wars before we succeeded in establishing stable democratic institutions." Russia interfered with sovereign states along its border, she agreed, but the United States had its own empire and was going far further than Stalin ever dared, acquiring strategic bases that circled the globe. Russia was not solely to blame for Cold War tensions, in other words; the United States was not an exceptional nation, but an imperial great power like any other.[19]

Even before the State Department had dreamt up the Marshall Plan, Dean had become a target of anticommunist activists. Alfred Kohlberg, a textiles exporter who waged a destructive legal fight against the Institute of Pacific Relations for its supposed harboring of radicals, eventually quit his Association membership in protest in April 1948, loudly accusing Dean of nothing less than "treason." Dean abandoned her admiration of Henry Wallace in advance of his run for the White House in 1948, but the FBI investigated her anyway, finally resolving in 1954 that if she had been "pro-Soviet in her writings," she had certainly never "engaged in any form of subversive activity." Controversy had long since turned to anger within the Association. Mrs. Percy Madeira, a member of the Philadelphia branch, fired off a twenty-seven-page critique of *Russia: Menace or Promise* to headquarters, declaring the book a "simply confusing" defense of the Soviets given the contradictory portrait offered in George F. Kennan's "X" article at the same time. Milwaukee officials reported that "at a time when terms like 'red-baiters' and 'fellow-travelers' are tossed about so indiscriminately," Dean's views were causing resignations. One Hartford branch veteran told Emeny that the Association's "curious pinkish aura" was making fundraising harder than ever. Even as some branches refused to let Dean appear on their stages, her response remained steadfast. For a scholar "to live at peace with his conscience, he must continue to speak his mind as long as the opportunity to do so exists," she wrote in 1953. "Only if we persist in the determination to maintain genuine democracy here can we hope to inject the same determination into foreign policy."[20]

For Dean, these attacks mattered not just as a mild personal irritant, but as evidence of the much more significant threat that the Cold War posed to the progressive vision of a democratic foreign policy. She feared that a "wall between the people and government" had been erected as early as October 1948, and suggested that the "reiteration of dramatic appeals to stave off impending catastrophes" to which the Truman administration resorted had created "a skeptical 'wolf, wolf!' attitude." She was deeply troubled by the increasingly prevalent notion that "world affairs are so complicated that the citizen has no way of making up his mind on controversial issues." Shortly after Truman announced that the United States would develop a hydrogen bomb in 1950, a judgment he had taken without public consultation despite its potentially dire consequences, she wrote that the "secrecy surrounding top policy decisions" was giving "even well-informed and civic-minded individuals a sense of fatalism which paralyzes the sense of personal responsibility." The entire conceptual framework of the conflict, she thought, undermined "popular democracy." "The term 'cold war' has encouraged the erroneous idea that 'our side' must register continuous clear-cut 'victories,'" she wrote in the spring of 1950, "otherwise our opponent will be victorious, and we shall suffer 'defeat.'" Perhaps democracy asked too much, she acknowledged, of citizens who needed to become "acquainted overnight with the thousand and one intricate details of relations between nations" and the "gradual, sometimes imperceptible, adjustments and readjustments" that marked diplomacy. But if the response was the removal of foreign policy from public consent, she wrote as Senator Joseph McCarthy began to slander the State Department, then the world would face "grave peril."[21]

As the second Red Scare showed educators like Dean how much they had left to do to educate the citizenry of primitive responses to world affairs, the same wave of anticommunism imperiled the institutions through which they hoped to do it. The Institute of Pacific Relations did not recover from the blow: its relationship with *Amerasia*, a leftist journal whose offices were found to contain classified documents during police raids in 1945, caused a lasting scandal. Several men tied to the Association as well as the Institute faced significant consequences. T. A. Bisson, a socialist who had undertaken a perilous voyage to Yan'an on a Rockefeller Foundation fellowship to interview Mao Zedong for the Association in 1937, was dismissed from his posting in the military government of Japan in 1947, interrogated before Congress in 1952, and fired by the University of California in 1953. Once the equal in stature of Owen Lattimore, Bisson spent the rest of his career teaching at a small women's college in Ohio. Bisson's replacement on the Association's research staff, Lawrence K. Rosinger, had moved on to the Institute in 1948; he asserted his fifth-amendment rights in front of McCarran Committee and wound up with a faculty position at a community college in Detroit. William Stone, so long a central figure at the Association and more briefly an *Amerasia* editor, became a *cause célèbre*, having risen through the State Department to play a key role in its overseas propaganda efforts. Barely left-wing at all, Stone was slurred by McCarthy himself, placed under loyalty review, and—despite receiving his clearance—forced to resign from the State Department in 1952 by Secretary Acheson, to the outrage of his mentor, Connecticut Senator William Benton, former assistant secretary for public affairs. Stone's obituaries remembered him only as a yachting journalist.[22]

Suspicion shuddered through the major foreign policy institutions. The FBI investigated the Association in 1950 but found nothing seriously amiss. Alger Hiss was brought before the House Un-American Activities Committee in 1948, tried for perjury in 1949, and convicted in 1950, almost tearing the Carnegie Endowment apart in the process. Congressmen Carroll Reece and E. E. Cox probed the Rockefeller and Carnegie foundations, searching for evidence of support for subversives. If all that had an undoubted chilling effect, so too did the ideological demands made of allies whose influence had been crucial to the Association's cause, whether the peace movement, which entered a period of relative quiescence, or the women's movement. Both the American Association of University Women and the League of Women Voters held faith in the United Nations well into the Korean War, urging conciliation with the Soviet Union much like Dean. Coming under constant government pressure and external attack, their leaders—now no longer drawn from the suffrage generation—had no choice but to take up the Cold War, eventually becoming combatants in the battle for hearts and minds through their voluntary work in civil defense programs, public diplomacy programs, and more. The League's membership rolls thickened, but at the cost of a conservative acceptance of domestic political structures, which compounded the ways in which the Cold War otherwise reinforced gender hierarchies, revitalized notions of female domesticity, and strengthened what Elaine Tyler May has called the "apolitical tenor" of the age, at least among the white middle class. If the League of Women Voters as an institution and League members as activists remained important to world affairs education, the radical edge of their commitment to participatory democracy was blunted.[23]

The Association could not ward off this stink. The branches distanced themselves from Emeny, who was caught in the tempest as an erstwhile treasure of the Institute. Outside the Northeast, there were places where public, contrarian discussion of foreign affairs came to endanger not just reputations, but livelihoods. By 1960, the Association would have to mount a legal defense against an Atlanta grand jury that issued a presentment declaring it to be "insidious and subversive," a judgment it made at the behest of the American Legion. John Birch Society members later disrupted meetings sponsored by the Association, especially in the South and West. Dan Smoot, a prominent conservative commentator who cut his teeth attacking the Dallas Council on World Affairs, accused the Association of being part of an "invisible government" trying to "convert America into a socialist state and then make it a unit in a one-world socialist system." If only, Dean might have said.[24]

More immediately, the second Red Scare coincided with a crisis in the model of foreign policy engagement promoted by the Association and its allies. Donors of a wealth comparable to the long-forgotten Thomas Lamont and Otto Kahn now faced immense income tax bills. Radio stations no longer needed Association research to write the news or Association researchers to interpret it. Regular members no longer depended on Association literature, one survey revealing that only one in eight of them considered it to be among their most valuable sources of information. The membership dropped below prewar numbers. Those who remained enrolled were as unrepresentative of American society as ever, with 80 percent of them being college graduates at a time when just 6 percent of Americans had degrees; the average age of a member, statistically highly likely to be a white woman, was about sixty. Even the structures of high-society life had shifted, the last remnants of the Gilded Age a distant memory. Harvey H. Bundy expressed the typical criticism with the common condescension at a State Department meeting in 1951. "The day of the great luncheon with 200," the former Boston branch chairman said, "three-quarters of them women who want to be politely stimulated so they can go home and talk about how much they can talk about foreign policy, is gone."[25]

Emeny knew all this: he was promoting a model in which educators improved the quality and quantity of foreign policy discussion in places where citizens already met and talked, rather than restricting themselves to institutions that spoke to foreign policy alone. But institutions are sticky and the upheaval involved threatened to be catastrophic. The Association faced insolvency at the end of 1950, and Dean was scapegoated as the cause. Eustace Seligman, a partner of Allen and John Foster Dulles at the Sullivan, Cromwell law firm, had never been a fan, warning Dean in July 1947 that the stridency of her views meant the Association had "ceased to be solely an objective fact-finding organization." Dean's interpretation of the facts had been welcome when they had supported intervention from 1939 to 1941, but they were less so when they led her to critique the government line after 1946. Seligman consequently proposed closing the research department, shuttering the Washington bureau, and creating a committee to consider what, if anything, the Association would publish after 1951. That committee—which included Hiss's replacement at the Carnegie Endowment, Joseph E. Johnson, as well as *Time* editor Thomas S. Matthews—advised the Association to end the *Reports*, curtail the Headlines, and make the *Bulletin* a forum for outside authors. All involved assumed that Dean would resign in protest, but she refused; the board reluctantly allowed her to edit a biweekly *Bulletin*, retaining her title even as she took on lectureships at Barnard College, Harvard, and other schools.[26]

If the Association's commitment to research and education in equal measure had cracked around Pearl Harbor, it had not then been clear to what extent it could rebuild its stature after the defeat of the Axis powers. It had its answer. Though not inevitable, its decline had become likely because of the specific form US primacy turned out to take; forged in war, it stoked war again. As historian Mary Dudziak has argued, there would be no peacetime now, only "wartime," a constant crusade that aimed to contain communism and sustain US leadership in the same breath. Even when it was "cold" rather than "hot," the Cold War cast foreign policy into a permanent state of emergency, one thought to justify the full extension of what James T. Sparrow has called the "warfare state" and that necessitated softer forms of the restrictions on democratic life that had so often been imposed during periods of war. This might have been the foreign policy of a democracy, but it was not the democratic foreign policy sought of old. The question now was whether the institutions that represented those hopes would collapse as well. Seligman feared so, telling the board in October 1951 that the Association should proceed with liquidation. It needed a savior.[27]

## The Ford Foundation and Adult Education

What was the Ford Foundation going to do with all that cash? Since its founding in 1936, the Foundation had given away only small amounts of money to causes around Detroit. But after the death of Henry Ford in 1947, the Foundation found itself with stocks worth nearly half a billion dollars. Such a sum made it the wealthiest philanthropy in the world, able to spend in quantities beyond the wildest dreams of any Rockefeller grant officer. How to distribute it was a problem the Foundation's board left to a committee led by a Californian lawyer, H. Rowan Gaither Jr., who tasked a staff with harvesting the suggestions of a thousand notable figures. Gaither's report, submitted in November 1949 and published the following year, therefore reflected an elite consensus on how such a fortune should be spent. Like Rockefeller before it, the Ford Foundation sought a more peaceful world through the exercise of US power, but a perhaps more surprising development, given recent decisions at the Rockefeller Foundation, was that Gaither urged Ford to throw itself into the problem of a democratic foreign policy. The Ford Foundation could best help, Gaither's report stated, by "assisting democracy to meet that challenge and to realize its ideals," strengthening it against those who tried to "stamp out dissent and measure loyalty by conformity" on the one hand and against the military establishment and the secrecy that surrounded decision-making on the other. Democracy in this view was not a set of "rigid rules" nor a set of institutions, but a freedom enacted in daily life; among its enemies were the "apathy, misunderstanding, and ignorance" that posed "a great danger to self-government."[28]

Progressive ideals, it seemed, died hard: the Gaither Report expressed the familiar view, in familiar terms, that an informed, active, educated public was necessary for the security of the United States as a bulwark against both "isolationism" and McCarthyism. Ford's International Affairs division should therefore support "independent and nonpartisan" means of getting the "relevant facts and judgments" on foreign policy to the "electorate at large," Gaither's staff wrote, for "our Government and the United Nations cannot effectively formulate or execute policy in international affairs without public understanding and support." In a slightly different context, though still under the rubric of strengthening democracy, Gaither also wrote that Ford should "encourage people to become better informed about, and to participate in, the solution of the different types of problems they share," above all through "the 'community workshop' in which scientists or educators act as social engineers." The tension was the old one, between the need to promote expert conceptions of foreign policy and the desire to create a public able to shape those conceptions from below, constraining policymakers when necessary. Right from the start, then, Ford struggled to define what, or who, a philanthropically-sponsored democratic foreign policy was supposed to be for.[29]

With the encouragement of John J. McCloy, formerly an inactive Association director who had served as the US High Commissioner for Occupied Germany and would chair the Council on Foreign Relations after 1954, Ford's International Affairs division spent its first years gestating a program to "establish a kind and degree of public understanding which would serve as a basis for wise planning and skillful operation by the U.S. government," as one memo put it. That program was stillborn, but other Ford projects grew quickly, especially the Fund for Adult Education, which it created soon after the arrival as its president of Paul G. Hoffman, who had risen from selling Studebaker cars to administering the Marshall Plan. Under C. Scott Fletcher, a protégé of Hoffman's at Studebaker and Benton's at the Encyclopedia Britannica and the Committee for Economic Development, the Fund's dominance over the adult education movement dwarfed even that of the Carnegie Corporation before it. Handed a $47 million budget and a significant amount of independence, Fletcher tried to fuse corporate marketing techniques, educational mass media, and small-group discussion to create "mature, wise, and responsible citizens who can participate intelligently in a free society."[30]

Brooks Emeny could barely believe what he was seeing. He had no links to any of the Ford Foundation's leaders, though Hoffman had occasionally given speeches at Association branches and World Affairs Councils; the similarity of Ford's vision to his own testified to the persistent power of his ideas even in a rapidly changing foreign policy community. "We believe that the Ford Foundation will have an especial interest in the work of the Association," Emeny wrote as soon as the Gaither Report came out, "because our aims and purposes so closely parallel the objectives of the Ford Foundation as expressed in its statement of policy." Unless the "average voter" came to learn "the fundamental facts and problems of our new world leadership, we cannot succeed in the development of a sound and effective foreign policy," he told Fletcher, explaining that radio, newspapers, and magazines were worse than useless without facilities that rooted discussion of the information within them in community life. Shocked to learn from the *New York Times* that the Foundation intended to spread programs "such as that of the Cleveland Council of World Affairs," despite having given him no warning at all, Emeny repeatedly sent proposals to Ford's offices in Pasadena, California, only to find them returned with requests for more ambition. By June, he had asked for a grant of $3 million, triple the total contribution of the Rockefeller Foundation over three decades, with $200,000 to be given up front to "provide proof of the soundness of our approach."[31]

Cleveland aside, however, there was scarce evidence that Emeny's approach was in fact sound. The Association's National Program had started slowly, mostly supporting new Councils that were formed in San Francisco, Philadelphia, and Boston, cities where foreign policy activism was already vibrant enough to make consolidation sensible. Emeny had helped where he could, making speeches and recommending graduates from Cleveland's training programs as candidates to staff new Councils, but the energy in these cases came from experienced local organizers who chafed at his interference. Emeny's rhetoric otherwise outstripped his limited administrative skills. He explained in the *Bulletin* that the days of "small lectureship societies and the distribution and sale of a limited number of world affairs studies" were gone, for it was clear by 1948 that "the knowledge and judgment of a few citizens on foreign policy do not automatically filter down through the mass of the population." But this criticism of the methods of trickle-down diplomacy alienated the existing membership, and even the more ambitious branches refused to expand their work along the lines he suggested. The board fired the first National Program director, Clarence Peters; the second, Thomas Power, made little headway.[32]

Emeny's vision still appealed to parts of the foreign policy community, though. With the Rockefeller Foundation withdrawn, the Carnegie Corporation stepped up, supporting new Councils with seed grants and offering to fund the Association itself. Claiming to have received expressions of interest from eighty-four communities, Emeny requested $150,000 in January 1949. Carnegie officials, including former Council on Foreign Relations staffer Whitney Shepardson, were enthused at the idea, if not at its lack of practicality. Even Shepardson's colleagues at Council House proved excited when they were asked for their views on the matter, suggesting that if Emeny's aim of creating a hundred Councils implied "a gross exaggeration of the degree of latent interest in international affairs," the fact that US foreign policy was taking on such vast responsibilities so far in advance of presumed public readiness still meant he deserved his chance at a "miracle." Carnegie agreed, cutting the target to twenty Councils and granting $93,000, a sum topped up by the Rockefeller Brothers Fund, which continued the Rockefeller family's personal support even as their Foundation pulled back.[33]

But at this critical point, with the Soviets in possession of atomic weapons, the Chinese Communist Party ascendant, and the Korean War convincing the White House to promote the apocalyptic confrontation envisaged in NSC-68 as the public basis for US foreign policy, the Association simply could not cope. As of August 1951, only eight of its thirty-two affiliates had professional direction; only three had more than one thousand members. Constant criticism of the branches eroded enthusiasm, while headquarters offered little more than flying visits from Emeny and Power. Some affiliates were innovating, with discussion forums ongoing in Philadelphia and Pittsburgh, television shows on the air in Milwaukee, and polls being taken in Providence, but progress otherwise was meager. Carnegie officials became so angry they considered asking for the Corporation's money back, a rare rebuke. Emeny was forced to admit in November 1952 that the Association had "not achieved in specific terms much of what it hoped." This was not just a personal failure, but a failure that risked discrediting the entire idea that the public could be relied upon when it came to foreign policy. Carnegie learned its lesson. One internal assessment concluded that its university grants for area studies and international relations programs had paid off, but "the more complex problem of discovering ways in which the American people can be given a clearer comprehension of the realities which condition their survival" was one "as yet unsolved." Its willingness to confront that problem was diminishing.[34]

Ford Foundation officials paid no attention to the complaints of their Carnegie counterparts, and even the State Department remained convinced for the time being that the Cleveland model could be replicated at scale. Assistant Secretary of State for Public Affairs Edward W. Barrett told Ford in May 1951 that if it wanted to help Foggy Bottom with "domestic information projects," as it was already assisting with propaganda initiatives abroad, it should fund World Affairs Councils to the extent that they could "make the community organization a real contributing part of the community as a whole." State offered its views on target cities, although the Association staff member who went to coordinate with its Office of Public Affairs, a Harvard-educated graduate of Emeny's training programs named Alexander Allport, was not impressed with its choices. Either way, in December 1951 the Fund for Adult Education granted $355,000 to Emeny's National Program, with so little due diligence that it seemed as if—following the Rockefeller and Carnegie pattern—this was the kind of thing that a big philanthropy ought, almost automatically, to be doing.[35]

Even if Ford had decided before consulting the State Department that it would support the Association, State's involvement might suggest that the Council project was merely one more weapon in the arsenal of elites seeking hegemony at home for their policies abroad. Councils, after all, received plenty of help from State, which sent them speakers for dinners, made them distribution centers for its publications, and worked with local activists to sponsor conferences. The appointment of Chester S. Williams as acting leader of the National Program in March 1952 might have given that sense too, but rather than proving how similar the approaches of State and the Association still were, the hiring of a warrior for adult education instead demonstrated how much ground participatory methods had lost at the Office of Public Affairs, not least because they were too slow and unreliable to secure support for specific policies compared to the more direct methods of ascendent psychological warriors. Educational forms still had their part to play in the early Cold War. Williams had spent 1949 working on the World Town Hall Meeting of the Air, a government-sponsored, thirty-four thousand-mile junket on which voluntary association leaders—including Emeny and League of Women Voters president Anna Lord Strauss—spread the word on behalf of the democratic method. But if voluntary association life still mattered to policymakers, it seemed to matter more as a propaganda tool than as a force in its own right.[36]

With the World Affairs Council program, Williams saw an opportunity to correct this drift towards state control, a chance to "develop a sense of self-confidence in large numbers of citizens concerning their ability to influence the direction of world affairs," as he put it in April 1952. Having spent a decade waging educational warfare against fascism at the Office of War Information and then against communism at State, Williams saw the Council project primarily in ideological terms, an effort to help citizens "encourage policies which will use American power to insure the survival of our free society." Fifty or so cities could support a full World Affairs Council, he thought after visiting a dozen of them. Others could set up an open World Affairs Forum, run by volunteers, or a smaller World Affairs Committee of up to one hundred people. Williams crucially proposed to link all these groups to state institutions, confronting a problem all too few Deweyans had dealt with. He imagined an annual World Affairs National Assembly, to be addressed by the president as well as officials from the State Department, the United Nations, and NATO, which would "provide an opportunity for the expression of views from the 'grass roots' of America." While Williams inquired with State as to whether President Truman could give the project impetus through a series of events "à la the cooperative forum technique," he asked the Fund for Adult Education for $491,500 as a prelude to a request for $2 million more. He planned to set up forty to sixty groups in advance of the first National Assembly, which he penciled in for January 1954.[37]

Again, the moment passed. Ford became even more willing to back the Association after Hoffman intervened in a fight in Los Angeles over whether the use of UNESCO publications in schools was unpatriotic. Hoffman defended the internationalist cause in ardent testimony before the city's school board in August 1952 but was heckled by nationalist opponents who ominously included several groups of the conservative, anticommunist women who were starting to mount a counterattack against progressive internationalists. Hoffman lost the battle but continued the war, plotting with other local

Republicans to form a Los Angeles World Affairs Council and handing the Association its massive grant. By then, though, Williams had already resigned, furiously telling Fletcher that the Association was beset by an arcane structure, a poor staff, a weak board, and a worrying habit of financial impropriety. "Only a few leaders in the field know the inside facts," Williams wrote, and without drastic change there would be "no future for the organization."[38]

Exactly when Emeny's dreams seemed about to come true, he had no choice but to quit. The Council project had been an extraordinarily personal enterprise, one in which a single man, albeit with his wife's wealth behind him, had convinced much of the foreign policy community to support an idiosyncratic, blinkered, yet powerful vision for how to reconcile diplomacy with democracy. But at the heart of this confluence of the individual, the institutional, and the ideological had always beat darkness. Tragedy had convinced the Emenys to start their quest, with the deaths of Winifred's parents and the Emenys' first, young daughter. Tragedy now ended it. Winifred had never recovered from that triple blow, her depression worsening until she had to spend a period in hospital in the summer of 1950. One day in March 1951, with Brooks and their eldest daughter touring colleges in Florida, she collected Winifred, aged twelve, and Josephine, aged six, from school, drove them into the garage of their mansion at Deer Park, Connecticut, and left the engine running, locking the doors. The governess found them too late. The suicide and the murders made national news; they destroyed Brooks. He held on for a while before resigning in October 1952.[39]

Emeny left a blueprint, one he lacked the ability and the will to carry out, but a blueprint all the same. He left his secret, too. The Emenys' investment in the Cleveland Council was still not widely known years after they had left town; it was a sum far larger than the Ford funds that the Association planned to distribute to any of the new Councils it hoped would prosper, despite its awareness that the culture of giving that had previously aided world affairs education had dissipated. The Emenys' investment in the Association was just as obscure. In March 1952, the board wrote off $57,388 in loans from Emeny, made up of his salary, his lecture fees, and sundry other contributions. Later that year, the Association told Congress that the Emenys had donated a further $61,365 since 1947. These amounts of money represented a greater personal investment in the Association than even the Carnegie Corporation had thought wise, keeping it alive. All this was rumored at most; if the secret had become public it would have cast fatal doubt on the viability of the project, even with the might of the Ford Foundation behind it. Staying on the committee that supervised the Council project, Emeny would now find out whether it would survive.[40]

## World Affairs Are Your Affairs!

The lights went down. There had been a procession, with the flags of the United States and the United Nations carried down the aisle of a radio station auditorium on Euclid Avenue, one night in March 1952. The Cleveland Heights Little Symphony had played; the Case Western Reserve Glee Club had sung; there had been remarks. A film clicked on. "Today," the narrator intoned, "issues between nations are so complex and baffling, that war and the threat of war have become the dominant forces in human affairs." A factory owner spoke, worrying that defense production left him without supplies. A boy told his parents that he wanted to be a doctor but was worried about the draft. A couple said goodnight, resolving to marry before the man, shown uniformed, went overseas. "Today," the narrator continued, "the need for a public understanding of the problems arising from the relationship of the United States and the rest of the world, is of compelling importance." But surveys revealed that citizens lacked basic facts, he continued, the camera eyeing a *New York Times* article headlined "What We Don't Know Can Hurt Us." "All over the nation," he said, "people are becoming acutely aware that they must have facilities which will help them to understand the great issues that confront them, and, as well, help them to formulate their own policies and make their own decisions." The picture panned to the Society for Savings Building, and to Emeny, behind his desk.

The Cleveland Council was the answer. Shots of a housewife washing dishes and mechanics at work illustrated that the Council represented "a cross-section of the entire community," with "volunteers in every age and income group." Scenes told how the fictional Walnut Hill Fortnightly Club, a suburban civic group, got speakers and films from the Council, then sent its members there to train in discussion theory before appearing on one of its television shows as citizen-expert panelists. More footage relayed how the Junior Councils on World Affairs had taken trips to the United Nations, coming back to speak to fifty adults per student. Still more outlined the Council's foreign student services, showing dances, international nights, even a young woman clasping a copy of Kennan's *American Diplomacy*, a paperback sensation at the time. Marshall, now retired, lectured a Cleveland ballroom about the need to "ascertain facts" and "shed ourselves of our emotions." At the end, a woman told her friends back in Port City that she had met Shepherd Witman and wanted to form a Council of her own. Would it make a difference, one asked? The secretary of state had told her it would, she replied. "We know that no policy will succeed unless it has the support of the people," he had said in a letter she had received a week earlier.[41]

This was the work of Louis de Rochemont, the most watched documentary filmmaker in America as the producer of Henry R. Luce's *March of Time* newsreels and, at the time *World Affairs Are Your Affairs* came out, planning an animated version of *Animal Farm* for the use of the Central Intelligence Agency. Presenting the Council less as a Cold War entity than in the classic sense of a democratic contribution to peace, the film employed the amateur dramatics of more than two hundred Clevelanders, cast Witman in a starring role, and cost the Fund for Adult Education an astonishing $65,000, just one part of its advertising campaign for its vision of a democratic foreign policy. De Rochemont's film imagined the Council appealing to the masses of the city, but it was hardly meant to reach masses in itself; the film was put to use at the end of one of the Fund's experimental study-discussion programs, also called "World Affairs Are Your Affairs," in which participants paid to view *March of Time* films, talk through a book of foreign policy essays, and finish by watching Witman at work. Otherwise, de Rochemont's film was intended for civic leaders, the kinds of people the Association hoped would follow the example of the fictional woman from Port City and establish a Council for themselves.[42]

Not every city was Cleveland, of course, and the Association had to fit what it could of the Cleveland model to communities of different types. The Fund provided the Association with the resources to start five regional offices and staff them with men who scoured cities, states, even entire coastlines for signs of interest in world affairs, wielding seed grants from their Ford-sponsored Community Investment Fund. When they found such signs, they might have been influenced by academic literature on how opinions moved or on how communities should be organized, but their work was mostly instinctive. Allport, deputy to the new Association chief, former Philadelphia World Affairs Council and Swarthmore University president John W. Nason, wrote that the typical first step was to research the "market," for while the "entire population" was the ultimate target of adult education, cities had to be ranked by "potential," a metric that comprised past activities, financial resources, and "strategic location." The staff then sought to find out who could run a Council, primarily by interviewing citizens assumed to be powerful as well as representatives of voluntary associations, above all the League of Women Voters. There would be a speech by a policymaker or other personality to flush activists and potential members into view and to demonstrate to them that the government and the foreign policy community really did believe in the "effect of public opinion on policy decisions." The nucleus thereby created would then decide what kind of Council made sense for the community, from a university-affiliated service bureau to a full-blown effort to replicate Cleveland's success.[43]

That, at least, was the theory. The reality was sketched in the composite scenario Nason compiled in his final report to the Fund in April 1957. Imagine Middletown, that fraught symbol of American normality, Nason wrote. Staffers had already picked Middletown as a target when the vice-president of a local bank wrote asking after the Council program. Field staff conducted a community survey, interviewing editors and media men, professors and labor leaders, taking six months to present their findings to the small group of Middletowners, perhaps fourteen strong, who were actively interested. It took another six months for them to raise money and hire a director, a former journalist, whose salary was paid with the help of an Association seed grant. Once the Council opened, it partnered with the public library to maintain a stock of books, pamphlets, and maps. It obtained State Department documents from an established Council a few hundred miles away. It started a neighborhood discussion series and a speakers bureau. It got a donation of half an hour a week of airtime from a radio station and rebroadcast its shows to schoolchildren. But there were problems in what Nason called this effort to create a culture "in which more people consciously allot interest and time to preparing themselves for their role in the final determination of foreign policy." There were local rivalries to contend with, and even if the Council's trustees eventually agreed on who they should work with and who they should target, their director still spent most of his time raising money. Without funding from local foundations, the business community, or the wealthy few, the Council had been "squeezed in an economic vice," too poor to make the splash necessary to bring in cash and stuck forever with such a small budget that it was unable to pay a professional director. Emeny's secret was out.[44]

The World Affairs Council brand proved malleable, applicable to institutions with quite different ideas about the kind of public that ought to be involved in a democratic foreign policy. While Councils in San Francisco, Seattle, and a few other cities came about through mergers of nonpartisan institutions, more emerged from alliances among action groups. Some succeeded, above all the

Philadelphia Council, where an Association branch and a United Nations Council combined in 1949 before making progress under the accomplished direction of Elizabeth Hallstrom and Ruth Weir Miller. But the transition was often difficult. In Baltimore, the United Nations Association formed a Maryland World Affairs Council but gave it nothing to do. Boston's United Council on World Affairs—a merger of the old Association branch, a United Nations Association chapter, and a moribund Joint Council for International Co-Operation—had a membership in the thousands but could not generate any coherence. The Association itself now saw US membership in the United Nations as a fact of life, and while it remained wary of outright promotional work, it moved into offices across from United Nations Plaza, working closely with the American Association for the United Nations.[45]

The more important divide among World Affairs Councils, however, was over the scale of the public they sought. The Cleveland Council, or at least the one presented on film, offered an ambitious example. Educators elsewhere were not convinced that their cities were ready for anything so radical. Some went back to the formats that Emeny had specifically inveighed against, especially in places where the foreign policy community had little foothold. The Los Angeles Council, for instance, operated purely as a lecture society, drawing big-ticket speakers like Vice President Richard Nixon, Secretary of State John Foster Dulles, and President Syngman Rhee of South Korea. Under the presidency of John McCone, a Republican shipping titan who had been Truman's undersecretary of the army and would lead Dwight Eisenhower's Atomic Energy Commission and John F. Kennedy's Central Intelligence Agency (neither institution being amenable to public scrutiny), the Council had no interest in waging a broad educational campaign to face down the right-wing radicals who had made the UNESCO fight so heated. Despite the escalating importance of defense jobs in Southern California, the Council appealed to corporate and social elites. Association officials never agreed with this approach, much as they appreciated the problems posed by suburban geography, rampant population growth, and a conservative civic culture, but there was nothing they could do about it. The ties between the Los Angeles Council and Ford, moreover, meant that a tenth of the Association's seed grants were assigned there, despite the Council's easy access to other funds.[46]

Other Councils skipped the high-society stage and aimed immediately for community engagement. The Dayton Council on World Affairs started life as a familiar collaboration, its chairman being paper magnate George H.

**THIS** or *THIS ?*

**5.1** From a promotional booklet for the Dayton Council on World Affairs, c. 1950. Dayton's booklet poses organized discussion as the alternative to nuclear war, guaranteeing peace, but the rise of nuclear weapons—and the secrecy that protected their development—seemed to some to make meaningful discussion on the World Affairs Council model impossible, or at least ineffectual. Special Collections and Archives, Wright State University Library.

Mead and one of its vice chairs being the president of the city's League of Women Voters. After its launch in July 1947, with Emeny acolyte Howard A. Cook on hand to lend advice and other Cleveland veterans later joining its staff, the Dayton Council used a phalanx of volunteers to overcome a small budget and start an eager program with discussion groups, a Junior Council on World Affairs, and a television program, *It's Your World*. First broadcast in June 1951 with a mix of panels, interviews, and reporting, this Sunday afternoon show was estimated to reach about one hundred thousand people in a fast-growing metropolitan area of half a million. Even the White House took note, President Eisenhower sending his congratulations when the Association presented the Dayton Council with an award in December 1954.[47]

If this was an unusual path for a Council premised, as they all were, on the idea that even explicitly educational mass media were not enough to create meaningful participation, Dayton's experiment only proved the point. There seemed to be "no end to the possibility for expansion" in terms of numbers reached through television, one of its annual reports noted, but "the value of the television program as an educational project" remained "difficult to determine." Fears persisted that television, combined with suburban patterns of leisure and consumption, would sate people rather than prompt further discussion. Dayton officials commissioned a survey in 1953 that found a "diffuse, favorable disposition to education and discussion about world affairs" among Daytonians, with 79 percent of respondents noting that efforts to help "people in this city get the facts about world affairs" were a good idea, and 49.5 percent agreeing that it was "absolutely true" that "world affairs are your affairs." But the Council was not converting ideals into action. Although nearly half of Daytonians claimed to have heard of the Council, only 4 percent of those respondents claimed to be members. Reaching a quarter of the population in even the most passive, limited sense, the survey concluded, would be "the Utopian goal for an agency like the Council."[48]

Even the most ambitious Councils found their ambitions dashed, then, most painfully the Cleveland Council itself. Witman had kept the faith at first, insisting that "no problem of world affairs is too difficult for any citizen to see" and maintaining the tempo of events that had made the Council an example seemingly worth following. But as white middle- and upper-class Clevelanders left the city for the suburbs, the Council drifted. Witman spent more time away, starting a series of residential seminars aimed at developing a more sophisticated awareness of world affairs among "civic, governmental and academic leaders." Staffers trained in Cleveland went off to replicate its workings elsewhere; those who remained had started to revolt by the end of 1953. One fear was that the Council was making little contribution to foreign policy, despite the promises policymakers often made. Another was that the Council's offerings were shallow. "I wonder whether we are not simply creating in the name of mass citizen education an elaborate system of filling stations," one internal critic wrote, "from which the local consumer chooses his brand of gas and oil and then has absolutely no clear idea of where to drive the contraption." And there was also the fact that the Council itself had remained so stubbornly elitist, whatever its achievements in the community. 89.8 percent of its members earned more than the national median wage, a survey found in 1955. 22 percent earned five times it.[49]

When Witman resigned in January 1955, the Council came under the control of its chairman, Kenyon C. Bolton. Son of Frances Bolton, that old friend of Emeny's, Kenyon set about turning the Council from what he said was a "wishy-washy" group, "cream-puff" and "pink," into a "virile, masculine" forum for businessman. He ploughed tens of thousands of dollars of his own money into promotional materials until the other board members broke ranks to accuse him publicly of running a "one-man" show to fulfil his aim of succeeding his mother—and joining his brother, Oliver—in Congress. Association officials were horrified, its Committee on National Program worrying in December 1955 that the Council was "tending to depart from the community education idea to work more with the elite" and the regional staff fearing the consequences for the entire movement if the "Cleveland Story" turned "into a façade." It did. Bolton held out and hired as Witman's eventual replacement Benjamin Brown, a former official at the US Mission to the United Nations who saw no value in community discussion and focused on big-ticket lectures. With the membership shrinking, debts rising, and the program neutered, New York staffers by 1958 were looking sadly at a Council in "serious illhealth." The Cleveland story had turned into a fairy tale.[50]

## *The Collapse of the Cleveland Model*

Nobody thought the World Affairs Council project had succeeded. Nason wrote in his final report to the Fund that the "'network' of world affairs organizations is larger and stronger than at any time in the past." Certainly it was larger, but stronger it was not. When Emeny had left the Association in November 1952, the list of Association branches, Councils, and similar groups ran to twenty-nine organizations, half of them in the Northeast. By the autumn of 1955, the list ran to sixty-eight such organizations, but many of them were general adult education committees with a flair for world affairs, or paper institutions, legal entities with no real budget or purpose. Fourteen of the seventy Councils founded by the end of the grant period soon collapsed, and more foundered later. Many struggled on without trying to fulfill the Cleveland promise; those that made the effort had their roots not in the heated years of the early Cold War, but in the fervor of conflicts past.[51]

Why did this effort not work? "Experience suggests," the Association told the Fund, "that most cities under 100,000 in population lack the financial and human base for supporting a real Council," an admission that sustained interest in world affairs in this form was vanishingly rare. 106 cities had a population of at least one hundred thousand by 1950, and thirty of the largest fifty had a Council of some sort by 1955. Those that did not were the booming metropolises of the South and West, so different in their geography and cultures to progressive-shaped cities of the Northeast and Midwest that the Association struggled to adapt. If the Association could not cope with urbanization on the scale of Los Angeles or Houston, nor could it cope with suburbanization in its traditional heartlands, despite the large proportion of Community Investment Fund grants earmarked for strengthening branches in places such as Albany and Hartford. Richard Rowson, the regional staffer with responsibility for the Northeast, reported early in 1955 that his "main problem was to deal largely with a number of metropolitan complexes, where the idea of a community is on the decline."[52]

This slippage between psychological and political definitions of "community"—assumed to be held among white, educated citizens and enacted through voluntary associations—and its physical equivalents was not new, but it was newly problematic. White flight became impossible to ignore. "It is clear," the Boston Council's director wrote in May 1954, "that most of those actively interested in world affairs education live in the suburbs and desire an active program in their own communities." Even so, the Association only weakly tackled the issue, funding a frail effort by the Rhode Island Council to support branches outside Providence but declining to sponsor the Boston Council's plans to develop satellite programs in commuter towns like Arlington, Salem, and Concord. Racism was the issue here, although usually an unspoken one, for despite the political sympathy of many educators with the civil rights movement, none of them seriously proposed tackling the basic orientation of the Council movement itself. Black engagement with world affairs was still treated as if it did not exist; almost entirely lacking Black leadership, with the odd Black trustee but certainly no Black professional directors, Councils cultivated Black participation only through schools rather than specific programs. If white flight was to be dealt with, it was to be dealt with by following the flight, not confronting the white.[53]

Race also played its part in the limited geographical reach of the Council project. The Association had little interest in allying with the politics of either racism or antiracism in the South, a reluctance which functioned only to entrench its whiteness. As its expensive efforts to prop up former branches in the Louisiana cities of New Orleans and Shreveport offered scant signs of progress, it left the region mostly alone. Failing to set up the office Ford required in the South before December 1954, it got nowhere in South Carolina, Florida, Mississippi, and Arkansas and little further in Georgia and Alabama. Further west the situation was no better. Nevada, Arizona, Utah, Wyoming, and Montana remained untapped. Where the Association did get involved, as in Texas, it quickly learned to stay in the shadows. The Dallas Council was a relatively strong one, its programs including a municipally endorsed World Affairs Week that in 1956 held a rodeo honoring ambassadors from Denmark, Finland, and New Zealand. But the Council got caught in a political struggle, its primary backer, Dresser Industries energy titan H. Neil Mallon, facing off against oil billionaire H. L. Hunt, whose feisty newsletter, *Facts Forum*, launched constant attacks on the Council from the ultranationalist conservative right. Dallas officials tried to prevent their Association colleagues setting foot in the state for fear of raising the specter of the Institute of Pacific Relations, while giving the regional staffers plenty of opportunities to indulge their intolerance, dubbing Texas the "land of the Philistines" and worse. The idea that world affairs education was a Yankee imposition endured.[54]

If the Fund for Adult Education, the Foreign Policy Association, and even some of the World Affairs Councils themselves started to doubt whether community institutions were the best answer to the problem of a democratic foreign policy, however, there was still little doubt within the field about the basic understanding that the foreign policy community could create mass participation through education, if only the right formats and messages could be found. The right money, too. Nason noted in his final report, rather pointedly, that the $1,090,250 received from the Fund over four years — less than a quarter of which went to Councils in seed grants from the Community Investment Fund — was nothing next to the $4 million advertising budget wielded annually at the Revlon cosmetics company. If the combined budgets of the Association and the Councils were slightly higher than the $1.3 million spent by the State Department on "domestic public information and liaison" in 1957, educators still alluded to the insignificance of such sums in the context of a defense budget nearing $40 billion. But it was clearer to some that cash was not really the problem. The World Affairs Council of Northern California had as much money as it knew what to do with, but its founder and chairman, three-time ambassador and former assistant secretary of state Henry F. Grady, informed the Fund that it was reaching an "infinitesimal" portion of the Bay Area population.[55]

Long before the end of the World Affairs Council project, then, the Association had come to see that it was unfit for its purpose. If Brooks Emeny had convinced much of the foreign policy community that every citizen ought to become a statesman, his failure to convince citizens of the proposition had immense costs. Intellectuals would now use the ongoing failure as evidence of the bankruptcy of the progressive conception of a democratic foreign policy. Once the intellectual basis of the vision was torn apart, as it would be among scholars by the end of the 1950s, the hopes of making it or anything like it a practical reality would soon follow.

# 6

# Who, Me?

Roger Mastrude was tired, and not a bit frustrated. The regional agent of
the Foreign Policy Association had spent the summer of 1953 driving up
and down the West Coast, hauling a trailer so laden with discussion materials, pamphlets, and film reels that the clutch and brakes on his family car
had given up. He covered more than twenty-five thousand miles that year,
from the foothills of the Rocky Mountains to the shores of the Pacific Ocean,
from the Canadian border in the north to the Mexican in the south. Born to
a Quaker family in Walla Walla, Washington, a month after Woodrow Wilson
had taken the United States to war, Mastrude saw this as a dream job, and it
was one he had worked hard for. He had no Ivy League education behind
him, taking his degree from the College of Puget Sound. He had missed out
on a Rhodes scholarship, paying for his graduate studies in Budapest himself.
He had seen war, working on the US Army staff of General George Patton as
an intelligence officer, and he had seen its deprivations too, running refugee
camps for the United Nations in occupied Germany. If he knew the world of
New York internationalism as a former director of education at International
House, his background led him to see the problem of a democratic foreign
policy differently to most in those circles. Out West, with only his books for
company, he was alone.[1]

"I must confess that I get a little glum now and then," Mastrude wrote to
his Manhattan colleagues on September 11, 1953. "I regret to say that I cannot
avoid being somewhat sensitive that so much hard work out here produces so
little." He already doubted that World Affairs Councils would ever take off
outside the Northeast, the idea being "so unfamiliar in most of these communities that they find it hard to absorb and take hold of." By Christmas, he
was thoroughly dissuaded. The West was too rural, he thought; it lacked

171

sufficient educational and associational infrastructure; its cities were too small, too far apart. "We must find our way experimentally," he reported to the Fund for Adult Education, "in terms of techniques, organizational framework, and even educational materials."[2]

Still, there were some sprouts at the grass roots. Portland, Oregon, had some experience with world affairs. Its wealthier men had created a Committee on Foreign Relations in 1938 and its liberal arts school, Reed College, put on an annual Northwest Institute of International Relations. There had been enough interest to bring together the World Affairs Council of Oregon in 1950, but it had struggled at first, like so many Councils. Even after Mastrude arrived to help it took a year to get the Council going, which he finally managed by arranging for a speech to be given to businessmen in 1954 by J. D. Zellerbach, an Association board member who had run the Marshall Plan in Italy and was opening a paper plant in the area. Fortunately, the Council had inspirational leadership. Its spiritual guide was Frank Munk, a leftist *émigré* who had run the Czechoslovak League of Nations Association before the war and, after teaching at Berkeley and working on refugee camps back in Europe, had found himself "taken up by Portland society and lionized as their special intellectual garlic," as Mastrude put it. Munk depended in turn on Louise Grondahl, formerly president of the League of Women Voters of Portland. "Never in the history of our country has it been so important for everybody to take an active interest in our foreign policy," she wrote in 1951 in the *Oregonian*, the major Portland newspaper, "since it will determine whether or not we are to be involved in global war."[3]

Grondahl's assumption was a common one still, constantly running through the speeches of politicians, policymakers, and activists like her. But it was an assumption under intellectual attack. Scholars in the immediate postwar decade, David Riesman of Harvard reflected in 1959, moved "from hopefulness about public opinion to complete despair," for it proved "hard for people like ourselves, in the educated upper middle class, to imagine the extent of the willingness of people to forget, to fail to register, to distort, and to overlook what all mass media seem so urgently to say." Confronted with statistics that measured the knowledge of individual citizens against elite expectations and found them wanting, postwar liberals gave in to the apathy their prewar predecessors had tried to overcome. Faced with a second totalitarian foe, one that seemed so threatening as to justify semi-permanent emergency measures, theorists and policymakers alike argued that it would be too risky to submit certain aspects of foreign policy to democratic control. Some scholars went further, arguing that

**6.1** Roger G. Mastrude, undated profile picture. Mastrude was the architect of the Great Decisions program and one of the most radical thinkers ever to work at the Foreign Policy Association. Wisconsin Historical Society.

basic understandings of democracy needed to be rethought. As this crisis of democracy played out in political theory, Kyong-Min Son has written, "'the masses' as the lethal threat to democracy overshadowed 'the people' as the legitimate foundation of popular sovereignty." Taking the ideal of an active, informed citizenry as their punching bag, these scholars erected what sociologist Seymour Martin Lipset called an "elitist theory of democracy" in the ruins of its progressive predecessor. That theory legitimized the increasing authority of state institutions that were sealed off from public oversight—above all the National Security Council and the Central Intelligence Agency—and encouraged the use of methods explicitly intended to manipulate consent.[4]

It is easy to forget what a radical moment this was, a time when no aspect of the polity was safe from remaking under Cold War imperatives. Worries about Harold Lasswell's "garrison state" staved off the worst, but global primacy transformed domestic politics even so. Built in the fears that world leadership both responded to and unleashed, the nascent national security state was "marked by antidemocratic pathologies," historian Ira Katznelson has written. Debates about this new state and decisions taken by it pulled power towards the executive branch, creating an entity of staggering reach; if the legislature retained some oversight powers, it eagerly consented to a stark weakening of its prerogatives. And if traditional democratic politics could not survive this frightening world, nor could traditional democratic theory. "Modern international politics is a rigorous testing ground for the classic instruments of government in a democratic society," the Yale political theorist Robert A. Dahl wrote in 1950. More and more, those instruments would be found wanting.[5]

What did this mean for those who kept the faith? After all, Dahl and his colleagues did not advocate new theories and new instruments of democracy merely because foreign policy now seemed to demand it. Their response to a threatening world could have been to place stronger emphasis on the old ways, to argue like Mastrude, Munk, and Grondahl that education in world affairs issues was more necessary than ever, that it should go further, deeper, that all should engage in it as a duty of democratic citizenship. But that was not the scholarly response, not for the most part. While political leaders continued to implore Americans to inform themselves and get involved, social scientists argued with blistering rhetorical force, at times even with derision, that educators had failed, that the foreign policy community needed to find ways of reconciling diplomacy with democracy that reflected realities, not dreams. It was an appealing argument, especially at the foundations that remained committed in principle to progressive conceptions of a democratic foreign policy but were tiring of its practical difficulties.

Portland was where the Foreign Policy Association counterattacked. With the support of the Ford Foundation, the Oregon Council launched Great Decisions, an attempt to demonstrate that the progressive dream was still plausible. Carefully designed to prove the emerging elitist theory wrong, Great Decisions claimed to offer Portlanders a chance to lead the world from their living rooms. After its pilot season in 1955, Great Decisions morphed into the most ambitious, popular, and enduring adult education program the foreign policy community has ever run, spreading to hundreds of towns and cities, involving thousands of volunteers, and drawing hundreds of thousands of participants into weekly discussion groups. But what mattered about this attempt to validate what one Association staffer called "the workability of the democratic process in the world affairs field" was not its scale. What counted was whether it reached a different kind of citizen, the kind of American who had to this point been beyond the reach of world affairs institutions, one thought unlikely by social scientists to be interested in the subject of foreign policy as they defined it—whether, put another way, educators could throw off their own elitism and make foreign policy a more truly democratic possession.[6]

## The "Elitist Theory of Democracy"

George F. Kennan, the father of containment and arguably the most famous Cold War diplomat in the United States, was the most celebrated critic of the idea of popular control over foreign affairs. *American Diplomacy*, the bestseller

Kennan wrote before he returned to Moscow as US ambassador to the Soviet Union in 1951, mercilessly attacked a political culture he had little immediate knowledge of, having spent most of his adult life on assignment overseas. Kennan bewailed the "histrionic" tendencies of legislators, decried the "trivial, superficial, and sensational trash that is permitted daily to flow out and to inundate the public attention," and suggested that half a century of evidence was plenty enough to prove that a democracy was "uncomfortably similar to one of those prehistoric monsters with a body as long as this room and a brain the size of a pin." Kennan retained some faith in the "common man," the diplomat said in 1953, but precisely because of his lack of inclination to "come up with answers at all about public matters." Conversely, Kennan declared himself irritated with the do-gooders who felt themselves "under an obligation to hold and voice opinions of international affairs," finding them "pontifical and opinionated, inclined to place the utterance before the thought, prone to hold views on inadequate evidence and then to be sensitive and stubborn in the exposition of them." If a citizen was interested and engaged, he would have nothing to do with them.[7]

Kennan's conviction that citizens could not cope with foreign policy was not a new one, but built on the theories of his sometime antagonist, Walter Lippmann. Lippmann had always been involved with foreign policy institutions, though his sympathies lay with the Council on Foreign Relations. Back in the 1920s, his *Public Opinion* and *The Phantom Public* had caused adult educators to double down on their Deweyanism, and his return to the theme, *Essays in the Public Philosophy* (1955), had much the same effect. The *Essays* savaged the abilities of the "mass" to act in the public interest, arguing that not even the wisest statesmen were able to hold back the mass's "enfeeblement, verging on paralysis, of the capacity to govern." Lippmann still believed in the pragmatist ideal that the truth could be discovered through discussion, but it was hard, now, to see how. Democracy required such "impassioned nonsense"—a war to "end all wars" or to "make the world safe for democracy"— to rouse it from its inertia that the truth was inevitably distorted in the process. Still a newspaper columnist, Lippmann inevitably thought the media had a role to play in creating opinions, but he worried that audiences, skimming the pages or flicking through the channels, never heard the relevant arguments and evidence well enough to make reasoned choices. Even if the common good could somehow be discerned, Lippmann paradoxically wrote, it "cannot be popular," for it had "to resist and to regulate those very desires and opinions which are most popular." Mass opinion therefore had to be curtailed "when the stakes are life and death"—"a mass," Lippmann concluded, "cannot govern."[8]

Public figures Kennan and Lippmann might have been, but their distance from mainstream views was suggested by the ferocity of the tone they felt it necessary to adopt. State Department officials, after all, constantly reiterated that policy was rooted in public consent. Not one but two assistant secretaries of state for public affairs wrote books after leaving office that outlined how citizens could contribute, while State itself published pamphlets with titles such as *How Foreign Policy is Made* (1954) and *Your Opinion Counts* (1954). Commentators easily dispatched these contrarian views, too. Dorothy Fosdick, a Columbia-trained political theorist who had worked for Kennan on State's Policy Planning Staff, titled her rebuttal *Common Sense and World Affairs* (1955). Foreign Policy Association member Dexter Perkins, president of the American Historical Association and a former State Department planner, took issue with the critics' jaundiced assessments of history, noting that public opinion had done well enough so far. Even if it had not, and more power did in fact have to be delegated to elites, Perkins reminded readers of his *Popular Government and Foreign Policy* (1956) that "folly is not confined to a democratic electorate." Experts could be wrong, too. Even the chief of the Council on Foreign Relations, former Brown University president Henry M. Wriston, defended the old ideals, tutting that the skeptics made people feel that "we are a nation, if not of morons, at least with moronic tendencies." "Schemes for the elimination of political forces in diplomacy are simply efforts to evade the facts of life," he wrote in *Diplomacy in a Democracy* (1956). "It is absurd to find men arguing for such a utopian program while pretending to deal realistically with world problems."[9]

But if it proved easy enough to rebuke Kennan and Lippmann at the public level, within the academic social sciences varieties of their views soon became the norm. Scholars had started to question Deweyan theory during the Great Depression, challenging the practicality of popular governance and the rationality of human nature. While the panic that eased the creation of the New Deal state faded, worries that democracy would capitulate in the face of deprivation and danger lingered. The American Political Science Association in 1934 heard its president call for "the ignorant, the uninformed, and the antisocial" to be disenfranchised so that the government could be controlled by "an aristocracy of intellect and character." Such calls grew louder even before the war, but they remained minority views, no threat to the dominance of Deweyan theory and its educational outlook within the academy and without. They became much more common after World War II.[10]

One crucial cause of this shift was the emergence of stark evidence for those who sought to argue for the incompetence of the masses, evidence that came from the surveys that the federal government had found so useful to acquire consent for its new world order. The National Opinion Research Center (NORC), based at the University of Chicago, could not have survived without State Department contracts; the Survey Research Center (SRC), located at the University of Michigan, grew out of Rensis Likert's pioneering work for the Department of Agriculture and the Strategic Bombing Survey, depending initially for over half of its budget on state funding. Many social psychologists and other scholars at places like these had been involved in wartime morale or propaganda work, and with the war won they had time to ponder what their results meant for democracy. Critics wondered whether their questions were too hard; some, such as sociologists David Riesman and Nathan Glazer, asked if it was at all fair to think of respondents as "responsible citizens" who considered the world in terms of "issues," who existed on "such single dimensions as left-right, or Republican-Democrat-Progressive," or who felt compelled "to take sides on public issues." But such quibbles about this imposition of a specific definition of citizenship on the population made little difference. Polls had already helped to set the agenda for debate on political issues; surveys now prodded academics to rethink what the public really was, and the answers continued less to empower citizens than to empower the state that sought to manage them in the name of national security.[11]

Despite a startling lack of debate about what citizens needed to know to fulfil their duties and how to assess whether they knew it, the evidence social scientists marshaled appeared to be devastating. Deweyans conceived of democratic citizenship as a collective manner of being; the limitations of the individual would be overcome when intelligence was pooled in discussion. But postwar surveys reduced citizens to their discrete, singular ability to recall facts. Most could not. One study found that half of Minnesota's urban residents could not name George Marshall as Truman's secretary of state, a number that rose to three-quarters of rural residents; even fewer could name Marshall's Soviet foe. One third of respondents, another report discovered, could not give "even the simplest answer" when asked about the purpose of the United Nations. Foreign policy remained detached from civic life for most. Almost half of Cincinnati adults were members of at least one voluntary association, NORC estimated, but only 15 percent thought they belonged "to any groups or organizations or attend any meetings where they talk about world affairs." Julian Woodward and Elmo Roper described merely one in ten adults as "very active" in politics, a category they defined to include voting, party and group membership, communication with policymakers, and regular discussion of politics with friends, family, and colleagues. The SRC told State that even its most informed respondents did no more than vote. Worse still, few people seemed to conceive of democracy in the sense that Deweyans urged. Just 43 percent of sampled residents in Albany, New York, believed that the State Department should listen to popular views, on the grounds that "that's the democratic procedure," while 47 percent thought State "should" or "must" do "what it thinks best." One in three said there was "nothing a citizen can do" to influence policy, compared to one in seven who said, "there is something and I've done it."[12]

Results like these confirmed doubts about the depth of the turn to internationalism that some within the foreign policy community had harbored since the end of the war. After all, the SRC reported, even Americans who said they supported a given policy tended not to "understand the issues well enough to know exactly why." SRC director Angus Campbell joined a colleague to write in *Public Opinion Quarterly* in 1951 that while popular views on world affairs had some structure, above all partisan structure, most people were so ill-informed that to think of them as "isolationists" or "internationalists" was to miss the point. The dilemma these data presented was clear to all. SRC staff wrote in 1949 that "a democratic society implies an informed and active electorate, but studies in the field of foreign affairs have revealed large numbers of people who have little information and few opinions about international events." Scholars with grander analytical ambitions went further. "If we accept the Greek's definition of an idiot as a privatized man," sociologist C. Wright Mills wrote, meaning men without concern for public affairs, "then we must conclude that the U.S. citizenry is now largely composed of idiots." Deweyans had never doubted that the people needed help, but even intellectuals less idiosyncratic than Mills agreed that their prospects were diminished. "The images of the public of classic democracy which are still used as the working justifications of power in American society" were no more than a "fairy tale," Mills wrote in *The Power Elite* (1956). "The public of public opinion is recognized by all those who have considered it carefully as something less than it once was."[13]

Why did intellectuals capitulate where once they had innovated? One answer is that the conflicts with fascism and communism—lumped together as species of "totalitarianism"—convinced many that participatory mass politics was a terrible idea, and that some degree of apathy would help to protect democratic institutions. Early interpretations of the rise of fascism, some advanced by émigrés who spoke with unfortunate authority, brought once-forgotten ideas about the perils of crowd psychology and mass society into democratic theory, creating among liberals an abiding fear of the "masses," imagined to be willing to renounce individuality under the spell of demagoguery and march into authoritarianism. As psychologists located the threat deep in the psyches of the people, warning ominously of an "authoritarian personality," other analysts warned that the shadow of dictatorship was already darkening American politics. "We have moved a considerable distance along the road to the mass society," Mills argued, noting that the power of the mass media made opinion expression, effective discussion, and the realization of popular views difficult. "At the end of that road," he went on, "there is totalitarianism." Given that democratic institutions as they stood seemed to work well enough for the time being, scholars wondered whether it would be better to stop pretending that participation was all that necessary, especially as so many experts were now trained to handle administrative government.[14]

When it came specifically to foreign affairs, postwar thinkers had another reason to doubt the Deweyan dream, namely that adult education clearly had not worked. The statistics compiled at NORC and the SRC came after thirty years of labor by the Association and its allies, as well as a war's worth of facts. Evidence grew that even propaganda campaigns succeeded only in highly limited circumstances, and more modest educational efforts still less. Over the winter of 1946–1947, the American Association for the United Nations and the United Nations Association of Cincinnati launched a self-described "crusade" to demonstrate "how a community may become so intelligently informed on world affairs as to be a dynamic force in the creation of an ordered and eventually a peaceful world." It did not go well. Despite a six-month blitz of 2,800 speeches, the printing of 59,588 pieces of literature, and the placement of ads on "blotters, matchbooks, streetcar cards, etc.," NORC found that the campaign "did not stir the interest of those who were not interested in the first place." Results like these suggested there were barriers to participation more difficult to overcome than the failings of any single institution involved. The evidence was not definitive, and even the Council on Foreign Relations still endorsed books that argued that education could solve the problem of public opinion at home and alleviate the causes of conflict overseas. But the evidence was becoming harder to deny.[15]

All this came together in two studies that emerged from the Yale Institute of International Studies. Since its founding in 1935, the Institute had helped to turn Yale into a hotbed of realism, so much so that its scholars became hostile to the project of their former colleague, Brooks Emeny. The first Institute book on the problem of public opinion, Dahl's *Congress and Foreign Policy* (1950), bade farewell to the old order. Popular control of foreign policy was unworkable, Dahl argued, not only for the traditional reason that foreign policy was remote from most people's daily experience, but because the cost of failure had now become annihilation. Dahl had few answers, though. Elite rule was impossible in an era of total war. "Expert authoritarianism" was unthinkable. But Deweyan democracy seemed implausible, too. Even if citizens accepted the "terrifying demand" that they should take responsibility for foreign policy, Dahl wrote, it was hard to see how their views could filter into policymaking. Certainly the "assorted foreign policy organizations" were useless, reaching "too restricted a clientele to be more than pitifully inadequate." Dahl therefore came to the disquieting conclusion that "discretion" would have to remain with elites for the time being. But his thinking moved quickly. Three years later, Dahl accepted that there were whole areas of foreign policy, especially relating to atomic weapons, "for which the traditional democratic processes are rather unsuitable and for which traditional theories of democracy provide no rational answer." And by the end of the decade, Dahl was theorizing democracy as a competition among pluralistic elites who could operate with limited reference to a citizenry that wore its "political indifference" like "impenetrable armor plate."[16]

Where Dahl prevaricated, Gabriel A. Almond wielded an old critique of progressive theory to offer clearer answers. Almond had joined Yale in 1947, and he had brought with him an intellectual outlook that gave him confidence where Dahl wrestled with confusion. Student to Harold Lasswell at the University of Chicago, Almond was trained in theories that insisted on the need for expert governance of politics, as well as for the democratic nature of propaganda. He was experienced in the practical aspects of those theories, too, having spent the war at the Office of War Information and the Strategic Bombing Survey. Influenced by *émigré* scholars such as Hans Speier and Hans Morgenthau who insisted that the public should not be trusted, Almond argued that public opinion needed to be managed in the name of strategy, and in the process he broke down distinctions between peacetime and wartime rules, domestic and foreign publics, democratic and totalitarian methods. Part of a groups of scholars who saw what Lasswell thought would be "the enormous importance of symbolic manipulation in modern society" and filtered into posts in the federal government, the foundations, and the academy during and

after the war, Almond also had philanthropy at his back. He had the intellectual firepower and the professional connections to make his theories the textbook treatment of the problem.[17]

In *The American People and Foreign Policy* (1950), Almond launched a
caustic attack on the traditional practices of the foreign policy community.
"The treatment of problems of public opinion and foreign policy" had been
"obscured and distorted by ethical bias and inhibition," he began, and approaches to it had not been scientific but evangelical. He described as "dema-
gogy" the belief that "the people" were "the real rulers of the republic,"
announced that "direct and literal control of public policy by public opinion"
was "obviously" precluded in real life, and savaged the dream of an informed
public as "apocalyptic." There was, he said, "no mass market for detailed information on foreign affairs" because facts lacked "immediate utility or meaning"
for most citizens. There was no point in trying to improve the knowledge that
surveys found so lacking in so many people, he continued, for it took "many,
many increments of knowledge plus much wisdom" to create "intelligent criticism of foreign policy." If Almond's target was not clear from his pillory of
"moralistic exhortations to the public to inform itself," he returned in his conclusion to suggest that "little more than self-intoxication" would come from "a
grass roots campaign in Middletown, Ohio, 'to relate Middletowners to the
world in which we live.'"[18]

No matter, for Almond saw a sharpening of elite focus on foreign policy as
a corollary to the mass inattention that threatened a return to "isolationism."
Almond was an uncomfortable elitist, like Dahl, and he noted that if elites
did dominate policymaking, foreign policy could only be imagined as
democratic—and safe—if opportunities for interested and educated citizens to
participate remained open. Almond was, however, willing to hand enormous
latitude to the few. He described society as a pyramid, with elites competing at the
top, a several-million-strong "attentive" public comprised of the "college-trained,
upper-income, 'mental-worker' stratum" below that, and the mass at the bottom,
superficial and unstable, looking to the tone and mood of elite cues and managed
by experts trained to manipulate consent. Almond erected a hierarchy of control in the wreckage of the Deweyan polity; this version of a democratic foreign policy was not one of rational, informed discussion at scale, but of
mobilization and morale, wartime concepts repurposed for an undeclared
Cold War. The foreign policy community should ignore the impulse to make
"experts and specialists of laymen," Almond suggested, to the extent that such
an impulse had ever existed. It should instead ensure that elites were trained,

that they competed, that they shared core values with the people—and, importantly, that ways existed to constrain them when necessary.[19]

The theories Almond codified provided plenty of justification for the rash of state-facing research centers, policy institutes, and social science programs that reared up after the war, all of them competing for funds that made Emeny right to fear the expansion of the professional—and overwhelmingly male— foreign policy community on terms that limited the place of the people in policymaking. Emeny was right, too, to fear the effect on what Almond—an acquaintance who had lent a hand to the Association president's attempt to abolish the research department— derided as the "democratic myth." Association operatives found it easy enough to rally like-minded volunteers with calls to "prove the Hamiltons, the de Tocquevilles, and the Lippmanns wrong!" It was another thing entirely to fend off academic ideas that came with significant institutional backing and general appeal to a foreign policy community becoming more wary about meaningful participation as it grew. Although the process took time and the outcome remained uncertain, the landscape in which the Association operated started to shift as the foundations started to listen to scholars like Almond to guide them in confronting the problem of a democratic foreign policy afresh.[20]

The Rockefeller Foundation was the philanthropy moving fastest away from world affairs education, but the Carnegie Endowment did the most to bridge theory and practice on the issue of public opinion. Turning Almond's ideas into practical recommendations became the task of Bernard C. Cohen, a student of Almond's who went with his mentor to start the Rockefeller-funded Center of International Studies at Princeton in April 1951. Cohen's doctoral thesis, which he sent to the Endowment that December, combined the latest scholarship with data acquired from the Association and its allies, including five World Affairs Councils. Cohen argued that there was now fundamental clash of democratic theories at work. "The objective of an informed and alert citizenry dispatching with acumen the complex problems of foreign policy has its roots in a traditional democratic theory," he wrote, holding that "apathy is one of the worst sins against democracy." But research and experience had come to show that the system could withstand apathy without descending into hell, and it had shown, too, that the social and psychological barriers protecting apathy from assault were significant. Cohen thought it would be as troubling for Deweyan educators "to discover that reality does not conform with time-hallowed theory" as to accept that their groups were as unrepresentative as they really were. But even if educators "dare not talk in terms that may be construed as 'undemocratic,'" he later advised, a change of goals was due; aiming for an impossible degree of participation might, after all, prove dangerous.[21]

What then should the Association and its allies do? Cohen showed that world affairs groups appealed overwhelmingly to educated, older, wealthy white people, mostly professional men and politically engaged women likely to be moderate Republicans. Participation among lower income groups and minorities was "sparse," an outcome not "due to a widespread conspiracy or even desire to exclude," Cohen generously allowed, but to the time, expense, and education needed to enjoy luncheons, seminars, and even extensive reading. More of the policy and opinion elite could and should be added to the academic, social, and financial elite that educators already reached, Cohen thought, but he argued that even if the educators perfected their methods they would never be able to appeal to the vast swathe of the population that paid little heed to foreign policy. Cohen insisted that the Association ought to shrink its ambitions its other ways, too. "So long as organizations continue to discuss 'foreign affairs' that may be unrelated to problems facing American policymakers," he wrote, or "to discuss American policy after unknown alternatives have been discarded by official policy-makers," making an "effective contribution" would be difficult. It was an argument symptomatic of a turn away from the people as the originators of the common good and toward policymakers as the definers of the national interest. How were the people to know what problems faced policymakers, in an age of rampant secrecy? How were they to know what options had already been set aside, or why? How were they to make clear that other issues ought to be made a priority, if their discussion of such issues was conceived, *a priori*, as irrelevant? Even the name Cohen gave to the diffuse field he studied, "citizen education in world affairs," implied that it was only the masses that needed teaching, not the experts whose education Deweyans had thought so important. Follow the logic and expert management would become the rule.[22]

The Association was given no choice but to engage with the Cohen report, which ended up shaping work in the field for more than a decade. Princeton's Center of International Studies published the report in October 1953, launching it at a conference at which Kennan declared his basic agreement with Almond's work. Association staffers soon asked the Ford Foundation for a grant to launch a rival study of the "what determines public opinion in a democracy," but without success. Nason was then asked to join a Carnegie Endowment study group that brought State Department, United Nations, and

UNESCO policymakers together with foundation officials, voluntary association leaders, and academics to learn from Almond, Cohen, and other social scientists. Those sessions concluded that "mass participation on a level of formal discussion" was an "impossibly ambitious goal," but the Association still felt able to dissent from that view. When some of its leaders met with Cohen at Emeny's mansion in New Jersey, they came away unimpressed. When the board met to discuss the Cohen report, it found no reason for dismay, but rather the opposite. Anna Lord Strauss, a former League of Women Voters president and United Nations delegate who was a trustee of both the Association and the Fund for Adult Education, summed up the consensus. Strauss ignored Cohen's basic assumption that there were structural, psychological impediments to popular participation, arguing that if it were Cohen was correct that foreign affairs groups had so far merely appealed to an elite, they should now start work "from the bottom up." Emeny himself, speaking from his retirement in 1955, similarly agreed with Cohen that "only a beginning has been made toward reaching the broader public of the land," but suggested that there were "half a dozen" communities, Cleveland in their lead, that gave "proof to the fact that such successful operations are practical."[23]

Far from having its intended effect, then, the earliest behavioral research on the problem of public opinion caused adult educators to double down on their convictions, just as Lippmann's polemics had in the 1920s. What Almond, Cohen, and others did give the Association, though, was an opportunity to classify more precisely the people it was interested in educating and those it was not. Before Nason engaged with their scholarship, he had spoken vaguely about reaching "the great majority of the American people who have not by custom and circumstance been accustomed to think in international terms." By the end of 1953, Nason was imagining the populace as a hierarchy, like Almond, with a 15 percent that was attentive and informed at the top and a 35 percent at the bottom that was unreachable, "politically inert." In between, Nason's Association told Ford, was the 50 percent of Americans "who may not be eager to learn about international affairs, but who are capable of taking an interest and forming judgments of their own." The minimum that ought to be expected of them was that they could think about the causes of war, grapple with the realities of interdependence, and, importantly, come to appreciate "the democratic principles which are the true sinews of our national power." The Association noted that this was "an uncomfortably large group for an educational venture," but it was the "crucial group in our democracy nonetheless." Ford applauded the idea.[24]

How was it possible for the Association to convince the Ford Foundation to go along with this deliberate misreading? For one thing, Nason and his colleagues tapped into suspicions that the Cold War was not quite an emergency requiring extraordinary measures. Education seemed more necessary than ever as international tensions slackened after the death of Joseph Stalin, the armistice in Korea, and the disgrace of Senator McCarthy, even if the democratic control of foreign policy was becoming more challenging in the face of steepling defense spending and stretching executive power. For another, though the Cold War lifted the social sciences to new heights of influence, their findings were never accepted without question, particularly not regarding an issue as charged as the basic meaning of democracy. Almond, Cohen, and their like merely further unsettled a confused debate. So fluid was the situation for the time being that Ford in fact found itself funding crusades against apathy on the one hand, through the Association and other groups tied to the Fund for Adult Education, and on the other supporting research programs overseen by a political scientist, Bernard Berelson, whose work argued that apathy was a good thing, that it was "unnecessary for the individual voter to be an 'average citizen' cast in the classic or any other single mold." Even so, if Deweyans had once had the run of the foreign policy community, they now had a fight on their hands. Educators had to win, they thought, were democracy to survive; all they needed was the right program.[25]

## Great Decisions in Portland

Great Decisions ran for the first time in Portland from February 20 to April 17, 1955. Overseen by the Association and the World Affairs Council of Oregon, it saw eighty to ninety discussion groups of a dozen or so men and women meet in living rooms, school halls, and public libraries for about three to four hours a week. Mastrude came up with eight, deliberately simple questions for the groups to discuss, before a concluding session that asked to what extent citizens could influence foreign policy:

1. Does US security, prosperity, and freedom depend on the rest of the world?
2. How shall we deal with the USSR?
3. Do we have a 'stake' in Asia?
4. Do we have a 'stake' in Europe?
5. Do we have a 'stake' in colonial Africa?

6. How should we defend ourselves?

7. Do we need friends and allies?

8. Is there an American way in foreign policy?

Each of these questions, intended to be basic enough for the uninitiated to grapple with, was the subject of what marketing experts called a "coordinated campaign" in the weeks the groups were supposed to discuss it. KOIN-AM, a local station in range of half a million radio sets, presented one half-hour program per week on Sunday afternoons. KOIN-TV, an affiliated television station, supplied the staff, films, sets, and airtime for a panel show screened every Wednesday night. KOIN's parent company also owned the *Oregonian*, which had a circulation of three hundred thousand readers. The *Oregonian* gave Great Decisions significant coverage, tracking its preparations for months in advance before lending the Council half a page in its editorial section every Sunday. Mastrude hoped that this bombardment would encourage Portlanders to set up discussion groups, but the Council also allied with the League of Women Voters, the American Federation of Labor, and many other voluntary associations to do the same task. "If you have a group of friends you haven't seen in a while," one organizer said to the *Oregonian*, "invite them in for an evening of conversation." 1,215 people, or thereabouts, ended up taking part in Portland, with more doing so in towns outside the city.[26]

Most Great Decisions discussions groups had experienced leaders, not foreign policy experts with credentials *per se*, but active citizens who had experience in the League or who took a course on discussion theory that Portland State University offered specially. Each of the participants was supposed to have either tuned in to a dedicated radio or television program before attending their discussion group or, preferably, to read one of the fact sheets the Association wrote to give the minimum necessary to contribute. Sold at $1.50 for a set of eight, the fact sheets—twenty-two by twenty-six inches and folded into eight—came illustrated with maps and cartoons and doubled as discussion outlines; after going over the basics of an issue, they posed questions the Association thought could be answered from general principles. The discussions were open, but if the Association was eager to include dissenters, it left no doubt about the answers it sought. The fact sheet for the session dealing with the USSR, for instance, explained that the United States had a "well-advertised increase in military and atomic strength" and "simply provided day-to-day assistance to Western European countries where economic instability and Communist tactics threatened democratic governments," whereas the Soviet Union

**6.2** John W. Nason, *right,* president of the Foreign Policy Association, shows a Decisions fact sheet on Western Europe to the co-chair of the Chicago Great Decisions program, Richard Schmidt, 1958. Wisconsin Historical Society.

had a strategy of "constantly shifting attacks on Europe and Asia" backed by a "huge military machine" that enabled "subversion, propaganda, trickery, obstruction, sabotage, and plotting through communist cells." Was it possible to coexist with such a power, it asked? "At what point should we defend against Communist aggression?" Each of the fact sheets also had an "opinion ballot" that let participants give their answers to questions like these. Participants were

187

asked to mail the ballots to the Council, which would pass them to the State Department. Some participants were so excited at this prospect that they forwarded their views with covering letters. Mrs. Gilbert Reeves of Yelm, Washington, wrote that the "'FINAL BALLOT' really awakened me!" "I'm not too well-versed in foreign policy," she continued, but even with her "average housewife's viewpoint" she knew "what I'd like to do if I had any influence or power."[27]

Letters like these gave Mastrude hope not just that he was reaching the kinds of Americans the Association had historically ignored, but that he was disproving the scholarship he and his colleagues in New York had spent so much time reading. If critics of a democratic foreign policy had long thought that foreign affairs were too distant to give citizens any reason to engage with them, then promoting discussion among friends, families, and work colleagues would give the citizen "good reason for *him* to learn about the subject," Mastrude wrote. If Almond thought that the "average American" felt an "infinitesimal share of influence over the developments of world politics," then Mastrude would use the statements of senior policymakers to insist that public opinion mattered. If Dahl warned that foreign policy was too complex for even some experts to deal with as a whole, then Mastrude would reduce it to a series of "basic issues," a tricky process the New York office dealt with, making problems seem simple enough that the typical citizen would feel that they "are not too 'deep' for him to understand" while also ensuring that the results of the ballots would not be useless for policymakers. With all that taken care of, Mastrude deployed the one chink of light left in communications theory, using evidence that small-group, face-to-face discussion could change minds if it was intimate enough. Even Cohen, after all, thought that "discussions might even be held on back porches on a summer's night."[28]

For the overall approach of Great Decisions, Mastrude drew on developments within the adult education movement. Although the rhetoric of adult education remained unchanged from the 1930s, its practice had become more innovative with the founding of the Fund for Adult Education. From 1951, the Fund invested in the corporate marketing techniques its president, C. Scott Fletcher, had once used to sell motor cars to promote a particular vision for democracy that grew out of small-group discussion. Its first effort was the Experimental Discussion Project, $2.1 million of programs that used prepackaged materials to teach the content and methods Fletcher thought would create "mature, wise, and responsible citizens" who might contribute to a "free world at peace." All the major world affairs groups joined in this work, including the Council on Foreign Relations, which received a grant to gloss *Foreign Affairs* articles for a discussion series that claimed to reach more than twelve hundred groups by 1954. Even dedicated internationalists found these groups daunting, expensive, and dull, however. An Oregon Council series put on with another adjunct of the Fund, the American Foundation for Political Education, convinced fewer than two hundred people to pay the twelve dollars needed to get involved in 1953, much more than the cost of Council membership.[29]

The Fund moved on to its Test Cities initiative, which sought to make adult education an inescapable part of community life. It quickly admitted that this project failed as the Carnegie Corporation's local adult education associations had before it, but there were some pockets of success for Mastrude to draw on. Mastrude liked what he saw in San Bernardino, California, where educator Eugene Johnson was showing that discussion groups could be made popular and effective if they were comprised of friends rather than strangers, if they took place at homes rather than the offices of some voluntary association, and if such groups could be served at scale by radio, television, and the press. Mastrude noted that these techniques managed to generate interest without requiring the presence of physical expertise, which helped him solve the difficulty world affairs groups still had with finding authoritative speakers, especially outside the Northeast. If this workaround threatened to betray the Deweyan faith that publics could educate experts, Mastrude believed that mass media shows featuring policymakers, scholars, and other experts would bridge the gap, especially as Ford was pouring tens of millions of dollars into educational television. Mastrude expressed his "extreme interest" in Johnson's work.[30]

Portland also seemed to be the ideal place to mount a counterattack. Oregon might not have benefitted all that much from defense spending, unlike Washington to the north, but such industries were anyway no guarantee of interest in world affairs on the foreign policy community's terms. Great Decisions fit into Portland's tradition of reformism, direct democracy, and (white) middle-class respectability, albeit one Mastrude complained had not left a culture of urban philanthropy or strong educational associations. Still, Mastrude increasingly believed that the Oregon Council was strong enough to reach "the great '50 percent group'" that had become Nason's target. Munk suggested something similar when he took the opportunity offered by Lippmann's *Essays*, which were coincidentally published just as Great Decisions got under way, to restate the case for participation. Lippmann might have attacked "the ability of the common voter to act intelligently," Munk wrote in the *Oregonian*, but it made no sense to "dispense with much of the democratic process." Rather, it remained worth the effort to try to replace the "ignorant electorate" with the "small but powerful voice of reason, sanity, and responsible citizenship." Not for nothing did an Association official now redefine its entire mission "in contradiction to Mr. Lippmann's 'public philosophy.'"[31]

Great Decisions was the test case for whether this vision of the democratic process was still workable, and there seemed to be signs, in its pilot season, that it had worked. Munk wrote in *Adult Leadership*, a Fund for Adult Education magazine that devoted a whole issue to Great Decisions, that while "the majority of the participants came from the middle-middle and upper-middle classes," the Oregon Council had penetrated "the 'sound barrier' that normally limits education in international affairs to the League of Women Voters type circuit." There was no easy way to measure its achievement, but a survey of group leaders suggested that two-thirds of participants had never joined a formal discussion of world affairs before. Somewhere between one-third and one-half of participants had gathered in parts of town where the average income was lower than the norm, even if only one group was comprised of Black residents in a highly segregated city. Warren Rovetch, Mastrude's deputy, reported that Great Decisions had "become a topic of social conversation," and that if one aim of the program was to create a buzz in the community, it certainly had. The opinion ballots indicated that the discussions had come to the desired results too. Of participants who submitted ballots, 97 percent "believed in working primarily with other countries," compared to just 2 percent who believed "we should 'go it alone.'" These Oregonians sought a foreign policy with a less militaristic tone, even if few of them called for defense spending to be cut. Almost all felt that "'the American brand' of foreign policy should be guided by an 'ideal of international cooperation and the United Nations,'" a position so typical among internationalists that it might have led the Association to reflect on whether it had merely reached its traditional clientele in larger numbers. For the moment, Great Decisions proved to Mastrude that people were indeed educable in the right environment.[32]

The State Department remained ambivalent. Publicly it supported Great Decisions, providing the Council with a note from Secretary of State John Foster Dulles saying that "our nation's foreign affairs should be discussed in every American home" and sending Assistant Secretary George V. Allen to give the Council an Association-sponsored award in December, cables from

President Eisenhower and other senior officials in hand. The reality was more tense. The Association pleaded with State to acknowledge letters from participants with sufficient enthusiasm to "convince people that in fact their opinion does really count," but public affairs officials were becoming less convinced that this was true. This was an institutional and financial issue as much as a philosophical one. State's Division of Public Liaison had been abolished; its successor, the Public Services Division, had to make do with roughly half the staff and half the cash. Its chief, former Emeny acolyte Howard A. Cook, was forced to retreat from promises made a decade earlier. Private individuals and voluntary associations should feel free to express their views on policy, Cook wrote in a memo when he quit in September 1955, but they should not be given the idea that they played "as important a role in the formulation of foreign policy as some have led them to believe." Cook had told Mastrude earlier that year that it was folly to claim that citizens contributed much at all, whatever State's pamphlets said. Warning that it was irresponsible for the Oregon Council to give "the impression that if a person joined one of the 'Great Decisions' groups he could directly influence foreign policy," Cook had written in March that "if these notions continue to be passed around," the organizers would appear "as naïve, which they are not." Mastrude admitted internally that the ballots had only "symbolic value"; Rovetch feared they came "too close to snake oil."[33]

Great Decisions counted most to convince the Ford Foundation to continue to fund the Association. Ford's International Affairs division now took responsibility for the Association from the Fund for Adult Education, which had moved on to other things. Nason asked for a grant of $10.75 million over ten years in January 1956, a sum that appears to have been entertained despite Shepard Stone, the division's chief, describing the figure as "out of this world." Great Decisions itself played only a minor role in the request, but the proposal was based on its animating idea that Nason's middle 50 percent, the "crucial group in our democracy," could be reached. Ford's referees were unenthused. Robert Hartley of the Brookings Institution said that it was simply not "realistic to hope to educate everybody about world affairs." Cook, for his part, said that the Association was deceiving itself, claiming to reach the masses while only enlarging its appeal to elites. But the Foundation was convinced, its staff told its trustees, that the "wisdom and effectiveness with which we manage our foreign relations depend ultimately on adequate public understanding of international problems," a process in which the Association remained "central." Unwilling to take control of the Association to the extent that a $10 million grant would imply, Ford endorsed a $1.5 million grant over five years, double what it had given the Council on Foreign on Relations two years earlier. Great Decisions had set precise demographic targets that could be reached or not; now it had to meet them.[34]

## Great Decisions Falters

Great Decisions took off nationwide. Participation was always difficult to measure because those taking part did not need to report their activities in any official sense, because their numbers were never quite the same from discussion group to discussion group, even evening to evening, and because the Association intended them to be able to share fact sheets if they preferred not to buy their own. Even so, in its first full year Great Decisions took place in fifty-four towns and cities in seven states, involving about sixty-five hundred adults, after which point it outgrew the ability of the Association's small staff to keep close track of it. By 1959, they guessed that the program reached 509 communities in forty-three states, involving about eighty thousand adults with the cooperation of 120 radio and television stations and 199 newspapers. Officials believed that more than 250,000 people were involved five years later, many of them high school students, but the numbers were shaky by that point. "The figures we have publicly used on Great Decisions participation have always puzzled me," one senior figure wrote in 1964, and rightly so. Whatever assessments the Association sent to Ford or quoted in public, the most rigorous internal estimates found that the program peaked at about forty to fifty thousand adults in 1962, dropping off after that.[35]

That is not to say that Great Decisions did not have its successes as the 1950s turned into the 1960s. Oregonians were so devoted to the program that when it outgrew the Council, its running was passed to a formal committee of statewide bodies that included the AFL-CIO, the public schools, and the Federal Cooperative Extension Service, an Agriculture Department agency that employed touring farm and home-economics specialists. Every television station in the state cooperated, along with most of its newspapers, and there were about six hundred discussion groups statewide in 1958. "World affairs and foreign policy were no longer matters a few 'thinkers' talked about," the Association's regional staff reported. For the same reason, officials tended to be most proud of the effect Great Decisions had in rural areas, where the foreign policy community had thus far left no mark. In Wyoming, federal extension services and the state university combined to create a hundred or so discussion groups in the 1959 season, even though there were no major television stations, radio shows, or newspapers available to coordinate messaging. Smaller towns offered opportunities too, as did cities where the suburbs had not yet proven quite so amenable as in the industrial cities of old. Of course, these successes were relative, limited by race and class. From its Portland pilot on, the Association assumed that Black and other minority involvement in Great Decisions was implausible, and that trying to involve certain neighborhoods and certain voluntary associations would therefore be a waste. This racism was more implicit than explicit, but not in much of the South. Few inroads were made there, and where Great Decisions did gain a foothold, as in a project in Macon, Georgia, the staff simply accepted segregation, expending little effort to have their program appeal outside of white communities. Only two of Macon's sixty-three discussion groups included Black members in 1959. Creating communities of foreign policy discussion seemed to require exclusion as well as inclusion.[36]

Even as the major World Affairs Councils struggled to deal with white flight, big cities with developed communications infrastructures offered a tempting target to the Association, when it could convince vested interests to give the program a shot. Educators in several places took advantage of the opportunity. The World Affairs Council of Boston was now in the hands of Christian A. Herter Jr., son of the former branch chairman and serving secretary of state. Great Decisions reached sixteen hundred Bostonian adults in 110 discussion groups in 1957 and became much more vibrant after that; even Henry A. Kissinger, an ambitious young Harvard professor who had set up a Center for International Affairs dedicated to the creation of expertise, took part in a television show that won a Peabody Award for educational programming in 1960. The Chicago Council on Foreign Relations tried its hand with Great Decisions, too, leading the creation of around three hundred discussion groups in 1958 before financial problems forced it to leave the program to others who saw its value, chiefly the editors of the *Chicago Daily News*.[37]

More often than instant success, though, Great Decisions brought fresh intensity to disagreements about the purpose and extent of a democratic foreign policy, showing that such debate was sharpening among grassroots activists as well as social scientists and national officials. While the old branch strongholds of the Northeast adopted Great Decisions as their own, many struggling Councils were skeptical about initiatives not explicitly aimed at their members, and especially about a program that was both a theoretical rebuke to the Council idea and a week-by-week competitor to Council activities. Bitter arguments strained relationships between Association staffers and Council directors, but their turf wars were, at their most fundamental, arguments about the publics educators sought. In Baltimore, the more progressive, mostly female cadres of the United Nations Association decided to start a Great Decisions series, but their push irritated their more traditionalist colleagues. "Some of the old-timers," Association staff noted, "feel that the 'common lot' have muddied their hands," even if there were just 925 participants in the city in 1959. Great Decisions became so popular in the Bay Area that many San Franciscans had to be denied entry to forty open, public discussion groups set up across the city in 1960. Calvin Nichols, executive director of the World Affairs Council of Northern California, looked on in derision. Attempting to create a kind of Council on Foreign Relations for the West, Nichols declared that Great Decisions had "no value whatever." In his view, it was "a delusion and unfair to the participants to give the impression that they were getting something significant out of such a brief exposure."[38]

What Great Decisions participants were in fact getting from the experience was hard to tell. The Association all but admitted that the program was an unwelcome imposition for many. On the cover of one promotional leaflet, for instance, a carpenter sawing, a father mowing, a secretary typing, and a mother cooking with a baby in her arms all looked out quizzically, asking "who, me?" "Do I really have anything to say about U.S. foreign policy?" wondered a shopper inside. "You bet you do!" the text replied, reiterating that while nobody expected ordinary people to know "the day-to-day details" of foreign policy, it was expected that most could take part in "the important, underlying decisions about which direction our foreign policy should follow." A man leaning on a globe asked, "but isn't foreign policy too difficult to understand?" "Not at all!" answered the Association. "You know you want peace, security, a better world for your children," and making an effort would represent "a constructive contribution to U.S. foreign policy." If you filled out a ballot, the leaflet claimed, it would be "tabulated in your own community and the results sent direct to the State Department and Congress." Every participating citizen would therefore "play a democratic role in the shaping of America's foreign policy," performing a duty of their citizenship. "Who, me?" asked the 1965 leaflet; "yes *you* should be interested in international problems."[39]

There were Americans for whom this experience was transformative. From the Western regional office, staffers reminded headquarters that "no counting of groups can set forth the gas station operator who had never before talked about his concerns for the world because he felt it would identify him as queer; the Methodist minister who 'rediscovered' his congregation; the women from the small mountain community who 'saw the world whole' for the first time." But concerns quickly developed that even the most eager of participants were not following through on the expectations the Association set, and that, critically, there were widespread doubts about the claim that individuals could and should have an impact on diplomacy. Troublingly, it was the opinion ballots, the very aspect of the program intended to symbolize ties between policymakers and the public, that made this clear. Philip Van Slyck, the Association official who took charge of the ballots from New York, wrote that the ballots were intended to "dramatize, as no other device can, the basic philosophy of the program that informed opinions do count in the democratic process." The choice of the verb "dramatize," was telling; the ballots remained a curiously performative exercise. The Association left their tabulations to local communities, and it took until 1959 for it to start to collate nationwide tallies. Even then, there was little interest in them. As H. Schuyler Foster of the State Department recalled, just a handful of towns and cities bothered to mail in their numbers each season, meaning that "most groups have not felt it worthwhile to send their conclusions to the State Department."[40]

Why participants were so reluctant to send their views to Washington was a puzzle, one that went to the heart of the difficulties educators now faced. Carnegie Endowment research on the Portland program found that of the 35 percent of 220 community leaders it interviewed who had taken part in 1956, just 16 percent had used a ballot. An observer in Buffalo reported that one group they questioned had not filled their ballots because they had run out of time, another group had "felt that they were really not qualified to form an opinion which would be of any value," and a third had downright refused. Van Slyck heard plenty of skepticism: the ballots were thought to be a "gimmick" because "users and sponsors are cynical about the value of communicating opinions to Washington." The State Department's obvious ambivalence did not help, a diffidence that often humiliated the Association. Van Slyck once told State officials about a lady from Massachusetts who became so convinced of her personal influence on international affairs during the Great Decisions season that she had written to Gamal Abdel Nasser of Egypt and Jawaharlal Nehru of India to express her view, as well as her congressional representatives and the State Department. All but the latter wrote back. There were enough of these stories for Foster to admit in 1963 that "some senders-in may unhappily conclude that the Department 'doesn't give a damn' about what they think," but even he, a former Association branch chair, never thought the ballots had more than "quite marginal" value. He declined to use them in the summaries of public opinion he wrote for departmental use, though the Association was assured that the results reached senior officials in some form.[41]

State's apprehension about Great Decisions, despite the letters it sent out and the speakers it provided, remained constant even as the Association tried to make the program more relevant to policymaking. This shift was not a response to expressed government needs, however, but an acknowledgement of the interests of the people being reached. Mastrude had initially sought to keep the discussions as broad as possible. Participants should not be asked whether they would defend Quemoy, the tiny island in the Taiwan Strait, he argued in 1955, but whether "we should fight, compete, cooperate with or woo China." Like other advocates of popular control, Mastrude did not want to "delude people" into thinking that they could make detailed policy choices, nor ask them to "clarify all the subtle, complex, contradictory, and domestic-political questions which go into decisions on specific policy acts." Citizens could hardly be asked to solve problems so intractable that few experts thought they themselves could cope. But Mastrude still believed that the people set the broad agenda for US foreign policy. Staffers found that "abstract questions like nuclear strategy" held little appeal to most, furthering suspicions that there were policy areas that would be hard, as Dahl had suggested, to submit to popular consent at all.[42]

The Association found increasing evidence, however, that a significant number of Great Decisions participants were simply repeating the program year after year. "People who have already been involved want something with more of an intellectual approach," one planning session noted. Satisfying these participants became so imperative for the program's continue success, even at the risk of scaring off the newcomers that the Association still sought. The one-page fact sheets, with their basic data, simple cartoons, and pocketbook size, were abandoned as the once-simplistic questions posed for discussion became anything but. A 1962 fact sheet on the war in Vietnam—one of eight subjects that year that included Berlin, the political economy of Brazil, and the state of Nigerian democracy—ran to twelve pages of dense prose filled with statistics, trade figures, and diplomatic history. If readers made it to the opinion ballot, which the Association now confined to "issues of policy on which action could be taken rather than on questions of attitude," they found nine policies available to deal with "indirect Communist aggression against South Vietnam" and fully twelve to deal with its 'internal problems of economic, social and political development."[43]

What drove this escalation? Was the average citizen Mastrude had thought he could reach more intelligent than he had presumed? Building a national picture was difficult, but in 1959 the Association ran surveys in four of its most successful target areas—Boston, Macon, Denver, and Oregon—with the intention of showing Ford that "'the people' are neither apathetic nor beyond communication." But the Association struggled to spin the results in that light. Great Decisions turned out to reach a similar kind of audience to other world affairs programs, albeit in greater numbers. Around Boston the program was aimed at the suburbs, on the assumption that the increasingly Black population within the city limits had no interest in foreign policy. Alfred Hero, the social psychologist who conducted the study as secretary of the World Affairs Council there, found that 93 percent of male participants and 87 percent of the women had attended college, half the men having gone on to graduate school. Roughly six in ten participants were women, and many of the group leaders were active in the League of Women Voters. The typical participant was one of the distinctly atypical Americans who belonged to four or more voluntary associations in addition to being a political junky "very far above average" in exposure to the "responsible" mass media. Hero did find that Great Decisions was effective at encouraging people who had a passive interest in world affairs to make a more concrete commitment, with less than half of participants recently having taken part in formal discussions on the subject. But the picture overall was "one of an upper-middle class group with considerable privilege in education, means and social status." Hero surmised that the participants were among "the better-informed, better-read, the more active and highly-motivated two or three percent of the population so far as international relations is concerned." If Great Decisions failed to break beyond a traditional public, with all its media coordination, all its specialist materials, all its forced intimacy, then it was "unrealistic" to try to do so in general, Hero concluded. If the "common man" did not care, "communication with a few of their more thoughtful and active associates seems to us one area where limited, gradual improvement may be practicable."[44]

Every Great Decisions survey taken in 1959—and for a decade and more afterwards—found similar results, even in places where the program was not aimed so directly at the white and well-to-do. Boston's program turned out, oddly, to be relatively progressive. In Denver, 28 percent of participants had graduate degrees; in the two counties surveyed in Oregon, it was 46 percent. Of participants across the country, only 20 to 30 percent had not been to college, most of them women; the men tended to be professionals, academics,

**6.3** Members of the Mile High Senior Citizens club meet at the Denver YMCA for a Great Decisions discussion, 1962. Wisconsin Historical Society.

lawyers, and the like. In Macon, 14 percent of participants were thought to earn less than $5,000 gross, but 24 percent took home over $10,000; the local Chamber of Commerce thought that 53 percent of families in the city earned less than $4,000 net, and just 5.4 percent over $10,000. Participants were also not only likely already engaged with world affairs, but demonstrably were. The best estimate available was that 1 percent of Americans had ever read a book on foreign affairs outside a classroom: half of Great Decisions participants claimed to read "not more than one" such book per year, leaving three-tenths who read two to four, and one-fifth who read at least five. Without question, such people benefitted from Great Decisions: two-thirds of discussants, for example, said that they read more foreign news than they had before taking part, and half took in more radio and television. But it was impossible for the Association to claim that Great Decisions had reached a new kind of citizen. The academic skeptics of participatory democracy, it turned out, were not the only ones working from an elitist theory of democracy.[45]

## *Deweyans Defeated*

Great Decisions did not fail alone. By the end of the decade there was a broad recognition that adult education in the forms favored at the Ford Foundation was an inherently elitist enterprise. The Fund for Adult Education made several studies that replaced normative assessments with statistical constructs, revealing the profoundly limited nature of its projects. Study-discussion programs attracted white, educated, wealthy, and professional types. NORC found that 84 percent of readers in the Great Books program—a Fund enterprise that taught classic literature and involved forty-two thousand people in eleven hundred communities by 1960—had a college transcript. Long before the Association gave up, others in Ford's networks had ceased aiming at the masses. The American Foundation for Political Education abandoned community programs for executive training in 1958, after scholars revealed that its world affairs initiatives had reached an even more exclusive clientele than Great Decisions. The Fund announced in 1959 that its most urgent task was now not to create the informed, interested citizenry that had seemed so imperative a decade earlier, but to "expand educational opportunities for those who bear public responsibilities." The Ford Foundation cut the Fund loose in 1961; it promptly collapsed. The Association meanwhile returned to Ford in 1960 to ask for $3.2 million that it proposed to aim at "community leaders" as opposed to its former target of "as many persons as possible." The Foundation dutifully sanctioned another grant of $1.5 million, but its staff told the trustees that it would start looking at alternatives. "Adult education in world affairs is important in helping American citizens to make informed judgments in the international sphere," the staff warned, "but it is a difficult and baffling field."[46]

Foreign policy, then, was not a special case in the death of the Deweyan dream: the very elitism of the models promoted by Deweyan educators pointed the way to the still greater elitism of the postwar democratic theorists. Great Decisions offered little that was genuinely new, after all. Its model of participation was still the same as much of what the foreign policy community had offered for decades, adding the innovations of the home discussion group, the coordinated media campaign, and the opinion ballot. Grassroots participation was to take place strictly on elite terms; there would be no engagement with the ways in which people otherwise involved themselves in politics, and while there would be boxes for discussants to tick if they sought to dissent from US foreign policy in whatever direction, there would be scarce opportunities for them to frame debates for themselves. With its politics of comfortable, middlebrow consensus, Great Decisions inscribed, endorsed, and made legitimate only a narrow form of participation familiar to (some) white, educated elites, even as Americans of all kinds were grappling with world affairs in countless ways. Yet even this stultifying form of politics made no impression at the State Department. Great Decisions did less to invigorate the progressive conception of a democratic foreign policy than to reveal just how moribund it had become. It survived the 1960s only as what one Association staffer called the "theoretically ideal" program to reach exactly the audience Mastrude had intended it to move beyond; it did better what the Association had always done. Politicians would continue to declare their allegiance to participatory ideals, but the doubts of scholars like Almond and Mills now became certainties to those in the know, as practitioners failed to show that they could create the democracy they sought.[47]

Roger Mastrude knew it. Writing privately in October 1959, he reminded himself that it was the gist of public opinion that mattered, that "the ordinary citizen with his endowment of common sense is about as well equipped as any of his more prestigious but still inexpert fellows" to deal with the modern world. "To deny the *capacity* of the people to think and choose well for their society *within these terms* is to assume that democracy is a preposterous sham," he warned. To leave them ignorant on the issues of the day was to abandon "rational grounds for continuing to believe democracy to be viable." Mastrude granted that educators like himself had probably made no real difference on any issue in the past, but that was no reason not to continue to try. New methods would be needed to reach the people, new technologies, new thinking; specialists would need to "outgrow our callous deprecation of their capacities to think." And if educators could not do better, they would have to admit they had "failed their civic responsibility." Soon enough, they would. Even Mastrude himself abandoned the masses, turning first to create events for corporate executives and then to invent simulations for school social studies classrooms, his final acceptance that adult education was unfit for the task he had set. When the Association fired him in 1970, it was close to insolvent, and the nation was in uproar.[48]

# 7

# The Diplomatic One Percent

The Foreign Policy Association's fiftieth birthday made the front pages and the opinion sections just as its birthdays had before. One thousand of its supporters gathered for dinner on the night of November 14, 1967, in the ballroom of the Manhattan Hilton. John D. Rockefeller III was there, a reliable patron ever since James G. McDonald had chaperoned him around the world. Secretary of State Dean Rusk came up from Washington, at least the third chief diplomat of the United States to have paid Association dues. "Yours has been a public service of profound importance," Rusk told the assembled dignitaries from the lectern. But Rusk revealingly did not go on to proclaim the necessity of an educated public or to insist that his policies were rooted in popular opinion, as his predecessors might have done. Rusk sought obeisance to policymakers instead. "Impatience is pretty dangerous in this modern world," he said, his speech turning to the worsening war in Vietnam. "I hope that each of you will try to put yourselves in the position of the President and Commander in Chief," he implored, for the world posed "questions which have to be approached on our knees."[1]

The *New York Times* had written earlier that morning that humility would indeed be in order. The Association had once resisted a "disastrous American retreat into isolationism," an editorial remembered; its supporters might now usefully spend "the rest of the twentieth century in studying the dangers of American overinvolvement and overcommitment." Even so, the *Times* still thought that the basic purpose of the Association was sound. "Officers of the organization believe that most Americans are poorly informed and apathetic about foreign affairs," a separate news report stated, citing the statistic that 30 percent of Americans were "unaware that China is ruled by a Communist regime." Setting the obvious contradiction aside, the editorial board nevertheless remarked that the Association's contribution to "public enlightenment of foreign problems cannot be measured but is surely substantial."[2]

The apathetic were riotous outside the Hilton that night. Three weeks earlier, students had laid siege to the Pentagon, a marked escalation in their antiwar campaign. Rusk had cancelled a meeting with the prime minister of Japan the morning before his Association address, hoping to arrive at the Hilton early enough to dodge trouble. Trouble came anyway. Three thousand demonstrators gathered around the hotel. Many of them were peaceful, but others pelted the thousand policemen on duty with stones, bottles, and eggs; some attacked the guards with bull's blood, gallon upon gallon of it, symbolic of casualties felled far away. The police lashed back, charging on scooters and stallions. "You want to be treated like animals," one screamed, "we'll treat you like animals." Groups of protestors broke off from the main picket, roaming Midtown. Part of this "roaring mob," as a reporter called it, locked arms and marched south down Sixth Avenue, singing "Hey, hey, LBJ, how many children were killed today?" Another part headed west for Times Square and the recruiting booth the military had erected on Forty-Third Street. "You're a bunch of Communists," one old man heckled from the sidewalk, "take a bath!" The protestors cheered when the news tickers high on the Times Square buildings blared out their actions and booed when the name of President Lyndon Johnson appeared. Meanwhile, activists associated with Students for a Democratic Society, whose Port Huron Statement had dedicated a new left to a democracy of participation and belonging in 1962, headed to Bryant Park, behind the New York Public Library. "We're not demonstrating against Rusk," one young man shouted through a bullhorn. "We're demonstrating against the Foreign Policy Association. We're demonstrating against the American establishment, against the liberal fascists."[3]

Forty-six protestors were taken into custody that night, and five police injured. The *Times* later reported that this was the first salvo in a new, more forceful strategy of antiwar dissent, one that would see previously nonviolent pacifists ally with an active "resistance." So it proved. A few weeks later, Rusk delivered another dinner speech, this time to the World Affairs Council of Northern California at the San Francisco Fairmont. Again there were rocks, eggs, and balloons filled with blood; the police, wielding nightsticks, arrested sixty or so. "Dean Rusk, wanted for murder," the chants went; the secretary of state retorted that the protestors were appeasers. Predictably, Rusk's allies were unimpressed. The Association's board met the day after the Hilton debacle, noting that while there had been some media coverage of the dinner itself,

**7.1** Antiwar demonstrators protest in front of the Century Plaza Hotel, where Secretary of State Dean Rusk was speaking to the Los Angeles World Affairs Council, October 25, 1967. This was one of several protests that took place as Rusk addressed world affairs institutions at the height of the Vietnam War, but one of the few that stayed peaceful.
Uncredited, Associated Press, Shutterstock.

"unfortunately most reports focused on the demonstrations outside." Some of the Association's staff saw the deeper implications of the fact that protestors whose own politics emerged from the participatory processes of teach-ins and the like were targeting Rusk specifically when he spoke to the semi-official institutions that had for so long worked to ensure that Americans felt a sense of engagement with their foreign policy: the Los Angeles World Affairs Council on October 24, the Association on November 14, the San Francisco Council on January 11. C. Dale Fuller, the Association's vice president, told a Kentucky newspaper on November 29 that while Great Decisions offered a "more meaningful" way to influence policy than rage, he could understand the anger. The protests, Fuller admitted, "may have sprung up around the country because individuals believe they have no other way to change America's stance."[4]

New concepts emerged in the wreckage of the educational ideal. The far right had long argued that US foreign policy was controlled by a Manhattan cabal plotting to install socialism and world government; elements of the left had embraced C. Wright Mills's less conspiratorial depiction of a "power elite." Now the conviction that there was a foreign policy "establishment" turned from the subject of satire into common sense, as it was revealed just as it seemed to breathe its death rattle. Council on Foreign Relations members had always differed on the nature and extent of a democratic foreign policy, and even some of its stalwarts were emboldened amid the criticism. John Kenneth Galbraith—economist, former ambassador to India, and veteran of the Democratic left—called in 1966 for progressives to oppose the "divine right" to rule of the "impeccably traditional member of the permanent foreign policy establishment." Rusk replied in a speech at Council House that the only "establishment" of which he was a member was the Smithsonian Institution, on whose board the secretary of state sits by statute. But Council members now joined journalists and historians in tracing their supposed elite all the way back to the Great War, obscuring past debates and writing onto the foreign policy community as a whole the taste for secrecy, lies, and insularity that the Pentagon Papers would expose in 1971. Surely, former State Department aide and founder of the Institute for Policy Studies Richard Barnet wrote, the permission that apathy and ignorance had given policymakers to do as they would had meant that their interest in "education" had been a "euphemism" for "subtle propaganda, the reinforcement of stereotypes, the stimulation of fears, and the quieting of disturbing doubts," even for "outright deception."[5]

Surely not, not quite. It was clear from the speed with which the "establishment" idea took hold that educators had failed to make world affairs anyone's affairs. But despite growing intellectual doubts, that failure had not been seen as complete even at the start of the 1960s. Back then, the Association and the Ford Foundation had then tried to reinvigorate the calcifying network of institutions they led, and the idea that foreign policy should be rooted in popular consent was not entirely forgotten among politicians, even if it had lost its radical edge. Secretaries of State Dean Rusk, Henry Kissinger, and Cyrus Vance each paid their respects to the Association while in office, and each sat on its board at one point or another—Rusk and Kissinger after they left the State Department, Vance before he swore his oath. Practically, however, the task came to appear impossibly challenging. As Ford withdrew, nothing more symbolized the fate of a project that had been central to the first age of American primacy—the decades from the trenches of the Great War to the jungles of Vietnam—than the near-collapse of the Association that had embodied the effort to make that primacy feel like a democratic possession. As the student in Bryant Park made viscerally clear, its humiliation meant it was now seen as no more than a branch of the "establishment" it had labored for half a century to avoid.

## The Collapse of "Public Opinion"

When Gabriel Almond wrote a preface to the second edition of his *The American People and Foreign Policy* in 1960, he saw more cause for satisfaction than he seen a decade before. Back in 1950, it had been "necessary to conclude that American mass opinion in foreign affairs was a 'mood' reaction, shifting radically in response to events," he now wrote. Since then, though, interest in foreign policy had steadied. Higher education had grown the "attentive public." Opinions had become more uniform as a result of narrowing class divisions, declining rates of immigration, and the "floor of information and communication" that the mass media buttressed. Almond did not go so far as to say that an adequate public had been built for US foreign policy, but he did argue that the public could no longer be so easily blamed for its faults.[6]

Almond made an optimistic case, but colleagues who were closer to the latest research on public opinion were far more skeptical. Take the idea that America was a "nation of joiners," as historian Arthur M. Schlesinger Sr. had written in 1944. Educators had always seen voluntary associations as the main means and even target of their work, believing them to be at the center of American political culture. But even as rising affluence and standards of education pulled association membership to a historic peak, scholars worried that such faith was folly. Research at the end of the 1950s revealed that just half of American families held memberships in at least one voluntary association, most likely a church group or a labor union; somewhere between one-fifth and one-sixth were members of two or more such groups and hence likely to be among the few who added civic or political affiliations to the more common religious and fraternal ties. Even if a person was a member of a voluntary association, the chance that they were an active one, enjoying the full, democratic benefits of participation, had worsened as such associations bureaucratized and became more hierarchical. Charles Wright and Herbert Hyman, the leading experts on the subject, concluded that "these findings hardly warrant the impression that Americans are a nation of joiners." Murray Hausknecht, a sociologist, predicted in 1962 that the voluntary association would soon "not be a significant factor in American life."[7]

If the prospects for reaching Americans through their associations looked dim, the hope that information might be taken in at scale had darkened too. No serious scholar believed in the postwar years that insufficient information about politics was available to citizens, as had been the consensus in the 1920s. "A fair flow of information is *accessible* to almost everyone in the society," sociologist Philip Converse wrote in 1962, continuing that "the fact that little attention is paid to it even though it is almost hard to avoid is a fair measure of lack of public interest." Scholars had once taken solace in studies showing that attitudes could shift in light of facts, at least under laboratory conditions. But most theorists now wrote of the audience not as the blank, manipulable slate Harold Lasswell had imagined, but as "obstinate," emphasizing that social, psychological, and technological barriers made effective communications almost impossible in the real world. As Robert A. Dahl put it in 1961, the "great flood of propaganda channeled through the mass media diminishes to a thin trickle when it encounters the desert of political indifference in which most citizens live out their lives." Converse and his colleagues at the University of Michigan's Survey Research Center also confirmed in *The American Voter* (1960)—the summit of postwar statistical research on democracy—that the most politically alert Americans were actually the least likely to change their minds on an issue. If the link between facts and opinions was in doubt, so was the personal touch. Opinion leaders had just a decade earlier been thought to connect media products to the masses, but Converse revealed that their existence was a theoretical fiction. "Very little information 'trickles down' very far," he concluded, because almost nobody had the cognitive structure to process it. Foreign policy beliefs were among the least stable political views of all, Converse found, suggesting that they had "extremely low centrality for the believer."[8]

Unlike at the start of the 1950s, when social scientific debate had been diffuse enough to leave openings for experiments like Great Decisions, there was now a consensus on all the major questions surrounding the Association's work. It had formed rapidly. The Carnegie Endowment study group that John W. Nason had participated in in 1953, for instance, had not convinced the Association's then president that an appeal to a broad public was certain to fail. But as that same study group had morphed into an effort to improve public understanding of the United Nations, its assumptions had hardened. Chaired by Paul G. Hoffman, sponsored by the Ford Foundation, and involving two former assistant secretaries of state for public affairs, that second

Endowment project had started from the conviction that it would be "fatuous" to advocate mass education, as one participant put it, for "'public opinion,' as such, is just too much to cope with." That belief only strengthened when the project's myriad surveys, interviews, and experiments found that even community leaders were not fulfilling the duties of their citizenship as the Endowment defined them. "Whence do people derive their information on which to base their vote on issues or give support to steps relating to foreign affairs?" political scientist Saul K. Padover asked in a version of the Endowment report that the Association published in 1958. "The answer is that they don't."[9]

Other scholars doubted that even the focus on community leaders that the Endowment consequently endorsed would work. Alfred Hero, the Great Decisions skeptic who was secretary of both the Boston World Affairs Council and the World Peace Foundation, edited a series of seven books in 1959 and 1960, offering educators a survey of the relevant recent scholarship. Hero set towering but not uncommon standards for the public, expecting voters to show explicit interest in foreign policy, to possess accurate information about it, to assess the issues "in a logical or rational way," and to be generally active in politics. Such citizens were vanishingly rare. Perhaps 3 percent of Americans were interested, informed, and active, but at best one in a hundred came "close to qualifying" in all four categories, Hero thought. The priority should therefore be to focus on the Americans who were already interested in foreign affairs or had significant political influence—to expand the one percent, in other words. Hero was not alone in this conclusion. Bernard C. Cohen continued to give what he knew was "uncomfortably regressive" advice along similar lines. The Endowment explicitly instructed educators to preach to the converted, for "a preacher who neglected his parishioners would soon find himself without a congregation." Practitioners in the Midwest wrote that since experience demonstrated that "the fully informed man in the street who takes an active interest in world affairs is clearly a fiction," ordinary citizens should be left alone, and not "held up to scorn and ridicule" for exercising their right to ignore politics. Even idealists were stuck. One dissenting Association staffer who decried Hero's "fallacy of the one percent," Hilton Power, still defined the task ahead as merely "turning the hundreds reached at present into thousands."[10]

The theoretical basis of the citizen education movement had been torn apart. Political science as a whole, indeed, was becoming premised on the assumption that policymakers had to govern where the people could not. Harvard's V. O. Key, for instance, wrote of public opinion as if it could not exist without the state at all, defining it in 1961 as "those opinions held by private persons which governments find it prudent to heed." Studies of administrative decision-making "migrated from the margins to the center of political science" from 1940 to 1960, Daniel Bessner and Nicolas Guilhot have written, whether in the form of systems theory, rational choice, or other genres of inquiry that explored how policymakers might decide, alone. Some academics still saw public opinion as one input into policy outcomes, not least because officials still told them it was, but even the best minds struggled to trace how such a process worked. "Officials simply do not think about public opinion very much or very explicitly," Cohen found. Key's colleague at Harvard, Ernest R. May, insisted that "American statesmen have traditionally thought themselves responsible to, and supported or constrained by, some sort of general will," but he, too, found "almost no evidence to support the proposition that officeholders have to heed public opinion when deciding issues of foreign policy." May decided that "public opinion" was a "fiction" needed "to cope with the chaos that is reality"; after a sabbatical at the Survey Research Center, where attitudes were measured to several decimal places, Key complained that "to speak with precision of public opinion is a task not unlike coming to grips with the Holy Ghost."[11]

Basic questions went unasked. Was too much being expected of the people? Were the right things being measured? Were people participating in ways that might mean that "apathy" was not what it seemed? Was it right to define the citizen's duties in ways that polls suggested very few Americans agreed with? One might reasonably wonder whether all this was intended to bolster the claims of expert power, but these men were not budding authoritarians in disguise and their work was not cynically antidemocratic. Dahl vigorously denied that the word "elitist" could be applied to his research, which he intended to be descriptive and not normative; he maintained that he felt that participation was in fact "deplorably low." Almond would later take offense at the claim that he was among the "power-security freaks, hirelings of World Wars I and II, and the Cold War." Key's last book, unfinished at his death in 1963, noted that while a "heroic conception of the voter" certainly did not emerge from postwar behavioral studies, a "perverse and unorthodox argument" could still be made that "voters are not fools." These were serious responses to serious times, to a world filled with frightening new dangers—but responses that had their own risks, too.[12]

## Behavioral Science Comes to the Association

The Foreign Policy Association had to move with the times. To think about public opinion in its circles was not now to redeploy knowledge from the women's movement or from peace activism, but to think in social scientific terms. When Nason quit under pressure from the Ford Foundation in January 1962, it was to a representative of that social science that the Association turned. Samuel P. Hayes Jr. was a Yale-trained social psychologist whose doctoral research on the presidential election of 1932 had led him to ask whether rational voters existed at all. Few academics had Hayes's breadth of insight into the practical uses of scholarship, particularly surveys: he had spent a post-doctoral year studying with Lasswell at Chicago, worked for George Gallup doing market research at a public relations agency, and served at the State Department, implementing the Marshall Plan and Point Four. Dabbling in development economics, he wrote a blueprint for the Peace Corps and helped set up the United States Agency for International Development. What mattered to the Association, though, was the expertise Hayes brought to the study of public opinion. More of an entrepreneur than an original thinker, Hayes had founded two initiatives at Michigan—the archetypal Cold War university— dedicated to exploring the utility of social scientific research and he was also a friend and co-author of the director of Michigan's Institute of Social Research, Rensis Likert, father of the Survey Research Center. Hayes was not a man to question an intellectual consensus, as his predecessor had been.[13]

The hiring of Hayes was symbolic not just of the Association's reluctant accommodation of scholarship, but of its acceptance of the primacy of policymakers too. Ironically, the Ford funding that had left Roger Mastrude room to experiment had also pulled the Association closer to the state, as the Foundation's prestige led to rebuilding of the board. John D. Rockefeller III had a spell as the Association's vice chairman. George Perkins and James Zellerbach served before becoming Dulles-era ambassadors, and legendary former Harvard president James Conant led the program committee after retiring as US ambassador to West Germany. Arthur Goldberg and Roswell Gilpatric left the board to take posts in the Kennedy administration; Henry Cabot Lodge Jr., President Eisenhower's United Nations ambassador and grandson of the enemy of the old League of Free Nations Association, came the other way. Lodge, like most of the others, joined on the condition he just be a "name on the list," endorsing the cause without advancing it, but at least one high-ranking official made their presence felt. Robert R. Bowie, protégé of

Council on Foreign Relations chairman John McCloy, had been the State
Department's director of policy planning under John Foster Dulles, quitting
in 1957 to found Harvard's Center for International Affairs with Henry A.
Kissinger. Serving as chair of the Association's program committee, Bowie
urged retrenchment at a time when Nason, confronting the failure of Great
Decisions, feared that educators were "fumbling for an adequate conceptual
scheme or framework within which to pursue our objectives."[14]

Hayes had a conceptual framework, and he applied it rigorously. After his
arrival in New York, he started to circulate bibliographies and plot a philosophy that would see the Association "advance the national interest" through
"more effective participation in the making of national decisions," as he put
it in March 1963. His plans gained academic approval that April at a conference of foundation officials, voluntary association leaders, and social scientists, with Hero and Angus Campbell—Hayes's friend and director of the
Survey Research Center—notably in attendance. "General education of 'attentive public' was recognized as tremendous task," Hayes noted, and "considerable doubt" was expressed about the "feasibility or desirability of general
public reaching 'decisions' on specific foreign policy issues." The board had
little option but to conclude likewise. "While all present agreed that it would
be desirable to educate the 'masses' on foreign policy," it resolved in October,
"it was generally recognized that 'operationally' this posed insurmountable
problems."[15]

By April 1964, Hayes had fully infused the once-radical effort for a democratic foreign policy with the conclusions of a social scientific field that denied the possibility of even minor reform. Citing Almond, Cohen, Hero,
Key, and others, Hayes declared in his final planning document that it would
be wasteful to direct resources to the 80 percent of Americans who were "inattentive" to politics, even to the 90 percent of Americans not "active" in
politics. "The size of the 'inattentive inactive' majority is so great," he wrote,
"the interest and attention aroused in it by foreign affairs treatment in the
media so low, the competition of other stimuli and interests so strong, and
the possibility of reaching the majority of the electorate through voluntary
organizations so limited, that it would be far beyond FPA's financial capabilities." The Association would target the seven million or so politically active
Americans who were not much interested in foreign policy, and beyond that,
the five million who were already both active and interested. Was this all that
different from the public the Association had cultivated so far? With the exceptions of its radio broadcasts and the odd state where Great Decisions had

broken through, not really. But the Association had never formally constrained its ambitions in such a way. Gone was Newton Baker's prayer that every man, woman, and child in Cleveland might be in reach. Gone was Brooks Emeny's trust that every citizen could be a statesman. Gone was John Nason's faith in the middlebrow. For Hayes, only a sliver of Americans could ever be party to a democratic foreign policy. One hundred million people would be unworthy of that.[16]

In practice, this meant a focus on leadership groups. Great Decisions remained at the core of the Association's work, although targeted at a more exclusive public than it had been designed to reach, and it now boasted National Educational Television shows and a series of "issues conferences" at which participants met with their congressional representatives. The rest of the Association's activities harkened back to its early days with a revival of the New York luncheons and the founding of Associates of FPA, which offered blue-chip speakers to wealthy benefactors. Several programs were remnants of the World Affairs Center, a quasi-independent attempt to coordinate the citizen education movement that Ford, Rockefeller, and Carnegie had forced the Association to lead in 1957. Operating from Carnegie Endowment facilities near the United Nations in Manhattan, the Center had a bookshop, auditorium, and conference rooms. It suffered severe budget cuts in 1961, but some of its initiatives went on, most importantly its Community Leaders Program, in which fifty or so notables at a time came to New York at the invitation of the US ambassador to the United Nations to hear briefings from members of the US mission, have lunch at the Association, and cross First Avenue to witness internationalism at work. The program seemed to be a welcome one, but it was revealing that Hayes had no interest in courting the million or so tourists who visited the United Nations every year, selecting instead—and at great expense—the businessmen and industrialists whose opinions he thought had more value.[17]

The same old problems marked this program. Set aside the obvious, troubling outlook of a philosophy aiming at the white, wealthy, and educated amid the civil rights movement and a war on poverty. Set aside, too, the precarity of the Association after the utter failure of its fortieth birthday celebrations to raise a significant endowment. Hayes's vision faced two significant issues on its own terms. One was that it left nothing for the World Affairs Councils to do, long abandoned and crumbling in the face of funding pressures. The other was that its focus on the impact of public opinion depended on convincing the public that opinions in fact mattered, a problem that

Great Decisions had tried to confront, without success. Solving that dilemma, though, was a question for the federal government.

### *"The Zeroest of Zero Jobs"*

On February 1, 1962, three members of the Association's board and one of its staff walked into the Oval Office. John F. Kennedy welcomed them as presidents had welcomed Association officials before, posing for photos and flicking through a Great Decisions kit. The Association's representatives told the *New York Times* that the president had given them "great encouragement" in their mission. But this brief reception was not a throwback to the years when James McDonald and Frank McCoy had gossiped with the men behind the White House desk; it was a mark of crisis, not a vote of confidence. The idea came from Chester Bowles. After Kennedy had fired Bowles as undersecretary of state late in 1961, the former business partner of William Benton became a troubleshooting ambassador-at-large. Bowles did not have to look far. Forget the "bomber gap" and the "missile gap," those Cold War campaign issues *par excellence*; Bowles was more concerned about the "information gap." There was, he told Kennedy in January 1962, a "dangerous" gulf between the "harsh, complex realities with which Washington policymakers must grapple and the generally limited understanding of these realities by most Americans, including the press and Congress." Hence the invitation to the Association, still the go-to authority on these issues.[18]

"I have been struck," Bowles wrote in a long critique of government information policies in March, "by the immensity of the problem and the tremendous effort that will be needed to do anything meaningful about it." Secretary Rusk had inherited a Bureau of Public Affairs with an annual appropriation of $1.4 million, puny compared to the $35 million the Pentagon spent on public relations. Just $31,000 was made available for State's publications program, a third of the budget of a typical college newspaper. When State had moved into its new building after World War II it had constructed its own media facilities, but its television studio was next to its air-conditioning system and its radio booth adjoined the delivery area, so neither had turned out to be much use. The Departments of Defense, Agriculture, and Interior—even the Bureau of Reclamation—had their own movie series, but State had not one reel of film available for distribution to the public. The Pentagon had four officers working in Hollywood; State had none. State's speakers bureau was "a one-woman operation," and she came nowhere close to fulfilling even

**7.2** President John F. Kennedy reads a Great Decisions fact sheet as he greets senior officials of the Foreign Policy Association in the Oval Office at the White House, February 1, 1962. Wisconsin Historical Society.

limited demand. Foreign service officers, often returning from abroad, were now put out to pasture in a public affairs unit where trained professionals had once thrived.[19]

How far the State Department had fallen. As World War II ended, the department had promised that a democratic foreign policy could be made a reality, one in which it would provide facts and take meaningful account of popular views. "If the foreign policy of the United States is to be democratically representative of the people," Office of Public Affairs chief Francis H. Russell had written in 1947 in an Association pamphlet that State ensured would promote the importance of the individual citizen, then "the people must participate in the making of policy and share responsibility for the outcome." These convictions were tempered but not abandoned as the growing threat of the Soviet Union appeared to require tougher forms of opinion management to ready the masses for the fight, in part because an ideal public was not yet felt to exist. "If we had a more enlightened public opinion," *Times* Sunday editor Lester Markel reflected in a Council on Foreign Relations study in 1949, "we would not have to use the shock technique to which the government believes it has to resort to awaken the Congress to the need for a Truman Doctrine."[20]

State's harsher methods blurred the line between the information campaigns it ran at home and the psychological warfare it waged with fewer scruples abroad, but the line did exist for the Truman administration, which tried not to oversell the Cold War and made little effort to push back on Congressional initiatives that constrained its action. Republican majorities put strict limits on the State Department's domestic reach in the Smith-Mundt Act (1948), raised the prospect of enforcing antiquated laws banning the use of appropriations to influence Congress, and even threatened to shut down State's *Bulletin*, a favorite target of Congressman Richard M. Nixon that did no more than reprint speeches, treaty texts, and communiqués. The resources at State's disposal therefore never matched the claims policymakers made from the secretary of state down. A sum of $115 million went to overseas information programs in 1952, but the Division of Public Liaison had a budget of just $250,000 that year, $180,000 less than an Association then flush with Ford Foundation grants.[21]

State Department operatives were forced to work through compliant private networks to guide public opinion, a collaboration that at least helped make its promotion of armed internationalism seem as if it were a spontaneous, voluntary, and even democratic occurrence. Just as they had with the campaign to join the United Nations, State officials outsourced their campaigns for the Marshall Plan and NSC-68 to private groups led by trusted former officials. Mass media cooperation was easy to acquire as broadcasters sought to fulfil their public service mandates; the shows that resulted, like CBS's *World Briefing* and *Diplomatic Pouch*, gave their audiences the impression of watching accountability at work as senior officials were subjected to interviews, but in fact remained tightly controlled behind the scenes. Journalists echoed official views, primed by their shared boys' club culture, their pack reporting methods, and the uncompetitive structure of a newspaper industry still local rather than national. Classification of official information meanwhile rose as a "more palatable method of securing secrets than the antidemocratic censorship of speech or publication," Sam Lebovic has written, walling the most consequential policy deliberations off from public scrutiny except when information leaked out. Wartime methods were carried over into the postwar period as State guided its information strategy with polling data it helped to fund and based its overall assumptions on the latest research.[22]

Contemporaries saw that the State Department was betraying its opportunity. The Hoover Commission on the operations of the federal government warned in 1949 that "neither the 'top command' level nor the Public Affairs units are presently organized to deal with public opinion in an adequate manner" and criticized a failure to include the public affairs staff in policy-making discussions. Russell, for his part, complained that his office was understaffed, underfunded, and underappreciated. His successor, Howard A. Cook, fared worse, writing in October 1952 that there was "a lack of appreciation and understanding of PA's [the Office of Public Affairs's] function within the Department and methods by which it achieves its purposes." The basic problem was that while nobody doubted that foreign policy was formulated with public opinion in mind, few thought that such institutional structures were necessary when policymakers already read newspapers, watched the evening news, and so on. "PA plays a relatively modest role in this process," one official told Russell, "which *goes on anyway.*"[23]

There was little resistance, then, when the Eisenhower administration pared State's public affairs infrastructure back, partly in the name of fiscal stringency, partly to clean house in the face of McCarthyism, and partly because of the trust it had in the corporate marketing techniques that had served it well in the presidential campaign of 1952. Secretary Dulles's first assistant secretary for public affairs, journalist Carl McCardle, had once served on the board of the Association's Philadelphia branch, but he saw his task primarily as press relations. His first budget slashed $430,000 and fifty-three staff from the Office of Public Affairs, curtailing the programs of the Public Services Division that replaced it. While McCardle was muting State's ability to speak he also covered its ears, halving H. Schuyler Foster's public opinion studies staff before his successor, Andrew Berding, stripped the political scientist of his contract with the National Opinion Research Center during a scandal in 1957. The real revelation of that debacle, which was sparked when Congress discovered that Foster's polling had been funded out of an appropriation supposedly set aside for consular emergencies, was that so few people really cared about an issue that had once been so fraught. Berding capitulated; Dulles never trusted polls; Clyde Hart, who ran the surveys at NORC, testified that they were "too niggardly an operation" to be much use. If the loss of the surveys made no difference to State's work, the breakdown of the "two-way" relationship that Dean Acheson had once imagined was clear. Public relations expert and Eisenhower adviser C. D. Jackson told one potential recruit that explaining foreign policy to the American people was "the zeroest of zero jobs." Vice President Nixon fumed that "if we indulge in the kind of thinking which assumes that foreign policy decisions should be made on the basis of opinion polls, we might as well decide now to surrender our position of world leadership to the Communists."[24]

The idea that mass participation was necessary in foreign policy died hard, though, and the Eisenhower administration less abandoned than reconceived it through public diplomacy initiatives, stoking the interest of attentive citizens and employing them as combatants in Washington's propaganda war abroad. Seeing foreign policy as a product to be sold like any other, its main effort was People-to-People, a massive program launched from the United States Information Agency (USIA)—which was supposed to target overseas populations alone—that encouraged a variety of contacts between Americans and foreign citizens. The program intended to give Americans the feeling that they were themselves waging the fight for a free and peaceful world when they wrote to a pen-pal abroad, hosted a touring orchestra, or consummated a sister-city alliance. But while People-to-People cleverly stole the rhetoric of the educational movement—"Your Community in World Affairs," announced one pamphlet—it employed citizens as the objects of government policy rather than as its makers. For many the thrill was irresistible; why debate China policy, after all, when one could play a small part in China policy? Brooks Emeny, no less, chaired People-to-People's foreign affairs committee after Nason turned the job down, touring the Middle East, Southeast Asia, and Africa to evangelize the democratic way on USIA-funded junkets. World Affairs Councils hosted hundreds of foreign visitors per year through State's Foreign Leader Program or on their own initiative. Doing your part for foreign policy, Berding told readers of his *Foreign Affairs and You!* (1962), might still mean joining a Council or reading a newspaper, as it had been in the past, but today it also meant serving as a soldier in a Cold War for hearts and minds.[25]

While the Kennedy administration offered Americans still more ways to join the fray, most powerfully the Peace Corps, it also tried to recover lost ground. Rusk increased the budget of the Bureau of Public Affairs to $1.75 million in 1964; it expanded its regional conferences, sending high-ranking officials to meet with community leaders or embedding junior officers in cities for several days, partnering with the few World Affairs Councils strong enough to cope. Rusk had refused to fund the Association as president of the

Rockefeller Foundation in the 1950s, but as secretary he endorsed it frequently, vouching for it when its grants came up at the Ford Foundation, recording radio ads for Great Decisions, and supporting funding that helped Councils defray the expenses of diplomats who otherwise had to spend their own money to address the public, a World War II–era policy to the contrary having lapsed. But it was too little, too late. One Cleveland educator had privately written back in 1953 that "unless we find ways to relate the educational groups to the actual processes of policy formulation and implementation, their growth will be stopped and perhaps they will even wither away." The prediction was not wrong.[26]

## Confusion at the Ford Foundation

The Ford Foundation had not given up yet, but its doubts were growing. Philanthropy had been at the center of the effort to create a democratic foreign policy almost as long as that effort had been around, shaping its direction and defining its reach, but Ford's power was far greater than any of its predecessors. Foundation officials had not paid much attention to how the $3.4 million Ford had granted since 1952 had been spent to this point; if they had quibbled with aspects of the Association's affairs, it said much about the lasting importance of the educational project that the necessity of continued funding was taken for granted. That had still held true as late as 1960, when Ford had stretched foundation support for the Association into a fourth decade, continuing one of the International Affairs division's largest commitments, albeit at a level that forced Nason to shutter the speakers bureau among other things. Grant officers heard from even skeptical sources that "if the FPA did not exist, it would have to be invented," and repeated the same line to Association staffers. Ford's trustees, who included at least one World Affairs Council board member, remained true to the mission, declaring themselves still dedicated to "efforts to increase American understanding of and participation in world affairs" in July 1962.[27]

What seemed desirable in theory, however, was becoming untenable on the ground. The relationship between the Association and the Councils had devolved into animosity after 1955, when the Association had started to use Great Decisions to appeal to a mass public at the same time as the Councils felt forced to restrict themselves to local elites in a desperate effort to rescue their finances. Association staffers increasingly believed, however, that Councils could prosper only in a few cities, with Mastrude suggesting in 1958 that just five were doing "a fairly effective job of community-wide education" and arguing in 1962 that the model had "no future." Councils required considerable private wealth to be viable, which Emeny had provided in Cleveland, as well as corporate buy-in, activist enthusiasm, and leadership as competent in civic organization as in foreign policy. Almost nowhere had this been possible. Several Council directors banded together to try their luck with the foundations, their individual inquiries having been dismissed, but their collective efforts went nowhere, with the Association still Ford's preferred vehicle and the Councils split over their needs and outlooks.[28]

Ford was willing to work out how bad the problem really was, though, and it turned to the most persistent Council director, Calvin Nichols, to do so. Director of the World Affairs Council of Northern California since 1955, in San Francisco Nichols had emphasized deep-dive study-discussion groups for the Council's up to four thousand members, hoping to influence policy. But despite a circumspect vision and a budget that rose from $91,500 in 1955 to almost $200,000 in 1962, Nichols faced such financial difficulties that he asked Carnegie and Ford for grants, without success, before leading his colleagues in a $2 million pitch to Ford in 1962. That was out of the question, so Nichols, whose bitter criticisms of the Association's ambition made his colleagues wonder whether he harbored some sort of vendetta, asked Ford for a grant to study the Councils' needs. "My guess is that the survey will not reveal a new promising opportunity," noted Ford official Stanley Gordon, as he set up a parallel internal evaluation under former Democratic party operative Matthew Cullen; "I hope I'm wrong." But he was not. Just four Councils, Nichols found, had more than four thousand members, and ten accounted for four-fifths of the total budget of about $700,000. "No council appears to be satisfied with the quality or adequacy of its program," he wrote, even as he defined citizen education—in the most conservative manner possible—as merely fostering "a climate in which leaders may lead and followers may follow intelligently in public criticism or support of foreign policy." Nichols sought $1.6 million to rebuild the movement from the ground up.[29]

Cullen's inquiries for the Ford Foundation found nothing more encouraging. "FPA is doing the kind of job that nobody else really wants to do," he told his boss, International Affairs division chief Shepard Stone, "and as a result there is little enthusiasm for what it is doing." One influential assessment came from Theodore Kaghan, a psychological warfare specialist who had worked for McCloy and Stone in occupied Germany. The idea that mass participation was even desirable was symptomatic of educators' basic "misconceptions about the democratic process," Kaghan wrote, and he felt that "encouraging the belief that knowledge about foreign affairs makes one a more 'effective citizen' is likewise misleading." It would be sufficient, he thought, to simulate the acquisition of consent through the mass media, whether the *New York Times*—in whose new Pacific edition Stone, once a *Times* reporter, had high hopes—or less salubrious means. "We don't have to descend to using Zsa Zsa Gabor as a bosomy interrogator of Dean Rusk on the Hungarian question," Kaghan wrote, "but other combinations of glamor and statecraft should not be ruled out." Other consultants had abandoned all hope. Former State Department official Charles E. Allen suggested terminating all philanthropic funding and clearing away "the existing debris"— and he actually sat on the board of Nichols's Council in San Francisco.[30]

When Hayes asked in the summer of 1964 for $3.9 million for new projects that would be exclusively aimed at adults assumed to be "significant in the democratic processes that shape foreign policy," on top of $1 million for general support, Ford officials felt discomfort, even embarrassment. Nichols suggested that $1.25 million would be more reasonable but told Cullen that "the record doesn't justify even this much assistance." Cullen agreed, yet consented to a terminal grant of $1 million. That was still too much for the Foundation's president, Henry T. Heald. Heald had despised adult education since before the downfall of the Fund for Adult Education, preferring to invest in educational television as an alternative to discussion groups. He forced Stone to halve the grant, throw out Nichols's scheme for the Councils, and insert a note in the materials for Ford's trustees that nodded to the "large amounts of money invested with only occasionally favorable results and limited improvement in world affairs education." When the trustees met in September, Heald instructed them to turn even this truncated plan down. Angrily noting their historic obligations and policy statements, they forced Heald to commission a fuller study before taking precipitate action. Cullen resigned in fury at Heald's duplicity, telling Hayes the gory details on his way out.[31]

No single view held sway at Ford, where a complex subject met a complex organization, but the Committee on Citizen Education in World Affairs that Heald formed was united in its dismay at what it found. Comprising four divisional chiefs from Ford's domestic programs, the group was chaired by Stone but run by director of policy planning Malcolm Moos, formerly a White House speechwriter who had drafted President Eisenhower's farewell address, with its plea for an "alert and knowledgeable citizenry" to balance the military-industrial complex. But creating that citizenry was no longer taken for granted as a job for the Foundation. All kinds of ideas—old and new—about the nature of a democratic foreign policy poured into the study. "Not the least of the concerns I have," wrote James Armsey, director of Ford's higher education programs, "is whether we shoot for the 'leaders' or the 'masses,' whether, in short, we espouse the elitist approach or the democratic approach to ultimate decision making in this society in the area of world affairs." (The choice of adjectives was telling.) "Who is trying to find out what we want citizens to know other than 'everything'" asked economist Marshall Robinson. "You simply cannot inculcate the idea of being interested in foreign policy matters," averred E. S. Staples. Moos knew that the likely end result of his inquiries would be difficult for the trustees to swallow. He fondly remembered the Association's glory days in the 1930s, but thought it had become "a little like a cat with nine lives that has used up eight of them but no one admits it."[32]

Moos dived deeper than any foundation official had dived before. He sent Staples to talk to the State Department. He spoke to Alfred Hero. He dined with Angus Campbell, whose Survey Research Center scholars wrote as optimistic a summary of the latest research as they could, as a favor to their old friend Hayes. Moos also hired a Johns Hopkins professor, Robert W. Tucker, to look over the field. Operating within the dominant paradigm of postwar social science, with all its deference to the decisionmaker, Tucker was troubled by the populism of a Great Decisions program he knew anyway appealed to a limited audience. "I see little to be gained and a great deal to be lost," he wrote, "by cultivating the idea that a few minutes of background material prepares one for making sound and responsible judgments on foreign affairs." By February 1965, Moos had finished a report that showed no trace of the zeal that not so long ago had linked the peace of the world to an informed populace at home. Rather, it betrayed a profound weariness that such a task, one that had already cost Ford almost $5 million, might still be necessary.[33]

"Every day Americans are made conscious of an uncomfortable world beyond our borders and that somehow we cannot disengage from it," the Moos report declared, yet nobody believed there was "any likelihood of a dramatic breakthrough in citizen education in world affairs." It was the difficulty that the field had long faced, put starkly: a changing, dangerous world did not prompt the kinds of activities that the foreign policy community saw as legitimate participation. The longer the perceived lack of engagement had gone on, the weaker the conviction that it could be created had become. After all, the field had not "aroused leading social scientists to bestir themselves," the Moos report claimed, and the issues now seemed "spongy and complex," evading the sorts of "scientific proof" acceptable to academics. How could a breakthrough come about? Through the media? Through a return to trickle down? "All in all," the report concluded, "no one knows very much about the subject."

The questions Ford posed, or declined to, spoke to the sheer range of issues that remained open. Ford did not ask whether the thawing of the Cold War made its effort more or less urgent, did not ask whether changes to the policy process were needed, did not challenge the basic idea—so susceptible to a growing elitism—that the relationship between policymakers and the people should be an educational one at all. Nobody challenged the conviction that the effort should aim at the "sophisticated American who is concerned and informed about world affairs," as the Moos committee wrote, not the "broad mass which is basically unconcerned and uninformed." Nobody confronted the stark whiteness of these institutions, even in the year of the Voting Rights Act. And if anybody asked whether any of this was an acceptable situation, they did not demand more ambition. When Ford's planners looked at the educational landscape as a whole, their impression was that the effort to create a citizenry fit for global responsibility had failed to make much of a difference at all.[34]

## The Ford Foundation Tries Again

The Ford Foundation resolved to try one more time, difficult as it still seemed to abandon the institutions most associated with the idea of a democratic foreign policy. The trustees granted $1 million to the Association, a check that was said to be the last from Ford unless Hayes showed some capacity to innovate and repaired his relationship with the Councils, some of which were to benefit from a further $300,000 put at the disposal of Ford's staff. But Hayes faced a new difficulty. Secretary Rusk wrote to Hayes as Ford completed its deliberations that he felt "it is especially important that younger Americans, particularly those at the secondary school level, study and discuss the basic subjects which lay the foundation for a mature understanding of foreign policy issues in depth." Indeed, the Association had already decided to move towards children, its board voting in January 1965 to accept federal grants—for the first time—to start a dedicated program for school classrooms.[35]

Schools had long been a subject of close internationalist attention, but the Association's concession that it was through children, rather than adults, that a foreign policy public could best be built was an acceptance of defeat, if one wrapped in opportunity. As President Johnson wielded national security

221

imperatives to put education at the heart of his Great Society, with the 89th Congress adding the Elementary and Secondary Education Act, the Higher Education Act, and the International Education Act to the resources that had been pumped into education since the orbit of Sputnik had prompted the National Defense Education Act of 1958, so the Association was able to draw on funds like never before. With Ford-backed pioneer James Becker at the helm of its schools program, it quickly gathered almost $1 million from the St. Louis-based Danforth Foundation, the education division of Ford, and the federal Department of Health, Education, and Welfare combined, driving its budget over $2 million by 1967. While Becker used his time to promote an influential concept of "global education," the Association used its $754,000 Danforth grant to add to its regional staff in the name of organizing conferences, workshops, and newsletters for social studies teachers. Mastrude also experimented with multimedia simulations, including one, "Dangerous Parallel," that split students into teams of government ministers dealing with a fictional conflict modeled on the Korean War.[36]

Schools offered educators ways to overcome challenges that had become intractable in the search for adult publics, given their omnipresence in metropolitan areas, their preexisting support systems, and their captive learners. Their appeal strengthened as the world affairs infrastructure neared collapse. At Ford's prompting, the Association tried to shore up its relationship with the Councils in July 1966 by hiring Zygmunt Nagorski, who had recently returned from serving as a USIA officer in Egypt, South Korea, and France. More used to overseas propaganda work, Nagorski paid over one hundred visits in two years to Councils large and small, even midwifing a reborn World Affairs Council in Detroit. But Nagorski quickly became convinced of the bankruptcy of the movement. He found bewildering unevenness, from decrepit Councils in small-town backwaters to the powerhouse Chicago Council on Foreign Relations, which had saved itself by offering its membership wildly popular chartered air tours of foreign hotspots. Nagorski estimated that the forty-three or so Councils in existence had a total budget of $1.3 million, a quarter of which was spent in three cities, and that they claimed fifty thousand members. He guessed that 180,000 people attended world affairs programs nationwide. This was not a diplomatic 1 percent, as Hero had imagined, but a 0.1 percent. "It does not sound enormous," Nagorski wrote, "but it is bigger than most of us, at this end of the operation, expected."[37]

With hopes dashed numerically, spirits weakened. Some of the members of this "small national fraternity" did not "even know that they belong to such a body of people," Nagorski wrote in December 1966, while others were "discouraged by the meagre results of their local efforts and the passive attitudes of their fellows." It was no surprise, then, that they had set aside their broader aims and settled for cherishing small communities among themselves. "Here we are, baffled and confused," Nagorski imagined them thinking in 1968, "frustrated and closed off from the main current of decision-making groups." Most merely wanted to "go through the motion of being closer to understanding foreign policy issues," to find "substitutes, palliatives to make us feel better" in the absence of anything more meaningful. Councils were no longer educational entities, Nagorski argued, if they ever had been, but the insular social clubs that the more ambitious of their founders had longed to avoid. "A sense of futility settles among many who object, e.g., to Vietnam," Nagorski wrote, "and see how little their objections count."[38]

Even the most elitist world affairs institutions were struggling, demonstrating that this crisis was structural and not limited to the Association and its partners. The Committees on Foreign Relations, set up by the Council on Foreign Relations from 1937 onwards, had 2,170 male members in thirty-four cities by 1966, but since the early 1950s New York officials had worried that they had become no more than gatherings for an aging, bored, if "faithful core of regulars." It would take until 1969 for a Committee to admit a Black man, and the year after to admit women. (Women had attended "ladies' nights" for years; one St. Louis stalwart noted wryly in 1958 that "some of the wives have proved to be more intelligent than their husbands.") Like the World Affairs Councils, the Committees were as ineffective as they were unrepresentative. Council House used them as a sounding board less often over time, and the State Department not at all. The Council stopped publishing surveys of Committee members' views from 1954 to 1959, and when they started taking the surveys again in 1960, far fewer members than before felt qualified to express their views. The Committees stopped talking about how a democratic foreign policy was supposed to work, a subject their leaders had taken up with authorities of the stature of Russell, Likert, and Lyman Bryson in the immediate postwar years; their pretensions to influence in their communities consequently disappeared too. "I have racked my brain and tried to find, if anyone was interested enough to do something about world problems as a direct result of a Committee meeting," wrote the Indianapolis secretary in 1963, when asked for evidence that opinions were in fact trickling down. "The answer is negative."[39]

Ford did nothing to prop up the Committees and the model they represented, focusing its work on the Association and its allies. The Foundation's reluctant embrace—or re-embrace—of the Councils included the hiring in June 1965 of James Huntley, who admitted to "very little direct experience in this field" but was nonetheless asked to spend the $300,000 the trustees had allotted. Nichols left Huntley a plan for granting two-thirds of the total to the six largest Councils—Boston, Philadelphia, Cleveland, Chicago, San Francisco, and Los Angeles—and the other third to ten more, but Huntley preferred to make large grants to the strongest outfits. San Francisco was the first beneficiary, receiving $97,000 to strengthen its study groups, restore a speakers bureau, and fund visits by State Department officials. Philadelphia asked for $42,000; Huntley doubled that sum, though his belittling of that Council's director, Ruth Weir Miller, as running a "matriarchy" out of its offices in the Wanamaker department store illustrated Ford's sour views of the movement's dependence on women. Huntley also supported proposals from Cincinnati and Cleveland, now a hotbed of antiwar protest where a longstanding member of the women's discussion group, Dorothy Binyon, was struggling to keep the Council afloat. By December, Huntley had earmarked a further $525,000 for Boston, Portland, Seattle, Minneapolis, Chicago, and sundry smaller groups. He had also given real thought to the decline in the quality of the Councils' directors, asking the Carnegie Endowment to create a career track that might involve graduate study and sabbaticals in government agencies, as well as a pipeline for diplomats to remain useful in retirement. Association officials sensed a "new mood."[40]

## The Ford Foundation Gives Up

Enter McGeorge Bundy. Descending to the presidency of the Ford Foundation from the White House in March 1966, Bundy took a while to sketch out his vision for the richest philanthropy in the world, a vision that eventually would be defined by a striking aversion to involvement in international affairs; an odd outlook for a former national security advisor, but one not so surprising amid the traumas of Vietnam. Long before that course was set, however, Bundy started to dispense with some of the more dubious responsibilities he had inherited.[41]

It would be easy to think it inevitable that McGeorge Bundy would look at world affairs education with disdain. Was he not the archetypal product, indeed the last true heir, of an eastern establishment that ruled from clubs and the Council on Foreign Relations? Was he not a product of Groton, Yale, and Skull and Bones, a dean of the Harvard faculty whose success was as much social as intellectual? Was he not among those accountable for a war so cavalier in its disregard for popular consent that its descent into a quagmire caused a ruinous crisis in American life? Indeed Bundy was. But in the previous fifty years even men like Bundy had tended to show some interest in educating some kind of public in foreign policy issues and had channeled that interest, to a greater or lesser extent, through the Association.

Think, after all, of Bundy's own father. Boston Brahmin Harvey H. Bundy may have been, but he had taken the time to knit himself into the public-facing side of the foreign policy community, succeeding Christian A. Herter as chairman of the Association's Boston branch in 1936 and retaining that position until 1941. This Bundy believed enough in the cause that he thought the branches to be dismayingly inadequate, supporting the nationwide spread of Cleveland model and serving as president of the World Peace Foundation and chairman of the Carnegie Endowment, organizations that saw value in progressive conceptions of a democratic foreign policy even if their ambitions diminished over time. Think of Bundy's mentors, too. John J. McCloy might have preferred the geniality of the Council on Foreign Relations himself, but the man who hired Bundy for Ford had funded the Association all the same, had sat briefly on its board, and had been offered its presidency in 1946. Henry Stimson was no populist, but the two-time secretary of war who had invited Bundy to draft his memoirs had cared enough about the Association to place it in the hands of General McCoy for the duration of World War II. Walter Lippmann doubted the power of education in theory, but the man who had told President-Elect Kennedy that Bundy would make a fine secretary of state had long supported the work of his old friend Newton Baker. And Dean Acheson, who had let Bundy edit his speeches and given him a post at the State Department, took no lectures on the importance of public opinion from anyone.[42]

Whatever use these men had for citizen education in world affairs, then, that Bundy had no use whatsoever for it was a surprise. Plenty of his colleagues in government, after all, were well aware of the movement, from President Kennedy and Secretary Rusk to Bundy's own deputy at the National Security Council, Walt Rostow, who had taken part in plenty of World Affairs Council events in the 1950s and whose wife Elspeth, the first woman to be receive tenure at the Massachusetts Institute of Technology, was a member of the Boston Council's board. Bundy was perfectly knowledgeable about the theoretical salience of public opinion, moreover. Teaching Government 135 to the young men of Harvard College, he had lectured on Alexis de Tocqueville, Lord Bryce, and the new political science; in Government 185, his students had been exposed to George Kennan's consuming bitterness about the public. But even if Bundy was more of an idealist than his syllabi implied, he had no experience with the organizations that for so many embodied the relationship between diplomacy and democracy. He seems never to have been a member of the Foreign Policy Association. He was never a member of the Committee on Foreign Relations in Boston, nor of his local World Affairs Council. He would not play along.[43]

Four weeks after Bundy arrived in New York, Stone found himself on the defensive. In a briefing note written at the end of March 1966, Stone painted the citizen education program in a remarkably positive light, describing it as one of the Foundation's historic responsibilities and even praising Great Decisions. "IA believes that the attitudes and opinions of the American people concerning international affairs," he wrote of the International Affairs division, "are a significant element in either inhibiting or in forming and sustaining enlightened public policies." Bundy disagreed. The grants to Cincinnati and Cleveland awaited his approval, as did Huntley's request to the trustees for funding for more Councils. Bundy could not do much about the Ohio grants, which Dorothy Binyon saw, rather unfortunately, as "especially significant because you have so recently come from the active political arena," but he had time to strip the $3,000 that each devoted to paying the expenses of foreign service officers, money that Secretary Rusk had asked for personally. "I remain *very* skeptical on this," Bundy scrawled on one memo from Stone. He seems to have gone further, too, without giving much clarity. "Didn't he indicate," one subordinate struggled to remember in September, that "that would be the end of Foundation activity in this area?"[44]

It would be, but not without a fight. Asking for a smaller grant for the Councils than the $525,000 he had hoped for, Huntley noted that Ford's trustees had "consistently backed" world affairs education, that the Foundation bore moral responsibility as the "consequences of FAE's failure still badly warp the field," and that "the very existence of local WACs inhibits extremist elements, strengthens the vital center, and—in many cases—makes world affairs a respectable topic for community discussion." Appealing to Bundy's liberalism, few at Ford doubted that the work remained necessary, even if debate about whether the Foundation ought to do it stepped up as Stone was replaced as director of the International Affairs division by David Bell, formerly budget director for President Kennedy. As one Ford official told a meeting of Council leaders in May, "we are so far short of a desirable state of affairs with respect to public knowledge, that we do not have to argue that." But when Bell sent

Huntley's $250,000 grant to Bundy, it received a frosty response. Huntley implored his superiors not to commit another error in a process Ford had "botched" for years, and Bell's staff proved that they still had some of their old clout. "Dear Mac," began a letter from Rusk: "I have for some time observed with great appreciation the Ford Foundation's imaginative support of efforts to strengthen world affairs education." It was no use. Bundy killed the grants in November. "All are now dead," Huntley lamented.[45]

Ending appropriations to the World Affairs Councils was one thing; ending grants to the Association was quite another. Convinced that Ford's offer of $1 million to prove its worth had been made in good faith in 1965, the Association's board had spent quickly. Hayes increased his office's tempo, raising more money from corporate sponsors and ploughing it into the schools and Council programs. Before Huntley left the Foundation in disgust, as Cullen had done before him, he noted that the Association was "headed in the right direction and moving fast," remaining the "essential core of any effective national effort in this field." Yet with inflation rising Ford's trustees curtailed the Foundation's lavish spending, setting Bundy's budget to the $200 million that its stocks earned annually and forbidding draws on the principal. Hayes was told to lower his expectations but asked for another $4 million in May 1967. "I fail to find this close to reality," Gordon snarked. Another official called the proposal "sophomoric."[46]

As Bundy turned Ford toward racial justice and the urban crisis, the Foundation cut away a grant that had defined not just its own programs, but that of big philanthropy for half a century. Bell used the progress the Association had made against it, as had his predecessors at the Rockefeller Foundation twenty years earlier. "The increased support that FPA has found in recent years gives us assurance that its continued existence is not critically dependent on the Foundation's general support," Bell told Bundy in December 1967, just a few weeks after Rusk had addressed the Association during the battle of Madison Avenue. Bell worried that his boss would not approve the $250,000 he sought to give the Association as a parting gift, but Bundy did. "My colleagues and I regret," Bell's assistant told Hayes just after Christmas, that the problems caused "do not appear to be easy ones, but we have confidence that they will be manageable without grievous damage to the good work of FPA."[47]

## "Defeat Known"

Grievous damage was done, but the destruction was rampant in any case. The solutions the Association and the Ford Foundation had offered to the problems they jointly perceived did not address fundamental issues, to the extent that those issues were perceptible at all—whether that meant the ineluctable drive to educate elites above all, or the intellectual construction of a public all but unwilling to enter politics, or the realities of the policymaking process, or the weakness of institutions still operating on patterns of urban life from thirty, forty, fifty years earlier. Even if the Foundation had given the Association the sums it had dreamed of, the general orientation of the educational movement would have remained the same; dollars here and there at this stage, even millions of dollars, were unlikely to have made much difference. If it was unfortunate that Bundy took over at Ford just as progress was seemingly being made, the realities on the ground were already darkening to black.

Four weeks after Bundy made his final decision, Viet Cong and North Vietnamese forces unleashed the Tet Offensive, making an already unpopular war so ruinously divisive that it dethroned a president. The Association's belief in reasoned discussion seemed ever more antiquated as 1968 went on, a year when authority was put under challenge more than at any point in living memory. There would be no benefit to world affairs institutions from this debate on the future of US power. "The U.S. is turning inward," Fuller wrote to Gordon after the election of Richard Nixon that November. "The staggering perplexities of the inner city, the struggle of minorities to find a suitable place in society, the disaffection of youth are the dominant concerns of many American community leaders." The Association had once been able to wield a formidable network of partners, but they were now "directing their program efforts toward the smoldering sections of their localities and away from those explosive situations abroad which could engulf us all." Quite a different women's movement was on the march for feminism, and the peace movement would have nothing whatsoever to do with an Association that had played its part in making the empire young activists decried. Neo-isolationism, as the new foreign policy mood came simplistically to be called, was not merely a subject taking up column inches, nor a figment of the opinion-poll imaginary, but a harsh reality for some. All educators lost their illusions; many lost their jobs.[48]

By the spring of 1968, the Association stood atop a financial cliff. It raised $1.24 million in its fiftieth anniversary campaign and Hayes induced more corporations than ever to give generously, but such figures could not cover the hole left as the Carnegie Endowment and the Rockefeller Brothers Fund joined Ford in withdrawing their support. Brutal inflationary pressures, themselves tied to the slow collapse of the economic order the United States had created two decades earlier, left Hayes half a million dollars short. As late as 1967, he had been eager to experiment. The Association for the first time saw Black Americans as worthy of special effort, even if a task force agreed that their "preoccupation with the civil rights movement," let alone barriers of economics and education, precluded much to rectify their "exceedingly limited" participation in white foreign policy institutions. Now experimentation ceased. Hayes closed Nagorski's department, curtailed publications, and began to draw on scarce reserves, shuttering all but one of the regional offices. The schools program imploded as the end of the Danforth grant necessitated wholesale firings. The board again considered liquidating the Association in April 1970; in August, Hayes found that he did not even have the money he needed to dismiss his staff with the severance they were legally owed. Whereas in 1967–1968 there had been a budget of more than $2 million and a staff of 104, Hayes thought he would have barely $900,000 and a staff of thirty-six by the end of 1971. By 1976 the Association's budget was $600,000, less than one-fifth of its income eight years earlier in real terms.[49]

Nor did the Councils prosper. At first, the turmoil appeared to offer a chance to reset; there was hope in the "malaise of disquiet about foreign policy," wrote William Messner of Cincinnati in July 1968, hope that could not be met with the "old banal slogan, 'World Affairs Are Your Affairs.'" But the newsletter of the Society for Citizen Education in World Affairs, founded earlier in the decade, took on a grim tone. Norman Pilgrim, now the Association's sole regional staffer, wrote in May 1970 that it was "a time to regain the moral strength in our profession of an idealism reborn through the temporizing hardness of cynicism, realism, and defeat known." In San Francisco the situation became so bad that Ford could not find anybody to write a grant report; an acting director reached fortuitously by telephone said that "the Council had gone through deep waters and that the administrative affairs had been left largely in the hands of the 'girls in the office.'" Binyon kept the Cleveland Council going, but its membership dropped to fifteen hundred in 1975, which the board attributed to "increasing isolationism." Good use of Ford money was made in Philadelphia, where the Council founded smaller regional Councils and pioneered programs at the request of Black students and teachers. The Cincinnati Council increased its budget by half. There was a goldrush on Lake Michigan, where the Chicago Council on Foreign Relations filled its membership rolls to twenty-five thousand residents by 1975. It would later reinvent itself as a think tank.[50]

Even so, no institution could escape this new reality. When the Council on Foreign Relations pleaded for help from Ford in 1973, the Foundation was as unsparing in its criticisms as any of the Council's critics. "There has clearly been an erosion in the Council's influence on the foreign policy thinking of both the American people and the government," one consultant wrote. The linkages between policymakers and even the narrowest of publics had broken down, and in the process even the Council had become too controversial for Ford's tastes. Bundy, whose brother William edited *Foreign Affairs*, permitted one last grant in 1974. "The objectives of these major grants were tied up with the main purposes of the Ford Foundation during its first quarter century," wrote the staffer who was later tasked with evaluating the $3.5 million that it had spent on the Council over two decades, words that could be applied to much of the Foundation's spending in this field. "We would probably do it rather differently today."[51]

## Henry Kissinger Surveys the Wreckage

Francis H. Russell had gone on to a significant career after stepping down from the Office of Public Affairs in 1952. His obituaries remembered him not for his most important contribution, as the architect of the structure the State Department had erected to give meaning to a democratic foreign policy after 1945, but as a three-time ambassador with spells in New Zealand, Ghana, and Tunisia to his name. Still, in retirement Russell wondered what his Office of Public Affairs might have been. "I hope that some day a new President and a new Secretary of State will look back at the operation and see that it's something valuable," he said in 1973. Russell knew all too well that the temptations of propaganda were the "easiest thing in the world," and his memory of his service in the Truman administration was rosy at best. But had that structure survived and been invested with meaning, he thought, perhaps public opinion might have been brought home to policymakers before disaster had struck, or the difficulties of policymaking at least made clearer to publics. "I think if we had had something like that *really* going on," Russell said, "a large part of the grief over Vietnam might have been alleviated."[52]

Might. The promises made at the end of the Second World War had gone unfulfilled, but they were powerful enough that policymakers returned to them as they surveyed what Charles Maier has called "the unraveling of the prior structures of American leadership," structures in which claims about the democratic nature of US policy might well be included. Even McGeorge

Bundy saw the light. Bundy did not often talk about the Vietnam War in public, but he did reflect from time to time on the nature of postwar policy, including at an anniversary dinner of the St. Louis Council on World Affairs in October 1973. "There is one element in the styles of the last 10 years," he said in an address that would have been perfectly generic if it had been given by any other Cold Warrior, "that will be profoundly out of place in the next 25 years—the apparent belief that there is an indispensable need for secrecy and loneliness in the conduct of our major international affairs." Bundy now sought openness, whether between the White House and other parts of the executive, the executive and the legislature, the government and the press, or the government and the "interested"—even the "general"—public. Probably unaware he was quoting the words of the secretary of state whose speeches he had once edited, Bundy called this "two-way communication based on trust."[53]

Henry Kissinger tried to rebuild what he thought had been lost. Committed to a style of diplomacy that prized quietude, secrecy, and freedom of maneuver, Nixon's national security advisor and eventual secretary of state nonetheless understood the importance of public opinion to a successful foreign policy. His academic research had made the point at length, and in his career he had made good use of the institutions of the foreign policy community. Kissinger supported State's efforts to revitalize networks that had broken down. "I attach the highest importance to developing a broad public consensus," he told a National Council of Community World Affairs Organizations in October 1974, a "consensus" that his subordinates informed the Association would be defined by "the broadest possible public discussion." That same month, Kissinger told the National Council on Philanthropy that world affairs groups were "suffering from inadequate resources, financial and human," that they "need help." It would not be forthcoming.[54]

What Kissinger sought, like policymakers before him, was support, as if to resurrect an imagined Cold War consensus around his ambivalent worldview. With détente under pressure in 1975, he embarked on a "heartland" tour, making speeches that were part philosophy seminar and part partisan fightback, made with one eye on the present and one eye on the history books. His realist message cut no ice, nor did his effort to recreate the institutional infrastructure of times long gone. As Kissinger traveled, his aides held a series of "town meetings," conferences in five cities that unknowingly recalled Chester Williams's initiatives from the early Cold War, with a full panoply of adult education devices that ranged from lectures and roundtables to forums and call-in media shows. Sponsored by the World Affairs Councils or equivalent institutions in Pittsburgh, Portland, San Francisco, Milwaukee, and Minneapolis and put on with the assistance of the Association, the sessions were intended to show that State "gives a damn about what individuals think about our foreign policy," Kissinger's assistant Lawrence Eagleburger told one audience. The aim, Deputy Assistant Secretary of State for Public Affairs Charles Bray wrote, was "the recreation of a national foreign policy 'establishment' and the invigoration of the private organizational infrastructure."[55]

But although the Councils had been symbols of the broad desire to root US foreign policy in public discussion, they had always been too weak to be the vehicles for public support that the State Department now sought to summon. Certainly, they had never been bastions of an "establishment"; their existence spoke to the necessity of avoiding one, and their memberships were never sufficiently incorporated into policymaking structures to deserve the dubious honor. Eagleburger and his colleagues felt the full force of that reality as the audiences they appeared before at the end of 1975 and the start of 1976 proceeded to humiliate them, as if the Deweyan dream that publics might educate experts had belatedly come true. Pittsburghers "do not understand many of the bedrock premises on which our foreign policy is based," Eagleburger and three other officials reported; State had "a fairly serious communications problem." Watergate had left its scars, as had sordid revelations about the Central Intelligence Agency and the Federal Bureau of Investigation. In Oregon, home of the Great Decisions program, there was a "generalized disenchantment with government institutions from which the Department also suffers." But the fiasco ran deeper than that: it revealed with painful immediacy the failure to build a democratic foreign policy worthy of the name.

"We know what kind of people we are," one exasperated man yelled at the State Department officials who had dared to appear in Portland. "Does the government know?"[56]

# Epilogue: A Foreign Policy for the American People?

"I know that foreign policy can sometimes feel disconnected from our daily lives." Secretary of State Antony Blinken was making the first major speech of his tenure from an empty dining room at the State Department on March 3, 2021. Diplomacy, Blinken continued, echoing the words of so many of his predecessors, is "often about people and events on the other side of the world, and it's about things you don't see," whether "crises stopped before they start, or negotiations that happen out of sight." Americans had good reasons for not understanding or wanting to understand their diplomacy, he suggested, reiterating the traditional explanations for the difficulty of subjecting foreign policy to democratic control. But Blinken went further than most who had held his office before. "Those of us who conduct foreign policy," he confessed, "haven't always done a good job connecting it to the needs and aspirations of the American people."

Revealingly, what mattered to Blinken about this oversight was not that it represented a betrayal of fundamental democratic principles, but that it had put the domestic basis of US leadership at risk. "For some time now Americans have been asking tough but fair questions about what we're doing, how we're leading," he said, "indeed, whether we should be leading at all." But if this pattern of miscommunication were fixed, Blinken argued, Americans would discover that their diplomats were taking care of things for them, that policymakers could be trusted to know what was best and act on it. He laid out an eight-point plan to revitalize the primacy he was determined would not crumble, rebranding it as an effort to restore the prosperity of the middle class. He would strengthen health security, fix immigration, restore

233

relationships with "allies and partners," tackle climate change, lead a "global technology revolution," and manage the rise of China, the sole nation that he said might "seriously challenge the stable and open international system."

Blinken also promised to "renew democracy." Nationalism was rising. Corruption was growing. Elections had become flashpoints for violence, and not just in the United States. He made clear that the threat to democracy was a global one. But while Blinken had offered specific examples of how the United States would right the balance of power and douse a world on fire, when it came to democracy he was out of ideas. He could reinstate a sense of nonpartisanship to foreign policy that he admitted some thought "quaint," he believed. He could build a "national security workforce that reflects America in all its diversity," he insisted. He could work with Congress "whenever we can," for "our foreign policy is stronger when the American people support it," as if that support were in some way optional. Blinken assured his listeners that, more than anything else, democracy would survive if "we and other democracies can show the world that we can deliver." Democracy was transactional, in this view; the citizenry bought what policymakers sold. This might have been, as the title of Blinken's speech had it, "A Foreign Policy for the American People," but it was not one to be made, by any means, by the American people.[1]

John Foster Dulles played an ambivalent role in the story of a democratic foreign policy, but Blinken's distant predecessor at least knew how to speak its language, even if his words gave only false hope. Right up until his appointment in 1953, Dulles was as committed a member of the Foreign Policy Association as anyone, donating to it generously, speaking often from its stages, and frequently peer-reviewing its publications. Dulles had been among the Association's seven legal incorporators in 1928, signing its charter alongside Felix Warburg and Eleanor Roosevelt. He took a stoutly paternalistic approach to public opinion in office from 1953 to 1959, however, believing that the way to rescue the reputation of a department beleaguered from McCarthyite attacks was to center attention on himself. But the first speech he made to the nation as secretary of state—laden though it was with rhetoric suggesting that his predecessors had tolerated a "gigantic" communist conspiracy—at least genuflected to participatory ideals. "Foreign policy isn't just something that's conducted by secretaries of state and by ambassadors in different parts of the world," he told a television and radio audience on January 27, 1953. "Every one of you has got a part in making a successful foreign policy for the United States." Dulles sought primarily to draft citizens as soldiers in a global war of hearts and minds, but he still gave far less of a sense than Blinken that foreign policy was to be made among a few and enjoyed, potentially, by the many. "I believe that our foreign policies should be open so that you can know what they are," Dulles said. "They should be sufficiently simple so that you can understand them and judge them, and they should be sufficiently decent and moral so that they will fit into your idea of what you think is right." Democracy here meant something more than deliverables.[2]

We should have no illusions that what Dulles expressed was a reality. It was not. Dulles himself faced criticism for impeding the ideal of a democratic foreign policy before and during his time as secretary. When he lent his Republicanism to the "bipartisan" foreign policy of the Truman administration in 1950, for example, the *New Republic* that was so close to the movement for democratic control attacked his appointment as a means "of removing foreign policy one stage farther from the people" at a time when it was crucial "the trickle-down theory of public engagement" be abandoned and Americans given "the sense that foreign policy is of their own making." Nor could the Eisenhower administration be considered the foremost example of what Dulles preached as the "principles" of "openness, simplicity, and righteousness." Within six months, Foster's brother, Allen, would lead the Central Intelligence Agency in secretly plotting a coup in Iran, before going on to do the same in Guatemala in 1954 and Cuba in 1961, if latterly with less success. Still, the outrage that followed the Bay of Pigs spoke to some degree to the ideals the Dulles brothers had once done their part to promote. Their power has long since diminished, their language forgotten. But the awareness has grown again that Americans have been unable to reconcile their foreign policy with their democracy. Can anything be done?[3]

THE PAST OFFERS LITTLE COMFORT. Foreign policy has always been pulled between the demands of what Acting Secretary of State John Jay in 1788 called the need for "perfect secrecy and immediate dispatch" on the one hand, and the democratic imperatives of transparency, participation, and consent on the other. The foreign policy community began to come together at the end of the Great War partly as a response to that dilemma. It was forged in the conviction that the United States, as a mass democracy though an imperfect one, would need a different kind of foreign policy, that matters could not be left to the State Department as the British left things to their Foreign Office. Popular diplomacy was inescapable in this view, a fact of life. "The fortunes of mankind are now in the hands of the plain people of the whole

world," Woodrow Wilson told the Paris Peace Conference in January 1919 as
he implored it to form a League of Nations. But the plain people of the world
would have to be educated, lest their supposed ignorance again turn peace
into war. DeWitt Clinton Poole, a State Department diplomat who would
become editor of the *Public Opinion Quarterly* in 1937, prayed to the Institute
of Politics in 1923 that "the popular sense of responsibility and restraint which
is essential to peace in a democratic world will grow as world affairs come increasingly within the popular knowledge" and argued that "the wisdom of the
popular judgment, when it is deliberately expressed, is a foundation upon
which a lasting edifice may be built." Perhaps so, perhaps not. There was no
guarantee that an educated public would be a pacific one, as Wilsonian progressives presumed. Poole understood, after all, that "those who have faith in
the democratic principle must suffer discouragement at times." Either way,
the question was not whether mass democracy would have an impact on foreign policy; it was how that impact could best be managed.[4]

While the Council on Foreign Relations sought to restrict serious discussion of foreign affairs to a select, male few, the Foreign Policy Association
harnessed the energies of the peace and suffrage movements to try to inform
a somewhat broader public about the shifting body of knowledge it steadily
defined as foreign policy. Broader, but not initially broad; if the foreign policy
community has always been more open to popular participation than has
often been assumed, it has always defined both "popular" and "participation"
in tightly limited ways. Gathering emerging networks of scholars and others
of notable credentials into the communities of expertise whose authority it
promoted from its stages, the Association first subjected those authorities to
the raucous participation of a fashionable, high society set. Even if the Association's luncheons were broadcast, even if they spread throughout the cities
of the nation, this public seemed an inadequate target at a time when it increasingly appeared that science could abolish war, if only it could be democratized. In the 1930s the Association's staff began to write for editors,
reporters, and scholars on the assumption that they would get the word out to
more and more Americans, eventually aiming still further through its education department. Yet trickle-down diplomacy never truly died. Democratization was to come strictly on terms of experts and policymakers; they could
abandon the effort at will.

Discouragement lurked. Getting information out did not seem to change
minds. Even those interventionists who had grown close to the State Department watched while it struggled to mount a muscular response to the rise of

Nazism, as the assumption that the distribution of facts about the world would lead Americans to accept greater involvement in it was tested to breaking point. The Association put its thumb on the scales, abandoning the commitment to balance that it had been easy to adopt when the stakes had been low, when the propaganda that progressives had so feared had not been wielded in support of a cause with which many of them agreed. The Second World War put the Association on the back foot. It acquiesced as harsher means took root at the heart of a new national security state, a vast edifice that borrowed the language of public participation without really requiring it, depending instead on a controlling dissent. There was a war to win, after all, and then a peace.

A colder war came, one that demanded proof of allegiance to the American way of life and to the foreign policy that seemed to flow from it. McCarthyism chilled speech, even made it dangerous in some parts of the country. Was not this modern world—with its atomic weapons, interdependent economic systems, and endlessly increasing number of actors, and non-state alike—too complicated, too dangerous, for ordinary people to cope with? Could even experts manage it? Might not encouraging popular participation drag the nation into totalitarianism, if the masses were to come under the sway of a demagogue who could play on their apathy and their ignorance? If elites and the masses anyway drew the same set of core values from their shared traditions— for this was the era of the "end of ideology," as the sociologist Daniel Bell famously put it—was there really any need for the citizenry to get involved? The Association insisted that there was, but its efforts to disprove the elitist theories of democracy that emerged from the academy now fell to the elitism that had always marked its work, as education came to mean something citizens received from policymakers, not the terrain on which the polity could come together in a common endeavor. Even those citizens the Association reached with Great Decisions no longer believed that they could make a difference, that world affairs were not really their affairs. Discouragement turned to disillusion. When a new kind of US leadership emerged from the wreckage of the 1970s, it did so from a fractured domestic political culture. The idea that foreign policy could be forged in popular participation, unrealized though it had been, disappeared; there would be attempts to remake the "establishment," but little more.[5]

"We do not pretend that we are successful," the director of the Cleveland Council on World Affairs, Donald Pryor, said in 1961. "We know that we are not." Nobody involved argued that the effort to create a democratic foreign policy along progressive lines had been a success, at least beyond a select few Americans. It was their ongoing failure, in fact, that was the underlying predicate both of the continuing experiments of educators and of the evolution of a policymaking environment that assumed the public's fundamental inability to contribute, a development that pushed educational success ever further out of reach. For some, the failure was a welcome one; there were safer means of running foreign policy than through a mass engagement few citizens in reality sought, and the United States in any case possessed procedures and institutions that made it a democracy, one that could survive and prosper despite what appeared to be an apathetic populace. For educators, the debacle threatened disaster. Speaking as a crisis in Berlin threatened to escalate into nuclear war, Pryor recalled Tocqueville's fear that a democracy would never be able to compete with an autocracy in foreign affairs and dwelled on the ruin of Athens at the hands of Sparta. "If we should try and fail, so be it; we shall have failed honorably," he said, reflecting on the wealth, the technology, and the fervor that had seemed to make the United States more likely to succeed than any of its forbears. "If we should fail without trying, who will grant us even the solace of self-respect?"[6]

THE PROSPECTS FOR RECONCILING DIPLOMACY with democracy today are much worse than they were when Donald Pryor still held out some hope, let alone when his predecessors in Cleveland, Brooks Emeny and Newton Baker, had believed that they might create their ideal of democracy, an informed public opinion. Theirs was in no sense a golden age and should not be imagined as such, but there were reasons for optimism, educators thought. The brief interlude of the Great Depression aside, the period after World War I and especially after World War II was a time when "engagement in community affairs and the sense of shared identity and reciprocity had never been greater in modern America," as Robert Putnam has written, "so the prospects for broad-based civic mobilization to address our national failings seemed bright." Civic engagement was inherently political then too, Theda Skocpol has argued, channeled through vast mass-membership associations that trained citizens in political action, so that "democratic governance and civic voluntarism developed together." Educators could work in media markets that verged on monopolies, endorsing a narrow range of opinions as legitimate. Newspapers were widely read, as were magazines; radio was heard, television watched. Commentators spoke with authority. Partisanship existed, whatever the myth that politics stopped at the water's edge, but not ruinously. Trust in government was appreciable. After 1941, there was something of a common purpose in foreign policy, one forged in wars that had asked for considerable collective sacrifice. Polls showed some support for the idea that citizens had a duty to engage with foreign policy; the claim was commonplace in political rhetoric well into the 1950s and beyond.[7]

Optimism is far harder to muster today; the barriers to success would be formidably high for any modern-day Brooks Emeny to surmount. Greater enfranchisement has given cover to what political philosopher Hélène Landemore has called the "enclosure of power." Putnam and legion other scholars have pointed to a decline of civic culture. Skocpol has written of a "diminished democracy." Voluntary associations have proliferated, but they exist now chiefly as lobbying groups with explicit policy perspectives, the participation they try to generate demanding little more than the answering of an email with a small donation. Mass media have diversified, bringing benefits in terms of the range of opinions represented, but at the same time siloing information so that it is more easily weaponized. Just as faith in the radio as the means of taking facts to the people was worked up and then abandoned in the interwar years, so faith in universal access to the internet has been smashed, as social media companies have undermined the conditions necessary for self-governance. Polarization rules all, and a reflexive, "negative" polarization at that, in which the taking of a position by one party automatically leads to criticism from the other. Political scientists see elites as fundamentally different from everyone else in their preferences, their values, even their cognitive architectures. Confidence in the federal government has collapsed, as has faith in expertise. The National Election Study found in 1958 that three in four Americans trusted the government to do the right thing; that number has risen and fallen since its peak of 77 percent in 1964, but it has not reached 30 percent since 2007. Whereas John Dewey had been able to inspire a whole movement to educate the public in the face of the "hokum" of the 1920s, writers warning of the need to defend democracy today have offered few concrete remedies, let alone fervor.[8]

Much the same has been true of the foreign policy community specifically, even after the fright of the 2016 election, when the flag of "America First" waved once again. Calls for the democratization of foreign policy have remained rare even as foreign policy institutions have tried to understand the nature of the domestic threat to their project of world leadership. The Carnegie Endowment for International Peace aped the Kissinger-era State Department by consulting in three "heartland" states in 2017, aiming to figure out what a foreign policy "for the middle class" might look like. Carnegie's team, which included future national security advisor Jake Sullivan, offered ideas on trade policy and other, primarily economic issues, but when it came to the issue of "rebuilding trust" the Endowment dodged, suggesting not only that any policy's benefits "will not be visible to, or verifiable by, most Americans at the local level," but that "the American people need to be able to trust that U.S. foreign policy professionals are managing this tremendous responsibility as best they can." How was that possible? Set aside the divisions unleashed amid the war on terror, and deeper analyses made clear that the people and the professionals now spoke an entirely different language. In 2019, the Center for American Progress asked focus groups about the words through which the foreign policy community thinks, catchphrases like "working with allies," "fighting authoritarianism and dictatorship," and "promoting democracy." Even voters who said they followed foreign policy news, the Center found, "simply did not understand what any of these phrases and ideas meant or implied." No wonder, as *Foreign Affairs* editor Gideon Rose put it in 2019, that "it has proved ever more difficult to generate popular support for the country's actual foreign policy."[9]

Even the more liberal members of the foreign policy community have largely given up. Obama administration official Ben Rhodes, decrier of the "Blob," admitted in 2016 that he had tried to create an "echo chamber" to sell the Joint Comprehensive Plan of Action to deal with Iran's nuclear program. "I mean, I'd prefer a sober, reasoned public debate, after which members of Congress reflect and take a vote," Rhodes shrugged in an interview with the *New York Times*, "but that's impossible." In foreign policy, Landemore's "enclosure of power" has hardened into more of an iron curtain than a picket fence. Public debate does of course exist, but so much policymaking is now done behind a veil of gratuitously overclassified secrets that leaks have to serve an invaluable democratic purpose, exposing areas of government controversy to publicity. Deliberation on foreign policy issues is now mostly internal, a discussion among the various interests comprising the state that is routed through the "interagency" at a National Security Council staffed by unelected appointees. The prerogatives of the executive have been encoded in deferential law. The Central Intelligence Agency takes care of what needs to be done; if not, the military does, and in secret. Undeclared wars have become the primary means of US leadership, and it has always been recognized that it is even harder to subject war to democratic consent than foreign policy.

As technologies have made armed conflict cleaner and more distant to most Americans, seemingly permanent congressional authorizations for the use of force have joined with an all-volunteer military apparatus—dependent on private contractors that are shielded from accountability—that affects few citizens except as an endless source of employment. While war has been outsourced, Congress has abandoned the limited powers it reclaimed in the fires of Vietnam, and bills proposed to right the balance with the executive have been met with silence. Even threat inflation has had little purchase after Iraq, as those proposing military action in Iran have found.[10]

Meanwhile, the methods the foreign policy community has brought to bear on public engagement have remained stuck, literally, in the 1950s. The main program of the Foreign Policy Association remains Great Decisions, though now it boasts an award-winning public television series as well as the traditional discussion groups. The Council on Foreign Relations has welcomed more members, by nomination only, but most of its energies still go to *Foreign Affairs* and its meetings program; it offers World101, an explanatory website, as well as a Model Diplomacy series, which gives students a simulation of a National Security Council meeting not far removed from Model League of Nations events that date back to the 1920s. More than ninety World Affairs Councils or similar institutions remain in existence, almost all of them affiliated to a convening group that emerged in 1986, World Affairs Councils of America. Roughly half are still so small that their revenues do not meet the threshold at which nonprofits must report their income to the tax authorities. The Cleveland Council on World Affairs still has a Committee on Foreign Relations at its heart, as well as a series of more open speaker forums. It runs "global competency workshops" for businesses and still hosts tourists through the State Department's International Visitor Leadership Program, a relic of Eisenhower-era public diplomacy. It focuses on schools, offering students its Model United Nations, Junior World Affairs Councils, and Academic World-Quest, a national quiz competition. Among the Council's leading donors is the Brooks Emeny Trust.[11]

Nor has the orientation of this limited work changed much. Paternalistic in conception, the elite effort to create a democratic foreign policy was historically premised on the conviction that only if the people—or some of them—were fully exposed to the thinking of an expert class and taught to define "foreign policy" in the same way as those authorities would their views be rendered as legitimate. Participation was conceived in a way few Americans recognized, involving a careful reading of texts, a parsing of speeches, an eagerness to engage in formal discussion. If that definition appealed to few beyond an educated, white upper-middle class, educators also labored to separate foreign policy from other forms of political activity, demanding it be treated on a "nonpartisan" basis. That did little to insulate foreign policy from party politics, but it did insulate what the foreign policy community saw as engagement with international affairs from the diverse ways in which Americans were actually approaching the world, from their faiths to their gender, their class to their labor—producing the appearance of apathy where historians have since seen only action. Rarely, if ever, did the Association or its allies ask those citizens they could not reach how *they* would like to relate to foreign policy, if at all. Far from the Association's work being part of a crusade to foist "globalism" on the populace, as some historians have thought, its records reveal constant frustration, a story of earnest, honest people doing what they could—of weakness, verging on a fiasco.[12]

NEVERTHELESS, that the Foreign Policy Association and related institutions have survived reveals an important continuity across the American Century: the impulse to reconcile diplomacy with democracy persists, even if it is not approached today with the intensity of old. This has been a sorry tale, a declension narrative, and it offers no easy answers and few successes on which to build. If it has a core lesson, it is that solving the problem of a democratic foreign policy has always been hard, and it is only getting harder. The United States is not now the country it was in 1945; reforms are trickier to imagine, let alone execute, after seventy-five years of bureaucratic development and with immense vested interests at play, not to mention jobs. Even if the patterns of primacy have long been set, however, the problem still needs to be raised more directly, as the United States once again looks out on an uncertain world. What does this story suggest ought to be kept in mind today?

Five things seem particularly important. The first is that processes must be designed through which the express will of the American people can be built into the making of strategy, routinely and explicitly so. The inability of educators to convince their targets that their opinions ever mattered was a fatal flaw in their work, one that eventually drove many of even the most committed citizens away. Educators were at least partly responsible for this shortcoming, for even those as commanding as Vera Micheles Dean and Chester S. Williams spent remarkably little time sketching out how a democratic foreign policy should operate. Most of their labor was dedicated to the confounding problem of how to take expert knowledge to the people, not to the equally important task of aiding the public to state its views and ensuring the government took them into account. When the time did come for adult educators to offer their ideas, during the Second World War, their proposals were timid, and the state set the tone. The State Department institutions that seemed to offer such promise at the end of World War II were hollowed out shortly after they were created; the Office of Public Liaison still exists today, but it comes nowhere close to being the vehicle for the "cooperative method of making foreign policy" that Dean Acheson once claimed was its aim. Where might reforms come from? There has been a strong revival of interest among scholars in participatory and deliberative forms of democracy, and while experiments to apply techniques such as deliberative polling to foreign policy issues have been neither all that common nor all that widely noticed, they have shown potential. Radical change seems unlikely in the short term, but the United States has little to lose by following allies such as Germany in dabbling with participatory forms of consultation.[13]

Should the foreign policy community experiment, secondly, it must do so in a spirit of humility. One of the preoccupations of current thinking about participatory democracy is to find ways to encourage citizens to write their political agenda for themselves. This was the difficulty Williams faced when he suggested, at the end of 1945, that State could use polling to bring the citizenry into the department *en masse*. Polling proved not to be a way of discovering the public's priorities, as George Gallup had hoped, but rather a way of assessing the degree of support people would give to proposals generated for them by others. US diplomats are not in control of world events, of course, and the American public is unlikely to be more so, but when it comes to setting the outlook of foreign policy in its broadest terms, institutional means must be found to expose the foreign policy community to the priorities of the people on their own terms. That requires a second dose of humility in turn, a recognition of the Deweyan injunction that experts value public input. Asking men and women who have spent their entire careers working on a diplomatic issue to adapt in the face of scrutiny, as Deweyans hoped, remains the tall order that it always was. After all, when even men as committed to popular prerogatives as Raymond Leslie Buell and Brooks Emeny confronted a public that did not share their views, they gave in to the temptation to simplify disagreements to the binary that pits expert authority against popular ignorance—and hence to scorn the public as illegitimate to decide on a subject. That temptation is still evident. In 2020, the president of the Council on

Foreign Relations, Richard Haass, wrote a book intended to make its readers "more globally literate," as several men in his position have before; the goal is worthy, but the means imagine education as an instructive tool, not a process of collective discovery. The democratic worth of a citizen is not reducible to the quantity of that citizen's knowledge—the temptation to make it so must be resisted.[14]

Third, the history told here shows the paramount importance of forging alliances with activist groups that have experience at the grass roots the foreign policy community lacks, especially those that could help diversify the outlook of an establishment that remains far from ideally inclusive. When the women's and peace movements were particularly vibrant, from the 1920s to the 1940s, the Foreign Policy Association was at its most energetic, even if those collaborations did not help it remove the blinders of race and class that marred its work. When the mainstream women's movement became more conservative in the 1950s, and McCarthyism pushed the peace movement out of bounds for an institution with semi-official connections, it became much more difficult for the Association to draw on inspirations other than its own. By then, the Association had already played a not inconsiderable role in creating a culture of foreign policy discussion that offered a loudspeaker to white, male voices and all but silenced others, even as it continued to depend on the labor of white, female organizers. The suffocating racism of the foreign policy community is a broader subject than can be dealt with here, but what bears repeating is that that racism was pervasive: from the efforts of Wilsonians who promoted public opinion as the way to manage a white world order to the Cold Warriors who simply followed their white members to the suburbs in cities across the country and ignored extensive Black engagement with the world, this vision of a democratic foreign policy was one conceived by white experts for white citizens. Other visions were available, of course: the foreign policy community is only just beginning to face the consequences of this, among other things, and even then within its own ranks; confronting those legacies in future work with the public and rectifying them would not only make that work more democratic, but might well reshape the content of "foreign policy" itself.[15]

Fourth, the history of the foreign policy community illustrates the continuing difficulties raised by the role of philanthropy in democratic reform, especially when that reform is conceived largely from the top down. This book has revealed that role to have historically been an ambivalent one. Without the grants made, often reluctantly, by the officers of the Rockefeller, Carnegie, and

Ford foundations, as well as the personal contributions of titans of industry, finance, and other fields, it is hard to imagine the progressive ideal of a democratic foreign policy becoming a matter of consensus within the foreign policy community at all. But philanthropists shaped the field in every imaginable way, wielding their cash to promote their own visions for what democracy ought to look like and tending to weaken reformist impulses. Often, that intervention was explicit, whether in the Rockefeller Foundation's demand that Frank McCoy buttress a branch network he knew would never reach a wide public during World War II, or in the Ford Foundation's retreat from what the Association claimed was mass education in the 1950s. Often, the intervention was implicit, as educators shaped their efforts around their perceptions of what the foundations would in the end demand. Either way, the immense influence of the foundations over this project, even in its failure, was a function of capital, whose power was heightened in this case because State Department officials thought they could not lead the educational effort themselves—for legal, political, and philosophical reasons—even if they could encourage and guide it. Historians of the role of philanthropy in US foreign policy have often taken a cynical, even conspiratorial view towards its relationship with democracy, one this story suggests is worth weakening. But as scholars today question the public responsibilities of private foundations, this history is a reminder that philanthropy's entanglements with even avowedly elitist modes of democratic reform have been long and frequently unhappy.[16]

All these suggestions, however, presuppose the success of the fifth and most pressing task: that we ask with renewed intensity the basic questions about how foreign policy should be conducted in a democracy that inspired such debate among earlier generations of Americans—and to keep asking them, as they did not. Simply talking about what a democratic foreign policy should consist of today would be an important prompt to rekindling an effort to have one. Does it hold true now that it is "the essence of a democracy that the people decide on foreign policy," as Brooks Emeny once had it? Do the people decide on foreign policy at all? Should they? If so, how can that be made feasible, made practical? Are there areas of foreign policy that should still be kept from democratic control, and if so, why? What more, if anything, does the public need to know, and how can they learn it, if misinformation already poses such a threat? What are the stakes? History can identify these questions. Only if Americans can answer them, and at last claim a democratic foreign policy for their own, might the United States finally prove equal to its mission, restore its confidence, and make whole its will.[17]

ABBREVIATIONS

ARCHIVES

NOTES

ACKNOWLEDGMENTS

INDEX

# ABBREVIATIONS

AES: Adlai E. Stevenson Papers, Seeley G. Mudd Manuscript Library, Princeton University

APP: *The American Presidency Project*

BE: Brooks Emeny Papers, Seeley G. Mudd Manuscript Library, Princeton University

BG: *Boston Globe*

BMC: Ben M. Cherrington Papers, Special Collections and Archives, University of Denver

CC: Carnegie Corporation Records, Rare Book and Manuscript Library, Columbia University

CCFR: Chicago Council on Foreign Relations Records, Special Collections, University of Illinois at Chicago

CCP: *Cleveland Call and Post*

CCWA: Cleveland Council on World Affairs Records, Western Reserve Historical Society

CEIP: Carnegie Endowment for International Peace Records, Rare Book and Manuscript Library, Columbia University

CF: Commonwealth Fund Records, Rockefeller Archives Center

CFR: Council on Foreign Relations Records, Seeley G. Mudd Manuscript Library, Princeton University

CP: *Cleveland Press*

CPD: *Cleveland Plain Dealer*

CSM: *Christian Science Monitor*

CSW: Chester S. Williams Papers, Special Collections, University of Oregon

DCWA: Dayton Council on World Affairs Records, Special Collections and Archives, Wright State University

EM: Emma McLaughlin Papers, Bancroft Library, University of California at Berkeley

FAE: Fund for Adult Education Records, Rockefeller Archives Center

FLA: Frederick Lewis Allen Papers, Manuscript Division, Library of Congress

FPA: Foreign Policy Association Records, Wisconsin Historical Society

FPB: *Foreign Policy Bulletin*

FPR: *Foreign Policy Reports*

FF: Ford Foundation Records, Rockefeller Archives Center

FRM: Frank Ross McCoy Papers, Manuscript Division, Library of Congress

FRUS: *Foreign Relations of the United States*

GFK: George F. Kennan Papers, Seeley G. Mudd Manuscript Library, Princeton University

HAS: H. Alexander Smith Papers, Seeley G. Mudd Manuscript Library, Princeton University

IPR: Institute of Pacific Relations Records, Rare Book and Manuscript Library, Columbia University

IPRSF: Institute of Pacific Relations, San Francisco Bay Region Records, Library and Archives, Hoover Institution

JFK: President's Office Files, John F. Kennedy Presidential Library

JWN: John W. Nason Papers, Library and Archives, Hoover Institution

KCB: Kenyon C. Bolton Papers, Western Reserve Historical Society

MB: McGeorge Bundy Papers, John F. Kennedy Presidential Library

McD: James G. McDonald Papers, Rare Book and Manuscript Library, Columbia University

McDD: Diaries of James G. McDonald, James G. McDonald Papers, United States Holocaust Memorial Museum

MH: Manley O. Hudson Papers, Historical and Special Collections, Harvard Law School

NDB: Newton Diehl Baker Papers, Manuscript Division, Library of Congress

NPC: National Policy Committee Records, Manuscript Division, Library of Congress

NYHT: *New York Herald Tribune*

## Abbreviations

NYT: *New York Times*

NYTM: *New York Times Magazine*

OMR: Office of the Messrs. Rockefeller Records, Rockefeller Archives Center

PCJ: Philip C. Jessup Papers, Manuscript Division, Library of Congress

PUK: Paul U. Kellogg Papers, Archives and Special Collections, University of Minnesota

RB: Rockefeller Brothers Fund Records, Rockefeller Archives Center

RBF: Raymond Blaine Fosdick Papers, Seeley G. Mudd Manuscript Library, Princeton University

RF: Rockefeller Foundation Records, Rockefeller Archives Center

RG 59: State Department Records, National Archives and Records Administration

RLB: Raymond Leslie Buell Papers, Manuscript Division, Library of Congress

RLW: Ray Lyman Wilbur Papers, Library and Archives, Hoover Institution

RRPA: Records Relating to Public Affairs Activities, 1944–1965, State Department Records, National Archives and Records Administration

SA: *Survey* Associates Records, Archives and Special Collections, University of Minnesota

TWL: Thomas W. Lamont Papers, Baker Library, Harvard Business School

VMD: Vera Micheles Dean Papers, Schlesinger Library, Radcliffe Institute

WB: William Benton Papers, Special Collections Research Center, University of Chicago

WP: *Washington Post*

WPF: World Peace Foundation Records, Digital Collections and Archives, Tufts University

# ARCHIVES

ARCHIVES AND SPECIAL COLLECTIONS, UNIVERSITY OF MINNESOTA, MINNEAPOLIS, MN

Paul U. Kellogg Papers
Minnesota World Affairs Center Records
*Survey* Associates Records

BANCROFT LIBRARY, UNIVERSITY OF CALIFORNIA AT BERKELEY, BERKELEY, CA

J. B. Condliffe Papers
Emma McLaughlin Papers

BRITISH LIBRARY, LONDON, UK

Lord Robert Cecil Papers

HISTORICAL AND SPECIAL COLLECTIONS, HARVARD LAW SCHOOL, CAMBRIDGE, MA

Judge Lawrence Brooks Papers
Manley O. Hudson Papers

JOHN F. KENNEDY PRESIDENTIAL LIBRARY, BOSTON, MA

President's Office Files
McGeorge Bundy Papers

LIBRARY AND ARCHIVES, HOOVER INSTITUTION, STANFORD, CA

Stanley Kuhl Hornbeck Papers
Institute of Pacific Relations, San Francisco Bay Region Records
John W. Nason Papers
Charles Easton Rothwell Papers

Eugene Staley Papers
Ray Lyman Wilbur Papers

LIBRARY AND ARCHIVES, UNITED STATES HOLOCAUST MEMORIAL
MUSEUM, WASHINGTON, DC

James G. McDonald Papers

MANUSCRIPT DIVISION, LIBRARY OF CONGRESS, WASHINGTON, DC

Frederick Lewis Allen Papers
Newton Diehl Baker Papers
Raymond Leslie Buell Papers
Norman H. Davis Papers
Norman Hapgood Papers
Philip C. Jessup Papers
Archibald MacLeish Papers
Frank R. McCoy Papers
National Policy Committee Records

NATIONAL ARCHIVES II, COLLEGE PARK, MD

Records of the Department of State, Record Group 59

RARE BOOK AND MANUSCRIPT LIBRARY, COLUMBIA UNIVERSITY,
NEW YORK, NY

American Institute of Pacific Relations Records
Nicholas Murray Butler Papers
Carnegie Endowment for International Peace Records
Carnegie Corporation of New York Records
Frederick P. Keppel Papers
James G. McDonald Papers

ROCKEFELLER ARCHIVES CENTER, SLEEPY HOLLOW, NY

Commonwealth Fund Records
Ford Foundation Records
Fund for Adult Education Records

Office of the Messrs. Rockefeller Records
Rockefeller Brothers Fund Records
Rockefeller Foundation Records

SCHLESINGER LIBRARY, RADCLIFFE INSTITUTE FOR ADVANCED STUDY,
CAMBRIDGE, MA

League of Women Voters of Cambridge, Massachusetts Records
League of Women Voters of Massachusetts Records
Louise Leonard Wright Papers
Vera Micheles Dean Papers
National Committee on the Cause and Cure of War Records

SEELEY G. MUDD MANUSCRIPT LIBRARY, PRINCETON UNIVERSITY,
PRINCETON, NJ

Council on Foreign Relations Records
Allen W. Dulles Papers
John Foster Dulles Papers
Brooks Emeny Papers
Raymond Blaine Fosdick Papers
George F. Kennan Papers
H. Alexander Smith Papers
Adlai E. Stevenson Papers

SPECIAL COLLECTIONS, BAKER LIBRARY, HARVARD BUSINESS SCHOOL,
BOSTON, MA

Thomas W. Lamont Papers

SPECIAL COLLECTIONS, UNIVERSITY OF ILLINOIS AT CHICAGO,
CHICAGO, IL

Chicago Council on Foreign Relations Records

SPECIAL COLLECTIONS, UNIVERSITY OF WASHINGTON LIBRARIES,
SEATTLE, WA

Charles P. Rockwood Papers
World Affairs Council of Seattle Records

SPECIAL COLLECTIONS AND ARCHIVES, UNIVERSITY OF DENVER, DENVER, CO

Ben Mark Cherrington Papers

SPECIAL COLLECTIONS AND ARCHIVES, WRIGHT STATE UNIVERSITY, DAYTON, OH

Dayton Council on World Affairs Records

SPECIAL COLLECTIONS RESEARCH CENTER, UNIVERSITY OF CHICAGO, CHICAGO, IL

William Benton Papers

WESTERN RESERVE HISTORICAL SOCIETY, CLEVELAND, OH

Cleveland Council on World Affairs Records
Kenyon C. Bolton Papers

WISCONSIN HISTORICAL SOCIETY, MADISON, WI

Foreign Policy Association Records

## Introduction

1 "America: Rich in Union," *Life*, June 5, 1939, 50–51; "LIFE on the Newsfronts of the World," *Life*, June 5, 1939, 24; Henry R. Luce, "The American Century," *Life*, February 17, 1941, 61–65.

2 Walter Lippmann, "The American Destiny," *Life*, June 5, 1939, 47, 72–73.

3 John Jay, "The Powers of the Senate," March 7, 1788, guides.loc.gov/federalist -papers/text-61-70; Alexis de Tocqueville, *Democracy in America*, trans. Arthur Goldhammer (New York: Library of America, 2004), 262, 476; William B. McAllister et al., *Toward "Thorough, Accurate, and Reliable": A History of the Foreign Relations of the United States Series* (Washington, DC: US Depart- ment of State, 2015), 17–43. Few histories of this problem exist, but see Eric Alterman, *Who Speaks for America? Why Democracy Matters in Foreign Policy* (Ithaca, NY: Cornell University Press, 1998). I thank Tom Arnold-Forster for the formulation that to think about foreign policy is also to think about democracy.

4 David Samuels, "The Aspiring Novelist Who Became Obama's Foreign-Policy Guru," *NYTM*, May 8, 2016, nytimes.com/2016/05/08/magazine/the-aspiring -novelist-who-became-obamas-foreign-policy-guru.html. For recent debates about the "elite," see e.g., Stephen M. Walt, *The Hell of Good Intentions: America's Foreign Policy Elite and the Decline of U.S. Primacy* (New York: Farrar, Straus, and Giroux, 2018); Patrick Porter, "Why America's Grand Strategy Has Not Changed: Power, Habit, and the U.S. Foreign Policy Estab- lishment," *International Security* 42, no. 4 (2018): 9–46; Hal Brands, Peter Feaver, and William Inboden, "In Defense of the Blob," *Foreign Affairs*, April 29, 2020, foreignaffairs.com/articles/united-states/2020-04-29/defense-blob; Emma Ashford, "Build a Better Blob," *Foreign Affairs*, May 29, 2020, foreignaffairs.com/articles/2020-05-28/build-better-blob; Robert Jervis, "Liber- alism, the Blob, and American Foreign Policy: Evidence and Methodology," *Security Studies* 29, no. 3 (2020): 434–456.

5  Richard H. Rovere, "Notes on the Establishment in America," *The American Scholar* 30, no. 4 (1961): 489–490; "Campus Violence Decried by Bundy," *NYT*, July 5, 1970, 28; "The Council on Foreign Relations—Is it a Club? Seminar? Presidium? 'Invisible Government'?" *NYTM*, November 21, 1971, 34, 123–131, 138, 142; William Appleman Williams, *The Tragedy of American Diplomacy* (New York: Dell, 1972), 6. Williams's phrase was notably absent from the 1959 and 1962 editions of *Tragedy*. See also Noam Chomsky, *American Power and the New Mandarins* (New York: Pantheon, 1969); Richard J. Barnet, *Roots of War* (New York: Atheneum, 1972); David Halberstam, *The Best and the Brightest* (New York: Random House, 1972); Joyce Kolko and Gabriel Kolko, *The Limits of Power: The World and United States Foreign Policy, 1945–1954* (New York: Harper & Row, 1972). For a useful genealogy of the term, see Priscilla Roberts, "'All the Right People': The Historiography of the American Foreign Policy Establishment," *Journal of American Studies* 26, no. 3 (1992): 409–434.

6  Brooks Emeny, "Every Citizen a Statesman," *The Kiwanis Magazine*, November 1946, 7, 30–31. For general histories of similar themes, see James A. Morone, *The Democratic Wish: Popular Participation and the Limits of American Government* (New York: Basic Books, 1990); James S. Fishkin, *The Voice of the People: Public Opinion and Democracy* (New Haven, CT: Yale University Press, 1995).

7  *Twenty-Five Years of the Foreign Policy Association, 1918–1943* (New York: Foreign Policy Association, 1943), 3. Little scholarship exists on the Association, but see Frank Winchester Abbott, "From Versailles to Munich: The Foreign Policy Association and American Foreign Policy," (PhD. diss, Texas Tech University, 1972); Alan Raucher, "The First Foreign Affairs Think Tanks," *American Quarterly* 30, no. 4 (1978): 493–513; Don Dennis, *Foreign Policy in a Democracy: The Role of the Foreign Policy Association* (New York: Foreign Policy Association, 2003).

8  For threat inflation, see John A. Thompson, "The Exaggeration of American Vulnerability: The Anatomy of a Tradition," *Diplomatic History* 16, no. 1 (1992): 23–42; Andrew Preston, "Monsters Everywhere: A Genealogy of National Security," *Diplomatic History* 38, no. 3 (2014): 477–500.

9  Broadly, this book agrees that the roots of US foreign policy are to be found more at home than abroad. See Daniel Bessner and Fredrik Logevall, "Recentering the United States in the Historiography of American Foreign Relations," *Texas National Security Review* 3, no. 2 (2020): 38–55. For Black engagement, see e.g., Brenda Gayle Plummer, *Rising Wind: Black Americans and U.S. Foreign Affairs, 1935–1960* (Chapel Hill: University of North Carolina Press, 1996); Sean L. Malloy, *Out of Oakland: Black Panther Internationalism during*

the *Cold War* (Ithaca, NY: Cornell University Press, 2017); Keisha N. Blain, *Set
the World on Fire: Black Nationalist Women and the Global Struggle for
Freedom* (Philadelphia: University of Pennsylvania University Press, 2018). For
labor, see e.g., Elizabeth McKillen, *Making the World Safe for Workers: Labor,
the Left, and Wilsonian Internationalism* (Urbana: University of Illinois Press,
2013); Dorothy Sue Cobble, "A Higher 'Standard of Life' for the World: U.S.
Labor Women's Reform Internationalism and the Legacies of 1919," *Journal of
American History* 100, no. 4 (2014): 1052–1085.

10  Harwood L. Childs, "'By Public Opinion I Mean' — ," *Public Opinion Quar-
terly* 3, no. 2 (1939): 327, 330; Anne Hartwell Johnstone, *American Foreign
Policy* (Washington, DC: The National League of Women Voters, 1938), 34;
Stephen Wertheim, "Reading the International Mind: International Public
Opinion in Early Twentieth Century Anglo-American Thought," in *The
Decisionist Imagination: Sovereignty, Social Science, and Democracy in the
20th Century*, ed. Daniel Bessner and Nicolas Guilhot (New York: Berghahn
Books, 2019), 34–36; Pierre Bourdieu, "Public Opinion Does Not Exist," in
*Communication and Class Struggle: An Anthology in 2 Volumes*, ed. Armand
Matterlart and Seth Siegelaub (New York: International General, 1976), 130.

11  Bernard C. Cohen, *The Public's Impact on Foreign Policy* (Boston: Little,
Brown, 1972), 7; Melvin Small, "Public Opinion," in *Explaining the History of
American Foreign Relations*, ed. Michael J. Hogan and Thomas G. Paterson
(New York: Cambridge University Press, 1991), 175–176; Ernest R. May, "An
American Tradition in Foreign Policy: The Role of Public Opinion," in *Theory
and Practice in American Politics*, ed. William H. Nelson and Francis L.
Loewenheim (Chicago: University of Chicago Press, 1964), 121–122.

12  For public opinion, see e.g., Steven Casey, *Cautious Crusade: Franklin D.
Roosevelt, American Public Opinion, and the War Against Nazi Germany*
(New York: Oxford University Press, 2001); Kenneth Osgood, *Total Cold War:
Eisenhower's Secret Propaganda Battle at Home and Abroad* (Lawrence:
University of Kansas Press, 2006); Steven Casey, *Selling the Korean War:
Propaganda, Politics, and Public Opinion in the United States, 1950–1953*
(New York: Oxford University Press, 2008); Daniel Bessner, *Democracy in
Exile: Hans Speier and the Rise of the Defense Intellectual* (Ithaca, NY: Cornell
University Press, 2018). For summaries of the literatures stemming from the
cultural turn, see Frank Costigliola and Michael J. Hogan, eds., *Explaining
the History of American Foreign Relations* (New York: Cambridge University
Press, 2016).

13  This definition of public opinion as a contest over an elite construction takes
its inspiration from scholars responding to Foucault, Bourdieu, and other
critics, as well as from histories that explore the limits of polling and tie its rise

to the state. See e.g., Benjamin Ginsberg, *The Captive Public: How Mass Opinion Promotes State Power* (New York: Basic Books, 1986); Jean M. Converse, *Survey Research in the United States: Roots and Emergence, 1890–1960* (Berkeley: University of California Press, 1987); Susan Herbst, "Surveys in the Public Sphere: Applying Bourdieu's Critique of Opinion Polls," *International Journal of Public Opinion Research* 4, no. 3 (1992): 220–229; Susan Herbst, *Numbered Voices: How Opinion Polling Has Shaped American Politics* (Chicago: Chicago University Press, 1993); Susan Herbst, "Public Opinion Infrastructures: Meanings, Measures, Media," *Political Communication* 18, no. 4 (2001): 451–464; Adam J. Berinsky, *Silent Voices: Public Opinion and Political Participation in America* (Princeton, NJ: Princeton University Press, 2004); Sarah E. Igo, *The Averaged American: Surveys, Citizens, and the Making of a Mass Public* (Cambridge, MA: Harvard University Press, 2007).

14  For this line of argument, this book is indebted to a new generation of historians working on women and international thought. See e.g., Patricia Owens and Katrina Rietzler, eds., *Women's International Thought: A New History* (New York: Cambridge University Press, 2021).

15  Gabriel A. Almond, *The American People and Foreign Policy* (New York: Harcourt, Brace, 1950), 4.

16  Heidi J. S. Tworek, *News from Germany: The Competition to Control World Communications, 1900–1945* (Cambridge, MA: Harvard University Press, 2019), 41; Jürgen Habermas, *The Structural Transformation of the Public Sphere: An Inquiry into a Category of Bourgeois Society*, trans. Thomas Burger (Cambridge, MA: MIT Press, 1991), 36. See also Michael Schudson, "Was There Ever a Public Sphere? If So, When? Reflections on the American Case," in *Habermas and the Public Sphere*, ed. Craig J. Calhoun (Cambridge, MA: MIT Press, 1992),143–164; Kate Lacey, "The Invention of a Listening Public: Radio and its Audiences," in *Mass Media, Culture and Society in Twentieth-Century Germany*, ed. Karl Christian Führer and Corey Ross (New York: Palgrave Macmillan, 2006), 61–79.

17  C. Wright Mills, *The Power Elite* (New York: Oxford University Press, 1956), 300.

18  Emeny, "The Responsibility of Citizenship in the World Today," September 29, 1964, CCWA, Box 2.

## Chapter 1

1  "In Attendance at Meeting Columbia University Club, April 23, 1918," PUK, Box 33; Wolfgang J. Helbich, "American Liberals in the League of Nations Controversy," *Public Opinion Quarterly* 31, no. 4 (1967): 568–596. Generally, see John A. Thompson, *Reformers and War: American Progressive Publicists and the First World War* (New York: Cambridge University Press, 1987).

2 "Minutes of Meeting of the 'Committee on Nothing at All,'" April 23, 1918, FPA, Box 2/15. For Kellogg, see Clarke A. Chambers, *Paul U. Kellogg and the Survey: Voices for Social Welfare and Social Justice* (Minneapolis: University of Minnesota Press, 1971); David S. Patterson, *The Search for Negotiated Peace: Women's Activism and Citizen Diplomacy in World War I* (New York: Routledge, 2008). For Wilson's fame, see Erez Manela, *The Wilsonian Moment: Self-Determination and the International Origins of Anticolonial Nationalism* (New York: Oxford University Press, 2007). For transatlantic influences on progressivism, see Daniel T. Rodgers, *Atlantic Crossings: Social Politics in a Progressive Age* (Cambridge, MA: Harvard University Press, 1998). The Foreign Policy Association's records are in two parts: an initial accession labeled Part 1 and Mss 2, and subsequent accessions, labeled Part 2 and M2011-044. References are given as Box [Part 1 or 2]/Box Number; "Box 2/15" therefore refers to Part 2, Box 15.

3 "Committee on American Policy: List of Members," July 1918, PUK, Box 33; "Committee on American Policy," June 27, 1918, FPA, Box 2/15; "Committee on American Policy," July 11, 1918, FPA, Box 2/15; Stephen P. Duggan to Paul U. Kellogg, July 31, 1918, PUK, Box 33; "Committee on American Policy in International Relations," October 3, 1918, FPA, Box 2/15; "Minutes of Meeting of Organizing Committee of League of Free Nations Association," November 13, 1918, FPA, Box 2/15; "Minutes of Meeting of Organizing Committee of League of Free Nations Association," November 19, 1918, FPA, Box 2/15. For Britain, see Helen McCarthy, *The British People and the League of Nations: Democracy, Citizenship and Internationalism, c. 1918–45* (Manchester: Manchester University Press, 2011).

4 "Statement of Principles," November 27, 1918, FPA, Box 2/224; Trygve Throntveit, *Power Without Victory: Woodrow Wilson and the American Internationalist Experiment* (Chicago: University of Chicago Press, 2017), 263–270.

5 "The League of Free Gratis Nations," *NYT*, November 28, 1918, 16; "Meeting of the Executive Committee," February 18, 1919, FPA, Box 2/15; "No 'Red Flag' in League, Says F. D. Roosevelt," *New York Tribune*, March 2, 1919, 4; "Hapgood for Danish Post," *NYT*, February 27, 1919, 7; "Conference of Members," March 8, 1919, FPA, Box 2/15; "Meeting of Executive Committee," April 1, 1919, FPA, Box 2/15.

6 "Minutes of the Executive Committee Meeting," May 27, 1919, FPA, Box 2/15; "The League of Free Nations Association," July 13, 1919, RBF, Box 12; "Observations by the Executive Committee of the League of Free Nations Association on the Treaty Reservations," November 24, 1919, FPA, Box 2/15; Richard Breitman, Barbara McDonald Stewart, and Severin Hochberg, eds., *Advocate for the Doomed: The Diaries and Papers of James G. McDonald, 1932–1935*

(Bloomington: Indiana University Press, 2007), 2–7; James G. McDonald to Members, December 20, 1919, TWL, Box 48; McDonald to Woodrow Wilson, May 28, 1920, FPA, Box 2/11.

7  Throntveit, *Power Without Victory*, 289–294; Stephen Wertheim, *Tomorrow, the World: The Birth of U.S. Global Supremacy* (Cambridge, MA: Harvard University Press, 2020), 27.

8  Woodrow Wilson, "Address at the Fairgrounds Auditorium in Billings, Montana," September 11, 1919, APP, presidency.ucsb.edu/node/317964; John A. Thompson, *A Sense of Power: The Roots of America's Global Role* (Ithaca, NY: Cornell University Press, 2015), 110. For organized internationalism, see Frank A. Ninkovich, *Global Dawn: The Cultural Foundation of American Internationalism, 1865–1890* (Cambridge, MA: Harvard University Press, 2009); Warren F. Kuehl, *Seeking World Order: The United States and International Organization to 1920* (Nashville: Vanderbilt University Press, 1969); Warren F. Kuehl and Lynne Dunn, *Keeping the Covenant: American Internationalists and the League of Nations, 1920–1939* (Kent, OH: Kent State University Press, 1997). For "isolationism," see e.g., William Appleman Williams, "The Legend of Isolationism in the 1920s," *Science & Society* 18, no. 1 (1954): 1–20; Warren F. Kuehl, "Midwestern Newspapers and Isolationist Sentiment," *Diplomatic History* 3, no. 3 (1979): 283–306; Brooke L. Blower, "From Isolationism to Neutrality: A New Framework for Understanding American Political Culture, 1919–1941," *Diplomatic History* 38, no. 2 (2014): 345–376. Cf. Christopher McKnight Nichols, *Promise and Peril: America at the Dawn of a Global Age* (Cambridge, MA: Harvard University Press, 2011); Charles A. Kupchan, *Isolationism: A History of America's Efforts to Shield Itself from the World* (New York: Oxford University Press, 2020).

9  For an introduction to progressivism after the Great War, see Alan Dawley, *Changing the World: American Progressives in War and Revolution* (Princeton, NJ: Princeton University Press, 2003).

10  Woodrow Wilson, "Address to a Joint Session of Congress on the Conditions of Peace," January 8, 1918, APP, presidency.ucsb.edu/node/206651; Quincy Wright, *The Control of American Foreign Relations* (New York: Macmillan, 1922), 363. Generally, see Jan Stöckmann, "The First World War and the Democratic Control of Foreign Policy," *Past and Present* 249, no. 1 (2020): 121–166.

11  James Bryce, *The American Commonwealth* (New York: Macmillan, 1888); Viscount Bryce, "Foreign Policy and the People," *International Review* 1 (1919): 9–13. For the Association's view of Bryce, see "James Bryce," FPB 1, February 3, 1922, 1.

12  Elihu Root, "The Declaration of the Rights and Duties of Nations Adopted by the American Institute of International Law," *American Journal of International*

*Law* 10, no. 2 (1916): 211; Elihu Root, "A Requisite for the Success of Popular Diplomacy," *Foreign Affairs* 1, no. 1 (1922): 4, 9; Elihu Root, "Steps toward Preserving Peace," *Foreign Affairs* 3, no. 3 (1925): 353; Benjamin Coates, *Legalist Empire: International Law and American Foreign Relations in the Early Twentieth Century* (New York: Oxford University Press, 2016), 73–74.

13 Elihu Root, "Public Opinion and Foreign Policy," *Foreign Affairs* 9, no. 2 (1931): vii; "Lashes Suffrage Foes," *Sun* (Baltimore), March 22, 1915, 14. For the gendered history of "Club World" see Clifton Hood, *In Pursuit of Privilege: A History of New York City's Upper Class and the Making of a Metropolis* (New York: Columbia University Press, 2017), 193–204. For club membership among Council members, see Inderjeet Parmar, "The Issue of State Power: The Council on Foreign Relations as a Case Study," *Journal of American Studies* 29, no. 1 (1995): 82. Traditional histories centering the Council include Laurence Shoup and William Minter, *Imperial Brain Trust: The Council on Foreign Relations and United States Foreign Policy* (New York: Monthly Review Press, 1977); Robert D. Schulzinger, *The Wise Men of Foreign Affairs: The History of the Council on Foreign Relations* (New York: Oxford University Press, 1984); Michael Wala, *The Council on Foreign Relations and American Foreign Policy in the Early Cold War* (Providence: Berghahn Books, 1994); Peter Grose, *Continuing the Inquiry: The Council on Foreign Relations from 1921 to 1996* (New York: Council on Foreign Relations, 1996); Priscilla Roberts, "'The Council Has Been Your Creation': Hamilton Fish Armstrong, Paradigm of the American Foreign Policy Establishment?" *Journal of American Studies* 35, no. 1 (2001): 65–94.

14 Kimberly Hutchings, "Now You See Them, Now You Don't: Women in the Inquiry 1917–19," *Women and the History of International Thought* (blog), *University of Sussex*, January 10, 2020, blogs.sussex.ac.uk/whit/2020/01/10/now-you-see-them-now-you-dont-women-in-the-inquiry-1917-19/; Mark T. Edwards, *Faith and Foreign Affairs in the American Century* (Lanham, MD: Lexington Books, 2019), 47; Whitney H. Shepardson, *Early History of the Council on Foreign Relations* (Stamford, CT: Overbrook Press, 1960), 9; Robert D. Schulzinger, "Whatever Happened to the Council on Foreign Relations?" *Diplomatic History* 5, no. 4 (1981): 278.

15 Martha S. Jones, *Vanguard: How Black Women Broke Barriers, Won the Vote, And Insisted on Equality for All* (New York: Basic Books, 2020), 178; Cynthia H. Enloe, *Bananas, Beaches and Bases: Making Feminist Sense of International Politics* (Berkeley: University of California Press, 1990), 133. See e.g., Allison L. Sneider, *Suffragists in an Imperial Age: U.S. Expansion and the Woman Question, 1870–1929* (New York: Oxford University Press, 2008); Mona L. Siegel, *Peace on Our Terms: The Global Battle for Women's Rights After the*

*First World War* (New York: Columbia University Press, 2020); Carrie A. Foster, *The Women and the Warriors: The U.S. Section of the Women's International League for Peace and Freedom, 1915–1946* (Syracuse, NY: Syracuse University Press, 1995); Leila J. Rupp, *Worlds of Women: The Making of an International Women's Movement* (Princeton, NJ: Princeton University Press, 1997); Christine von Oertzen, *Science, Gender, and Internationalism: Women's Academic Networks, 1917–1955* (New York: Palgrave Macmillan, 2014); Keisha N. Blain, *Set the World on Fire: Black Nationalist Women and the Global Struggle for Freedom* (Philadelphia: University of Pennsylvania Press, 2018); Keisha N. Blain and Tiffany M. Gill, eds., *To Turn the Whole World Over: Black Women and Internationalism* (Urbana: University of Illinois Press, 2019).

16  Jane Addams, Emily G. Balch, and Alice Hamilton, *Women at the Hague: The International Congress of Women and its Results* (New York: Macmillan, 1915), 153–154; "The Change of Name," *Bulletin of the Foreign Policy Association 2*, June 1921, 4. For internationalism and women, see e.g., Glenda Sluga, "Women, Feminisms and Twentieth-Century Internationalisms," in *Internationalisms: A Twentieth-Century History*, ed. Glenda Sluga and Patricia Clavin (New York: Cambridge University Press, 2017), 61–84; Jan Stöckmann, "Women, Wars, and World Affairs: Recovering Feminist International Relations, 1915–39," *Review of International Studies 44*, no. 2 (2018): 215–235.

17  *Ten Years of the F.P.A.* (New York: Foreign Policy Association, 1929); "Contributions of $500 and Over, October 1927–September 1928," undated, CC, Box 147. For the Institute of Pacific Relations, see John N. Thomas, *The Institute of Pacific Relations: Asian Scholars and American Politics* (Seattle: University of Washington Press, 1974); Tomoko Akami, *Internationalizing the Pacific: The United States, Japan, and the Institute of Pacific Relations in War and Peace, 1919–45* (New York: Routledge, 2002); Priscilla Roberts, "The Institute of Pacific Relations: pan-Pacific and pan-Asian visions of international order," *International Politics 55*, no. 6 (2018): 836–851.

18  *Ten Years*; "Minutes of the Meeting of the Executive Committee," March 4, 1925, FPA, Box 2/15.

19  "Meeting of the Executive Committee F.P.A.," December 14, 1922, FPA, Box 2/15; "Contributions to the Foreign Policy Association of $100 and Over," September 1, 1926, CF, RG 1, Series 18.1, Box 110; "Agnes Leach Dies; A Civic Leader, 90," *NYT*, August 28, 1975, 36.

20  Raymond Leslie Buell, "Memorandum on Washington Trip," October 4, 1927, RLB, Box 41; "'Lie' Is Passed, Fists Menace in Fascism Debate," *NYHT*, January 24, 1926, 2. For donors, see "Contributions to the Foreign Policy Association"; Buell to T. W. Lamont, February 24, 1938, FPA, Box 2/11; "Cox Committee Questionnaire," November 14, 1952, FPA, Box 2/2. On Lamont, see

Edward M. Lamont, *The Ambassador from Wall Street: The Story of Thomas W. Lamont, J. P. Morgan's Chief Executive* (Lanham, MD: Madison Books, 1994); Emily S. Rosenberg, *Financial Missionaries to the World: The Politics and Culture of Dollar Diplomacy* (Cambridge, MA: Harvard University Press, 1999); Susie Pak, *Gentleman Bankers: The World of J. P. Morgan* (Cambridge, MA: Harvard University Press, 2013).

21 "See 'Red Hysteria' in Sedition Curb," *NYT*, February 29, 1920, 14; Throntveit, *Power Without Victory*. For pragmatism and internationalism, see Charles F. Howlett, "John Dewey: A Pragmatist's Search for Peace in the Aftermath of Total War," in *Progressivism and US Foreign Policy Between the World Wars*, ed. Molly Cochran and Cornelia Navari (New York: Palgrave Macmillan, 2017), 117–141; Molly Cochran, "The 'Newer Ideals' of Jane Addams's Progressivism: A Realistic Utopia of Cosmopolitan Justice," in Cochran and Navari, *Progressivism and US Foreign Policy*, 143–165. For the Committee on Public Information and its legacies, see John Maxwell Hamilton, *Manipulating the Masses: Woodrow Wilson and the Birth of American Propaganda* (Baton Rouge: Louisiana State University Press, 2020).

22 "Call Soviet Money Mere 'Dirty Paper'," *NYT*, January 26, 1919, 23; Edwin Björkman, "The League of Free Nations Association of the United States," April 1919, FPA, Box 2/15; "Final Plea Here for Free Filipinos," *NYT*, April 20, 1919, E1; "Puts Peace Delay on Reactionaries," *NYT*, April 6, 1919, 12.

23 "Meeting of the Executive Committee F.P.A.," December 14, 1922, FPA, Box 2/15. For women's clubs in New York reform, see Elisabeth Israels Perry, "Women's Political Choices After Suffrage: The Women's City Club of New York, 1915–1990," *New York History* 71, no. 4 (1990): 415–434; Johanna Neuman, *Gilded Suffragists: The New York Socialites Who Fought for Women's Right to Vote* (New York: New York University Press, 2017). For New York's elite and the persistence of inequality, see Sven Beckert, *The Monied Metropolis: New York City and the Consolidation of the American Bourgeoisie, 1850–1896* (New York: Cambridge University Press, 2001); David Huyssen, *Progressive Inequality: Rich and Poor in New York, 1890–1920* (Cambridge, MA: Harvard University Press, 2014).

24 Kellogg to McDonald, February 3, 1926, SA, Box 95; "Luncheon Discussion," December 1, 1928, FPA, Box 1/80; Elizabeth MacCallum Oral History, 1977, Queen's University, Canada; "1,000 at Astor Hiss Defender of Soviet Rule," *NYHT*, January 18, 1925, 5; "Saturday, January 17, 1925," McDD, Box 1; "Kellogg Attack Booed at Forum on Mexico Issue," *NYHT*, February 28, 1926, 3; "Saturday, November 13, 1926," McDD, Box 1.

25 Kellogg to McDonald, February 3, 1926; "Memorandum on Present Work and Proposed Expansion of Activities of the Foreign Policy Association," April 1925,

FPA, Box 2/110; "Proceedings of the Annual Meeting of the Foreign Policy Association," April 6, 1927, FPA, Box 2/110; *Ten Years*, 17.

26 "Lord Robert Cecil," *FPB* 2, April 6, 1923, 1; McDonald to Lamont, April 16, 1923, FPA, Box 2/10; "Disarmament and the League of Nations," April 2, 1923, FPA, Box 2/110.

27 "'Towaco Shows the Way,'" *FPB* 5, February 19, 1926, 2; "Proceedings of the Annual Meeting of the Foreign Policy Association," April 14, 1928, NDB, Box 153; "Our Policy in Haiti Scored in Debate," *NYT*, December 22, 1929, 20. For listeners' clubs, see David Goodman, "A Transnational History of Radio Listening Groups I: The United Kingdom and United States," *Historical Journal of Film, Radio and Television* 36, no. 3 (2016): 436–465.

28 Owen D. Young to Raymond Blaine Fosdick, March 8, 1928, McD, Box 5; McDonald, "Europe Convalescent," April 23, 1928, SA, Box 73; "Friday, May 18, 1928," McDD, Box 1; McDonald to Kellogg, January 31, 1929, SA, Box 73; James G. McDonald, "International Broadcasting—A Humanizing Force," 1933, McD, Box 36; *The World Today*, 1928 (New York: National Broadcasting Company, 1928), 3. McDonald's activities anticipated the educational work that swept the airwaves in the 1930s. See David Goodman, *Radio's Civic Ambition: American Broadcasting and Democracy in the 1930s* (New York: Oxford University Press, 2011).

29 Courtenay Crocker, "Early Days of the Foreign Policy Association of Massachusetts," undated, FPA, Box 2/1; Kenneth T. Jackson, *Chicago Council on Foreign Relations: A Record of Forty Years* (Chicago: Chicago Council on Foreign Relations, 1963), 7; "Proceedings of the Annual Meeting," April 14, 1928.

30 "Miss Merriman, Foreign Affairs Expert, Suicide," *NYHT*, December 24, 1930, 9; Neil Earle, "Public Opinion for Peace: Tactics of Peace Activists at the Washington Conference on Naval Armament (1921–1922)," *Journal of Church and State* 40, no. 1 (1998): 149–169; Lisa Hendrickson, "Biographical Sketch of Esther Gracie Ogden," *Biographical Database of NAWSA Suffragists, 1890–1920*, documents.alexanderstreet.com/d/1010026830; "Esther G. Ogden, Suffragist, Dies," *NYT*, January 15, 1956, 92. The foreign policy activities of the League of Women Voters deserve more attention, but see Louise M. Young, *In the Public Interest: The League of Women Voters, 1920–1970* (New York: Greenwood Press, 1989), esp. 71–88; Helen Laville, *Cold War Women: The International Activities of American Women's Organisations* (Manchester: Manchester University Press, 2002).

31 "The Foreign Policy Association: Its Women Workers," *CSM*, March 17, 1931, 8; "Minutes of a Meeting of the Executive Board," February 9, 1927, FPA, Box 2/15; "Minutes of a Meeting of the Board of Directors," May 8, 1929, FPA, Box 2/15; "The Annual Meeting," April 22, 1930, NDB, Box 99. For examples of lists

of speakers, see e.g., "The Kellogg Pact," "Manchuria," and "Dictatorship of Democracy," October 1928, MH, Box 137; "Foreigners in the United States," September 7, 1928, MH, Box 137.

32  "Meeting of the Executive Committee F.P.A.," December 14, 1922, FPA, Box 2/16; "Meeting of the Executive Committee," March 19, 1924, FPA, Box 2/15; "F.P.A. Notes," *FPB* 3, March 28, 1924, 2; "Thursday, February 26, 1925," McDD, Box 1; "Friday, 27, 1925," McDD, Box 1; "Friday, May 15, 1925," McDD, Box 1. For the suffragists' return to educational forms of politics after 1920, see Michael McGerr, "Political Style and Women's Power, 1830–1930," *Journal of American History* 77, no. 3 (1990): 864–885.

33  Crocker, "Early Days"; "Monday, May 24, 1926," McDD, Box 1; Herbert Gibbons to Manley O. Hudson, March 25, 1924, MH, Box 7. For Andrews and broader arguments about women's international thought that inform this section, see Valeska Huber, Tamson Pietsch, and Katharina Rietzler, "Women's International Thought and the New Professions, 1900–1940," *Modern Intellectual History* 18, no. 1 (2021): 121–145.

34  Marguerite Hopkins to Hudson, February 16, 1924, MH, Box 7; Hopkins to Hudson, April 3, 1929, MH, Box 137; Hudson to Andre Siegfried, October 3, 1929, MH, Box 137.

35  "Report of the Annual Meeting of the Foreign Policy Association," May 3, 1928, WPF, Series 1, Box 14; "Annual Report, 1936–1937," undated, WPF, Series 1, Box 14; Meeting of the Executive Committee of the F.P.A.," January 9, 1924, FPA, Box 2/15.

36  "Report of the Annual Meeting of the Foreign Policy Association," May 31, 1927, WPF, Series 1, Box 14; "Report of the Annual Meeting of the Foreign Policy Association," May 3, 1928; "Report of the Annual Meeting of the Foreign Policy Association (Boston Branch)," May 9, 1929, WPF, Series 1, Box 14; "Report of the Annual Meeting of the Foreign Policy Association (Boston Branch)," April 29, 1930, WPF, Series 1, Box 14; "Report of the Annual Meeting of the Foreign Policy Association (Boston Branch)," May 9, 1931, WPF, Series 1, Box 14. I am indebted here to Katharina Rietzler, whose work builds extensively on earlier findings of mine; see Katharina Rietzler, "U.S. Foreign Policy Think Tanks and Women's Intellectual Labor, 1920–1950," *Diplomatic History* (forthcoming).

37  John Carter, *Man Is War* (Indianapolis: Bobbs-Merrill, 1926), 253–258; "Minutes of a Meeting of the Board of Directors," December 12, 1928, FPA, Box 2/15.

38  John Carter, "Foreign Policy on the Half-Shell," *Outlook and Independent*, November 28, 1928, 1249–1250, 1260; "John Franklin Carter, 70, Dies," NYT, November 29, 1967, 47.

39  Hopkins to Hudson, December 3, 1928, MH, Box 137; "Meeting of the Executive Committee of the F.P.A.," January 9, 1924, FPA, Box 2/15; "Executive Committee Meeting," October 16, 1936, CCFR, Box 9.

## Chapter 2

1 "Tuesday, August 20," 1929, McDD, Box 2; "J. G. McDonald Visits Premier in Scotland," *NYT*, August 22, 1929, 7; "Monday, September 2nd," 1929, McDD, Box 2; "Thursday, November 21, 1929," McDD, Box 2; "Rockefeller III is at Shanghai," *BG*, October 18, 1929, 28; "Tuesday, December 3, 1929," McDD, Box 2.

2 Judith Sealander, *Private Wealth, Public Life: Foundation Philanthropy and the Reshaping of American Social Policy from the Progressive Era to the New Deal* (Baltimore: Johns Hopkins University Press, 1997), 244. On foundations and US foreign policy in this period, see e.g., Katharina Rietzler, "Before the Cultural Cold Wars: American Philanthropy and Cultural Diplomacy in the Inter-War Years," *Historical Research* 84, no. 223 (2011): 148–164; Inderjeet Parmar, *Foundations of the American Century: The Ford, Carnegie, and Rockefeller Foundations in the Rise of American Power* (New York: Columbia University Press, 2012); Katharina Rietzler, "Fortunes of a Profession: American Foundations and International Law, 1910–1939," *Global Society* 28, no. 1 (2014): 8–23; Katharina Rietzler, "From Peace Advocacy to International Relations Research: The Transformation of Transatlantic Philanthropic Networks, 1900–1930," in *Shaping the Transnational Sphere: Experts, Networks, and Issues from the 1840s to the 1930s*, ed. Davide Rodogno, Bernhard Struck, and Jakob Vogel (New York: Berghahn Books, 2015), 173–193. Generally, see Olivier Zunz, *Philanthropy in America: A History* (Princeton, NJ: Princeton University Press, 2012); Elisabeth S. Clemens, *Civic Gifts: Voluntarism and the Making of the American Nation-State* (Chicago: University of Chicago Press, 2020).

3 Andrew Jewett, *Science, Democracy, and the American University: From the Civil War to the Cold War* (New York: Cambridge University Press, 2012), 12.

4 James G. McDonald to John D. Rockefeller Jr., May 18, 1932, OMR, Series Q, Box 1; William T. Stone, "Memorandum," January 5, 1932, McD, Box 32; "Report of the Washington Bureau," January 12, 1932, FPA, Box 2/15; "September 1, 1932," McDD, Box 2.

5 "Fictions About Russia," *NYT*, January 15, 1921, 11; "Free Nation League Replies to Davis," *NYT*, January 17, 1921, 11; "Has No Proof of Intervention Plot," *NYT*, September 11, 1919, 17; "Demand Americans Quit Haiti at Once," *NYT*, April 29, 1922, 3; "The Secretary of State Replies," *FPB* 1, May 5, 1922, 2; "U.S. Russian Policy Defended," *FPB* 1, January–February 1921, 11.

6 "Minutes of the Executive Committee," December 14, 1922, FPA, Box 2/15; "Foreign Policy Association," November 29, 1926, OMR, Series Q, Box 1; "Friday, February 20, 1925," McDD, Box 1; "Wednesday, February 25, 1925," McDD, Box 1; "Minutes of the Meeting of the Executive Board," April 1, 1925, FPA, Box 2/15. On opium, see William O. Walker III, *Opium and Foreign Policy: The Anglo-American Search for Order in Asia, 1912–1954* (Chapel Hill:

University of North Carolina Press, 1991). On newspapers, see Julia Guarneri, *Newsprint Metropolis: City Papers and the Making of Modern Americans* (Chicago: University of Chicago Press, 2018).

7   "The Locarno Security Conference," *Information Service* 1, no. 1 (1925): 1; Raymond Leslie Buell, *International Relations* (New York: Henry Holt and Company, 1925); "Wednesday, March 18, 1925," McDD, Box 1; David Ekbladh, "Present at the Creation: Edward Mead Earle and the Depression-Era Origins of Security Studies," *International Security* 36, no. 3 (2011): 107–141; "Minutes of the Meeting of the Executive Board," January 6, 1926, FPA, Box 2/15. For simplicity, these publications are referred to as *Reports* throughout the main text. The Association has been ignored in histories of think tanks in US foreign policy, but its research staff represented the first think tank on a model recognizable today. See Alan Raucher, "The First Foreign Affairs Think Tanks," *American Quarterly* 30, no. 4 (1978): 493–513. Cf. Donald E. Abelson, "Old world, new world: the evolution and influence of foreign affairs think-tanks," *International Affairs* 90, no. 1 (2014): 125–142; Priscilla Roberts, "A century of international affairs think tanks in historical perspective," *International Journal* 70, no. 4 (2015): 535–555.

8   "'Who's Who' in the Research Department," attached to Christina Merriman to Members of the National Council and Executive Board, January 9, 1928, SA, Box 73; *Ten Years of the F.P.A.* (New York: Foreign Policy Association, 1929), 26–28; "Foreign Policy Association, Inc.," May 29, 1929, OMR, Series Q, Box 1; "The Foreign Policy Association: Its Women Workers," CSM, March 17, 1931, 8.

9   Elizabeth MacCallum Oral History, 1977, Queen's University, Canada.

10  "Text of Owen D. Young's Address at Johns Hopkins Celebration," *Baltimore Sun*, February 24, 1925, 4; "Proceedings of the Annual Meeting of the Foreign Policy Association," April 6, 1927, FPA, Box 2/110; "Minutes of a Meeting of the Executive Board," October 13, 1926, FPA, Box 2/15; McDonald to Rockefeller Jr. November 16, 1926, OMR, Series Q, Box 1.

11  "Report of the Field Secretary, Raymond T. Rich, to the Executive Board," January 5, 1927, FPA, Box 2/15; Charles P. Howland to McDonald, March 11, 1927, FPA, Box 2/9; "Foreign Policy Association," October 20, 1926, CF, RG 1, Series 18, Box 110; Newton D. Baker to Elizabeth Ogden, June 12, 1929, NDB, Box 99. For the "objectivity" debate in the social sciences, see Mark C. Smith, *Social Science in the Crucible: The American Debate Over Objectivity and Purpose, 1918–1941* (Durham, NC: Duke University Press, 1994). For the lasting influence of Great War propaganda, see J. Michael Sproule, *Propaganda and Democracy: The American Experience of Media and Mass Persuasion* (New York: Cambridge University Press, 1997); Brett Gary, *The Nervous Liberals: Propaganda Anxieties from World War I to the Cold War* (New York: Columbia University

Press, 1999); Jonathan Auerbach, *Weapons of Democracy: Propaganda, Progressivism, and American Public Opinion* (Baltimore: Johns Hopkins, 2015).

12 "Memorandum on Present Work and Proposed Expansion of Activities of the Foreign Policy Association," April 1925, FPA, Box 2/110; "Minutes of a Special Meeting of the Foreign Policy Association," November 10, 1928, FPA, Box 2/15; "Friday, May 14, 1926," McDD, Box 1; "Tuesday, December 28, 1926," McDD, Box 1; "Foreign Policy Association," October 1926, SA, Box 73; Foreign Policy Association: Annual Meeting," April 14, 1928, FPA, Box 1/80. The Association's turn to objectivity also had financial roots. Donors could deduct contributions to "educational" groups from their taxes, but not those to pressure groups. Although the FPA had declared in 1922 that its activities were "purely educational," the Treasury Department did not agree until 1929, a change that came about because of the success of the research department. See McDonald to Members of the Executive Committee, July 10, 1922, FPA, Box 2/15; C. B. Allen and L. K. Sunderlin to H. Maurice Darling, April 26, 1929, FPA, Box 2/15; "Minutes of a Meeting of the Board of Directors," May 8, 1929, FPA, Box 2/15.

13 "Friday, September 24, 1926," McDD, Box 1; Raymond Leslie Buell, *The Native Problem in Africa* (New York: Macmillan, 1928); Susan Pedersen, *The Guardians: The League of Nations and the Crisis of Empire* (New York: Oxford University Press, 2015), 238–239, 258–259, 322–324; Quincy Wright, Review of *The Native Problem in Africa, Political Science Quarterly* 44, no. 2 (1929): 276–279; Raymond Leslie Buell, "The American Occupation of Haiti," *Information Service* 5, no. 19–20 (1929): 327–392; "Memorandum on the Work of the Research Department of the Foreign Policy Association," attached to McDonald to the Trustees of the Rockefeller Foundation, November 25, 1932, RF, Box 333; Buell, "Memorandum to the Board," February 4, 1930, SA, Box 73. (All RF references are to RG 1.1, Series 200, unless otherwise stated.)

14 "The Annual Meeting: April 29, 1931," July 1931, FPA, Box 2/111.

15 Richard Breitman, Barbara McDonald Stewart, and Severin Hochberg, eds., *Advocate for the Doomed: The Diaries and Papers of James G. McDonald, 1932–1935* (Bloomington: Indiana University Press, 2007), 12–18.

16 McDonald to FPA, April 3, 1933, McDD, Box 2; Breitman et al., *Advocate for the Doomed*, 47–50; Greg Burgess, *The League of Nations and the Refugees from Nazi Germany: James G. McDonald and Hitler's Victims* (New York: Bloomsbury, 2016), 33; "League Aid Asked by McDonald to End Nazi Persecution," *NYT*, December 30, 1935, 1.

17 Buell to Stone, May 1, 1933, RLB, Box 42.

18 Stephen Wertheim, "Reading the International Mind: International Public Opinion in Early Twentieth Century Anglo-American Thought," in *The Decisionist Imagination: Sovereignty, Social Science, and Democracy in the*

*20th Century*, ed. Daniel Bessner and Nicolas Guilhot (New York: Berghahn Books, 2019), 48; Francis Pickens Miller to Richard F. Cleveland, November 4, 1935, NPC, Box 1; Buell to Vera Micheles Dean, July 17, 1944, RLB, Box 5; Buell, "National Program of Public Education," March 1935, RLB, Box 44.

19 "The Annual Meeting," April 22, 1930, NDB, Box 99; "Memorandum on the Work."

20 Robert Vitalis, *White World Order, Black Power Politics: The Birth of American International Relations* (Ithaca, NY: Cornell University Press, 2015), 11–13, 55–61, 74–90; McDonald to Rockefeller Jr., April 27, 1929, OMR, Series Q, Box 1; "Miss Wertheimer, Expert on Europe: Research Associate of Foreign Policy Association Dies in California at 41," *NYT*, May 7, 1937, 30.

21 Buell, "Memorandum on Washington Trip," October 4, 1927, RLB, Box 41; Office of the Historian, "Frequently Asked Historical Questions," 1997-2001. state.gov/about_state/history/faq.html#personnel; Frank B. Kellogg to McDonald, December 16, 1927, RG 59, Central Decimal File, 1930–1939, 811.43 Foreign Policy Association, Box 5071; Stone to McDonald, May 24, 1927, McD, Box 19. For Association support for State, see William T. Stone, "The Administration of the Department of State: Its Organization and Needs," *Information Service* 4, special supplement no. 3 (1929): 1–44; Buell to Cordell Hull, February 24, 1937, FPA, Box 2/7.

22 "Foreign Policy Association," June 16, 1932, OMR, Series Q, Box 1; "Memorandum on the Work"; "Minutes of a Meeting of the Board of Directors," April 10, 1931, FPA, Box 2/15.

23 Ogden to McDonald, November 22, 1929, McD, Box 11; "Foreign Policy Association," June 15, 1933, OMR, Series Q, Box 1; "Minutes of a Meeting of the Board of Directors," February 1, 1934, FPA, Box 2/15; "Minutes of a Meeting of the Board of Directors," March 18, 1936, FPA, Box 2/15; "Foreign Policy Association," January 20, 1933, RF, Box 333; "Foreign Policy Association," December 11, 1935, RF, Box 333; "The Six International Organizations," July 28, 1933, HAS, Box 225; "Minutes of a Meeting of the Board of Directors," May 8, 1935, FPA, Box 2/15.

24 Buell, "Proposed Five Year Plan for the F.P.A.," March 14, 1933, SA, Box 73; Committee on the Philippines, "Recommendations regarding the Future of the Philippines," January 1935, RLB, Box 43; Norma S. Thompson to Buell, April 23, 1934, RF, Box 335; *Problems of the New Cuba: Report of the Commission on Cuban Affairs* (New York: Foreign Policy Association, 1935); Andres Pastoriza to Secretary of State, April 30, 1936, RG 59, Central Decimal File, 1930–1939, 811.43 Foreign Policy Association/70, Box 5072; Laurence Duggan to Hull, July 11, 1936, RG 59, Central Decimal File, 1930–1939, 811.43 Foreign Policy Association/73, Box 5072.

25  Buell, "Proposal to Expand the Scope of the Foreign Policy Association,"
    October 23, 1934, RLB, Box 42; "Minutes of a Meeting of the Board of Direc-
    tors," June 12, 1935, FPA, Box 2/15; "Meeting of Branch Chairmen," September
    29, 1934, FPA, Box 2/1. For Buell and Miller, as well as for the policy groups as
    a species of participatory democracy, see Mark Thomas Edwards, *Faith and
    Foreign Affairs in the American Century* (Lanham, MD: Lexington Books,
    2019), 79–82.

26  Walter Lippmann, *Liberty and the News* (New York: Harcourt, Brace, and
    Howe, 1920), 99–100; Walter Lippmann, *The Phantom Public* (New York:
    Harcourt, Brace, 1925), 22, 26–27; Ronald Steel, *Walter Lippmann and the
    American Century* (New Brunswick: Transaction, 1998), 212; John Dewey,
    "Public Opinion," *New Republic*, May 3, 1922, 286–288; John Dewey, "Practical
    Democracy," *New Republic*, December 2, 1925, 52–54. For the rise of "realism,"
    see Edward A. Purcell, *The Crisis of Democratic Theory* (Lexington: University
    of Kentucky Press, 1973); Leon Fink, *Progressive Intellectuals and the Dilemmas
    of Democratic Commitment* (Cambridge, MA: Harvard University Press, 1997).
    For a rejoinder, see Jewett, *Science, Democracy*. For the "Lippmann-Dewey
    debate," see Michael Schudson, "The 'Lippmann-Dewey Debate' and the
    Invention of Walter Lippmann as an Anti-democrat, 1986–1996," *International
    Journal of Communication* 2 (2008): 1031–1042; Sue Curry Jansen, "Phantom
    Conflict: Lippmann, Dewey, and the Fate of the Public in Modern Society,"
    *Communication and Critical/Cultural Studies* 6, no. 3 (2009): 24–45.

27  John Dewey, "Education as Politics," *New Republic*, October 4, 1922, 139–141.
    For the international aspects of Dewey's thinking, see Molly Cochran,
    "Dewey as an international thinker," in *The Cambridge Companion to
    Dewey*, ed. Molly Cochran (New York: Cambridge University Press, 2010),
    309–336; Charles F. Howlett and Audrey Cohan, "John Dewey and the
    Significance of Peace Education in American Democracy," *Journal of the
    Gilded Age and Progressive Era* 16, no. 4 (2017): 456–472. Generally, see
    Joseph F. Kett, *The Pursuit of Knowledge Under Difficulties: From Self-
    Improvement to Adult Education in America, 1750–1990* (Stanford: Stanford
    University Press, 1994).

28  John Dewey, *The Public and its Problems* (New York: Henry Holt, 1927), 109;
    Frederick P. Keppel, *Education for Adults and Other Essays* (New York:
    Columbia University Press, 1926). For postwar adult education, see William M.
    Keith, *Democracy as Discussion: Civic Education and the American Forum
    Movement* (Lanham, MD: Lexington Books, 2007); Jewett, *Science, Democ-
    racy*, 109–147, 196–244; David Goodman, *Radio's Civic Ambition: American
    Broadcasting and Democracy in the 1930s* (New York: Oxford University Press,
    2011). For Carnegie, see Amy D. Rose, "Beyond Classroom Walls: The

Carnegie Corporation and the Founding of the American Association for Adult Education," *Adult Education Quarterly* 39, no. 3 (1989): 140–151.

29  Morse A. Cartwright, *Ten Years of Adult Education: A Report on a Decade of Progress in the American Movement* (New York: Macmillan, 1935), 14; Walter Lippmann, *Public Opinion* (New York: Macmillan, 1922), 364; Lyman Bryson, *Adult Education* (New York: American Book, 1936), 3–4; Ben M. Cherrington, *Methods of Education in International Attitudes* (New York: Teachers College, 1934); Ben M. Cherrington, "The Meaning of Adult Education in America," undated [1934], BMC, Box 3. For race and the Carnegie Corporation, see Maribel Morey, *White Philanthropy: Carnegie Corporation's* An American Dilemma *and the Making of a White World Order* (Chapel Hill: University of North Carolina Press, 2021).

30  John W. Studebaker and Chester S. Williams, foreword to *Education for Democracy: Public Affairs Forums* (Washington, DC: Government Printing Office, 1935); A. Caswell Ellis to General Education Board, undated [1935], NDB, Box 67. On forums, see Robert Kunzman and David Tyack, "Educational Forums of the 1930s: An Experiment in Adult Civic Education," *American Journal of Education* 111, no. 3 (2005): 320–340; Keith, *Democracy as Discussion*, 221–329.

31  Ben M. Cherrington, "Democratic versus Authoritarian Adult Education," *Journal of Adult Education* 6, no. 3 (1939): 242–245; John W. Studebaker, *Plain Talk* (Washington, DC: National Home Library Foundation, 1936), 160.

32  Eduard C. Lindeman, *The Meaning of Adult Education* (New York: New Republic, 1926), 188–189.

33  Alfred Dwight Sheffield, *Creative Discussion* (New York: Association Press, 1927), 24, 48–49; Lindeman, *Meaning of Adult Education*, 138; Goodman, *Radio's Civic Ambition*, 183; Cherrington, "Adult Education in Public Affairs," April 15, 1937, BMC, Box 3. Broadly, see Laura M. Westhoff, "The Popularization of Knowledge: John Dewey on Experts and American Democracy," *History of Education Quarterly* 35, no. 1 (1995): 27–47; Tom Arnold-Forster, "Democracy and Expertise in the Lippmann-Terman Controversy," *Modern Intellectual History* 16, no. 2 (2019): 561–592.

34  "Verbatim minutes of meeting of the Board," February 10, 1932, FPA, Box 2/15; Buell to Keppel, September 30, 1938, CC, Box 147.

35  "Foreign Policy Association," May 17, 1935, RF, Box 336; Buell to Sydnor Walker, May 9, 1935, RF, Box 336; Frank R. McCoy, "Informal Report of the President for the Year 1945," undated [March 1946], RF, Box 334.

36  Kett, *Pursuit of Knowledge*, 370–375; John B. Hench, *Books as Weapons: Propaganda, Publishing, and the Battle of Global Markets in the Era of World War II* (Ithaca, NY: Cornell University Press, 2010), 11–18; "Report of the

Department of Popular Education," undated [1935], FPA, Box 2/21; "Report on the Experimental Education Program, July 1, 1935–June 30, 1936," October 3, 1936, RF, Box 336; Stone to John D. Rockefeller III, November 29, 1940, OMR, Series Q, Box 1.

37 "Experimental Program of Popular Education," October 21, 1937, RF, Box 336; "Report to the Rockefeller Foundation on the Program of Popular Education of the Foreign Policy Association for the Year 1938," March 31, 1939, RF, Box 336; Tracy Kittredge to Joseph H. Willits, November 29, 1940, RF, Box 336.

38 Douglas B. Craig, *Fireside Politics: Radio and Political Culture in the United States, 1920–1940* (Baltimore: Johns Hopkins University Press, 2000), xi; Sarah Ellen Graham, *Culture and Propaganda: The Progressive Origins of American Public Diplomacy, 1936–1953* (Farnham, UK: Ashgate, 2015), 33; Buell, "Radio and Foreign News," April 17, 1939, RLB, Box 32; McDonald, "Radio: A Two-Way Instrument of Democracy," November 27, 1942, McD, Box 14. For radio in the 1930s, see Goodman, *Radio's Civic Ambition*; Bruce Lenthall, *Radio's America: The Great Depression and the Rise of Modern Mass Culture* (Chicago: University of Chicago Press, 2007).

39 "Minutes of a Meeting of the Board of Directors," September 27, 1939, FPA, Box 2/15; "Minutes of a Meeting of the Board of Directors," October 25, 1939, FPA, Box 2/15; "Radio Report," January 23, 1940, FPA, Box 2/21; "Application to the Rockefeller Foundation for Renewal of Existing Grants in Support of the Foreign Policy Association," attached to McCoy to Raymond Blaine Fosdick, October 16, 1941, RF, Box 334; "Radio Report," February 28, 1940, FPA, Box 2/21.

40 "Radio Report," April 21, 1941, FPA, Box 2/21; "Excerpts from Broadcast Letters," December 12, 1939, FPA, Box 2/21; "Radio Report," October 17, 1941, FPA, Box 2/21.

41 Paul F. Lazarsfeld, *Radio and the Printed Page: An Introduction to the Study of Radio and its Role in the Communication of Ideas* (New York: Duell, Sloan and Pearce, 1940); "Radio Report," March 24, 1941, FPA, Box 2/21; "Division of Public Liaison, July 1944–June 1945," November 7, 1945, RG 59, RRPA, Box 3; "Minutes of a Meeting of the Board of Directors," April 29, 1942, FPA, Box 2/15.

42 Francis Buell, "Buell: A World New Deal," March 1962, RLB, Box 42; "Congressman Treadway Facing Toughest Campaign in 30 Years," BG, July 26, 1942, C28; "For Congress; A Man of Vision Knowledge and Action," undated [1942], RLB, Box 40.

43 Buell to Stone, November 9, 1934, RLB, Box 32; Raymond Leslie Buell, *Isolated America* (New York: Knopf, 1940), 419, 452–453.

44 Buell, *Isolated America*, 24, 71, 92, 287–288, 297.

45 Joseph Schumpeter, *Capitalism, Socialism, and Democracy* (New York: Harper, 1942), 262–265; Buell to Dean, January 26, 1945, RLB, Box 5.

46 Buell to Benjamin Gerig, September 28, 1943, RLB, Box 6; Buell to Henry R. Luce, August 9, 1945, RLB, Box 23; Buell to Archibald MacLeish, February 21, 1945, RLB, Box 22.

## Chapter 3

1 Vera Micheles Dean, "Toward A New World Order," *FPR* 17, no. 5 (1941): 50–68. A draft of these proposals was read by Leo Pasvolsky, who was in charge of postwar planning at the State Department. See note on Dean, "Toward A New World Order," April 29, 1941, VMD, Box 3.

2 "The F.P.A.," *WP*, December 8, 1938, 10; "Foreign Policy Group Birthday Is Hailed by Hull and Halifax," *NYHT*, December 4, 1938, A1; Charles A. Beard, "Giddy Minds and Foreign Quarrels," *Harper's*, September 1939, 338; *Twenty Years of the Foreign Policy Association* (New York: Foreign Policy Association, 1939), 28.

3 *Twenty Years*, 17–31.

4 Malcolm Moos, "Toward Greater Public Understanding of Foreign Policy and the Achievement of World Affairs Education at the Community Level," October 16, 1964, FF, FA582, Box 8; "Conquest of U.S. Seen as Planned," *NYT*, March 19, 1939, 33; "Divergent Views on Germany Given," *NYT*, January 15, 1939, 30. For a contemporary review of the debate, see Charles O'Donnell, "American Foreign Policy: A Review of Some Recent Literature on Isolation and Collective Security," *Review of Politics* 1, no. 3 (1939): 333–347.

5 Dean, "Hitler at Grips with Allies in Low Countries," *FPB* 19, May 17, 1940, 2; "Report of the Washington Bureau," May 8, 1934, FPA, Box 2/21; William T. Stone, "The Munitions Industry: An Analysis of the Senate Investigation," *FPR* 10, no. 20 (1934): 250–268; "Minutes of a Meeting of the Board of Directors," January 9, 1935, FPA, Box 2/15; "Washington Bureau Report," May 8, 1935, FPA, Box 2/21; "Minutes of a Meeting of the Board of Directors," June 12, 1935, FPA, Box 2/15; William T. Stone, *War Tomorrow: Will We Keep Out?* (New York: Foreign Policy Association, 1935); Thomas W. Lamont to Raymond Leslie Buell, May 15, 1936, TWL, Box 29; Lamont to Florence Lamont, November 4, 1938, TWL, Box 29; James Wechsler, "War in the Peace Movement," *Nation*, March 19, 1938, 323; John C. de Wilde, David H. Popper, and Eunice Clark, *Handbook of the War* (Boston: Houghton Mifflin, 1939). Cf. Inderjeet Parmar, *Foundations of the American Century: The Ford, Carnegie, and Rockefeller Foundations in the Rise of American Power* (New York: Columbia University Press, 2012), 65–90.

6 Note, *FPB* 18, September 15, 1939, 1; Dean, "The United States Faces a New World Order," *FPB* 19, May 24, 1940, 1–2; Lamont to Frank R. McCoy, April 1, 1940, FPA, Box 2/11; William T. Stone, *America Rearms: The Citizen's Guide to*

*National Defense* (New York: Foreign Policy Association, 1941), 62–63; "America and the Next War: II," *New Republic*, June 21, 1939, 176; Marquis W. Childs and William T. Stone, *Toward a Dynamic America: The Challenge of a Changing World* (New York: Foreign Policy Association, 1941), 7; Dean, "Is A Negotiated Peace Possible?" *FPB* 20, January 10, 1941, 1–2; "U.S. 'Bill of Duties' Urged by Wallace," *NYT*, April 9, 1941, 1; Dean, "America Must Choose," *FPB* 20, May 20, 1941, 1–2.

7   Dean, "Writing Contemporary History," May 10, 1939, RLB, Box 5; Tracy Kittredge, "International Relations Programs in the United States," September 30, 1941, RF, Box 334; "White Unit Widens British Aid Stand," *NYT*, December 28, 1940, 3; "Minutes of a Meeting of the Board of Directors," January 22, 1941, FPA, Box 2/15; "General McCoy and Mrs. Dean," December 4, 1940, RF, Box 336.

8   A. J. Bacevich, *Diplomat in Khaki: Major General Frank Ross McCoy and American Foreign Policy, 1898–1949* (Lawrence: University of Kansas Press, 1989), 126, 211–213.

9   "Minutes of a Meeting of the Board of Directors," September 27, 1939, FPA, Box 2/15; "Notes on the New England Branch Meeting," May 2, 1941, FPA, Box 1/70; "Minutes of a Meeting of the Board of Directors," September 24, 1941, FPA, Box 2/15.

10  "Report of Special Drafting Committee," September 23, 1941, HAS, Box 227; "Minutes of a Meeting of the Board of Directors," October 22, 1941, FPA, Box 2/15; Kittredge, "Program of the Foreign Policy Association," October 29, 1941, RF, Box 334; "Roosevelt Says U.S. Aim is End of Hitler Peril," *NYHT*, October 26, 1941, 20; "Minutes of a Meeting of the Board of Directors," December 17, 1941, FPA, Box 2/15; "The FPA in the War," *FPB* 21, December 26, 1941, 2–3. Generally on this debate, and especially the radicalism of the interventionist cause, see Stephen Wertheim, *Tomorrow, the World: The Birth of U.S. Global Supremacy* (Cambridge, MA: Harvard University Press, 2020).

11  Franklin D. Roosevelt, "Address at the Annual Dinner of White House Correspondents' Association," March 15, 1941, APP, presidency.ucsb.edu/node/210670. Generally, see John A. Thompson, "Conceptions of National Security and American Entry into World War II," *Diplomacy & Statecraft* 16, no. 4 (2005): 671–697; Andrew Preston, "Monsters Everywhere: A Genealogy of National Security," *Diplomatic History* 38, no. 3 (2014): 477–500; Steven Casey, *Cautious Crusade: Franklin D. Roosevelt, American Public Opinion, and the War Against Nazi Germany* (New York: Oxford University Press, 2001); Andrew Johnstone, "Spinning War and Peace: Foreign Relations and Public Relations on the Eve of World War II," *Journal of American Studies* 53, no. 1 (2019): 223–251. It is not entirely clear whether Roosevelt was an Association member.

The Association did not claim him as one, which it would have done if it could, but Eleanor's involvement makes it likely. On Roosevelt, internationalism, and public opinion, see Graham Cross, *The Diplomatic Education of Franklin D. Roosevelt, 1882–1933* (New York: Palgrave Macmillan, 2012). On noninterventionists, see Justus Doenecke, *Storm on the Horizon: The Challenge to American Intervention, 1939–1941* (Lanham, MD: Rowman & Littlefield, 2000).

12 Vera Micheles Dean, "U.S. Foreign Policy and the Voter," *FPR* 20, no. 13 (1944): 156. For the State Department, see e.g., *Peace and War: United States Foreign Policy, 1931–1941* (Washington, DC: Government Printing Office, 1942), 3.

13 Justin Hart, *Empire of Ideas: The Origins of Public Diplomacy and the Transformation of U.S. Foreign Policy* (New York: Oxford University Press, 2013), 83.

14 Buell, "Confidential Interviews in Washington," November 19, 1934, RLB, Box 42; Stone to Research Staff, February 18, 1939, FPA, Box 2/10; Stone to Dean, December 1, 1938, FPA, Box 2/6; George Messersmith to Dean, January 16, 1939, FPA, Box 2/11; Henry F. Grady to Stone, October 11, 1940, RG 59, Central Decimal File, 1940–1944, 811.43 Foreign Policy Association/107; Sumner Welles, "Visit of Mr. Charles A. Thomson of the Foreign Policy Association to South America," August 10, 1938, RG 59, Central Decimal File, 1930–1939, 811.43 Foreign Policy Association/81; "Address of the Honorable Sumner Welles," October 19, 1936, FPA, Box 2/96.

15 Cordell Hull to Buell, January 14, 1937, FPA, Box 2/7; "The Foreign Policy Association Looks to the Future," June 18, 1941, RF, Box 336. For the Council and the IPR, see Yukata Sasaki, "Foreign Policy Experts as Service Intellectuals: The AIPR, the CRF and Planning the Occupation of Japan during World War Two," in *The United States and the Second World War: New Perspectives on Diplomacy, War, and the Home Front*, ed. G. Kurt Piehler and Sidney Pash (New York: Fordham University Press, 2010), 293–332; Dayna Barnes, "Think Tanks and a New Order in Asia," *Journal of American-East Asian Relations* 22, no. 2 (2015): 89–119.

16 Buell, "The Churches and the World Outside," October 17, 1939, RLB, Box 32; Buell to McCoy, September 3, 1939, RLB, Box 10.

17 Wertheim, *Tomorrow, the World*, 65–67; Stone to McCoy, September 14, 1939, FPA, Box 2/12; "Minutes of a Meeting of the Board of Directors," September 27, 1939, FPA, Box 2/15; "Minutes of a Meeting of the Board of Directors," November 15, 1939, FPA, Box 2/15.

18 Wertheim, *Tomorrow, the World*, 115–172; Andrew Johnstone, *Dilemmas of Internationalism: The American Association for the United Nations and US Foreign Policy, 1941–1948* (Farnham, UK: Ashgate, 2009); "Minutes of a

Meeting of the Board of Directors," September 27, 1939, FPA, Box 2/15;
"Minutes of a Meeting of the Board of Directors," November 15, 1939, FPA,
Box 2/15; "Proposed activities of the Council on Foreign Relations in the field
of research and collaboration with the Department of State," September 12,
1939, attached to "Memorandum for Under Secretary Stettinius from Mr.
Armstrong," November 24, 1943, RG 59, Central Decimal File, 1940–1944,
811.43 Council on Foreign Relations/220; Kittredge, "Application for a New
Appropriation FPA," September 22, 1941, RF, Box 334.

19 Buell to Charles A. Thomson, October 11, 1938, RLB, Box 15; "Minutes of a
Meeting of the Board of Directors," May 28, 1941, FPA, Box 2/15; "Minutes of a
Meeting of the Board of Directors," October 22, 1941, FPA, Box 2/15; "Minutes
of a Meeting of the Board of Directors," December 17, 1941, FPA, Box 2/15;
Dean to McCoy, May 12, 1942, RLB, Box 5; "Minutes of a Meeting of the
Board of Directors," November 26, 1941, FPA, Box 2/15; "FPA Staff in Govern-
ment Service," *FPB* 21, August 28, 1942, 3.

20 Sheila Isenberg, *A Hero of Our Own: The Story of Varian Fry* (New York:
Random House, 2001); McCoy to Joseph Willits, March 20, 1942, RF, Box 334;
"Branch Conference, May 7, 1943," FPA, Box 1/70; Dean to George H. Chase,
April 7, 1943, FPA, Box 2/91; "56 U.S. Women Nominated for Peace Parleys,"
*NYT*, August 31, 1944, 6; "Poll Shows Growing Sentiment for Woman at the
Peace Table," *NYHT*, September 10, 1944, A4; "Minutes of a Meeting of the
Board of Directors," April 29, 1943, FPA, Box 2/15.

21 Dean, "Writing Contemporary History," May 10, 1939, RLB, Box 5; Andrew
Jewett, "Collective Security for Common Men and Women: Vera Micheles
Dean and US Foreign Relations," in *Women's International Thought: A New
History*, ed. Patricia Owens and Katrina Rietzler (New York: Cambridge
University Press, 2021), 309; Dean, untitled memorandum, October 21, 1942,
RF, Box 334; "Informal Report of the President for the Year 1941," undated,
HAS, Box 227; "Informal Report of the President for the Year 1942," April 27,
1943, BE, Box 39; "Informal Report of the President for the Year 1943,"
February 24, 1944, BE, Box 39; "Informal Report of the President for the Year
1945," undated, BE, Box 39; Vera Micheles Dean, *United Nations Discussion
Guide* (New York: Reader's Digest, Time, Newsweek, 1942).

22 Willits to Raymond Blaine Fosdick, July 27, 1943, RF, Box 334; Alan Brinkley, *The
Publisher: Henry Luce and His American Century* (New York: Knopf, 2010), 282–312.

23 "Branch Conference, October 2, 1942," FPA, Box 1/70; "Minutes of a Meeting
of the Board of Directors," March 24, 1943, FPA, Box 2/15; "Minutes of a
Meeting of the Board of Directors," December 1, 1943, FPA, Box 2/15; "Minutes
of a Meeting of the Board of Directors," October 25, 1944, FPA, Box 2/15;
"Branch Conference, October 15, 1943," FPA, Box 1/70.

24 "Minutes of a Meeting of the Board of Directors," May 22, 1940, FPA, Box 2/15; "Informal Report of the President for the Year 1943," "Foreign Policy Association," May 7, 1942, FPA, Box 1/70; "Branch Conference, May 8th, 1942," FPA, Box 2/70; "Branch Conference, October 15, 1943."

25 "Branch Conference, October 15, 1943"; "Dorothy F. Leet, 99, Director of Reid Hall," *NYT*, March 9, 1994, 10; Christine von Oertzen, *Science, Gender, and Internationalism: Women's Academic Networks, 1917–1955* (New York: Palgrave Macmillan, 2014), 9–26.

26 "Gives 7-Point Plan for Allies in Peace," *NYT*, May 13, 1942, 8; Dorothy F. Leet to McCoy, April 29, 1943, FPA, Box 1/71; Hull to Walter Parker, April 24, 1944, RG 59, Central Decimal File, 1940–1944, 811.43 Foreign Policy Association/123, Box 3854; "Minutes of a Meeting of the Board of Directors," April 26, 1944, FPA, Box 2/15; "Branch Conference, October 19, 1945," FPA, Box 2/71.

27 "Branch Officers and Chairmen of Special Committees," November 1944, FPA, Box 1/73; "Foreign Policy Association Meetings and Attendance for the Calendar Years 1943–1945," undated, BE, Box 39.

28 "Branch Conference, October 6, 1944," FPA, Box 1/71; "Branch Conference, October 19, 1945."

29 "Minutes of a Meeting of the Board of Directors," February 28, 1945, FPA, Box 2/15.

30 John K. Jessup, "America and the Future," *Life*, September 20, 1943, 105, 114.

31 Senator Alexander Wiley, "Cooperation between the Senate and Executive in Formulation and Consideration of Post-War Peace Treaty," *Congressional Record* 88 (November 25, 1942): 9132–9135; "Role of Congress in Peace Provided in Senator's Plan," *CSM*, September 18, 1942, 19; "Senators Hit Treaty Plan," *Sun*, December 4, 1942, 13; Hugh Gibson, *The Road to Foreign Policy* (Garden City, NY: Doubleday, 1944), 174–228.

32 Joseph M. Jones, "The U.S. State Department," *Fortune*, September 1943, 186; Joseph M. Jones, "A Modern Foreign Policy," *Fortune*, August 1943, 194. See also Joseph M. Jones, *A Modern Foreign Policy for the United States* (New York: Macmillan, 1944). For State's earlier efforts, see William O. Chittick, "The Domestic Information Activities of the Department of State," (PhD diss., Johns Hopkins University, 1964); Robert C. Hilderbrand, *Power and the People: Executive Management of Public Opinion in Foreign Affairs, 1897–1921* (Chapel Hill: University of North Carolina Press, 1981).

33 "Foreign Policy and Public Opinion," February 8, 1944, CFR, Series 3B, Box 135; Walter Lippmann, *U.S. Foreign Policy: Shield of the Republic* (Boston: Little, Brown, 1943), 9; Cordell Hull, "Foreign Policy of the United States of America," *Department of State Bulletin* 10, no. 251 (1944): 335; Michael Leigh, *Mobilizing Consent: Public Opinion and American Foreign Policy, 1937–1947*

(Westport, CT: Greenwood Press, 1976), 128; Dean, "Hull Welcomes Public Participation in Shaping Foreign Policy," *FPB* 23, April 14, 1944, 1–2.

34  Andrew Jewett, *Science, Democracy, and the American University: From the Civil War to the Cold War* (New York: Cambridge University Press, 2012), 9; Robert E. Riggs, "Overselling the UN Charter—Fact and Myth," *International Organization* 14, no. 2 (1960): 277–290; Susan A. Brewer, *Why America Fights: Patriotism and War Propaganda from the Philippines to Iraq* (New York: Oxford University Press, 2009), 136; Robert A. Divine, *Second Chance: The Triumph of Internationalism in America During World War II* (New York: Atheneum, 1967), 252.

35  Andrew Buchanan, "Domesticating Hegemony: Creating a Globalist Public, 1941–1943," *Diplomatic History* 45, no. 2 (2021): 301–329; Wertheim, *Tomorrow, the World*, 149–172; H. Schuyler Foster, "Domestic Information Activities of the State Department," March 30, 1946, RG 59, RRPA, Box 1; "Division of Public Liaison, July 1944–June 1945," November 7, 1945, RG 59, RRPA, Box 3; Charlene Mires, *Capital of the World: The Race to Host the United Nations* (New York: New York University Press, 2013); Vera Micheles Dean, *On the Threshold of World Order* (New York: Foreign Policy Association, 1944), 60; "Peace by Propaganda," *NYHT*, April 4, 1945, 24.

36  Dean Acheson, "Government-Citizen Cooperation in the Making of Foreign Policy," *Department of State Bulletin* 13, no. 336 (1945): 893–894.

37  "John S. Dickey Oral History Interview," Harry S. Truman Presidential Library, trumanlibrary.gov/library/oral-histories/dickeyjs; "Francis Russell Oral History Interview," Harry S. Truman Presidential Library, trumanlibrary.gov/library/oral-histories/russellf; Francis H. Russell, "Referendum Backs League in Bay State," *WP*, November 19, 1934, 9; "Boston Lawyer Urges War on Germany," *Hartford Courant*, July 10, 1940, 9; "Francis Russell of Boston to Help U.S. Find Out the Facts About Foreign Policy," *BG*, January 17, 1946, 10. For progressive anti-propaganda ideas in the shaping of US public diplomacy, see Sarah Ellen Graham, *Culture and Propaganda: The Progressive Origins of American Public Diplomacy* (Farnham, UK: Ashgate, 2015). For varieties of interventionists, see Andrew Johnstone, *Against Immediate Evil: American Interventionists and the Four Freedoms on the Eve of World War II* (Ithaca, NY: Cornell University Press, 2014).

38  Russell to William Benton, July 18, 1946, RG 59, RRPA, Box 1; "What Becomes of Queries on Foreign Policy," *CSM*, March 30, 1945, 11; Chester S. Williams, "Democratic Process at San Francisco," *Department of State Bulletin* 12, no. 313 (1945): 1163–1165. On the Division of Public Liaison, see Nancy E. Bernhard, "Clearer than Truth: Public Affairs Television and the State Department's Domestic Information Campaigns, 1947–1952," *Diplomatic History* 21,

no. 4 (1997): 545–567; Andrew Johnstone, "Creating a 'Democratic Foreign Policy': The State Department's Division of Public Liaison and Public Opinion, 1944–1953," *Diplomatic History* 35, no. 3 (2001): 483–503; Autumn Lass, "Fact Givers or Fact Makers? The Dilemma of Information-Making in the State Department's Office of Public Affairs during the Truman Administration," in *The Cold War at Home and Abroad: Domestic Politics and US Foreign Policy Since 1945*, ed. Andrew L. Johns and Mitchell B. Lerner (Lexington: University Press of Kentucky, 2018), 9–35.

39  Williams, "Report and Recommendations on Group Relations Section of Division of Public Liaison," July 16, 1946, RG 59, RRPA, Box 3.

40  Williams to Russell, "Various Means of Establishing Closer Public Liaison," November 2, 1945, RG 59, Records of the Bureau of Public Affairs, Public Services Division, Subject Files, 1945–1952, Lot File 56D33, Box 132; Johnstone, "Creating," 496.

41  Inderjeet Parmar, "'To Relate Knowledge and Action': The Impact of the Rockefeller Foundation on Foreign Policy Thinking during America's Rise to Globalism, 1939–1945," *Minerva* 40, no. 3 (2002): 253–256; David B. Truman, "Public Opinion Research as a Tool of Public Administration," *Public Administration Review* 5, no. 1 (1945): 62–72; Rensis Likert, "Opinion Studies and Government Policy," *Proceedings of the American Philosophical Society* 92, no. 5 (1948): 341–350; Martin Kriesberg, "What Congressmen and Administrators Think of the Polls," *Public Opinion Quarterly* 9, no. 3 (1945): 337. The stoutest critic of polling was Lindsay Rogers, *The Pollsters: Public Opinion, Politics and Democratic Leadership* (New York: Knopf, 1949).

42  George Gallup and Saul Forbes Rae, *The Pulse of Democracy: The Public Opinion Poll and How It Works* (New York: Simon & Schuster, 1940), 245; Russell to Benton, October 1945, RG 59, RRPA, Box 3. For the limitations of early polling, see Adam J. Berinsky, *Silent Voices: Public Opinion and Political Participation in America* (Princeton, NJ: Princeton University Press, 2004).

43  See e.g., Robert Lynd, "Democracy in Reverse," *Public Opinion Quarterly* 4, no. 2 (1940): 218–220; Elmo Roper, "So the Blind Shall Not Lead," *Fortune*, February 1, 1942, 102; Edward L. Bernays, "Attitude Polls-Servants or Masters?" *Public Opinion Quarterly* 9, no. 3 (1945): 264–268b. On polling and the war, see Jean M. Converse, *Survey Research in the United States: Roots and Emergence, 1890–1960* (Berkeley: University of California Press, 1987), 131–238; Steven Casey, *Cautious Crusade: Franklin D. Roosevelt, American Public Opinion, and the War Against Nazi Germany* (New York: Oxford University Press, 2001).

44  Brett Gary, *The Nervous Liberals: Propaganda Anxieties from World War I to the Cold War* (New York: Columbia University Press, 1999), 57; Harold D. Lasswell,

"The Garrison State," *American Journal of Sociology* 46, no. 4 (1941): 455–468. For Lasswell, who could do with a biographer, see Gary, *Nervous Liberals*, 55–174; Raymond Seidelman, *Disenchanted Realists: Political Science and the American Crisis* (Albany: State University of New York Press, 2015), 130–145.

45  Harold D. Lasswell, *Propaganda Technique in the World War* (New York: Knopf, 1927); Gary, *Nervous Liberals*, 104; Harold D. Lasswell, *Democracy Through Public Opinion* (Menasha, WI: George Banta, 1941), 15. Foster's graduate work was partly published in H. Schuyler Foster, "How America Became Belligerent: A Quantitative Study of War News, 1914–17," *American Journal of Sociology* 40, no. 4 (1935): 464–475; H. Schuyler Foster, "Charting America's News of the World War," *Foreign Affairs* 15, no. 2 (1937): 311–319; H. Schuyler Foster and Carl Friedrich, "Letters to the Editor as a Means of Measuring the Effectiveness of Propaganda," *American Political Science Review* 31, no. 1 (1937): 71–79.

46  Robert E. Elder, "The Public Studies Division of the Department of State: Public Opinion Analysts in the Formulation and Conduct of American Foreign Policy," *Political Research Quarterly* 10, no. 4 (1957): 783–792.

47  Susan Herbst, "Surveys in the Public Sphere: Applying Bourdieu's Critique of Opinion Polls," *International Journal of Public Opinion Research* 4, no. 3 (1992): 223; Benjamin I. Page and Robert Y. Shapiro, *The Rational Public: Fifty Years of Trends in Americans' Policy Preferences* (Chicago: University of Chicago Press, 1992), 176. This view of polling draws on the work of Herbst and Berinsky, as well as Benjamin Ginsberg, *The Captive Public: How Mass Opinion Promotes State Power* (New York: Basic Books, 1986); James R. Beniger, "The Impact of Polling on Public Opinion: Reconciling Foucault, Habermas, and Bourdieu," *International Journal of Public Opinion Research* 4, no. 3 (1992): 204–219; Limor Peer, "The Practice of Opinion Polling as a Disciplinary Mechanism: A Foucauldian Perspective," *International Journal of Public Opinion Research* 4, no. 3 (1992): 232–242.

48  Benton to Russell, March 10, 1947, RG 59, Records of the Assistant Secretary of State for Public Affairs, 1947–1950, Lot File 52–202, Box 2; H. Schuyler Foster, "Domestic Information Activities of the State Department," March 30, 1946, RG 59, RRPA, Box 1; Francis H. Russell, "Oil for the Lamps of Democracy," *Department of State Bulletin* 15, no. 376 (1946): 502.

49  Lester Markel, "Opinion—A Neglected Instrument," in *Public Opinion and Foreign Policy*, ed. Lester Markel (New York: Harper, 1949), 5; Lasswell, *Democracy*, 79–80; Benton to Russell, March 10, 1947.

50  James T. Sparrow, *Warfare State: World War II Americans and the Age of Big Government* (New York: Oxford University Press, 2011), 114–127, 261–264; Ira Katznelson, *Fear Itself: The New Deal and the Origins of Our Time* (New York: Liveright, 2013), 345–346.

51  Dennis Showalter, "Global Yet Not Total: The U.S. War Effort and Its Consequences," in *A World at Total War: Global Conflict and the Politics of Destruction, 1937–1945*, ed. Roger Chickering, Stig Förster, and Bern Greiner (New York: Cambridge University Press, 2005), 105–133; Daniel Immerwahr, *How to Hide an Empire: A History of the Greater United States* (New York: Farrar, Strauss, Giroux, 2019); Mary L. Dudziak, "'You didn't see him lying . . . beside the gravel road in France': Death, Distance, and American War Politics," *Diplomatic History* 41, no. 1 (2018): 1–16; Jerome S. Bruner, *Mandate From the People* (New York: Duell, Sloan, and Pearce, 1944), 223; W. Harold Dalgleish, *Community Education in Foreign Affairs: A Report on Activities in Nineteen American Cities* (New York: Council on Foreign Relations, 1946), vii–viii.

52  George F. Kennan to Russell, August 23, 1946, GFK, Box 298; Margaret Carter to Russell, September 4, 1946, RG 59, Subject Files of Francis H. Russell, 1944–1952, Lot 54D202, Box 5.

53  Nicholas Guilhot, *After the Enlightenment: Political Realism and International Relations in the Mid-Twentieth Century* (New York: Cambridge University Press, 2017), 42–48; Willits to Fosdick, August 9, 1943, RF, Box 334; Fosdick to Willits, May 17, 1945, RF, RG 3, Series 910, Box 1; Willits, "General Frank R. McCoy," August 28, 1945, RF, Box 334; Willits to McCoy, October 31, RF, Box 334.

54  "Minutes of a Meeting of the Board of Directors," December 13, 1944, FPA, Box 2/15; Dean, "U.S. Foreign Policy and the Voter," 152; "Minutes of a Meeting of the Board of Directors," April 25, 1945, FPA, Box 2/15; Margaret Carter, Memorandum of Conversation, December 17, 1946, RG 59, Records of the Office of Public Affairs, Subject Files of the Chief, 1945–1951, Lot File 53D387, Box 110; "Notes on a Meeting of the Board of Directors," March 27, 1946, FPA, Box 2/15; "Membership Chart—1931–1949," FPA, Box 2/21; "Minutes of a Meeting of the Board of Directors," February 26, 1947, FPA, Box 2/15; "Recommendations to the Planning Committee," February 20, 1946, FLA, Box 7; "Minutes of a Meeting of the Board of Directors," December 18, 1946, FPA, Box 2/15.

55  William W. Lancaster to McCoy, March 26, 1947, FRM, Box 73.

## *Chapter 4*

1  "Foreign Council to Change Name," CPD, February 3, 1943, 15; Brooks Emeny to Raymond Blaine Fosdick, April 3, 1943, CCWA, Box 1; Samuel Zipp, "When Wendell Willkie Went Visiting: Between Interdependency and Exceptionalism in the Public Feeling for *One World*," *American Literary History* 26, no. 3 (2014): 485.

2  "Mr. Hull Makes a Wise Appointment," *Christian Century*, August 17, 1938, 981.

3 "Mr. Baker's Speech," *NYT*, June 30, 1924, 14; William Allen White, *Politics: The Citizen's Business* (New York: Macmillan, 1924), 281; Newton D. Baker, "The New Spirit and Its Critics," *Foreign Affairs* 12, no. 3 (1933): 3. For Baker, see C. H. Cramer, *Newton D. Baker: A Biography* (Cleveland: World Publishing Company, 1961); Douglas B. Craig, *Progressives at War: William G. McAdoo and Newton D. Baker, 1863–1941* (Baltimore: Johns Hopkins University Press, 2013).

4 Baker to Emeny, January 9, 1934, BE, Box 32; Brooks Emeny, *A History of the Founding of the Cleveland Council on World Affairs, 1935–1948* (Cleveland: Council on World Affairs, 1975), 29–32; Craig, *Progressives at War*, 382. Emeny's *History* is the fullest source for the Council's story, containing facsimiles of primary sources of which some are now otherwise lost. Documents reprinted in the *History* lack page numbers.

5 Newton D. Baker, "The Answer is Education," *Journal of Adult Education* 3, no. 3 (1931): 265–267; Baker, "Adult Education," *Proceedings of the Ohio State Educational Conference*, 1931, NDB, Box 248.

6 "Women to Brave Critics in Parade Today for Peace," *CPD*, May 18, 1924, 1; "Cleveland Club Women Plan Varied Programs for Fall and Winter," *CPD*, September 12, 1926, 6; "Peace Council Passes," *CPD*, June 14, 1929, 14; "Women's Council for Peace Meets Friday," *CPD*, May 12, 1929, 4.

7 Craig, *Progressives at War*, 376; "Annual Report of the Adult Education Association of Cleveland," 1928, NDB, Box 17; "Wizard of Geneva Purse Will Open Institute Tonight," *CPD*, February 14, 1927, 3; "U.S. 'Imperialism' Drubbed in Forum," *CPD*, March 11, 1928, 1.

8 Harrison B. McGraw to Former Members of the Adult Education Association, November 25, 1933, NDB, Box 98; "Report of the Executive Secretary for the work of the Foreign Affairs Council, Sept. 1934 to April 15, 1935," NDB, Box 97; Baker to Raymond Leslie Buell, January 23, 1934, NDB, Box 99.

9 Emeny, "Autobiography of Brooks Emeny: The International Phase," April 1975, BE, Box 1.

10 "On the Threshold," *Daily Princetonian*, March 1, 1923, 2; "Elections Are Held for Round Table Committee," *Daily Princetonian*, May 9, 1923, 1.

11 Emeny, "Autobiography"; Paulo J. Ramos, "Role of the Yale Institute of International Studies in the construction of the United States National Security Ideology, 1935–1951," (PhD diss., Manchester University, 1993), 134. For Spykman, see Or Rosenboim, *The Emergence of Globalism: Visions of World Order in Britain and the United States, 1939–1950* (Princeton, NJ: Princeton University Press, 2017), 56–99.

12 Emeny, "An outline of a study on 'The United States as a World Power' in which is contained an outline of another study (Division V) on 'Geographic

Location as a Factor of World Power,'" undated [1932], BE, Box 1; Brooks Emeny, *The Strategy of Raw Materials: A Study of America in Peace and War* (New York: Macmillan, 1934), 174; Emeny, *Cleveland Council*, 89.

13  Frank Simonds and Brooks Emeny, *The Great Powers in World Politics: International Relations and Economic Nationalism* (New York: American Book, 1935), 129–132, 350, 357, 369.

14  "Flunked History, Now He's Expert," CPD, February 2, 1936, 12; Emeny, "Autobiography," 16–17.

15  Baker to A. Caswell Ellis, November 9, 1934, NDB, Box 67.

16  Emeny, *Cleveland Council*, 3–8.

17  Thomas F. Campbell and Edward M. Miggins, eds., *The Birth of Modern Cleveland, 1865–1930* (Cleveland: Western Reserve Historical Society, 1988).

18  Selig Adler, *The Isolationist Impulse: Its Twentieth-Century Reaction* (New York: Abelard-Schuman, 1957), 43–44; "Myth of Midwest Isolationism Exploded in National Survey," WP, April 11, 1945, 7; Julian L. Woodward, *Foreign News in American Morning Newspapers: A Study in Public Opinion* (New York: Columbia University Press, 1930); Quincy Wright, "The Middle West and American Isolation," *Christian Science Monitor*, January 10, 1934, WM7; Thomas A. Bailey, *The Man in the Street: The Impact of American Public Opinion on Foreign Policy* (New York: Macmillan, 1948), 108; Emeny to Malcolm W. Davis, April 30, 1943, CEIP, Series VI, Box 228.

19  "Fish Rips Baker World View Here," CPD, March 16, 1935, 11; Buell to Emeny, March 25, 1937, RLB, Box 5; Baker to Polly Prescott, October 10, 1935, NDB, Box 97; Emeny, *Cleveland Council*, 51–58; "Statement of Purpose," 1936, CCWA, Box 1.

20  "Raw Materials Give U.S. Balance of World Power," CP, February 22, 1936, 5; "Calls Trade Peace Key," CPD, December 3, 1935, 17; "The Passing Week," CCP, November 19, 1936, 6; "Flunked History, Now He's Expert," CPD, February 2, 1936, 12.

21  "Plans for World Peace and Efforts to Attain It Occupied Clubs in 1935," CPD, January 5, 1936, 8; "Report of the Executive Secretary of the Foreign Affairs Council, April 15, 1935 to May 1, 1936," CCWA, Box 1; Emeny, *Cleveland Council*, 59–71.

22  Emeny, *Cleveland Council*, 57, 59, 67; "Report of the Executive Secretary of the Foreign Affairs Council, April 2, 1937 to April 23, 1938," CCWA, Box 1.

23  "Report of the Executive Director to the Board of Directors, for the Period from August 1, 1937 to August 1, 1938," CFR, Series 1, Box 13; Morse A. Cartwright to Frederick Keppel, September 27, 1937, CC, Box 127; "Peace Plan," October 26, 1937, CC, Box 127; Walter H. Mallory, "Memorandum from W.H.M.," November 1, 1937, CFR, Series 1, Box 3; R. C. Leffingwell to Keppel, November 3, 1937, CC, Box 127.

24 Mark Thomas Edwards, *Faith and Foreign Affairs in the American Century* (Lanham, MD: Lexington Books, 2019), 84–88; Francis P. Miller, "A Report on the First Eight Months," November 21, 1938, CC, Box 127; Untitled notes, 1940, CFR, Series 7, Box 595; Miller, "Report to Research Committee on Foreign Relations," June 22, 1939, CFR, Series 1, Box 3.

25 George Messersmith to Breckenridge Long, March 25, 1940, RG 59, Central Decimal File, 1940–1944, 811.43 Council on Foreign Relations/199; "Council on Foreign Relations," November 25, 1946, CC, Box 529; Percy W. Bidwell, "Seven-Year Survey of an Educational Project in International Relations," attached to Mallory to Devereux Josephs, June 11, 1945, CC, Box 127; Bidwell, "Report on Work of the Foreign Relations Committees, Season 1941–42," April 14, 1942, CFR, Series 1, Box 3.

26 Emeny, *Cleveland Council*, 79; Bidwell to Shepherd L. Witman, October 31, 1947, BE, Box 36.

27 Vera Micheles Dean to Emeny, October 17, 1941, FPA, Box 2/5; Emeny, *Cleveland Council*, 83.

28 "Report of the Executive Secretary of the Foreign Affairs Council, May 1, 1940 to May 1, 1941," CCWA, Box 1; "Experiments in Democracy," *CP*, April 12, 1939, in Emeny, *Cleveland Council*.

29 Nicholas J. Spykman, *America's Strategy in World Politics: The United States and the Balance of Power* (New York: Harcourt, Brace, 1942), 457; Emeny to Baker, October 3, 1936, NDB, Box 98; Emeny, "Now America Must Decide," October 27, 1939, BE, Box 29. For an argument that Emeny was correct and Spykman wrong, see Robert J. Art, "The United States, The Balance of Power, and World War II: Was Spykman Right?" *Security Studies* 14, no. 3 (2005): 364–406.

30 "Summary of Speech by Brooks Emeny," *National Peace Conference Bulletin* 2, October 30, 1940, BE, Box 29; "British Minister Discusses War in Talk at Principia," *St. Louis Post-Dispatch*, May 3, 1941, 5; *Hearings before the Committee on Foreign Affairs, House of Representatives, Seventy-Seventh Congress, First Session, on H. R. 1776* (Washington, DC: Government Printing Office, 1941), 465–477.

31 Brooks Emeny, *Frontiers of National Defense* (Cleveland: Foreign Affairs Council of Cleveland, 1941).

32 "Asks Harder Push for Allies' Cause," *CPD*, June 19, 1940, 19; "Finds 'Hysteria' in U.S. War Reaction," *CPD*, June 8, 1940, 8; "Praises 'Embargo' On Metal and Oil," *CPD*, July 26, 1940, 3.

33 "Lindberg Right, Says Dr. Emeny," *CPD*, May 11, 1941, 7; "Has Hitler Done Nothing?" *CPD*, May 12, 1941, 6; "Biographical Sketch of Josephine Saxer Irwin," *Biographical Database of NAWSA Suffragists, 1890–1920*,

documents.alexanderstreet.com/d/1009860129; "Education for What?" *CPD*, June 1, 1941, 21.

34  "Candidate for Taft?" *CPD*, November 17, 1943, 6; "Emeny Denies Story of Senate Candidacy," *CP*, January 7, 1944, 5; Emeny, *Cleveland Council*, 129.

35  "Mustn't Lose Peace Again, Says Emeny," *Hartford Courier*, October 30, 1941, 19.

36  Jon C. Teaford, *Cities of the Heartland: The Rise and Fall of the Industrial Midwest* (Bloomington: Indiana University Press, 1993), 180–206; "World War II," *Encyclopedia of Cleveland History*, case.edu/ech/articles/w/world-war-ii. On suburbanization, see Todd M. Michney, *Surrogate Suburbs: Black Upward Mobility and Neighborhood Change in Cleveland, 1900–1980* (Chapel Hill: University of North Carolina Press, 2017); Jonathan Mark Souther, *Believing in Cleveland: Managing Decline in 'The Best Location in the Nation'* (Philadelphia: Temple University Press, 2017).

37  "All on Civilian Front Must Know U.S. World Position, Emeny Says," *CPD*, May 17, 1942, 25; Emeny to Nelson A. Rockefeller, September 2, 1941, BE, Box 32; Emeny to Sumner Welles, June 6, 1942, BE, Box 2; Harley A. Notter, *Postwar Foreign Policy Preparation, 1939–1945* (Washington, DC: Department of State, 1950), 73, 114, 136–139; Brooks Emeny, *Mainsprings of World Politics* (New York: Foreign Policy Association, 1943), 35.

38  Emeny, "War for Survival," June 10, 1942, BE, Box 29; Emeny, *Cleveland Council*, 107–139.

39  Emeny to Davis, April 30, 1943; "Statistical Report – June 1935 to June 1945," BE, Box 32; "Dr. Emeny Is Elected," *CPD*, October 7, 1943, 14; "World Council's Director on Job," *CPD*, June 28, 1944, 13.

40  Shepherd L. Witman, "Let's Talk Things Over Right," *National Municipal Review* 36 (1947): 312–313; Witman to Board of Trustees, May 15, 1945, in Emeny, *Cleveland Council*; Witman to Malcolm W. Davis, May 21, 1945, CEIP, Series VI, Box 228.

41  Emeny to George Finch, January 11, 1946, CEIP, Series VI, Box 228; "Report Submitted to the Board of Trustees of the Council on World Affairs," May 1946, CCWA, Box 1; Witman to Ray M. Gidney, March 5, 1951, FAE, FA716, Reel 4734.

42  Emeny, *Cleveland Council*; Paul F. Lazarsfeld, Bernard Berelson, and Hazel Gaudet, *The People's Choice* (New York: Duell, Sloan and Pearce, 1944), 49–51.

43  Arthur M. Schlesinger, "Biography of a Nation of Joiners," *American Historical Review* 50, no. 1 (1944): 24–25; James E. Benjamin, "A Study of the Council on World Affairs, Cleveland, Ohio" (MA diss., University of Chicago, 1948), 68; Emeny to Frances P. Bolton, February 10, 1947, BE, Box 3; Bolton to Emeny, February 14, 1947, BE, Box 3.

44 "The Passing Week," *CCP*, February 20, 1936, 6; Emeny to Finch, January 11, 1946; "Central Takes Part in Student Int'l Conference," *CCP*, March 17, 1945, 7; "Negro Organizations to Be Well Represented at World Affairs Meet," *CCP*, January 21, 1950, 14; "Liberian Believes UN Best Formula for African Strife," *CCP*, February 7, 1953, 3; "African Experts Duck Questions About Mau Mau," *CCP*, February 7, 1953, 1.

45 "Institute Opening Today Brings World Affairs Experts," *CPD*, January 9, 1947, 1; "Institute Opens in Pomp of Flags," *CPD*, January 10, 1947, 1.

46 "Speech by Henry R. Luce, Editor-in-Chief of Time, Life, Fortune, and the March of Time," *A Report from the World*, attached to Emeny to Finch, March 26, 1947, CEIP, Series VI, Box 228.

47 "Town Hall," *Time*, March 8, 1943, 48; Emeny, *Cleveland Council*, 155; Edward C. Carter to MAS, December 30, 1946, IPR, Box 203; "The Bill Is Presented at Cleveland," *Chicago Tribune*, January 6, 1947, 18; "Mr. Luce Comes to Town," undated, CCWA, Box 4; "Speech by James Francis Byrnes, former Secretary of State," *A Report from the World*; "Report from the World," *Time*, January 20, 1947, 53–60; "We Will Keep Faith With World, Says Secretary Byrnes," *NYT*, January 12, 1947, 1.

48 "Cleveland Committee on Foreign Relations," October 2, 1946, CC, Box 127; Oswald Garrison Villard to Emeny, August 11, 1944, CFR, Series 2, Box 33; Emeny, *Cleveland Council*, 59; Emeny to Josephs, March 12, 1947, CC, Box 127; Witman to John Gardner, March 6, 1950, CC, Box 127.

49 Fosdick to John D. Rockefeller Jr., August 30, 1944, OMR, Series Q, Box 4; Adm. John Greenslade to Emeny, May 4, 1945, IPRSF, Box 3; Emeny, *Cleveland Council*.

50 Emeny to Nelson A. Rockefeller, October 11, 1941, BE, Box 39.

51 Emeny to Nelson A. Rockefeller, November 28, 1941, BE, Box 39; Emeny to Henry S. Haskell, November 3, 1941, BE, Box 39; Emeny to Frank R. McCoy, August 20, 1941, BE, Box 39; "Memorandum on Mr. Emeny's letter of August 20, 1941 regarding Branches," BE, Box 39; "Minutes of a Meeting of the Board of Directors," October 22, 1941, FPA, Box 2/15; "Minutes of a Meeting of the Board of Directors," December 17, 1941, FPA, Box 2/15; W. W. Waymack to Emeny, December 26, 1941, BE, Box 39; "Foreign Affairs Council Cleveland," February 11, 1942, CC, Box 147.

52 Emeny to Members of the Committees on Foreign Relations, March 5, 1942, BE, Box 39; Leffingwell to Mallory, March 16, 1942, CC, Box 127; Bidwell, "Report on Work of Foreign Relations Committees, Season 1941–42," April 4, 1942, CFR, Series 1, Box 3.

53 John W. Davis and George O. May to Emeny, June 22, 1944, BE, Box 39; Emeny to John W. Davis, July 21, 1944, BE, Box 36.

54 John W. Davis to Emeny, August 2, 1944, CFR, Series 2, Box 33; Mallory to
Arthur W. Packard, September 7, 1944, OMR, Series Q, Box 4; W. L. Clayton
to Emeny, CFR, Series 2, Box 33; Leland Goodrich to Emeny, CFR, Series 2,
Box 33; Owen Lattimore to Emeny, August 10, 1944, BE, Box 36; Philip C.
Jessup to Emeny, August 2, 1944, CFR, Series 2, Box 33.

55 John D. Rockefeller Jr. to Emeny, September 5, 1944, CFR, Series 2, Box 33;
Emeny circular, March 28, 1945, BE, Box 32; McCoy to Emeny, April 18, 1945,
BE, Box 36; Emeny to Buell, September 28, 1945, RLB, Box 5; Emeny to
Welles, March 3, 1943, BE, Box 2; Emeny to Malcolm W. Davis, April 10, 1945,
BE, Box 36.

56 S. Sheperd Jones to Francis H. Russell, October 1, 1946, RG 59, Russell
Subject Files, Box 1; "Minutes of a Meeting of the Board of Directors,"
February 26, 1947, FPA, Box 2/15.

57 Henry Stimson to William W. Lancaster, December 28, 1945, PCJ, Box I.211;
"Vera Micheles Dean," March 4, 1946, RF, Box 334; Lancaster to Adlai
Stevenson, May 21, 1946, AES, Box 369; Stevenson to Lancaster, October 26,
1946, AES, Box 369; Alger Hiss to Dean Acheson, April 4, 1946, RG 59, Central
Decimal File, 1940–1944, 811.43/Foreign Policy Association 4-446; Emeny to
Dean, February 19, 1947, BE, Box 39; "Special Meeting of the Board of
Directors," March 18, 1947, FPA, Box 2/15; Secretary to Lancaster, March 21,
1947, CC, Box 147.

## Chapter 5

1 "Remarks by the Honorable George C. Marshall, Secretary of State, at Harvard
University on June 5, 1947," in *FRUS, 1947*, vol. III, *The British Commonwealth; Europe* (Washington, DC: Government Printing Office, 1972),
237–239.

2 George C. Marshall Foundation, "The Marshall Plan Speech," transcription
version, June 5, 1947, marshallfoundation.org/marshall/the-marshall-plan/
marshall-plan-speech/; Marshall S. Carter to Frank R. McCoy, December 10,
1946, FRM, Box 73.

3 Melvyn P. Leffler, *A Preponderance of Power: National Security, the Truman
Administration, and the Cold War* (Stanford: Stanford University Press, 1992),
145–146; Fredrik Logevall and Campbell Craig, *America's Cold War: The
Politics of Insecurity* (Cambridge, MA: Harvard University Press, 2012), 79;
Dean Acheson, *Present at the Creation: My Years in the State Department*
(New York: Norton, 1969), 375; "Consultative Conference with Representatives
of Foundations on Problems of Information and Education on Foreign Affairs,"
April 18–19, 1951, RG 59, Lot File 56D33, Box 133. For the argument that "the
Cold War" was an invention, see Anders Stephanson, "Cold War Degree

Zero," in *Uncertain Empire: American History and the Idea of the Cold War,* ed. Joel Isaac and Duncan Bell (New York: Oxford University Press, 2012), 19–50.

4 Harry S. Truman to McCoy, October 13, 1945, *Department of State Bulletin* 13, no. 331 (1945): 678.

5 The literature here is enormous, but see e.g., Stephen J. Whitfield, *The Culture of the Cold War* (Baltimore: Johns Hopkins University Press, 1996); Christina Klein, *Cold War Orientalism: Asia in the Middlebrow Imagination, 1945–1961* (Berkeley: University of California Press, 2003); Kenneth Osgood, *Total Cold War: Eisenhower's Secret Propaganda Battle at Home and Abroad* (Lawrence: University of Kansas, 2006); Margot Canaday, *The Straight State: Sexuality and Citizenship in Twentieth-Century America* (Princeton, NJ: Princeton University Press, 2009); Jonathan P. Herzog, *The Spiritual-Industrial Complex: America's Religious Battle Against Communism in the Early Cold War* (New York: Oxford University Press, 2011); Michael Brenes, *For Might and Right: Cold War Defense Spending and the Remaking of American Democracy* (Amherst: University of Massachusetts Press, 2020).

6 Brooks Emeny, "America's Role As Super Power," September 30, 1946, in Brooks Emeny, *A History of the Founding of the Cleveland Council on World Affairs, 1935–1948* (Cleveland: Council on World Affairs, 1975); Brooks Emeny, "'Freedom from thought' . . . the immediate danger," *Vogue,* April 15, 1947, 120–121, 167–169.

7 "National Leaders Write for 30th Anniversary," attached to Emeny to Joseph H. Willits, April 12, 1949, RF, Box 334; W. Harold Dalgliesh, *Community Education in Foreign Affairs: A Report on Activities in Nineteen American Cities* (New York: Council on Foreign Relations, 1946), 19, 24; Emeny to Alger Hiss, May 27, 1947, CEIP, Series I, Box 48.

8 "Foreign Policy Association," August 26, 1947, CC, Box 147; "Minutes of Executive Committee Meeting," April 28, 1947, FRM, Box 73; William W. Lancaster to McCoy, April 29, 1947, FRM, Box 73; Edward C. Carter to Herbert S. Little, May 6, 1947, MP, Carton 4; John N. Thomas, *The Institute of Pacific Relations: Asian Scholars and American Politics* (Seattle: University of Washington Press, 1974), 30–34, 57–61; Carter to Board of Trustees, April 16, 1947, IPR, Box 101; "Memorandum to Dr. Robert Gordon Sproul," May 27, 1947, EM, Carton 3; "World Affairs Groups Formed in California," *NYT,* June 22, 1947, 23; Bryce Wood, "Amalgamation of FPA & IPR," January 13, 1948, RF, Box 334.

9 Patricia L. Rosenfield, *A World of Giving: Carnegie Corporation of New York—A Century of International Philanthropy* (New York: Public Affairs, 2014), 155–170.

10 Willits to Raymond Blaine Fosdick, May 14, 1945, RF, RG 3, Series 910, Box 7; Bryce Wood, "The Program of the Division of the Social Sciences in the Field of International Relations," August 1947, RF, RG 3, Series 910, Box 8; Wood to Willits, March 5, 1948, RF, RG 3, Series 910, Box 7; Nicolas Guilhot, *After the Enlightenment: Political Realism and International Relations in the Mid-Twentieth Century* (New York: Cambridge University Press, 2017), 40–61.

11 Nicholas Guilhot, ed., *The Invention of International Relations Theory: Realism, the Rockefeller Foundation, and the 1954 Conference on Theory* (New York: Columbia University Press, 2011); Emeny to Nelson A. Rockefeller, November 28, 1941, BE, Box 39; Emeny to the Board of Trustees, April 1948, FRM, Box 73; "Foreign Policy Association, Incorporated, to the Carnegie Corporation of New York," December 31, 1948, CC, Box 147.

12 Wood to Willits, February 4, 1948, RF, Box 334; Ludovic Tournès, "American membership of the League of Nations: US philanthropy and the transformation of an intergovernmental organisation into a think tank," *International Politics* 55, no. 6 (2018): 852–869; Ron Robin, *The Making of the Cold War Enemy: Culture and Politics in the Military-Intellectual Complex* (Princeton, NJ: Princeton University Press, 2001); Daniel Bessner, *Democracy in Exile: Hans Speier and the Rise of the Defense Intellectual* (Ithaca, NY: Cornell University Press, 2018).

13 Vera Micheles Dean to Lancaster, May 3, 1948, FRM, Box 73. For the Foundation's contributions, see Wood, "Program"; "Excerpt from Minutes of SS Staff Meeting #73, May 24, 1950," RF, Box 335. For the research department, see "Memorandum for Consideration by Members of the Executive Committee," April 29, 1948, FRM, Box 73; Dean to Lancaster, May 3, 1948, FRM, Box 73; Emeny to Branch Chairmen and Secretaries, May 18, 1948, RLW, Box 37.

14 Vera Micheles Dean, *Russia: Menace or Promise* (New York: Henry Holt, 1947), vii; Dean, "Proud to Live in Our Times," VMD, Box 1.

15 Vera Micheles, "Governments de facto with special reference to the Soviet government" (PhD diss., Radcliffe College, 1928); Raymond Leslie Buell to Dean, April 16, 1928, RLB, Box 5; "Report of the Executive Secretary of the Foreign Affairs Council, May 1, 1940 to May 1, 1941," CCWA, Box 1.

16 Vera Micheles Dean, *Russia at War: Twenty Key Questions and Answers* (New York: Foreign Policy Association, 1942), 11; Buell to Dean, January 26, 1945, RLB, Box 5; Dean to Buell, January 30, 1945, RLB, Box 5; Dean, *Russia: Menace or Promise*, viii. Generally, see David C. Engerman, *Modernization from the Other Shore: American Intellectuals and the Romance of Russian Development* (Cambridge, MA: Harvard University Press, 2003).

17 Dean, "UNO Offers Best Means of Reconciling Big-Three Conflicts," FPB 25, March 22, 1946, 2; Dean, "Marshall Plan Offers Opportunity to Strengthen

UN," *FPB* 26, June 27, 1947, 1–2; Michael Wala, "Selling the Marshall Plan at Home: The Committee for the Marshall Plan to Aid European Recovery," *Diplomatic History* 10, no. 3 (1986): 254.

18  Dean, "Can Allies Reconcile War Policies With War Aims?" *FPB* 22, December 11, 1942, 3.

19  Dean, "U.S. In New Role Must Do More Than Stop Russia," *FPB* 26, March 21, 1947, 1; Dean, "Korean Conflict Tests U.S. Containment Policy," *FPB* 29, July 28, 1950, 1; Dean, "Great Powers Differ On Approach to World Security," *FPB* 24, May 4, 1945, 2; Dean, "Will U.S. Use its Economic Power to Aid Democracy Abroad?" *FPB* 24, August 31, 1945, 3; Dean, *Russia: Menace or Promise*, 63–70.

20  Alfred Kohlberg to Emeny, April 5, 1948, FPA, Box 1/66; SAC, New York, to Director, FBI, March 31, 1954, case 62–68549, FOIA release in author's possession; Mrs. Percy Madeira to Emeny, September 10, 1947, FPA, Box 2/92; "Minutes of a Meeting of the Board of Directors," September 25, 1947, FPA, Box 2/15; Roger Shaw to Emeny, November 26, 1948, BE, Box 59; "Executive Session of Board of Directors Meeting," May 24, 1951, FPA, Box 2/15; Vera Micheles Dean, *Foreign Policy Without Fear* (New York: McGraw-Hill, 1953), x, 208.

21  Dean, "What Are Americans Thinking About Foreign Policy?" *FPB* 28, October 22, 1948, 1–2; Dean, "Secrecy on Defense Weakens Civic Responsibility," *FPB* 29, February 10, 1950, 2; Dean, "Long View Needed in Assessing Cold War," *FPB* 29, April 7, 1950, 2; Dean, "Do U.S. Terms Offer Basis for Cold War Truce?" *FPB* 29, March 24, 1950, 1. On nuclear weapons and secrecy, see Alex Wellerstein, *Restricted Data: The History of Nuclear Secrecy in the United States* (Chicago: University of Chicago Press, 2021).

22  Harvey Klehr and Ronald Radosh, *The Amerasia Spy Case: Prelude to McCarthyism* (Chapel Hill: University of North Carolina Press, 1995); Howard B. Schonberg, *Aftermath of War: Americans and the Remaking of Japan, 1945–52* (Kent, OH: Kent State University Press, 1989), 90–110; "L.K. Rosinger, 78, An Expert on China," *NYT*, September 21, 1994, D18; "Raps Acheson for Permitting Stone to Resign," *Chicago Tribune*, March 18, 1852, 4; "McCarthy, Benton Exchange Charges," *NYT*, July 4, 1952, 5; "Longtime Sailing Writer William Stone Dies at 94," *WP*, December 6, 1993, B8. For the second Red Scare's derailing of progressive politics, see Landon R. Y. Storrs, *The Second Red Scare and the Unmaking of the New Deal Left* (Princeton, NJ: Princeton University Press, 2013).

23  "Foreign Policy Association, Inc.," July 6, 1950, archive.org/details/foia _Foreign_Policy_Assn-HQ-2/page/n211; Mark Solovey, *Shaky Foundations: The Politics-Patronage-Social Science Nexus in Cold War America* (New Brunswick:

Rutgers University Press, 2013), 120–123; Helen Laville, *Cold War Women: The International Activities of American Women's Organisations* (Manchester: Manchester University Press, 2002), 96–129; Susan Levine, *Degrees of Equality: The American Association of University Women and the Challenge of Twentieth-Century Feminism* (Philadelphia: Temple University Press, 1995), 53–82; Elaine Tyler May, *Homeward Bound: American Families in the Cold War Era* (New York: Basic Books, 2008), 17. See also this period's crises of masculinity and panics over homosexuality, e.g. Canaday, *Straight State*; Robert D. Dean, *Imperial Brotherhood: Gender and the Making of Cold War Foreign Policy* (Amherst: University of Massachusetts Press, 2001).

24 "Brief Review Concerning Extremist Attacks," October 6, 1961, FPA, Box 2/39; Dan Smoot, *The Invisible Government* (Dallas: Dan Smoot Report, 1962), iv.

25 "Results of the FPA Questionnaire," undated, FPA, Box 2/75; "Consultative Conference."

26 Minutes of a Meeting of the Board of Directors," September 28, 1950, FPA, Box 2/15; "Minutes of a Meeting of the Board of Directors," October 26, 1950, FPA, Box 2/15; Eustace Seligman to Dean, July 25, 1947, BE, Box 59; "Report to the President of F.P.A.," February 5, 1951, FPA, Box 2/15; "Main Conclusions of Ad Hoc Committee on Publications of the FPA," March 21, 1951, FPA, Reel 1/4; "Minutes of a Meeting of the Board of Directors," May 24, 1951, FPA, Box 2/15.

27 Mary L. Dudziak, *War Time: An Idea, Its History, Its Consequences* (New York: Oxford University Press, 2012); James T. Sparrow, *Warfare State: World War II Americans and the Age of Big Government* (New York: Oxford University Press, 2011); "Memorandum to the Trustees of the Foreign Policy Association," October 9, 1951, BE, Box 42.

28 *Report of the Study for the Ford Foundation on Policy and Program* (Detroit: Ford Foundation, 1949), 20–21, 28, 32.

29 *Report of the Study*, 58–59, 68.

30 Volker R. Berghahn, *America and the Intellectual Cold Wars in Europe: Shepard Stone Between Philanthropy, Academy, and Diplomacy* (Princeton, NJ: Princeton University Press, 2001), 147–53; Christopher P. Loss, *Between Citizens and the State: The Politics of American Higher Education in the 20th Century* (Princeton, NJ: Princeton University Press, 2012), 148–149; *1951–1961: A Ten Year Report of the Fund for Adult Education* (New York: Fund for Adult Education, 1961), 12.

31 Emeny to B. J. Craig, November 13, 1950, FPA, Box 2/84; Emeny to C. Scott Fletcher, April 25, FPA, Box 2/84; "Ford Fund Grants Emphasize 'Deeds,'" *NYT*, June 3, 1951, 46; Emeny to Fletcher, June 7, 1951, FPA, Box 2/84.

32 Emeny, "Citizens and Foreign Policy: II, The Problem," *FPB* 27, July 2, 1948, 4.

33  Emeny to Members of the Board, January 27, 1949, FPA, Box 2/15; "WHS, CD, and Brooks Emeny," February 2, 1949, CC, Box 147; Joseph Barber to Walter Mallory, January 25, 1949, CC, Box 147; "Comments on F.P.A. Proposal," undated, CC, Box 147; "Foreign Policy Association," undated, CC, Box 148; John D. Rockefeller III to Emeny, July 28, 1949, RB, RG 3.1, Box 344.

34  "FA and Thomas L. Power," August 16, 1951, CC, Box 147; "Proceedings of the Council of Associates," September 21–22, 1951, FPA, Reel 1/4; "Foreign Policy Association," October 8, 1952, CC, Box 147; Florence Anderson to Charles Dollard, October 17, 1952, CC, Box 147; Anderson to Dollard, November 14, 1952, CC, Box 147; Emeny to Anderson, November 12, 1952, CC, Box 147; Rosenfield, *World of Giving*, 166.

35  Edward W. Barrett to James Webb Young, May 18, 1951, RG 59, Russell Subject Files, Box 3; Alexander Allport, "Report on Trip to Washington, D.C., for the Community Development Committee," February 14–15, 1952, FPA, Box 1/4; "Minutes of a Meeting of the Board of Directors," December 20, 1951, FPA, Box 2/15.

36  "Minutes of Meeting of Executive and Finance Committees," March 17, 1952, FPA, Box 2/16; "Report to the President of the United States from the Members of the World Town Hall Seminar Meeting," October 18, 1949, FPA, Box 1/54; Helen Laville, "The Importance of Being (In) Earnest: Voluntary Associations and the Irony of the State-Private Network During the Early Cold War," in *The US Government, Citizen Groups and the Cold War: The State-Private Network*, ed. Helen Laville and Hugh Wilford (New York: Routledge, 2006), 65–83.

37  "Detailed Outline of Report and Recommendations of Acting Director," April 24, 1952, FPA, Box 2/87; "Report of the Acting Director on Field Survey," June 8, 1952, CSW, Box 10; "Report on FPA and Community World Affairs Education," June 12, 1952, FPA, Box 2/39; Chester S. Williams to Marshall Schumann, June 25, 1952, FPA, Box 1/57; "Request for Additional Grants," June 25, 1952, FPA, Box 2/16.

38  "UNESCO Friends, Foes Clash at Board Meeting," *Los Angeles Times*, August 26, 1952, 2; Williams to Fletcher, September 16, 1952, FF, FA716, Reel 4737; Michelle Nickerson, *Mothers of Conservatism: Women and the Postwar Right* (Princeton, NJ: Princeton University Press, 2012), 32–102.

39  "Emeny Deaths Called Suicide and Homicide," *NYHT*, March 17, 1951, 11; "Emeny and Daughter Home for Funerals," *NYT*, March 17, 1951, 14; "Minutes of Executive Committee Meeting," October 1, 1952, FPA, Box 2/15.

40  "Minutes of Meeting of Executive and Finance Committees," March 17, 1952, FPA, Box 2/16; "Cox Committee Questionnaire," November 14, 1952, FPA, Box 2/2; Seligman to Delbert Clark, October 1, 1952, RB, RG 3.1, Box 344.

41 "New 'World Affairs' Film by De Rochemont Praised," *CPD*, March 14, 1952, 14; *World Affairs Are Your Affairs* (Louis de Rochement Corporation, 1952), Michael Schwartz Library, Cleveland State University Library.

42 Tony Shaw, *Hollywood's Cold War* (Edinburgh: Edinburgh University Press, 2007), 72–85; "Excerpt from Minutes of Meeting of Board Directors," January 18, 1952, FF, FA716, Reel 4734; "Peace Depends On You," undated, FF, FA716, Reel 4737; *World Affairs Are Your Affairs* (Pasadena: Fund for Adult Education, 1952).

43 Allport to Richard C. Rowson, January 23, 1953, FPA, Box 1/78.

44 John W. Nason, "Terminal Report to the Fund for Adult Education," April 15, 1957, FF, FA732C, Grant 56–117, Reel 4159.

45 Rowson, "Report on World Affairs Council of Philadelphia Conference on US Foreign Policy," May 19, 1953, FPA, Box 1/31; Rowson "Maryland Council on World Affairs and UN Association, Baltimore, Maryland, June 21, 1956," July 24, 1956, FPA, Box 1/8; Nason, "Field Report: Boston, Massachusetts," March 24, 1954, FPA, Box 1/9; "Minutes of Meeting of the Board of Directors," February 17, 1955, FPA, Box 2/16.

46 Roger Mastrude, "Los Angeles," November 24, 1952, BE, Box 43; "Field Report," July 24, 1953, FPA, Box 1/1; Dorothy B. Robins, "Field Report on Los Angeles, California" March 16, 1954, FPA, Box 1/1; Nason, "Terminal Report."

47 "Dayton World Affairs Council Organized To Provide Public Information On Trends," *Dayton Daily News*, July 15, 1947, 15; "Dayton Group Wins World Affairs Honor," *CSM*, December 14, 1954, 18.

48 "Annual Report – 1952–1953," DCWA, Box 3; "A Report of 1953 Community Survey," DCWA, Box 10.

49 Witman to Edward S. Morris, November 3, 1952, CCWA, Box 2; Witman to Ronald Shilen, April 26, 1955, FF, FA716, Reel 4737; "Minutes of the Meeting of the FPA Committee on National Program," April 2–3, 1954, BE, Box 44; Katherine C. Bang et al. to Ralph Beese, March 17, 1954, CCWA, Box 2; "Analysis of 422 Questionnaire Replies From Members," January 31, 1955, FPA, Box 1/48.

50 "Basic Statement on the Cleveland Council on World Affairs," September 9, 1955, KCB, Box 8; "Bolton Charged With 'One-Man' Rule of World Affairs Unit," *CP*, July 15, 1955, 2; "Minutes of the Meeting of the FPA Committee on National Program," December 6, 1955, BE, Box 45; Rowson to Nason, July 13, 1955, BE, Box 45; Bill Cowan, "Field Report: Cleveland, Ohio," February 28, 1956, FPA, Box 1/27; Jarvis Freymann to Nason, May 15, 1958, FPA, Box 1/11.

51 Nason, "Terminal Report"; "Non-Partisan Community Foreign Policy Associations, World Affairs Councils, & Similar Organizations," November 1, 1952, FPA, Box 1/73; "Three Year Report to the Fund for Adult Education," September 23, 1955, FF, FA716, Reel 4737.

52 "Three Year Report"; "Conference of FPA Regional Representatives," February 14–16, 1955, FPA, Box 2/84.

53 John S. Gibson to Rowson, May 13, 1954, FPA, Box 1/34; Rowson to Arthur E. Whittemore, February 25, 1955, FPA, Box 1/10.

54 "Dallas Council on World Affairs: A Five Year Report," 1956, AES, Box 369; Nason to Warren Rovetch and Mastrude, January 22, 1958, FPA, Box 1/36; "Field Report: Dallas, Texas, March 5–9, 1954," Box 1/35.

55 Nason, "Terminal Report"; "Three Year Report"; "Executive Committee," June 4, 1957, FPA, Box 2/16; *The Budget of the United States Government for the Fiscal Year Ending June 30, 1959* (Washington, DC: Government Printing Office, 1958), 763; Henry F. Grady to Fletcher, May 26, 1954, FPA, Box 1/2.

## Chapter 6

1 Roger G. Mastrude, "Resume of Professional Experience," 1970, JWN, Box 34.

2 Mastrude to Alexander Allport, September 11, 1953, FPA, Box 1/77; Mastrude to John W. Nason, September 9, 1953, FPA, Box 1/77; Mastrude, "Summary Regional Report, Region IV, Western States," December 28, 1953, FF, FA732G, Reel 4159, Grant 56-117.

3 Mastrude "Seattle, Washington—December, 1952," January 5, 1953, FPA, Box 1/77; "Group to Center on World Affairs," *Oregonian*, January 22, 1951, 3; Mastrude, "Portland, Oregon, January 6–9, 1953," January 26, 1953, FPA, Box 1/77; "Local World Affairs Council," *Oregonian*, April 3, 1951, 18.

4 David Riesman, "Private People and Public Policy," *Bulletin of the Atomic Scientists* 15, no. 5 (1959): 206, 203; Kyong-Min Son, *The Eclipse of the Demos: The Cold War and the Crisis of Democracy before Neoliberalism* (Lawrence: University Press of Kansas, 2020), 3; Jack L. Walker, "A Critique of the Elitist Theory of Democracy," *American Political Science Review* 60, no. 2 (1966): 286. Generally, see Nils Gilman, *Mandarins of the Future: Modernization Theory in Cold War America* (Baltimore: Johns Hopkins University Press, 2003); Joy Rohde, *Armed with Expertise: The Militarization of American Social Research During the Cold War* (Ithaca, NY: Cornell University Press, 2013); Daniel Bessner, *Democracy in Exile: Hans Speier and the Rise of the Defense Intellectual* (Ithaca, NY: Cornell University Press, 2018).

5 Harold D. Lasswell, "The Garrison State," *American Journal of Sociology* 46, no. 4 (1941): 458; Ira Katznelson, *Fear Itself: the New Deal and the Origins of Our Time* (New York: Liveright, 2013), 485; Robert A. Dahl, *Congress and Foreign Policy* (New York: Harcourt, Brace, 1950), 3. See also Michael J. Hogan, *A Cross of Iron: Harry S. Truman and the Origins of the National Security State* (New York: Cambridge University Press, 1998); James T.

Sparrow, *Warfare State: World War II Americans and the Age of Big Government* (New York: Oxford University Press, 2011).

6 Richard C. Rowson, "Whither FPA?" August 25, 1955, FPA, Box 1/64.

7 George F. Kennan, *American Diplomacy* (Chicago: University of Chicago Press, 1984), 61–62, 66, 93; Kennan, "Public Opinion and Foreign Policy," October 23, 1953, FPA, Box 2/230.

8 Walter Lippmann, *Essays in the Public Philosophy* (Boston: Little, Brown, 1955), 14–15, 20–21, 25, 162.

9 Edward W. Barrett, *Truth Is Our Weapon* (New York: Funk & Wagnalls, 1953); Andrew H. Berding, *Foreign Affairs and You!* (Garden City, NY: Doubleday, 1962); Dorothy Fosdick, *Common Sense and World Affairs* (Boston: Harcourt, Brace, 1955); Dexter Perkins, *Popular Government and Foreign Policy* (Pasadena: Fund for Adult Education, 1956), 63; Henry M. Wriston, *Diplomacy in a Democracy* (New York: Harper, 1956), 63–64, 106.

10 Edward A. Purcell, *The Crisis of Democratic Theory* (Lexington: University Press of Kentucky, 1973), 109.

11 Jean M. Converse, *Survey Research in the United States: Roots and Emergence, 1890–1960* (Berkeley: University of California Press, 1987), 305–378; Amy Fried, *Pathways to Polling: Crisis, Cooperation and the Making of Public Opinion Professions* (New York: Routledge, 2012), 69–133; Fay Terris, "Are Poll Questions Too Difficult?" *Public Opinion Quarterly* 13, no. 2 (1949): 314–319; David Riesman and Nathan Glazer, "The Meaning of Opinion," *Public Opinion Quarterly* 12, no. 4 (1948): 635.

12 Ralph O. Nafziger, Warren C. Engstrom, and Malcolm S. Maclean, "The Mass Media and an Informed Public," *Public Opinion Quarterly* 15, no. 1 (1951): 107–108; Leonard S. Cottrell and Sylvia Eberhart, *American Opinion on World Affairs in the Atomic Age* (Princeton, NJ: Princeton University Press, 1948), 19; NORC, *Cincinnati Looks at the United Nations* (Chicago: National Opinion Research Center, 1948), 27–28; Julian L. Woodward and Elmo Roper, "Political Activity of American Citizens," *American Political Science Review* 44, no. 4 (1950): 875–876; SRC, "Citizen Participation in Problems of World Affairs," February 1948, RG 59, Bureau of Public Affairs, Miscellaneous Records, Lot File 53D350, Box 40; SRC, *Interest, Information, and Attitudes in the Field of World Affairs* (Ann Arbor: University of Michigan, 1949), 82–84.

13 SRC, *Public Attitudes Toward American Foreign Policy: A Nationwide Survey* (Ann Arbor: University of Michigan, 1947), 3; George Belknap and Angus Campbell, "Political Party Identification and Attitudes Toward Foreign Policy," *Public Opinion Quarterly* 15, no. 4 (1951): 603; C. Wright Mills, *White Collar: The American Middle Classes* (New York: Oxford University Press, 1951),

328; C. Wright Mills, *The Power Elite* (New York: Oxford University Press, 1956), 300.

14  Mills, *Power Elite*, 304; Purcell, *Crisis*, 216–261; Son, *Eclipse*, 37–58.

15  Shirley A. Star and Helen MacGill Hughes, "Report on an Educational Campaign: The Cincinnati Plan for the United Nations," *American Journal of Sociology* 55, no. 4 (1950): 389–390, 393, 399; Lester Markel, ed., *Public Opinion and Foreign Policy* (New York: Harper, 1949); Frederick S. Dunn, *War and the Minds of Men* (New York: Harper, 1950).

16  Robert A. Dahl, *Congress and Foreign Policy* (New York: Harcourt, Brace, 1950), 78, 89–90, 93; Robert A. Dahl, "Atomic Energy and the Democratic Process," *Annals of the American Academy of Political and Social Science* 290, no. 1 (1953): 6; Robert A. Dahl, *Who Governs? Democracy and Power in an American City* (New Haven, CT: Yale University Press, 1961), 264. See also Son, *Eclipse*, 59–70.

17  Lasswell, "Garrison State," 459; Ido Oren, *Our Enemies and US: America's Rivalries and the Making of Political Science* (Ithaca, NY: Cornell University Press, 2003), 134–147; Gilman, *Mandarins*, 51–55.

18  Gabriel A. Almond, *The American People and Foreign Policy* (New York: Harcourt, Brace, 1950), 3–6, 82, 231–233.

19  Almond, *American People*, 6, 76, 127, 138–139, 231.

20  "Main Conclusions of Ad Hoc Committee on Publications of the FPA," undated, BE, Box 42; Bill Cowan, "Preliminary Comments on the 'Decisions' program," February 29, 1956, FPA, Box 2/233.

21  Bernard C. Cohen, "Private Organizations and Public Education in World Affairs" (PhD diss., Yale University, 1951), 201; Bernard C. Cohen, *Citizen Education in World Affairs* (Princeton, NJ: Center of International Studies, 1953), 70.

22  Cohen, *Citizen Education*, 73–88, 127.

23  Rowson, "Field Report," December 22, 1953, FPA, Box 1/16; Robert H. Cory, *Communicating Information and Ideas about the United Nations to the American People* (New York: Carnegie Endowment for International Peace, 1955), 24; "Minutes of the Meeting of the FPA Committee on National Program," April 2–3, 1954, FPA, Reel 1/4; "Minutes of Meeting of the Board of Directors," May 20, 1954, FPA, Box 2/16; Brooks Emeny, "Non-Governmental Organizations in International Affairs," May 4, 1955, BE, Box 29. For Cohen's influence, see Stanley T. Gordon to Francis Sutton, July 21, 1971, FF, FA732C, Grant 72-134, Reel 2362.

24  Nason, "Some Reflections on Program relating to the Foreign Policy Association," October 28, 1952, JWN, Box 3; "Regional Conference on World Affairs Education, Asilomar, December 4–6, 1953," FPA, Box 1/1; Nason, "Foreign

Policy and the American Citizen," November 2, 1955, FPA, Box 1/20; "Proposal to the Ford Foundation from the Foreign Policy Association," January 23, 1956, FF, FA732G, Reel 4159, Grant 56-117; "Some Points on FPA Proposal to the Ford Foundation," February 20, 1956, FF, FA732G, Reel 4159, Grant 56-117.

25 Bernard R. Berelson, Paul F. Lazarsfeld, and William N. McPhee, *Voting: A Study of Opinion Formation in a Presidential Campaign* (Chicago: University of Chicago Press, 1954), 322. For the limits of social science, see Lawrence Freedman, "Social Science and the Cold War," *Journal of Strategic Studies* 38, no. 4 (2015): 554–574; Nils Gilman, "The Cold War as Intellectual Force Field," *Modern Intellectual History* 13, no. 2 (2016): 507–523. For the funding of the behavioral sciences, see Mark Solovey, *Shaky Foundations: The Politics-Patronage-Social Science Nexus in Cold War America* (New Brunswick: Rutgers University Press, 2013), 103–47.

26 Mastrude, "The 'Basic Issues' Test Program in Oregon, Locally Called the 'Great Decisions' Program," 1955, FPA, Box 2/28; "'Decisions' on American Foreign Policy Aimed to Reach Into Portland Homes," *Oregonian*, February 2, 1955, 12.

27 "Great Decisions No. 2," *Oregonian*, February 27, 1955, 33; "Policy Study Clinic Dated," *Oregonian*, February 11, 1955, 8; Mastrude to Allport, April 14, 1955, FPA, Box 2/28; "Excerpts From a Few Letters Received with Ballots," 1955, FPA, Box 2/244.

28 Roger Mastrude, "Bringing World Affairs to the People," *Adult Leadership* 4 (March 1956): 15; Almond, *American People*, 70; Bernard C. Cohen, "What Voluntary Groups Can Do," *Adult Leadership* 1 (July–August 1953): 12; Elihu Katz, "The Two-Step Flow of Communication: An Up-To-Date Report on an Hypothesis," *Public Opinion Quarterly* 21, no. 1 (1957): 61–78. On the fetish for small-group thinking, see Daniel Immerwahr, *Thinking Small: The United States and the Lure of Community Development* (Cambridge, MA: Harvard University Press, 2015), 15–39.

29 C. Scott Fletcher, "The Program of the Fund for Adult Education," *Adult Education* 2, no. 2 (1951): 66; Byron Dexter, *Let's Talk About: John Foster Dulles, 'Policy for Security and Peace'* (New York: Council on Foreign Relations, 1954), 1; "Discussion Groups," 1954, FPA, Box 1/29.

30 Eugene I. Johnson, "Groups with a Future—in a New Communication System," *Journal of Communication* 5, no. 3 (1955): 89–101; Mastrude to Dorothy Robins, March 4, 1954, Box 1/77, FPA. Generally, see Paul J. Edelson, "Socrates on the Assembly Line: The Ford Foundation's Mass Marketing of Liberal Adult Education," October 1991, eric.ed.gov/?id=ED340885; Christopher P. Loss, *Between Citizens and the State: The Politics of American Higher Education in the 20th Century* (Princeton, NJ: Princeton University Press, 2012), 147–156.

31  Christopher P. Foss, *Facing the World: Defense Spending and International Trade in the Pacific Northwest Since World War II* (Portland: Oregon State University Press, 2020), 65–69; Robert D. Johnston, *The Radical Middle Class: Populist Democracy and the Question of Capitalism in Progressive Era Portland, Oregon* (Princeton, NJ: Princeton University Press, 2006); Mastrude to Committee on National Program, August 23, 1954, FPA, Box 1/29; "Great Decisions No. 9," *Oregonian*, April 17, 1955, 45; Rowson, "Whither FPA?".

32  Frank Munk, "Oregon Makes Great Decisions," *Adult Leadership* 4 (March 1956): 18–21; Warren Rovetch, "Report on the Great Decisions Program," April 1955, FPA, Box 2/40; Mastrude, "'Basic Issues'"; Mastrude, "Bringing World Affairs," 14–17.

33  Munk, "Oregon Makes," 20; Allport to Howard A. Cook, January 21, 1955, FPA, Box 1/57; William O. Chittick, "The domestic information activities of the Department of State" (PhD diss., Johns Hopkins University, 1964), 59–68; Cook to John Meagher, September 28, 1955, RG 59, RRPA, Box 1; Cook to Mastrude, March 17, 1955, FPA, Box 1/57; Mastrude, "'Basic Issues'"; Rovetch, "Report."

34  Charles P. Noyes, "Foreign Policy Association," February 10, 1956, RB, RG 3.1, Box 345; "Proposal to the Ford Foundation from the Foreign Policy Association," January 23, 1956, FF, FA732C, Grant 56-117, Reel 4159; "FPA – Views of Mr. Hartley," February 1, 1956, FF, FA732C, Grant 56-117, Reel 4159; "FPA – Views of Mr. Cook," January 30, 1956, FF, FA732C, Grant 56-117, Reel 4159; "Foreign Policy Association," March 9–10, 1956, FA732C, Grant 56-117, Reel 4159, FF; "Council on Foreign Relations," February 19–20, 1954, FF, FA732B, Grant 54-27, Reel 1344.

35  "Decisions . . . USA," June 18, 1956, FPA, Box 2/16; "Board of Directors Meeting," May 27, 1959, FPA, Box 2/16; "Great Decisions – 1962 and 1964: Reported and Estimated Kit Sales and Participation," 1964, FPA, Box 2/59; Samuel P. Hayes Jr. to Mastrude, October 22, 1964, FPA, Box 2/205; C. Dale Fuller, "Program Review and Evaluation: Great Decisions," undated, FPA, Box 2/55.

36  "Roundup from Field Reports," March 14, 1958, FPA, Box 2/39; "Report on Oregon 'Decisions . . . 1957' Program," November 1957, FPA, Box 1/28; "Minutes of Regional Meeting," May 19–20, 1959, FPA, Box 2/230; "Great Decisions 1959 in Macon, Georgia," September 1959, FPA, Box 2/55.

37  "Report on the Decisions—1957 Program," August 20, 1957, FPA, Box 1/10; "Some Local 'Great Decisions' Programs," undated, FPA, Box 2/180; "Subcommittee on Regional Operations and Cooperation with Other Organizations," May 20, 1959, FPA, Box 2/40.

38  "Summary Baltimore 'Great Decisions' Program 1958," May 15, 1958, FPA, Box 2/207; "Summary and Evaluation of Great Decisions – 1959," undated, FPA,

Box 1/9; "San Francisco," February 16, 1960, FPA, Box 2/260; "Roundup From Field Reports," March 14, 1958, FPA, Box 2/39; "Memo of Conversation with Cal Nichols," November 28, 1962, FPA, Box 2/79.

39  *Who, Me?* (New York: Foreign Policy Association, 1958), FPA, Box 2/180; *Who, Me?* (New York: Foreign Policy Association, 1965), FPA, Box 2/78.

40  "Report on Oregon 'Decisions . . . 1957' Program"; Philip Van Slyck to Nason, May 22, 1959, FPA, Box 2/16; H. Schuyler Foster to Hayes, January 8, 1963, FPA, Box 2/60.

41  Mastrude to Regional Representatives, November 8, 1956, FPA, Box 1/73; "Evaluation of the Decisions Program 1957," March 1957, FPA, Box 2/230; Van Slyck to Nason, April 23, 1959, FPA, Box 2/16; Cook to Meagher, September 28, 1955; Van Slyck to Nason, February 28, 1958, FPA, Box 2/40; Foster to Hayes, January 8, 1963, FPA, Box 2/60; Foster to Hayes, February 27, 1963, FPA, Box 2/51.

42  Mastrude to Allport, April 14, 1955, FPA, Box 2/28; "Great Decisions No. 3," *Oregonian*, March 6, 1955, 41; "Minutes of Regional Meeting – June 11–13, 1957," FPA, Box 2/230.

43  "Minutes of Policy Planning Group Meeting, December 18, 1958," January 6, 1959, FPA, Box 2/69; "Meeting of Regional Directors, May 19–21," FPA, Box 2/230; Great Decisions Packet, 1962, FPA, Box 2/111.

44  Mastrude to Nason, April 20, 1959, FPA, Box 1/242; Alfred O. Hero, "Participation in 'Great Decisions' Discussions in Greater Boston," May 1959, FPA, Box 1/10; "A Joint Report on 'Great Decisions: 1959' in Boston," August 25, 1959, FPA, Box 2/55.

45  "Great Decisions . . . 1959: A Report to Colorado," FPA, Box 2/40; "Highlights of Surveys of Great Decisions . . . 1959," FPA, Box 2/55; "Great Decisions 1959 in Macon, Georgia," September 1959, FPA, Box 2/55; "Working Paper on FPA's Role in Citizen Education in World Affairs," June 25, 1959, FPA, Box 2/242; "Response to Questions from the Ford Foundation," June 1, 1964, FF, FA732C, Grant 56-117, Reel 4159; Alfred O. Hero, *Mass Media and World Affairs* (Boston: World Peace Foundation, 1959), 33.

46  James A. Davis, *A Study of Participants in the Great Books Program, 1957* (White Plains, NY: Fund for Adult Education, 1960), 11; Kenneth P. Adler and Davis Bobrow, "Interest and Influence in Foreign Affairs," *Public Opinion Quarterly* 20, no. 1 (1956): 89–101; *Education for Public Responsibility* (White Plains, NY: Fund for Adult Education, 1959), 11; *1951–1961: A Ten Year Report of the Fund for Adult Education* (New York: Fund for Adult Education, 1961), 32–33, 49–51; "Notes on Future Program Activities of the Foreign Policy Association–World Affairs Center," May 20, 1960, FF, FA732C, Grant 56-117, Reel 4159; "Foreign Policy Association–World Affairs Center," October 25, 1960, FF, FA732C, Grant 56-117, Reel 4159.

47  Fuller, "Evaluation and Planning of 'Great Decisions,'" January 31, 1969, FPA, Box 2/17.

48  Mastrude, "The 'Plebs' and World Affairs," October 1959, FPA, Box 2/226.

### Chapter 7

1  Dean Rusk, "The Political Future of the Family of Man," *Department of State Bulletin* 57, no. 1484 (1967): 735–741.

2  "The F.P.A. at Fifty," *NYT*, November 14, 1967, 46; "Rusk, Here, Renews Offer to Talk with Hanoi," *NYT*, November 15, 1967, 2.

3  "War Foes Clash with Police Here as Rusk Speaks," *NYT*, November 15, 1967, 1; "Pickets Besiege Hotel as Rusk Talks in N.Y.," *WP*, November 15, 1967, A1; "Roaring Antiwar Mob Pickets Rusk in New York," *Hartford Courant*, November 15, 1967, 8A; "Anti-Viet Pickets Fight City Cops," *Newsday*, November 15, 1967, 1.

4  "Leaders of Rusk Demonstration Cite New Techniques of Protest," *NYT*, November 16, 1967, 4; "War Foes Protest A Speech by Rusk In San Francisco," *NYT*, January 12, 1968, 1; "S.F. Rusk Protest," *Los Angeles Times*, January 12, 1968, 1; "Meeting of the Executive Committee," November 15, 1967, FPA, Box 2/17; "Rusk Likens War Protest to Appeasers," *Los Angeles Times*, October 25, 1967, 2; "Policy Association Favors Concern, Not Disorder," *Courier-Journal* (Louisville), November 29, 1967, A15. For participatory politics and antiwar protest, including their influence on "realists" who had previously denigrated public opinion, see Francesca Polletta, *Freedom is an Endless Meeting: Democracy in American Social Movements* (Chicago: University of Chicago Press, 2002); Udi Greenberg, *The Weimar Century: German Émigrés and the Ideological Foundations of the Cold War* (Princeton, NJ: Princeton University Press, 2014), 237–255.

5  "Galbraith, Opening ADA Convention, Attacks Foreign Policy Establishment," *WP*, April 23, 1966, A1; "Rusk Defense U.S. Foreign Policy," *WP*, May 25, 1966, A1; Richard J. Barnet, *Roots of War* (New York: Atheneum, 1972), 242; Brian S. Mueller, *Democracy's Think Tank: The Institute for Policy Studies and Progressive Foreign Policy* (Philadelphia: University of Pennsylvania Press, 2021).

6  Gabriel A. Almond, *The American People and Foreign Policy* (New York: Praeger, 1960), xi–xxviii.

7  Arthur M. Schlesinger Sr., "Biography of a Nation of Joiners," *American Historical Review* 50, no. 1 (1944): 1–25; Charles R. Wright and Herbert H. Hyman, "Voluntary Association Memberships of American Adults: Evidence from National Sample Surveys," *American Sociological Review* 23, no. 3 (1958): 286; John C. Scott, "Membership and Participation in Voluntary Associations," *American Sociological Review* 22, no. 3 (1957): 315–326; Murray Hausknecht,

*The Joiners* (New York: Bedminster, 1962), 124–125. Generally, see Robert D. Putnam, *Bowling Alone: The Collapse and Revival of American Community* (New York: Simon & Schuster, 2000).

8  Philip E. Converse, "Information Flow and the Stability of Partisan Attitudes," *Public Opinion Quarterly* 26, no. 4 (1962): 592–593; Raymond A. Bauer, "The Obstinate Audience: The Influence Process from the Point of View of Social Communication," *American Psychologist* 19, no. 5 (1964): 319–328; Robert A. Dahl, *Who Governs? Democracy and Power in an American City* (New Haven, CT: Yale University Press, 1961), 264; Angus Campbell, Philip E. Converse, Warren E. Miller, and Donald E. Stokes, *The American Voter* (New York: Wiley, 1960); Philip E. Converse, "The Nature of Belief Systems in Mass Publics (1964)," *Critical Review* 18, nos. 1–3 (2006): 10, 47.

9  *Ford Foundation Annual Report: October 1, 1954 to September 30, 1955* (New York: Ford Foundation, 1956), 79; John Howe to Saul K. Padover, August 13, 1957, WB, Box 436; Saul K. Padover, *U.S. Foreign Policy and Public Opinion* (New York: Foreign Policy Association, 1958), 44.

10 Alfred O. Hero, *Americans in World Affairs* (Boston: World Peace Foundation, 1959), 2, 4; Bernard C. Cohen, *The Influence of Non-Governmental Groups on Foreign Policy-Making* (Boston: World Peace Foundation, 1959), 21; *The United States Public and the United Nations* (New York: Carnegie Endowment for International Peace), 42–43; Robert W. Hattery, Carolyn P. Hattery, William C. Rogers, and Barbara Stuhler, *A Midwest World Affairs Audience: Interest in World Affairs and Its Origins* (Madison: University of Wisconsin, 1959), 30–31; Leonard Freedman and Hilton Power, *The Few and The Many: Two Views on Public Affairs Education* (Chicago: Center for the Study of Liberal Education, 1963), 16, 26.

11 V. O. Key Jr., *Public Opinion and American Democracy* (New York: Knopf, 1961), 8, 14; Daniel Bessner and Nicolas Guilhot, "Who Decides?" in *The Decisionist Imagination: Sovereignty, Social Science, and Democracy in the 20th Century*, ed. Daniel Bessner and Nicolas Guilhot (New York: Berghahn, 2019), 1; Bernard C. Cohen, *The Public's Impact on Foreign Policy* (Boston: Little, Brown, 1972), 33–34; Ernest R. May, "An American Tradition in Foreign Policy: The Role of Public Opinion," in *Theory and Practice in American Politics*, ed. William H. Nelson and Francis L. Loewenheim (Chicago: University of Chicago Press, 1964), 117–118, 121–122.

12 Robert A. Dahl, "Further Reflections on 'The Elitist Theory of Democracy,'" *American Political Science Review* 60, no. 2 (1966): 297–298, 301; Gabriel A. Almond, "Responses to Oren, Ido (2000)," *European Journal of International Relations* 7, no. 3 (2001): 401–402; V. O. Key Jr., *The Responsible Electorate: Rationality in Presidential Voting, 1936–1960* (Cambridge, MA: Harvard University Press, 1966), 4–7.

13 Ethan Schrum, *The Instrumental University: Education in Service of the National Agenda after World War II* (Ithaca, NY: Cornell University Press, 2019), 164–182. For Michigan, see David A. Hollinger, *Science, Jews, and Secular Culture: Studies in Mid-Twentieth-Century American Intellectual History* (Princeton, NJ: Princeton University Press, 1996), 121–154.

14 Henry Cabot Lodge Jr. to Eustace Seligman, March 17, 1961, FPA, Box 2/24; John W. Nason, "Foreign Policy and the National Consensus," *Adult Leadership* 8 (February 1961): 236.

15 "Some References," April 4, 1963, FPA, Box 2/57; "Draft Statement of Purposes and Principles of FPA," March 27, 1963, FPA, Box 2/17; "List of Participants," April 3, 1963, FF, FA732C, Grant 56-117, Reel 4159; "Summary of April 5–6, 1963, Meeting with Social Scientists," April 23, 1963, FF, FA732C, Grant 56-117, Reel 6307; "Joint Meeting of the Executive & Special Committees," October 1, 1963, FPA, Box 2/17.

16 "The Purpose, Priorities and Operating Principles of FPA," April 15, 1964, FPA, Box 2/49.

17 "Report on Program Activities of FPA, July 1, 1963–June 30, 1964," August 7, 1964, FPA, Box 2/84; "10 Millionth U.N. Visitor Is Welcomed by Thant," *NYT*, May 15, 1964, 3.

18 "Kennedy Gets Kit," *NYT*, February 2, 1962, 3; Chester Bowles to the President, "Need for Improving Public Understanding of American Foreign Policy and World Affairs," January 17, 1962, JFK, Staff Memoranda, Box 62.

19 Bowles, "The Government's Information Program in Foreign Affairs," March 27, 1962, FPA, Box 2/60. Bowles and State officials consulted with the Association on this, e.g., C. Dale Fuller to Bowles, January 22, 1962, FPA, Box 2/42; Richard Winslow to Lucius Battle, February 5, 1962, FPA, Box 2/60; Winslow and Temple Wanamaker, "Proposal for Improving Public Information and Education Concerning Foreign Policy Matters," July 1962, FPA, Part 2/60.

20 Blair Bolles, *Who Makes Our Foreign Policy?* (New York: Foreign Policy Association, 1947), 93; Lester Markel, "Opportunity or Disaster?" in *Public Opinion and Foreign Policy*, ed. Lester Markel (New York: Harper, 1949), 215.

21 Andrew Johnstone, "Creating a 'Democratic Foreign Policy': The State Department's Division of Public Liaison and Public Opinion, 1944–1953," *Diplomatic History* 35, no. 3 (2001): 500–501; Kenneth Osgood, *Total Cold War: Eisenhower's Secret Propaganda Battle at Home and Abroad* (Lawrence: University of Kansas Press, 2006), 43; "Division of Public Liaison," May 2, 1952, RG 59, RRPA, Box 1; "Division of Public Liaison," October 30, 1952, RG 59, RRPA, Box 1; *The Thirty-Fifth Year: Annual Report* (New York: Foreign Policy Association, 1953), 15.

22 Michael Wala, "Selling the Marshall Plan at Home: The Committee for the Marshall Plan to Aid European Recovery," *Diplomatic History* 10, no. 3 (1986): 247–265; Steven Casey, "Selling NSC-68: The Truman Administration, Public Opinion, and the Politics of Mobilization, 1950–51," *Diplomatic History* 29, no. 4 (2005): 655–690; Nancy E. Bernhard, *US Television News and Cold War Propaganda, 1947–1960* (New York: Cambridge University Press, 1999); Kathryn McGarr, "'We're All in This Thing Together': Cold War Consensus in the Exclusive Social World of Washington Reporters," in *Media Nation: The Political History of News in Modern America*, ed. Bruce J. Schulman and Julian E. Zelizer (Philadelphia: University of Pennsylvania Press, 2017), 77–95; Sam Lebovic, *Free Speech and Unfree News: The Paradox of Press Freedom in America* (Cambridge, MA: Harvard University Press, 2016), 165.

23 "Hoover Commission Foreign Affairs Task Force Report on the Organization of the Government for the Conduct of Foreign Affairs (Excerpts Relating Particularly to the Work of PA)," undated, RG 59, Russell Subject Files, Box 8; Howard A. Cook to John French, October 16, 1952, RG 59, RRPA, Box 1; "Our Meeting with Schuyler Foster," January 25, 1950, RG 59, Office of the Assistant Secretary of State for Public Affairs, Office of the Executive Director, Subject Files, 1946–1953, Lot File 60D412, Box 21.

24 Cohen, *Public's Impact*, 43–48; MacAlister Brown, "The Demise of State Department Public Opinion Polls: A Study in Legislative Oversight," *Midwest Journal of Political Science* 5, no. 1 (1961): 13; Nancy E. Bernhard, "Clearer than Truth: Public Affairs Television and the State Department's Domestic Information Campaigns, 1947–1952," *Diplomatic History* 21, no. 4 (1997): 549; "Nixon Scores Disclosure of Adverse Quemoy Mail," *NYT*, September 28, 1958, 1.

25 Mara Oliva, *Eisenhower and American Public Opinion on China* (Cham: Palgrave Macmillan, 2018), 50–58; Osgood, *Total Cold War*, 214–252; Christina Klein, *Cold War Orientalism: Asia in the Middlebrow Imagination, 1945–1961* (Berkeley: University of California Press, 2003), 49–57; Andrew Berding, *Foreign Affairs and You!* (Garden City, NY: Doubleday, 1962), 229–248. Although it does not put the issue in these terms, for how the language of a democratic foreign policy bled into public diplomacy see Justin Hart, *Empire of Ideas: The Origins of Public Diplomacy and the Transformation of U.S. Foreign Policy* (New York: Oxford University Press, 2013).

26 William O. Chittick, "The domestic information activities of the Department of State" (PhD diss., Johns Hopkins University, 1964), 74–78, 156–170; E. S. Staples, "Discussion at State Department concerning citizens' education in world affairs, December 3, 1964," December 9, 1964, FF, FA 582, Box 8; "Text of statement recorded by Secretary of State Dean Rusk," December 26, 1962,

FPA, Box 2/50; Rusk to Samuel P. Hayes Jr., January 3, 1965, FPA, Box 2/17; Rusk to McGeorge Bundy, November 16, 1966, FF, FA617, Box 37; SLN, "The Status of Citizen Education in World Affairs," December 1954 [1953], CCWA, Box 2.

27 "Recommendations for 1961–62," March 24, 1961, FPA, Box 2/242; Hayes, "Memo of Conversation," October 3, 1962, FPA, Box 2/44; Hayes, "Memo of Discussion with Shep Stone and Joe Slater of the Ford Foundation," September 19, 1962, FPA, Box 2/242; *Ford Foundation in the 1960s: Statement of the Board of Trustees on Policies, Programs, and Operations* (New York: Ford Foundation, 1962), 11.

28 Mastrude, "Outline on World Affairs Councils," October 27, 1958, FPA, Box 2/26; Mastrude, "Background comments for consideration re a policy for relations with World Affairs Councils," October 17, 1962, FPA, Box 2/79; Calvin Nichols, "Report of Exploratory Meeting on Financial Problems of World Affairs," May 20, 1959, KCB, Box 9; Lionel Landry to Nason, July 20, 1959, FPA, Box 2/26.

29 Nichols, "Proposal for Strengthening World Affairs Education at the Community Level," March 24, 1962, FF, FA732I, Grant 63-157, Reel 680; John L. Simpson to Nason, March 20, 1959, FPA, Box 2/16; Nichols, "Proposal for Study of the Problems and Needs of World Affairs Education at the Community Level with Special Reference to the Role of World Affairs Councils," December 19, 1962, FF, FA732I, Grant 63-157, Reel 680; Matthew Cullen to Joe Slater and Stanley Gordon, January 2, 1963, FF, FA732I, Grant 63-157, Reel 680; Nichols, "Summary Report of the National Study of the Problems of and Needs for World Affairs Education at the Community Level with Special Reference to the Role of World Affairs Councils or Similar Community Organizations," March 16, 1964, FPA, Box 2/232.

30 Cullen to Shepard Stone, June 17, 1964, FF, FA732C, Grant 56-117, Reel 4159; Theodore Kaghan, "Foreign Affairs and Mass Media: U.S. Public Understanding of World Affairs," January 4, 1963, FF, FA582, Box 8; Charles E. Allen to Slater, July 17, 1964, FF, FA617, Box 37.

31 "Response to Questions from the Ford Foundation," June 1, 1964, FF, FA732C, Grant 56-117, Reel 4159; Hayes, "Memo of conversation at the Ford Foundation," June 3, 1964, FPA, Box 2/44; Nichols to Cullen, June 24, 1964, FF, FA732C, Grant 56-298, Reel 2257; Cullen to Stone, June 17, 1964; "Citizen Education in World Affairs," September 1964, FF, FA739A, Box 123; Hayes, "Memo of conversation, October 1, 1964 with Matt Cullen," FPA, Box 2/41; Hayes, "Memo of luncheon conversation on November 10th with Matt Cullen," FPA, Box 2/41. For Heald and adult education, see Waldemar A. Nielsen, *The Big Foundations* (New York: Columbia University Press, 1972), 89–93.

32  Dwight Eisenhower, "Farewell Radio and Television Address to the American People," January 17, 1961, *APP*, presidency.ucsb.edu/node/234856; H. T. Heald, "Citizen Education in World Affairs," October 6, 1964, FF, FA633, Box 28; James W. Armsey to Stone, December 28, 1964, FF, FA582, Box 8; Marshall A. Robinson to Stone, December 23, 1964, FF, FA633, Box 28; E. S. Staples, "Foreign Policy Association and Citizens Education in World Affairs," October 16, 1964, FF, FA582, Box 8; Malcolm Moos, "Toward Greater Public Understanding of Foreign Policy and the Achievement of World Affairs Education at the Community Level," October 16, 1964, FF, FA582, Box 8.

33  Staples to Moos, December 9, 1964, FF, FA582, Box 8; "Citizen Education in World Affairs committee meeting," January 19, 1965, FF, FA633, Box 28; SRC, "World Affairs Information, Exposure, And Interest—And Some Of Their Determinants," March 1965, FF, FA582, Box 8; Martin Patchen to Hayes, June 25, 1965, FPA, Box 2/47; Robert W. Tucker, "Memorandum on FPA's 'Great Decisions' Program," undated [1965], FF, FA582, Box 9.

34  "Report of Committee on Citizen Education in World Affairs," February 15, 1965, FF, FA739A, Box 112.

35  "Citizen Education in World Affairs," March 25–26, 1965, FF, FA732C, Grant 56-298, Reel 2257; Fuller, "Conversation with Ford Foundation 4/20/65," April 22, 1965, FPA, Box 2/44; Rusk to Hayes, January 3, 1965, FPA, Box 2/17; "Meeting of Board of Directors," January 12, 1965, FPA, Box 2/17.

36  Julian E. Zelizer, *The Fierce Urgency of Now: Lyndon Johnson, Congress, and the Battle for the Great Society* (New York: Penguin, 2015), 174–184; "Draft Budget for 1967–68," FPA, Box 2/17; Hayes to Board Members, "Strategic Briefing for 'Dangerous Parallel,'" January 2, 1969, FPA, Box 2/17; James M. Becker, *An Examination of Objectives, Needs and Priorities in International Education in U.S. Secondary and Elementary Schools* (New York: Foreign Policy Association, 1969). Generally, see Katie Day Good, *Bring the World to the Child: Technologies of Global Citizenship in American Education* (Cambridge, MA: MIT Press, 2020).

37  Zygmunt Nagorski, "Trip to Detroit," February 15, 1968, FPA, Box 2/224; Nagorski, "Chicago Council on Foreign Relations," November 18, 1966, FPA, Box 2/47; Nagorski, "WACs and What They Are: A Study Summary," *Society for Citizen Education in World Affairs Newsletter*, January 1968, 10–12, CFR, Series 7, Box 592.

38  Nagorski to Hayes, December 29, 1966, FPA, Box 2/79; Nagorski, "Program Planning and Evaluation: WAC Unit," March 12, 1968, FPA, Box 2/79.

39  "Committees on Foreign Relations: Twenty-Eighth Annual Conference, June 10th and 11th, 1966," CFR, Series 7, Box 598; "Committees on Foreign Relations: Eighteenth Annual Conference, June 8th and 9th, 1956," CFR,

Series 7, Box 597; "Committees on Foreign Relations: Twentieth Annual Conference, June 6th and 7th, 1958," CFR, Series 7, Box 597; William L. Lieber to Rolland Bushner, August 14, 1963, CFR, Series 7, Box 613.

40 James Huntley to Slater, June 15, 1965, FF, FA732I, Grant 66-11, Reel 1439; "Administration of the Appropriation for Grants to World Affairs Councils for Support of Community World Affairs Programs," April 1965, FF, FA739D, Box 434; "Proposed Grant to the World Affairs Council of Northern California," August 10, 1965, FF, FA732I, Grant 66-11, Reel 1439; Huntley, "Visit to Philadelphia World Affairs Council – August 19, 1965," FF, FA732I, Grant 66-11, Reel 1478; F. F. Hill to Heald, October 1, 1965, FF, FA732I, Grant 66-11, Reel 1439; Huntley to Stone, December 8, 1965, FF, FA617, Box 37; Huntley to Stone, March 17, 1966, FF, FA739D, Box 434; CHB to Hayes, December 10, 1965, FPA, Box 2/79.

41 For Bundy at Ford, see Karen Ferguson, *Top Down: The Ford Foundation, Black Power, and the Reinvention of Racial Liberalism* (Philadelphia: University of Pennsylvania Press, 2013).

42 For Bundy's mentors and worldview, see Andrew Preston, *The War Council: McGeorge Bundy, the NSC, and Vietnam* (Cambridge, MA: Harvard University Press, 2006).

43 Notes in folder "Government 135: X, XI, XII, Public Opinion," MB, Box 30; "Government 185 – Reading List I – Fall Term 1955," MB, Box 31; "Government 185 – Reading List I – Fall Term 1956," MB, Box 31.

44 Stone to Bundy, March 30, 1966, FF, FA617, Box 7; Dorothy Binyon to Bundy, May 3, 1966, FF, FA732B, Grant 66-184, Reel 1454; Stone to Bundy, April 1, 1966, FF, FA732B, Grant 66-184, Reel 1454; William Watts to W. McNeil Lowry, September 14, 1966, FF, FA582, Box 8.

45 Huntley to Stone, April 29, 1966, FF, FA748, Box 1; Huntley to Stone, May 24, 1966, FF, FA739D, Box 434; "Summary: Meeting on World Affairs Education," May 24, 1966, FF, FA739A, Box 115; David E. Bell to Bundy, October 26, 1966, FF, FA748, Box 1; Huntley to Slater, October 10, 1966, FF, FA748, Box 1; Rusk to Bundy, November 16, 1966, FF, FA617, Box 37; Huntley, "Transfer of Responsibility," January 27, 1967, FF, FA748, Box 1. For the skepticism about public opinion in "vital center" liberalism, see Kyong-Min Son, *The Eclipse of the Demos: The Cold War and the Crisis of Democracy before Neoliberalism* (Lawrence: University Press of Kansas, 2020), 39–41, 51–52.

46 Huntley to Slater, January 23, 1967, FF, FA732C, Grant 56-117, Reel 4158; Nielsen, *The Big Foundations*, 94–95; "The Foreign Policy Association and Its Program: A Proposal to the Ford Foundation," May 16, 1967, FF, FA732C, Grant 56-298, Reel 2257; Gordon to Slater, May 31, 1967, FF, FA732C, Grant 56-298, Reel 2257; Howard Swearer to Francis Sutton, August 8, 1967, FF, FA732C, Grant 56-298, Reel 2257.

47  Bell to Bundy, December 18, 1967, August 8, 1967, FF, FA732C, Grant 56-298, Reel 2257; Sutton to Hayes, December 28, 1967, FF, FA732C, Grant 56-298, Reel 2257.

48  Fuller to Gordon, November 27, 1968, FPA, Box 2/87.

49  "Board-Staff Task Force on Inter-Racial Participation," July 6, 1967, FPA, Box 2/17; "Joint Meeting of the Executive Committee and the Program Methods Committee," May 15, 1968, FPA, Box 2/17; "Special Meeting of Budget Committee of the FPA Board," April 8, 1970, FPA, Box 2/17; "Emergency Minutes of the Executive Committee," August 24, 1970, FPA, Box 2/17; "Board of Directors," September 24, 1970, FPA, Box 2/17; Sutton to John Doran, March 23, 1976, FF, FA732, Grant 72-134, Reel 2362.

50  William C. Messner Jr., "This Pivotal Period in Public Opinion," *Society for Citizen Education in World Affairs Newsletter*, July 1968, 14–15, CCWA, Box 2; Norman W. Pilgrim, "Programming Trends in World Affairs," *Society for Citizen Education in World Affairs Newsletter*, July 1970, 1, CCWA, Box 2; Moselle Kimbler, "Evaluation of grant to the World Affairs Council of Northern California," October 17, 1972, FF, FA732I, Grant 66-11, Reel 1439; "Board of Trustees," March 8, 1976, CCWA, Box 3; Kimbler, "Evaluation of grant to World Affairs Council of Philadelphia," May 13, 1970, FF, FA732I, Grant 66-13, Reel 1478; Kimbler, "Evaluation of grant to Cincinnati Council on World Affairs," August 5, 1970, FF, FA732B, Grant 66-185, Reel 1846; *The Chicago Council on Foreign Relations, 1973–1975* (Chicago: Chicago Council on Foreign Relations, 1975).

51  Anthony Solomon, "An Evaluation of the Council on Foreign Relations," November 14, 1973, FF, FA732B, Grant 54-27, Reel 1344; Craufurd D. Goodwin, "Evaluation of Council on Foreign Relations Grants," May 25, 1977, FF, FA732B, Grant 54-27, Reel 1344.

52  "Oral History Interview with Francis H. Russell," July 13, 1973, Harry S. Truman Presidential Library, trumanlibrary.org/oralhist/russellf.htm.

53  Charles S. Maier, *Among Empires: American Ascendancy and Its Predecessors* (Cambridge, MA: Harvard University Press, 2006), 241; "Toward an Open Foreign Policy," WP, October 22, 1973, A28.

54  Henry A. Kissinger, "Message to The National Council of Community World Affairs Organizations," October 8, 1974, CCWA, Box 3; "Notes on SPH Conversation with Carol Laise and Charlie Bray, Department of State, June 4, 1974," FPA, Box 2/51; Kissinger, "Message to the National Council on Philanthropy," October 21, 1974, FPA, Box 2/18. For more, see David Allen, "Realism and Malarkey: Henry Kissinger's State Department, Détente, and Domestic Consensus," *Journal of Cold War Studies* 17, no. 3 (2015): 184–219.

55  "District Residents' Views Vary on Foreign Policy," *Pittsburgh Post-Gazette*, February 19, 1976, 9; Charles W. Bray, untitled memorandum, undated [1976], RG 59, Director's Files of Winston Lord, Lot File 77D112, Box 358.

56 "Verbatim Text: Principal Findings from Pittsburgh "Town Meeting" on Foreign Policy," September 16, 1976, RG 59, Central Foreign Policy Files, 1973–79, Electronic Telegrams, 1976STATE229191; William E. Schaufele to Kissinger, April 30, 1976, RG 59, Records of Henry Kissinger, 1973–77, Lot File 91D414, Box 1.

## *Epilogue*

1  Antony J. Blinken, "A Foreign Policy for the American People," March 3, 2021, state.gov/a-foreign-policy-for-the-american-people/.

2  John Foster Dulles to Esther G. Ogden, November 3, 1928, JFD, Box 8; John Foster Dulles, "A Survey of Foreign Policy Problems," *Department of State Bulletin* 28, no. 711 (1953): 212, 216.

3  "Foreign Policy is the People's Business," *New Republic,* April 24, 1950, 5–6.

4  John Jay, "The Powers of the Senate," March 7, 1788, guides.loc.gov/federalist-papers/text-61-70; Woodrow Wilson, "Address to the Peace Conference in Paris, France," January 25, 1919, *APP,* presidency.ucsb.edu/node/317821; DeWitt C. Poole, *The Conduct of Foreign Relations Under Modern Democratic Conditions* (New Haven, CT: Yale University Press, 1924), 196–197.

5  Daniel Bell, *The End of Ideology: On the Exhaustion of Political Ideas in the Fifties* (Cambridge, MA: Harvard University Press, 2000).

6  Donald J. Pryor, "Must Athens Fall Again?" November 7, 1961, CCWA, Box 2.

7  Robert D. Putnam, *Bowling Alone: The Collapse and Revival of American Community* (New York: Simon & Schuster, 2000), 16–18; Theda Skocpol, *Diminished Democracy: From Membership to Management in American Civic Life* (Norman: University of Oklahoma Press, 2003), 13.

8  Hélène Landemore, *Open Democracy: Reinventing Popular Rule for the Twenty-First Century* (Princeton, NJ: Princeton University Press, 2020), 3; Skocpol, *Diminished Democracy,* 11; Pew Research Center, "Public Trust in Government: 1958–2021," pewresearch.org/politics/2021/05/17/public-trust-in-government-1958-2021/.

9  Salman Ahmed and Rozlyn Engel, eds., *Making U.S. Foreign Policy Work Better for the Middle Class* (Washington, DC: Carnegie Endowment for International Peace, 2020), 67–69; Richard Haass, "How a World Order Ends: And What Comes in Its Wake," *Foreign Affairs* 98, no. 1 (2019): 30; John Halpin et al., *America Adrift: How the U.S. Foreign Policy Debate Misses What Voters Really Want* (Washington, DC: Center for American Progress, 2019), 3–4; Gideon Rose, "The Fourth Founding: The United States and the Liberal Order," *Foreign Affairs* 98, no. 1 (2019): 21. Cf. Daniel Bessner and Stephen Wertheim, "Democratizing U.S. Foreign Policy," *Foreign Affairs,* April 5, 2017, foreignaffairs.com/articles/united-states/2017-04-05/democratizing-us-foreign-policy.

10  David Samuels, "The Aspiring Novelist Who Became Obama's Foreign-Policy
    Guru," *NYTM*, May 8, 2016, nytimes.com/2016/05/08/magazine/the-aspiring-
    novelist-who-became-obamas-foreign-policy-guru.html. For secrecy and leaks,
    see David E. Pozen, "The Leaky Leviathan: Why the Government Condemns
    and Condones Unlawful Disclosures of Information," *Harvard Law Review* 127,
    no. 2 (2013): 512–635. Generally on these points, see Mary L. Dudziak, "Death
    and the War Power," *Yale Journal of Law and the Humanities* 30, no. 1 (2018):
    25–62; Michael Brenes, *For Might and Right: Cold War Defense Spending and
    the Remaking of American Democracy* (Amherst: University of Massachusetts
    Press, 2020); Mark Philip Bradley and Mary L. Dudziak, eds., *Making the
    Forever War: Marilyn B. Young on the Culture and Politics of American
    Militarism* (Amherst: University of Massachusetts Press, 2021); Samuel Moyn,
    *Humane: How the United States Abandoned Peace and Reinvented War* (New
    York: Farrar, Straus and Giroux, 2021).
11  "Member Councils," worldaffairscouncils.org/About/index.cfm?PageID=5;
    *2020–2021 Annual Report* (Cleveland: Cleveland Council on World Affairs,
    2021), ccwa.org/about/annual-reports/.
12  Cf. Edward H. Berman, *The Ideology of Philanthropy: The Influence of the
    Carnegie, Ford, and Rockefeller Foundations on American Foreign Policy*
    (Albany: State University of New York Press, 1983); Inderjeet Parmar, *Founda-
    tions of the American Century: The Ford, Carnegie, and Rockefeller Foundations
    in the Rise of American Power* (New York: Columbia University Press, 2012).
13  Generally, see James S. Fishkin, *When the People Speak: Deliberative Democ-
    racy and Public Consultation* (New York: Oxford University Press, 2011); "The
    Prospects & Limits of Deliberative Democracy," *Daedalus* 146, no. 4 (2017):
    6–166; James S. Fishkin, *Democracy When the People Are Thinking: Revital-
    izing Our Politics Through Public Deliberation* (New York: Oxford University
    Press, 2018); John S. Dryzek et al., "The crisis of democracy and the science of
    deliberation," *Science* 363, no. 6432 (2019): 1144–1146. For an early application,
    see Henry E. Brady, James S. Fishkin, and Robert C. Luskin, "Informed Public
    Opinion About Foreign Policy: The uses of deliberative polling," *Brookings*,
    June 1, 2003, brookings.edu/articles/informed-public-opinion-about-foreign
    -policy-the-uses-of-deliberative-polling/. For Germany, see Hanna Pfeifer,
    Christian Opitz, and Anna Geis, "Deliberating Foreign Policy: Perceptions and
    Effects of Citizen Participation in Germany," *German Politics* 30, no. 4 (2021):
    485–502.
14  Richard Haass, *The World: A Brief Introduction* (New York: Penguin, 2020),
    xvii.
15  Generally, see Robert Vitalis, *White World Order, Black Power Politics: The
    Birth of American International Relations* (Ithaca, NY: Cornell University Press,

2015); Adriane Lentz-Smith, "The Unbearable Whiteness of Grand Strategy," in *Rethinking American Grand Strategy*, ed. Elizabeth Borgwardt, Christopher McKnight Nichols, and Andrew Preston (New York: Oxford University Press, 2021), 329–345.

16 See e.g., David Callahan, *The Givers: Money, Power, and Philanthropy in a New Gilded Age* (New York: Penguin, 2018); Rob Reich, *Just Giving: Why Philanthropy is Failing Democracy and How It Can Do Better* (Princeton, NJ: Princeton University Press, 2018); Anand Giridharadas, *Winners Take All: The Elite Charade of Changing the World* (New York: Penguin, 2019).

17 Brooks Emeny, "The Responsibility of Citizenship in the World Today," September 29, 1964, CCWA, Box 2.

ACKNOWLEDGMENTS

Writing a book is not exactly a democratic exercise, but it is certainly one that requires mass participation. This one started at Columbia University, where Matthew Connelly was a model mentor, personally and professionally. I am not aware of many advisors who genuinely want their graduate students to think with them, let alone to collaborate and publish with them; my work with Matt on official secrecy animated the concerns that lie behind this book. At Columbia, I also benefited from the advice of Eric Foner, Robert Jervis, Mark Mazower, and Anders Stephanson, and I was lucky to be able to take advantage of the extended visits to Morningside Heights of David Greenberg and Mario del Pero. Lien-Hang Nguyen and Ira Katznelson helped to guide my eventual revisions with typical insight; I doubt that these pages make the profound statement about American democracy that Ira once asked me for, but his work on politics and the state has inspired many of them all the same. So too has the example and scholarship of Andrew Preston. Among many debts, I owe Andrew for welcoming me into his Clare College office at the start of a postgraduate year back at Cambridge by encouraging me immediately to apply to leave for a doctoral program in the United States. For more than merely academic reasons, he was, as ever, right.

Although I began this project at Columbia, almost all of it has been written at the Harvard Kennedy School, where by some miracle I spent all but one of my last six years in academia, the exception being a trip down the road to the Massachusetts Institute of Technology, where Owen Cote, M. Taylor Fravel, Barry Posen, and Joli Divon Saraf provided a genial welcome to the Security Studies Program. Months before I had even arrived at Harvard, Odd Arne Westad had asked me to teach with him; it was the first act of generosity in what has since become a long, long list. Debating with Arne how to teach the rise and fall of the great powers in a way that would be useful to public policy students remains the most enthralling intellectual experience of my career; doing it for myself, at his invitation, was at first the most frightening and then,

313

as my anxieties were eased by the fine students of the Yale Jackson Institute for Global Affairs, the most fulfilling. At Harvard, Fredrik Logevall similarly took me on as if I were one of his own students, buying the drinks as we swapped notes on how to write a biography—his of John F. Kennedy, mine of an institution—and lamented the direction of our field. Both Arne and Fred have always made me feel as if we were engaged as equals in a shared endeavor, and I could not be more grateful for that, as well as for much else. Stephen Walt and Steven Miller preside over a famously productive atmosphere at the International Security Program at the Belfer Center for Science and International Affairs, and I thank them in particular for going beyond the call of duty to arrange just one more fellowship year. Susan Lynch deserves special mention for the boundless patience with which she has looked after me and the many other junior scholars who have taken up residence at One Brattle Square. Leverett House turned Harvard into a home; I am indebted to Ann and Howard Georgi, as well as to the maintenance crew, the dining hall staff, and so many of the tutors and undergraduates for making it so.

Much of this book is about how money matters in the creation of knowledge. For grants, office space, and more, I thank the staff of the Charles Koch Foundation, particularly Haley Ast and Michelle Newby; the Belfer Center for Science and International Affairs and the Ash Center for Democratic Governance at the Harvard Kennedy School; the Security Studies Program at the Massachusetts Institute of Technology; the Department of History, the University Library, and the Brown Institute for Media Innovation at Columbia University; the Eisenhower Institute at Gettysburg College; the Friends of the University of Wisconsin-Madison Libraries; the Clements Center for National Security of the University of Texas at Austin; and the Society for Historians of American Foreign Relations. Some of those grants enabled me to visit the depositories across the country where I was graced with the assistance of innumerable kind archivists. Lee Grady at the Wisconsin Historical Society and Margaret Snyder at the Rockefeller Archives Center—that incomparable paradise for researchers—were essential in making their holdings comprehensible. I also profited from aid at the Manuscript Division of the Library of Congress; the Rare Book and Manuscript Library at Columbia University; the Schlesinger Library at the Radcliffe Institute for Advanced Study; the Seeley G. Mudd Manuscript Library at Princeton University; and the Library and Archives at the United States Holocaust Memorial Museum. Ross Coen, Nanosh Lucas, and Emily Masghati scanned and sent records that would otherwise have been out of my reach. Alexander

Messman of the Los Angeles World Affairs Council was kind enough to give me that Council's early board minutes. Kyle Haddad-Fonda, David Heidelberger, and MacDara King of the Foreign Policy Association eagerly answered my inquiries even as it became clear that the history of the Association for which they work has not always been a happy one. I hope that I did not entirely ruin the Great Decisions episode that they invited me to appear on in 2020.

This book has been improved under the criticism, often sympathetic, of panel members, commentators, and audience members at events arranged by the Ash and Belfer Centers at the Harvard Kennedy School; the ISS-Brady Johnson Colloquium in Grand Strategy and International History at Yale University; the Organization of American Historians; and the Society for Historians of American Foreign Relations. Portions of Chapter Six were first published as "Great Decisions, the Foreign Policy Association, and the Triumph of Elitism in the U.S. Foreign Policy Community," *International History Review* 43, no. 4 (2021): 701–719, © Taylor & Francis, available at doi.org /10.1080/07075332.2020.1840416. Two peer reviewers did me the tribute of engaging substantively with the book manuscript for Harvard University Press, where Kathleen McDermott has been as fine and understanding an editor as any author could hope for. I am grateful to the team at Harvard, and to Jamie Armstrong, for making this book a reality.

Over the years, I have been fortunate to benefit from the time and insights of Tom Arnold-Forster, Paul Behringer, Daniel Bessner, Lindsay Dayton, Alexandra Evans, Julian Gewirtz, David Goodman, Mattias Fibiger, Stephanie Freeman, Gretchen Heefner, Eric Herschthal, Michaela Hoenicke-Moore, Daniel Hummel, Elizabeth Ingleson, Daniel Jacobs, William James, Andrew Johnstone, Jason Kelly, Alexander Keyssar, Mookie Kideckel, Kathryn Lasdow, Aroop Mukharji, Jack Neubauer, Katharina Rietzler, Ben Serby, Elizabeth Shackelford, Peter Slezkine, Jan Stöckmann, John A. Thompson, Heidi Tworek, and Emily Whalen. Writing on classical music for the *New York Times* remains the great privilege of my professional life. It has been an honor to work with Joshua Barone, Michael Cooper, Corinna da Fonseca-Wollheim, Myra Forsberg, Jim Oestreich, Anthony Tommasini, Dan Wakin, Seth Colter Walls, Jessie Wender, and above all my longtime editor, Zachary Woolfe, whose patience, protection, and persistence in excising Oxford commas have been unending.

It might be my name that appears on the cover of this book, but it is above all a tribute to the friends and family who have suffered and sustained me through its writing. I met Fr. Stephen M. Koeth, CSC, within hours of stepping foot on Columbia's campus; that he was there to greet me within hours of stepping off it, several degrees and more than seven years later, is a blessing undisguised. George Ward kept me on an even keel in Cambridge, or at least properly fed and watered. Daniel Cohen has always been there, and he always will. Yan Zheng and He Feng have welcomed me into their family, offered support, and improved my Mandarin. My grandfather, John Gardner, inspired my youthful interest in history when he took me through his Royal Air Force log books; those hours in his study remind me, still, that history happens to real people. My sister, Katie Allen, has tolerated me being, well, me, and with rare humor as well; my father, Jeremy Allen, has read every word of every draft of this manuscript with a keen eye and without complaint; my late mother, Patricia Allen, could not possibly have done more for us all, nor done it more loyally.

This book is for Tian. Tian has made it possible for me to be a writer, commas and all. She has borne us three children whose smiles make me happier than I ever thought I could be, and she has been by my side come what may, and come what has. It turns out that I can indeed do it, Tian, and only because of you.

# INDEX

*Page numbers in italics refer to illustrations.*

317

American Political Science Association, 101, 176

American University Women's Club, 88

*American Voter, The* (Survey Research Center), 206

Andrews, Fannie Fern, 22, 39

Angell, Norman, 17, 19, 52–53

anticommunist scares, 20, 30. *See also* McCarthyism

anti–Vietnam War protests, 202–205, 224, 228

Armsey, James, 220

arms race. *See* nuclear weapons

Armstrong, Hamilton Fish, 83

*Atlantic Monthly,* 67

Atoms for Peace, 141

Austin, Warren, 138

Avenol, Joseph, 54

Bache-Wiig, Ruth, 49–50

Bailey, Thomas A., 116

Baker, Newton D.: adult education movement and, 109–110; assessment of democratic foreign policy, 108–109, 238; belief in need for informed United States public and, 107, 109, 238; Council on Foreign Relations and, 107–108; Emeny and, 115; on Emeny's scholarship, 115; Foreign Affairs Institute of 1927, 117; Foreign Policy Association and, 108–109, 111; foreign policy community and, 108–109; propaganda and, 115; on *Reports* (FPA), 52; success of Cleveland Foreign Affairs Council and, 107; temperament of, 109; Wilsonian legacy and, 108

Barnet, Richard, 204

Barrett, Edward W., 158

Bay of Pigs, 235

Beard, Charles A., 17–18, 49, 75–76, 80

Becker, James, 222

Bell, David A., 226–227, 237

Bemis, Samuel Flagg, 77, 113

Benton, William, 93, 101–102, 152

Berding, Andrew, 215–216

Bernays, Edward, 99

Bessner, Daniel, 146, 208

Biddle, Francis, 76

Bidwell, Percy, 121

Binyon, Dorothy, 224, 226, 229

Bisson, T. A., 58, 84, 151

Blinken, Anthony, 233–234

Bliven, Bruce, 29

Bolton, Chester, 121

Bolton, Frances, 121, 123

Bolton, Kenyon C., 167

Bonfield, Margaret, 41

Borah, William, 28

Borchard, Edwin, 32, 113

Bourdieu, Pierre, 8

Bowie, Robert R., 209–210

Bowles, Chester, 212

Bradley, Omar, 131

Brookings Institution, 191

Brooks Emeny Trust, 241

Brown, Benjamin, 167

Brown, Bernice, 39

Bruner, Jerome, 103

Bryson, Lyman, 63, 68, 223

Buell, Raymond Leslie: on American "imperialism," 73; black scholars and, 57; as critic of America neutrality in the 1930s, 60; Dean and, 147–148; death of, 73; departure from FPA and, 72, 86; disillusionment of, 13, 70–73; FPA appearance of nonpartisanship and, 53; Great Depression and, 66; as head of FPA, 56–59; hiring policies and, 57–58; Hull and, 81; *International Relations* of, 49; McDonald's hiring of, 49, 53; New Deal and, 71;

primary of Treadway and, 71; proposed policy groups and, 60–61; research department and, 82–83; Roosevelt and, 73; on the strategy on impartiality, 53–54; studies after World War I, 62; under Luce, 72–73; World War II and, 77, 83
*Bulletin* (Foreign Policy Association), 26, 47, 57, 154
*Bulletin* (State Department), 214
Bunche, Ralph, 127, 130
Bundy, Harvey H., 40, 76, 153, 225
Bundy, McGeorge, 4, 224–227, 230–231
Bureau of Social Hygiene (Rockefeller), 46, 48
Burton, Harold, 121
Busch, Henry Miller, 124
Butler, Nicholas Murray, 8, 18
Byrnes, James F., 131–132, 138

*Call and Post*, 130
Campbell, Angus, 178, 220
Cantril, Hadley, 98
Carnegie Corporation: adult education and, 62, 66; Baker and, 108; Cleveland Council on World Affairs and, 121, 134; conviction of Hiss and, 152; Council on Foreign Relations Committees and, 119–120; Emeny's Foreign Policy Foundation proposal and, 143; FPA funding and, 137, 143–144, 157–158; McCarthyism and, 152
Carnegie Endowment for International Peace, 18, 46, 59, 111, 119, 210, 224, 228, 239–240
Carnegie Endowment study group on the United Nations, 206–207
Carter, Edward C., 132–133
Carter, John Franklin, 41–42
Carter, Margaret, 103–104
Cartwright, Morse A., 63

Catt, Carrie Chapman, 36, 52
Cecil, Robert, 33
censorship, 30, 214
Center for American Progress, 240
Center for International Affairs (Harvard), 193, 210
Center of International Studies (Princeton), 183
Central Intelligence Agency, 173, 232, 240
Chafee, Zachariah, Jr., 30
Chang Hsueh-Liang, 45
Chatham House (Royal Institute of International Affairs), 25
Cherrington, Ben M., 63–65, 107
Chicago Council on Foreign Relations, 28, 35, 89, 193, 222, 229
*Chicago Daily News*, 193
*Chicago Tribune*, 51, 133
Childs, Harwood, 8
Chinese Communist Party, 157
*Christian Century*, 107
civic engagement, 205, 238–239
Clayton, Will, 136
Cleveland: adult education and, 106–107; America First Committee and, 124; Black migration from the South and, 126; civic spirit of, 115–116; dearth of foreign policy groups in the post–World War I decade and, 110; Foreign Affairs Institute of 1927, 110; Great Depression and, 110–111, 116; reception of Emeny in, 117–118; segregation and, 130; stereotypes about midwestern cities and, 116; women and foreign policy groups in, 110; World War II and, 126. *See also* Cleveland Council on World Affairs
Cleveland Adult Education Association, 110–111

Fosdick, Raymond Blaine, 49, 86, 104, 108, 133
Foster, H. Schuyler, 100–101, 195, 215
Frankfurter, Felix, 18
Frechtling, Louis, 85
*Freedom and Culture* (Dewey), 72
Fry, Varian, 66, 85
Fuller, C. Dale, 203, 228
Fund for Adult Education, 156, 158, 162, 188, 190–191, 199, 219

Gaither, H. Rowan, Jr., 154–155
Galbraith, John Kenneth, 204
Gallup, George, 92, 98, 209, 243
Gasperi, Alcide de, 131
G. I. Bill, 144
Gibson, Hugh, 91
Gideonse, Harry, 43
Gildersleeve, Virginia, 88, 135
Gilpatric, Roswell, 209
Glazer, Nathan, 177
Goetz, Delia, 66
Goldberg, Arthur, 209
Goodman, David, 65
Goodrich, Leland, 136
Gordon, Stanley, 218, 227
Goslin, Ryllis Alexander, 66
government trust, 239–240
Grady, Henry F., 170
Great Books program, 199
Great Decisions: adult education methods and, 188–189; American Federation of Labor and, 186; arguments about oversight, 193–194; Bay Area and, 194; Chicago Council on Foreign Relations and, 193; class and, 193, 196–197, 199; current-day, 241; education level of participants and, 199; effect on participants, 194–195; failure of, 15, 199–200; Ford Foundation and, 174, 191; FPA fact

sheets and, 186; FPA oversight and, 192; Fund for Adult Education and, 190; Hayes and, 210; League of Women Voters and, 186, 196; marketing for, 194; meetings with congressional representatives and, 211; nationwide rollout, 192–193; opinion ballots and, 187–188, 190, 195–196; participation and, 192, 196–198; Portland and, 174, 185–188, 192; race and, 190, 193, 196; Rusk and, 217; State Department and, 187–188, 190–191, 195–196; television and, 211; United Nations Association and, 194
Great Depression, 13, 55, 110–111, 116, 176, 238
*Great Powers in World Politics, The* (Emeny and Simonds), 114–115
Green, James Frederick, 84
Greenslade, John, 133–134
Grew, Joseph, 138
Griswold, A. Whitney, 113
Grondahl, Louise, 172, 174
Gruening, Ernest, 60
Guilhot, Nicholas, 208

Haass, Richard, 244
Habermas, Jürgen, 12
Hallstrom, Elizabeth, 164
Hamilton, Alice, 40
Hand, Frances, 32
Hanfstaengl, Ernst, 54
Hapgood, Norman, 18–19
Harbord, James, 33
Hart, Clyde, 215
Hartley, Robert, 191
Hausknecht, Murray, 205
Hayes, Samuel P., Jr.: background of, 209; financial crisis at FPA and, 228–229; Ford Foundation and, 219,

Nason, John W.: Carnegie Endowment study group and, 206; departure from the FPA of, 209; Ford Foundation and, 191; Great Decision program and, 187; leadership of FPA and, 162–163, 167, 169; People-to-People program and, 216; response to elitist scholarship and, 184–185

*Nation*, 17, 19, 22

National American Woman Suffrage Association, 36

National Association for the Advancement of Colored People, 130–131

National Conference on US Foreign Policy, 96

National Council for Limitation of Armament, 36

National Council for Prevention of War, 67

National Council of Community World Affairs Organizations, 231

National Council on Philanthropy, 231

National Defense Education Act of 1958, 222

National Election Study, 239

nationalism, 234

National Opinion Research Center (NORC), 100, 177, 179, 199, 215

National Peace Conference, 67

National Security Council, 173, 240

*Native Problem in Africa, The* (Buell), 53

Nazis, FPA luncheon invitation to fascist to defend, 77

neoisolationism, 228

Ness, Eliot, 121

New Deal, 71, 107

New Orleans Branch of FPA, 88–89

*New Republic*, 17, 19, 22, 26, 29, 57, 235

newspapers, 48–49, 51, 62–63, 117, 186, 214. *See also individual papers*

*New York Herald Tribune*, 94

*New York Times*, 4, 57, 108, 132, 156, 161, 201–202

Nichols, Calvin, 194, 218–219, 224

Nichols, Rose Standish, 40

Nixon, Richard M., 164, 214, 216

North Atlantic Treaty, 94

NSC-68 paper, 157, 214

nuclear weapons, 141–142, 151

Nuremberg trials, 76

Nye, Gerald, 77

Office of Public Opinion Research, 98

Office of Strategic Services (OSS), 84–85

Office of the Coordinator of Inter-American Affairs, 121

Office of War Information, 95

Ogden, Esther G., 36–37, 43

*One World* (Willkie), 106

opinion polling: academic anti-democratic beliefs and, 99–100, 178–179; democratic foreign policy and, 176–179; on lack of malleability of public opinion, 206; oversimplifications and, 100–101; as propaganda tool, 98–100; Rockefeller Foundation, 97–98; State Department and, 96–97, 100, 215, 243; trust in government and, 239–240; World War II and, 98–99

*Oregonian*, 172, 186, 190

*Our Foreign Policy*, 70, 93

*Outlook and Independent*, 41

Padover, Saul K., 207

Palmer, A. Mitchell, 20

Park, Julian, 89

Parker, Phyllis, 133

Peace Corps, 209, 216

Pearl Harbor, 80, 114, 125

People-to-People program, 216

religion, 141
"Report from the World" (Cleveland), 131–132
Rhee, Syngman, 164
Rhodes, Ben, 3, 240
Rich, Raymond T., 38, 52
Riesman, David, 172–173, 177
Rightor, Edward, 89
Ringwood, Ona, 57
Robin, Ron, 146
Robinson, Marshall, 220
Rockefeller, Abby, 49
Rockefeller, John D., III, 44–46, 67, 201, 209
Rockefeller, John D., Jr., 47, 49, 58, 108, 137, 146
Rockefeller, Nelson A., 127, 134, 145
Rockefeller, Winifred, 114, 119, 131, 134, 160
Rockefeller Brothers Fund, 157, 228
Rockefeller Foundation: Cleveland Council on World Affairs and, 134–135; Council on Foreign Relations War and Peace Studies program and, 83; FPA funding and, 13, 59, 66, 68, 70, 103–104, 137, 143–146, 155, 245; interest in Lasswell of, 99–100; League of Nations and, 146; McCarthyism and, 152; opinion polling and, 97–98; post-World War II funding priorities and, 144–146; professionalism in foreign policy and, 182
Rogers, James Grafton, 138
Romulo, Carlos, 131
Roosevelt, Eleanor, 55, 143, 234
Roosevelt, Franklin D.: address to the League of Free Nations Association, 19; FPA as mouthpiece for, 14, 79–80; McDonald's attempt for appointment in Berlin, 55; Office of Public

Opinion Research and, 98; pictured, 87; public opinion and, 8; relationship between foreign policy and public opinion and, 90–91; support for FPA branches and, 86–87, 89–90; support of Great Britain in World War II and, 6, 74
Root, Elihu, 23–25
Roper, Elmo, 177–178
Rose, Gideon, 240
Rosinger, Lawrence K., 151
Ross, Colin, 77
Rovere, Richard H., 4
Rovetch, Warren, 190–191
Royal Institute of International Affairs (Chatham House), 25
Rusk, Dean, 201–204, 212, 216–217, 221, 227
Russell, Francis H., 95, 98, 101–102, 213, 215, 223, 230
*Russia: Menace or Promise* (Dean), 148, 150

Sachs, Arthur, 59
Sayre, Francis B., 95
Schacht, Hjalmar, 47
Schlesinger, Arthur M., Sr., 130, 205
schools, Johnson administration and, 221–222
Schulzinger, Robert, 25
Schumpeter, Joseph, 72
Sealander, Judith, 46
Seligman, Eustace, 54, 153–154
settlement house movement, 62
Seward, William, 3
sexism, 25, 31–32, 89–90, 119, 120–121. *See also* women
Sheffield, Alfred, 65
Shepardson, Whitney, 133, 157
Simkhovitch, Mary, 32
Simonds, Frank, 114